The Rise and Fall of America's Concentration Camp Law

In the series *Asian American History and Culture*, edited by Cathy Schlund-Vials, Shelley Sang-Hee Lee, and Rick Bonus. Founding editor, Sucheng Chan; editors emeriti, David Palumbo-Liu, Michael Omi, K. Scott Wong, and Linda Trinh Võ.

Also in this series:

Shirley Jennifer Lim, *Anna May Wong: Performing the Modern*
Edward Tang, *From Confinement to Containment: Japanese/American Arts during the Early Cold War*
Patricia P. Chu, *Where I Have Never Been: Migration, Melancholia, and Memory in Asian American Narratives of Return*
Cynthia Wu, *Sticky Rice: A Politics of Intraracial Desire*
Marguerite Nguyen, *America's Vietnam: The* Longue Durée *of U.S. Literature and Empire*
Vanita Reddy, *Fashioning Diaspora: Beauty, Femininity, and South Asian American Culture*
Audrey Wu Clark, *The Asian American Avant-Garde: Universalist Aspirations in Modernist Literature and Art*
Eric Tang, *Unsettled: Cambodian Refugees in the New York City Hyperghetto*
Jeffrey Santa Ana, *Racial Feelings: Asian America in a Capitalist Culture of Emotion*
Jiemin Bao, *Creating a Buddhist Community: A Thai Temple in Silicon Valley*
Elda E. Tsou, *Unquiet Tropes: Form, Race, and Asian American Literature*
Tarry Hum, *Making a Global Immigrant Neighborhood: Brooklyn's Sunset Park*
Ruth Mayer, *Serial Fu Manchu: The Chinese Supervillain and the Spread of Yellow Peril Ideology*
Karen Kuo, *East Is West and West Is East: Gender, Culture, and Interwar Encounters between Asia and America*
Kieu-Linh Caroline Valverde, *Transnationalizing Viet Nam: Community, Culture, and Politics in the Diaspora*
Lan P. Duong, *Treacherous Subjects: Gender, Culture, and Trans-Vietnamese Feminism*
Kristi Brian, *Reframing Transracial Adoption: Adopted Koreans, White Parents, and the Politics of Kinship*
Belinda Kong, *Tiananmen Fictions outside the Square: The Chinese Literary Diaspora and the Politics of Global Culture*
Bindi V. Shah, *Laotian Daughters: Working toward Community, Belonging, and Environmental Justice*
Cherstin M. Lyon, *Prisons and Patriots: Japanese American Wartime Citizenship, Civil Disobedience, and Historical Memory*
Shelley Sang-Hee Lee, *Claiming the Oriental Gateway: Prewar Seattle and Japanese America*
Isabelle Thuy Pelaud, *This Is All I Choose to Tell: History and Hybridity in Vietnamese American Literature*

A list of additional titles in this series appears at the back of this book.

Masumi Izumi

The Rise and Fall of America's Concentration Camp Law

Civil Liberties Debates from the Internment to McCarthyism and the Radical 1960s

TEMPLE UNIVERSITY PRESS
Philadelphia • Rome • Tokyo

TEMPLE UNIVERSITY PRESS
Philadelphia, Pennsylvania 19122
tupress.temple.edu

Copyright © 2019 by Temple University—Of The Commonwealth System of Higher Education
All rights reserved

Paperback edition published 2022
Cloth edition published 2019

Library of Congress Cataloging-in-Publication Data

Names: Izumi, Masumi, 1966– author.
Title: The rise and fall of America's concentration camp law : civil liberties debates from the internment to McCarthyism and the radical 1960s / Masumi Izumi.
Description: Philadelphia : Temple University Press, 2019. | Series: Asian American history and culture | Based on author's thesis (doctoral —Doshisha University. Graduate School of American Studies, 2003) issued under title: Japanese American internment and the Emergency Detention Act (Title II of the Internal Security Act of 1950), 1941–1971 : balancing internal security and civil liberties in the United States | Includes bibliographical references and index. |
Identifiers: LCCN 2018057936 (print) | LCCN 2018060130 (ebook) | ISBN 9781439917268 (E-book) | ISBN 9781439917244 (cloth : alk. paper)
Subjects: LCSH: United States Emergency Detention Act of 1950. | Internal security—Law and legislation—United States—History—20th century. | Political crimes and offenses—Law and legislation—United States—History—20th century. | Detention of persons—United States—History—20th century. | Japanese Americans—Evacuation and relocation, 1942–1945.
Classification: LCC KF4850.A328195 (ebook) | LCC KF4850.A328195 .I995 (print) | DDC 344.7303/545—dc23
LC record available at https://lccn.loc.gov/2018057936

ISBN 9781439917251 (paperback : alk. paper)

Printed in the United States of America

081222

To my husband and daughter, Hitoshi and Mana Kamada;

my parents, Yoshiko and Shinzo Izumi;

my grandmother, Teiko Onda;

and all my mentors and "sempai" activists

Contents

A Note on Terminology ... ix

Introduction: The Emergency Detention Act: A "Concentration Camp Law" ... 1

1 Alienable Citizenship: Race, Loyalty, and the Mass Incarceration of Japanese Americans ... 11

2 Legalizing Preventive Detention: The Passage of the Emergency Detention Act of 1950 ... 44

3 The Shifting Ground of Civil Liberties: McCarthyism, the FBI, and the Supreme Court in the Age of Concentration Camps ... 76

4 Quiet Americans No More: The Expansion of Political Dissent and the Grassroots Campaign to Repeal Title II ... 110

5 Recommitting to Civil Liberties: The Repeal of Title II and the Passage of the Non-Detention Act ... 145

Conclusion: A New Age of Concentration Camps? ... 171

Acknowledgments ... 181

Notes ... 185

Bibliography ... 233

Index ... 247

A Note on Terminology

How to describe what Japanese Americans experienced during World War II is a contested matter in itself. As the U.S. government decided to exclude "all persons of Japanese ancestry" from the one-hundred-mile coastal zones on the Pacific, it invented official terminologies to legitimize its actions. The exclusion and removal of people of Japanese ancestry from the "defense zone" while no combat was imminent on the West Coast was called the "evacuation." The term implied that the policy was a safety measure for its victims. The forced removal of ethnic Japanese was called "relocation," and the makeshift facilities in which Japanese Americans were housed within the defense zone were called "assembly centers." The camps built inland, outside the defense zone, were called "war relocation centers," even though these facilities were surrounded by barbed-wire fences and guarded by armed soldiers with guns pointed inward. The "evacuees" were allowed to move freely inside the camps, but they could not leave the camps without permission. The whole process, including exclusion and removal from the West Coast and confinement in inland camps, was called "internment."

Over the years scholars of Japanese American history and concerned Japanese Americans have uncovered the true nature of these wartime policies and the conditions that the victims of the policies were forced to endure. Thus, there arose a need to replace the euphemisms that had been used to disguise reality.[1] To that end, the Japanese American Citizens League (JACL) published *Power of Words Handbook: A Guide to Language about Japanese Americans in World War II* (2013), which explains various euphemistic terms used during the war and recommends alternatives that accurately reflect reality.² For example, the handbook recommends that the terms "evacuation" and "relocation" be replaced with "forced removal," that "assembly center" be replaced with "temporary detention center," and that "relocation center" or "internment camp" be replaced with "concentration camp." It also suggests that "internment" should be used only to describe the apprehension and detention of Issei (Japanese-born immigrants) in Department of Justice facilities and that terms such as "incarceration" and "illegal detention" should be used to describe the confinement of Nisei (second-generation U.S. citizens) in the camps managed by the War Relocation Authority.

I wholeheartedly share the JACL's concerns about euphemistic terms and agree that accurate terms that reflect reality are needed. Thus, I use "forced removal" and/or "exclusion" to refer to the relocation of Japanese Americans from the West Coast and "incarceration" or "detention" to describe their confinement in inland camps. I use "concentration camps" instead of "relocation centers" to describe the War Relocation Authority camps and "detention camps" to refer to Justice Department camps, except when the context necessitates the inclusion of the name of a camp (e.g., Gila River War Relocation Center).

When referring to the governmental power to forcibly remove and incarcerate enemy aliens, I do not rule out the use of the generic term "internment." The JACL handbook argues that because "internment" is defined as "the confinement or impounding of enemy aliens in a time of war," it should not be used to describe the confinement of Nisei—who accounted for three-quarters of Japanese Americans during World War II—because they were U.S. citizens. While this argument makes sense on the basis of a legal definition, I fear that it might suggest that although Nisei confinement was unconstitutional, Issei confinement was justifiable. I contend that Issei detention and Nisei detention were equally problematic, as the entire policy of removal and incarceration was justified by the discourse of "preventive detention of enemy aliens," through which Nisei citizens were discursively "alienated" from their birthright citizenship. Because my main focus is the critical analysis of the precarious borderline between citizens and aliens, I want to avoid drawing a simple, fixed line between Nisei citizens and Issei aliens.

I also have reservations about using the term "illegal detention" to describe the wartime incarceration of Japanese Americans. The removal and confinement of Japanese Americans who were branded enemy aliens and non-aliens—the "internment"—was conducted at the very brink of legality, and the Supreme Court managed to uphold it in the *Hirabayashi* and *Korematsu* decisions, albeit on extremely narrow constitutional grounds.³ The essence of the problem, which this book scrutinizes, is not the fact that the government carried out illegal actions against American citizens but the fact that the U.S.

Constitution allowed for the preventive mass incarceration of both citizens and aliens under the rubric of governmental war power. The story of the passage and repeal of Title II, which is the focus of this book, illuminates how Americans viewed this problem in terms of the tension between national/internal security and civil liberties and how they tried to cope with this essential weakness within the constitutional protection of civil liberties when confronted with various "enemies" of the state.

The Rise and Fall of America's Concentration Camp Law

Introduction

*The Emergency Detention Act:
A "Concentration Camp Law"*

On September 25, 1971, President Richard Nixon was on his way to Anchorage, Alaska, to meet Emperor Hirohito of Japan. He stopped in Portland, Oregon, to sign HR234, a bill that repealed the Emergency Detention Act of 1950.[1] Nixon, on signing the bill, reiterated the nation's faith in its democratic tradition:

> This strong country has no reason to fear that the normal processes of law—together with those special emergency powers which the Constitution grants to the Chief Executive—will be inadequate to deal with any situation, no matter how grave, that may arise in the future. But we do have a great deal to fear if we begin to lose faith in our constitutional ideals.[2]

The law that fell on that autumn day had passed in Congress by an overwhelming majority exactly twenty-one years earlier. The Emergency Detention Act (hereafter Title II) formed Title II of the Internal Security Act of 1950. The Internal Security Act, also popularly called the McCarran Act, was one of the antisubversion laws passed by Congress in the context of early Cold War anticommunist fervor. The law gave the president power to apprehend and detain any person who the government suspected might engage in acts of espionage and sabotage in the event of invasion, war, or insurrection.[3] It authorized the Justice Department to construct detention facilities to lock up potential spies and saboteurs as soon as the president declared the existence of an internal security emergency. Drafted, debated, and passed a few months after the start of the Korean War and the arrests of Julius and Ethel Rosenberg, Title II greatly expanded the government's power to restrict civil liberties. Soon after its drafting, it acquired the nickname of "the concentration camp law," and this label lingered for the duration of the law's existence.

Title II was one of many laws Americans passed as they struggled to balance individual freedom and internal security. One characteristic, however, distinguished it from other pieces of legislation that restricted citizens' liberty for the nation's security: Title II embodied the idea of *preventive detention.*

Preventive detention is a measure to protect internal security by restricting the freedom of a certain individual or a group of individuals on the basis of actions that *might be* taken to threaten the security of a nation or region. It differs from criminal punishment, which is based on actions *already* taken that violate existing criminal laws. In preventive detention, the accused cannot be tried beyond a reasonable doubt, the principal guideline in criminal trials, since the accusation is based on the assumed probability of certain future actions. It also differs from military tribunals or enemy combatant cases, because the apprehension involves civilians who are not necessarily engaged in military or pseudo-military actions. Finally, preventive detention requires special detention facilities, or concentration camps, to house those who are apprehended, instead of prisons, which jail people found guilty and sentenced in criminal trials.

Because preventive detention depends heavily on government officials' discretion, it conflicts with the Fifth Amendment of the U.S. Constitution, which prohibits depriving any person of "life, liberty, or property, without due process of law." Such a policy is considered acceptable only when there is a grave danger to national or internal security (such as war, espionage, or terrorist attacks) that outweighs the constitutional protection of civil liberties.

Under the U.S. constitutional system, the government cannot make a law that violates the Constitution, even if the president or Congress believes such a law is necessary. How, then, did Congress justify Title II so that it passed by an overwhelming majority? The obvious background for the passage of law was the rising tide of McCarthyism and the imminent threat of nuclear espionage in the early Cold War period. As today we confront the fear of terrorist attacks in major cities and heightening military tension in East Asia, we may be living in a similar political atmosphere. Many democratic nations are now implementing systems of closer governmental surveillance on their citizens' lives, and there is stronger public support for stricter law enforcement at the expense of civil liberties. The late 1940s and early 1950s were when the world experienced the threat of nuclear annihilation for the first time. The ideological schism between the Eastern and Western blocs as well as the escalating arms race between the United States and the Union of Soviet Socialist Republics (USSR) made the majority of Americans feel that extreme security measures such as preventive detention were acceptable and even necessary.

On the other hand, when I examined the congressional debates at the passage of Title II, I noticed that the repressive nature of the law severely disturbed the consciences of federal lawmakers, legal experts, and even mainstream journalists. Many were concerned about the possibility of governmental abuse of power, and some lawmakers tried to provide human rights protections within the bill and restrictions on its implementation.

An even more peculiar thing about Title II was that the law was repealed by Congress twenty-one years after its passage, despite the facts that it was never invoked during its statutory life and the possibility of its future invocation was minimal. And although the law was designed to deal with internal security crises, the repeal took place in 1971, a year when there was widespread protest against the government on city streets and university campuses.

Nixon explained the repeal as follows:

> The mere continued existence of these legal provisions has aroused concern among many Americans that the act might someday be used to apprehend and detain citizens who hold unpopular views. Some have feared that it might someday be used to permit a situation comparable to the detention of Americans of Japanese ancestry during World War II.[4]

This speech shows two reasons for ending Title II. Nixon hoped that the repeal would ease public anxiety about the government's repression of social and political dissent among minorities and radical dissidents, symbolized in the image of U.S. "concentration camps." Nixon's speech also suggests that the memory of Japanese American wartime incarceration gave impetus to the repeal. This indicates that Americans in 1971 associated Title II with Japanese American incarceration during World War II, an incident that predated the law's passage. To elucidate the connection between Japanese American internment and Title II, this book scrutinizes the debates concerning civil liberties in three historical moments of national crisis: the forced relocation and incarceration of Japanese Americans during World War II, the passage of Title II in 1950, and the law's repeal in 1971.[5]

Although Title II has been studied in three academic fields, it has received comparatively little attention considering the potential severity of its impact on the freedoms of citizens. In the 1950s and 1960s, several articles analyzed Title II in law journals. Political analyses of its passage began to appear in the 1970s, when New Left historians engaged in the revision of the political history of the early Cold War era. Title II is mentioned occasionally in Japanese American historiography, but there is only one article-length work on the relationship between Title II and the mass incarceration of Japanese Americans, other than my own work and articles written by those directly involved in the repeal campaign.[6] One obvious reason for this neglect is that this law never actually came into effect in American legal processes. Title II was to be activated only when the government declared the existence of a national emergency (i.e., war, invasion, or insurrection). The American government did not make such a declaration between 1950 and 1971.

Unlike Title II, which has rarely been discussed in scholarly works in any substantial way, the wartime removal and incarceration of Japanese Americans has become one of the most heavily studied civil rights violations in U.S. history. Yet past studies have approached the events as two separate phenomena. During World War II, the American government forcibly removed and detained American citizens and resident aliens suspected to be linked to an enemy state through racial affiliations. Not a single Japanese American—including Issei, who were legally Japanese nationals—was convicted of espionage or sabotage. After the end of World War II, Japanese Americans never again became a target for mass detention, nor was their loyalty to the United States collectively placed in doubt. Title II, a law passed in the context of early Cold War national insecurity, was a manifestation of the severe prosecution of communists during the 1950s and had the potential to be used against radical social dissenters in the 1960s. The persecution of racial/ethnic minorities and that of political spies and radicals have conventionally been treated as separate issues in ethnic studies or American studies. Even when the connection is made through the study of Title II, the relationship between these two issues has been rendered a simple one.[7]

In the past two decades, however, an increasing number of works have started to link civil rights issues with the Cold War. Mary Dudziak, one of the pioneering scholars on Cold War racial politics, elucidated how the Cold War motivated the U.S. government's effort to tackle domestic racial inequality in order to promote an image of the nation as a leader of democratic regimes in the international sphere.[8] Recently, Asian American scholars have come to juxtapose the post–World War II construction of Asian Americans as a "model minority" against the negative representations of African Americans as a group socially dependent on governmental intervention for their racial ascendancy. They have analyzed this contrast in light of the United States' Cold War desire to be the leader of the so-called free world while facing strong domestic resistance against the liberalization of race relations. Works such as Ellen Wu's *Color of Success* (2014) and Cindy I-fen Cheng's *Citizens of Asian America* (2014) show how Asian Americans actively participated in the advancement of Cold War liberalism by demonstrating their patriotism and desirability as citizens, on the one hand, and striving to remove racially exclusive conventions such as restrictive covenants and immigration quotas on the other.[9]

Other recent works investigate the link between antiradicalism and racial persecution. For example, Jeff Woods analyzes smear campaigns and scare tactics against civil rights activists in the U.S. South during the early Cold War period.[10] Utilizing anticommunist rhetoric, those campaigners ultimately aimed to maintain the southern way of life founded on the social principles of segregation and white supremacy. Woods elucidates how segregationist southerners worked with the anticommunist and antiradical FBI director, J. Edgar Hoover, to conduct persistent surveillance on civil rights organizations. He concludes that these concerted efforts were successful in derailing the civil rights organizations' efforts to pursue African American rights and desegregation lawsuits, as they were pressed into defensive positions regarding communist infiltrations in the 1950s.

In line with these recent findings in American studies and Asian American studies, this book analyzes the entangled discourses of race, national security, and civil liberties during what I call the "age of concentration camps" between 1941 and 1971. It closely examines rhetorical as well as direct historical links between Japanese American incarceration and the passage of Title II to elucidate how Cold War liberalism created a regime that confined American citizenship within the boundary of loyalty and patriotism, while the nation tried to rid itself of overt racial oppression and exclusion. Cold War liberalism expanded the boundary of discursive citizenship to include racial minorities, but at the same time, it placed individuals considered not loyal or patriotic outside the national boundary.

This book adopts critical discourse analysis as its primary method. Based on a constructionist view of history, discourse analysis focuses on how language produces knowledge, shapes meaning, and influences social practice. Constructionism frees us from being concerned with the intentionality of historical actors and helps us focus on the relationship between one action and another by looking at power and the practice of representation. Critical discourse analysis looks at historical texts within their contexts and illuminates the social structures, often including uneven power relationships, that legitimate, enact, or reproduce particular forms of social interaction.[11] Rather than trying to fix the definitions of terms such as "loyalty," "American," and "un-American," this book analyzes the contested usage of such terms and explores how the boundaries of citizenship shifted as domestic and international political contexts changed between 1941 and 1971.

To see how the concept of citizenship was manipulated through the construction or threat of concentration camps, this book looks at the wartime mass incarceration of Japanese Americans, a legal precedent of Title II, in the history of American national and internal security. In reality, the camps, euphemistically named War Relocation Centers, were concentration camps for American citizens and long-term residents of Japanese ancestry, who were deprived of constitutional freedoms. Officially, however, the policy enacted the wartime internment of enemy aliens and their dependents. Issei, first-generation immigrants who constituted one-third of camp residents, were de jure enemy aliens, because they were barred from naturalization and thus had retained their Japanese citizenship. Nisei and Sansei, the second and third generations who were American citizens by birth, were treated *like* enemy aliens, and to do so the government devised terms such as "non-aliens" to legally and constitutionally justify the forced removal and detention of American citizens.

Rather than drawing a fixed line between Issei and Nisei based on legal citizenship statuses, this book looks at the fluidity of such categories to illuminate the *alienability* of citizenship based on factors such as race, loyalty, and political beliefs, particularly at times of national and internal security crisis. Chapter 1, "Alienable Citizenship: Race, Loyalty, and the Mass Incarceration of Japanese Americans," explains Japanese American mass incarceration as a wartime measure of preventive detention by analyzing its administrative process and related Supreme Court decisions. By manipulating words to label Japanese Americans as enemy aliens or non-aliens and racially and culturally marking them as potentially disloyal, the government succeeded in justifying mass incarceration based on race. In 1943, the government forced incarcerated Japanese Americans over the age of sixteen to answer a "loyalty questionnaire." Those who did not answer "yes" to two crucial questions—whether they were willing to serve in the U.S. Army and whether they would forswear any allegiance to the Japanese emperor—were branded as disloyal and sent to Tule Lake Segregation Center as potential renunciants of American citizenship. The rest of the incarcerees, now determined as loyal to the United States, were allowed to leave the camps and encouraged to reintegrate into the society after being cleared for indefinite leave.[12]

While the government defended its decision as based on military necessity, the incarceration of a racial group en masse disturbed those who administered the policy. The Supreme Court justices who ruled on its constitutionality were reluctant to give the military unrestricted discretion over civilians even in wartime. The sense of guilt ironically led liberal lawmakers in 1950 to draft a bill that allowed the government to construct concentration camps and lock up subversive citizens, based on individual assessment, in an emergency. Chapter 2, "Legalizing Preventive Detention: The Passage of the Emergency Detention Act of 1950," explains the legislative process in which Title II was passed. Ironically, Title II was a product of liberal lawmakers' attempts to defeat the communist registration and anti-immigration bill advocated by conservatives in Congress. Title II was drafted to set the rules for preventive detention, so that the government could remove ostensibly dangerous persons from society and lock them up in camps while maintaining liberty for the rest of the American people. The bill's drafters modeled it after Japanese American incarceration, and they installed provisions to protect the detainees' rights in order to prevent the arbitrary detention of innocent citizens, even minorities. The drafters and sponsors of the bill included liberal lawyers and politicians directly involved in the administration of wartime incarceration or resettlement of Japanese Americans as government officials.

Chapter 3, "The Shifting Ground of Civil Liberties: McCarthyism, the FBI, and the Supreme Court in the Age of Concentration Camps," elucidates how Title II contributed to the strengthening of the FBI as an internal security agency and also led to the construction of detention camps designated specifically for Title II in case the law was invoked. Throughout the McCarthy era, Title II also provided statutory justification for expanding the FBI's power of surveillance and creating a blacklist of potentially subversive persons. Contrary to the intentions of Title II's liberal drafters, the procedural protections of civil liberties provided by the law had limited effects. The FBI grew in size and influence as a domestic intelligence agency during the 1950s and 1960s, and the information it gathered was used for anticommunist congressional and state investigations. The list was also utilized to watch civil rights and labor activists. The Justice Department built six detention camps in accordance with the provisions of Title II. One of the camps was Tule Lake, the former segregation center for the "disloyal" Japanese Americans, which was partly rehabilitated for the new law. Title II legitimized the development of a formidable surveillance agency that transcended racial and political boundaries and infiltrated private spheres to monitor even the minds and thoughts of individuals as loyalty came to be used to draw the boundary between Americans and un-Americans. The shadow of concentration camps loomed throughout the society, even though Title II was never enforced.

The later chapters connect the Japanese American internment with the rise of political radicalism in the late 1960s. In this period, notions such as loyalty and patriotism came to be questioned by various groups. Chapter 4, "Quiet Americans No More: The Expansion of Political Dissent and the Grassroots Campaign to Repeal Title II," explains how the campaign to repeal Title II started within the Japanese American community and spread to other groups. As a rumor arose that the government was preparing concentration camps to lock up African Americans and radical antiwar activists, a few Japanese American social activists moved to involve the Japanese American Citizens League (JACL), an ethnic organization led by mainstream Japanese

Americans, to formally oppose Title II and advocate its repeal. After joining the JACL, grassroots activists worked with the long-term leftist opponents of the Internal Security Act as well as radical African American organizations and emerging Asian American student groups to repeal Title II. Through the campaign, Japanese Americans started talking about their wartime experiences in public, and this helped the repeal campaign gain popular support.

Chapter 5, "Recommitting to Civil Liberties: The Repeal of Title II and the Passage of the Non-Detention Act," explains the congressional process that ended the law. The debates and discussions that took place suggest that the shared memory of the wartime incarceration of Japanese Americans was crucial to the consensus building for repeal. Many civic organizations, ethnic groups, and politicians advocated repeal—but for different reasons. Liberal politicians had a chance to express their regret for Japanese Americans' wartime treatment and, for some, to alleviate their own sense of guilt for passing Title II. Conservative politicians and the Nixon administration took advantage of the opportunity to appease public anxiety about the political repression of dissidents. Minorities, particularly African Americans, narrated their own historical oppression in relation to the tragic wartime persecution of Japanese Americans. Japanese Americans connected their wartime experiences to Title II in the image of barbed-wire fences and watchtowers, and they succeeded in obtaining support from groups with a wide range of views on internal security and civil liberties. Opponents of the repeal tried to separate the Title II issue from Japanese American removal, but the very presence of Japanese Americans in the repeal campaign ensured the symbolic connection between the two. The historical memory of mass incarceration, acknowledged by all participants in the repeal process, made opposition to repeal virtually impossible.

In 1971, Americans of various racial, ethnic, religious, and political affiliations came together to repeal Title II, and Congress declared once and for all that the United States did not need concentration camps. The images of barbed-wire fences and watchtowers haunted the law, as the memory of Japanese American internment was resurrected after two decades of amnesia. The public discussions that led to the repeal of Title II elucidate how unsettling memories shaped Americans' understanding of preventive detention vis-à-vis changing race relations and contested political perceptions about social resistance in the 1960s. The Title II repeal campaign was a precursor to the Japanese American Redress movement—the movement to demand official governmental apology and compensation for the wartime mass incarceration—as it gave political voice to Japanese Americans as victims of U.S. historical racism.

Americans looked into the past when they passed Title II, and again when they repealed the act and found Japanese American mass incarceration to be an important reference point in dealing with the civil liberties of those whose loyalty to the nation was rendered questionable. Shedding light on the notion of preventive detention reveals the shift in the discursive boundaries of citizenship, precisely because preventive detention as an emergency measure lies at the very fringe of the constitutional protection of civil liberties and citizenship. Preventive detention, often justified by a discourse of danger, places detainees outside the citizenry, notwithstanding Fifth Amendment protections. Careful scrutiny of the discursive shifts in language used in the wartime policy for Japanese Americans and Title II reveals the performative construction of U.S. identity and the boundaries of citizenship.

Cold War liberalism necessitated the inclusion of "desirable" racial minorities to showcase American superiority in the ideological competitions against the socialist bloc and the decolonizing third world. Japanese Americans who passed the loyalty screening perfectly embodied a desirable racial minority that the postwar United States could use as an example of a successfully integrated population. Title II, designated as an improvement over mass internment, nominally credited Cold War liberals for their advocacy of liberal democracy. In practice, however, it advanced Cold War conservatives by allowing the passage of a concentration camp law, which tremendously expanded the discretion of the executive branch by granting it power to watch over citizens and to label and lock up certain individuals as undesirables. Two decades later, in the Title II repeal campaign, Americans revisited the wartime incarceration of Japanese Americans, whose experiences were now understood in the context of the historical exclusion and oppression of racial minorities. As the nation went through a wholesale reevaluation of its past in terms of civil rights and liberties, people felt that a concentration camp law needed to be struck down in a legislative spectacle.

Now is a peculiar time to be contemplating how the United States in the past has tried to balance civil liberties with national and internal security. Title II was passed early in the Cold War, when the anticipation of a nuclear war hovered over people's everyday thinking. The law was repealed while the United States was fighting an imperialistic war in Asia and massive protests were organized in almost every city in the nation. Today, we are witnessing rising military tensions in East Asia, with the expansion of Chinese naval power and an unclear schedule or process for North Korea's nuclear disarmament.[13] Japan's looming remilitarization is a cause of concern as well.

Writing history is writing in hindsight—we know what happened after the incident we are describing. However, today I am writing with uncertainty about tomorrow. The "shadow of war," as Michael S. Sherry titles his book, covers our lives.[14] As a citizen of Japan, I realize that it has been a luxury to have lived for several decades without fear of random destruction by military might, thanks to the nation's pacifist constitution. But it has been merely a geopolitical and historical contingency that many of us living in the Global North did not have to live in such fear.

As the feeling of insecurity rises, we are witnessing the increase of discriminatory and hateful messages around issues such as immigration, security, labor, and diversity throughout the Global North. In the United States, a presidential candidate who used racist and sexist language throughout the election process proved to have run the most successful campaign. Even after taking office in January 2017, Donald J. Trump has continued to tweet inflammatory and divisive language. Moreover, he has introduced policies that exclude certain people from entering the United States based on nationality and religion, as well as policies that would limit civil rights for people within the nation. In Japan, Prime Minister Shinzo Abe is trying to introduce a constitutional change to remilitarize the country and curtail civil liberties. While the majority of Japanese citizens support the retention of the pacifist clause, the administration touts a need for change. The draft of the new constitution proposed by the ruling Liberal Democratic Party (LDP) significantly weakens the protection of human rights, and it strengthens governmental power to restrict individual civil liberties for the sake of maintaining public order.

One way of coping with this fear is to acknowledge the ephemerality of our lives in *ukiyo*, or the floating world, and go with the flow—let fate take its own way. But as a historian and a parent, I know I have another choice, which is to write and act in order to prevent or at least postpone massive destruction, and to search for an alternative destiny for humankind. This book, like many other history books, describes how people acted to defend human rights in a time of social crisis. These events offer many lessons from which we can learn to resist the general apathy that the fears of war and political oppression are generating today. People came together, shared their histories, and developed consciousness about the legal and executive structure of one form of political oppression—preventive detention—and repealed the law that authorized the government to exercise such power.

I never wanted this research to be timely. I wish that the fear of concentration camps was a story of the past. But we know that detention—whether threatened or enforced, massive or arbitrary—based on the mere suspicion of subversive future actions is a governmental apparatus for silencing dissent. As the shadow of war grows more imminent, telling the story of Title II's enactment and repeal becomes increasingly important. In this sense, this publication is a timely one. I deliver this book with help and support from so many people who share the feeling that we need to value civil liberties for all, especially at a time when those in power propagate the idea that the repression of liberties is necessary to keep us safe.

1

Alienable Citizenship

Race, Loyalty, and the Mass Incarceration of Japanese Americans

On December 8, 1941, a day after the Pearl Harbor attack, *Newsweek* carried an advertisement by an asbestos company, Keasbey and Mattison.[1] Three bomber airplanes, drawn in silhouette, flew over an otherwise peaceful home with a couple standing outside, looking up into the sky. The "shadow of war" was spreading over the lives of ordinary Americans. Historian Michael S. Sherry writes that this ad "offered a simple visual statement of war as an external force that Americans were loath to engage, rendering it as a set of menacing shadows hovering over a scene of domestic tranquility."[2]

In fact, the war had already affected many Americans even before the country declared its participation in World War II. A large number of Jews had escaped Nazi persecution and sought asylum in the United States. Certain ethnic organizations, including groups of Japanese and Germans, had kept close ties with their states of origin and supported the war effort of their home countries. For most Americans, however, war was an external menace happening far away. But once the war that had swallowed Europe and Asia finally reached America, it covered the entire world.

In the same *Newsweek* issue, an advertisement for Fleischmann's Enriched Hi-B$_1$ Yeast Bread appeared. It warned readers, "Get this shocking fact: Four out of ten American men—at the peak of youth—aren't quite good enough for the Army!" It blamed a lack of essential diet factors for the unfitness of millions of men. Fleischmann's enriched yeast, the ad claimed, would make "a more alert, calm and confident America, ready and unafraid," and thus contribute to the nation's preparedness for war.[3]

The Pearl Harbor attack literally brought war to American homes. Bread, a toothbrush, Coca-Cola, and life insurance were all advertised under military images in the same issue of *Newsweek*.[4] The militarization of society, however, did not happen overnight. Sherry defines "militarization" as "the process by which war and national security became consuming anxieties and provided the memories, models, and metaphors that shaped broad areas of national life," arguing that this started in the United States in the 1930s.[5] Using evidence ranging from statistics on the growth of military expenditure to representations in popular culture, Sherry contends that this process not only affected the government and military but also "reshaped every realm of American life—politics and foreign policy, economics, technology, culture and social relations—making America a different nation" from the country before the 1930s.[6]

The militarization of the United States was a result of the global shift in the nature of war and, more importantly, in the nature of modern society. Modern war involved technological weaponry, such as aircraft carriers, radar, and strategic bombers. Enemies at a great distance could now do much damage not only to military facilities but also to civilian lives. Technological advancement, particularly in aviation, was "tearing down the barriers that once had insulated America."[7] America's defense spending rose by 50 percent in the latter half of the 1930s, and army manpower increased eightfold between 1939 and 1941.[8]

Technological war enlarged the menace of enemies close by as well as those farther away. Advancements in communication and information technology, as well as in weapons, meant that information involving these innovations could make a crucial difference in the competition over military strength and in the damage the enemy could do. Espionage and sabotage, or the "fifth column," became a great source of anxiety in this process.[9]

Modern war was also a "total war." The result of a conflict depended on not only the country's military power—the number of army and navy personnel and amount of munitions—but also the country's economic and industrial ability to produce these resources. The central factor in the war effort was a nation's ability to continue its mobilization of domestic and international resources longer than the enemy nations could. The concept of a total war existed before the 1930s, but it was President Franklin D. Roosevelt who fully utilized his cultural resources to hammer the notion into people's minds. He reiterated over the radio the menace of enemy air raids on cities. He asked for total defense, because no attack was "so unlikely or impossible that it may be ignored."[10]

A total war permeated citizens' everyday lives. As it was crucial for the state to mobilize all segments of national life into the war effort, mundane things, such as what kind of bread people ate, became vital concerns. Commitment to the interests and security of the nation was essential for the maintenance of social coherence, without which the country became vulnerable to foreign attack. In preparation for a total war, the state required loyalty from every single citizen. The Pearl Harbor attack proved that FDR was not crying wolf, confirming his claims that there was "no such thing as impregnable defense against powerful aggressors who sneak up in the dark and strike without warning."[11] Posters appeared depicting cunning enemies that might sneak up from behind and stab one in the back.[12] The dreadful sentiment arose that enemies were close and invisible.

After Pearl Harbor, even though the United States was at war with Japan, Italy, and Germany, the main target of suspicion for the general population as well as the military on the West Coast was Japanese Americans. The general animosity toward Japanese Americans reflected not only traditional mistrust of Asians as inscrutable aliens but also American insecurity about national defense. Pearl Harbor had a dramatic effect on both ordinary citizens and high military officials sensitive to the potential threat of espionage and sabotage. Since a small number of disloyal citizens could bring great peril, those perceived to be associated with the enemy nation seemed to threaten the United States' integrity in its war effort. Japanese Americans were therefore considered suspect.

When military or other kinds of insecurity arise in a society, it is often the case that an unpopular racial, ethnic, and/or other minority becomes a target of focused antagonism. Because the government singled out Japanese nationals from other enemy aliens such as Germans and Italians, and included American citizens of Japanese ancestry in the enemy alien category, the majority of scholars of the internment point to racist aspects of the policy. On the other hand, a few scholars have focused on its implications for the military or internal security. Brian Hayashi, who explored military records both inside and outside the United States, argues that the army was more concerned about the tactical aspects of the war in the Western Hemisphere than racial relations.[13] Roger W. Lotchin criticizes what he calls "the race paradigm" of internment scholarship in his 2018 book *Japanese American Relocation in World War II: A Reconsideration*.[14] Lotchin contends that historians have asserted a deterministic and dogmatic paradigm of American racism as a single cause of the policy, oversimplifying the complex political, military, psychological, and economic factors that led to the government's decision to "evacuate/relocate" Japanese Americans.[15] Lotchin's book ultimately fails to disprove the notion that Japanese American "relocation" was triggered by West Coast racism and approved because of general American racial prejudice. But his claim that the policy requires consideration of multiple factors other than racism, such as psychological and military concerns, cannot simply be pushed aside: as this book shows, the policy was a rather complex phenomenon.

Debating whether the Japanese American removal and incarceration policy was caused by military necessity or racial prejudice is somewhat futile, because the two were not mutually exclusive; rather, they worked together. Economic, political, social, and military concerns are often expressed in the language of race, and they are frequently channeled into and played out through racial divisions. To elucidate how this mass removal and incarceration of an ethnic group was possible within the American constitutional democracy and to assess its legal as well as political impact on the civil liberties of the nation as a whole, this chapter scrutinizes the relationship among racial prejudice, internal security policy, and a growing sense of national insecurity.

Japanese historian Akihiro Yamakura points out that the incarceration of Japanese Americans should be considered in tandem with the detention of Japanese nationals during World War II, as both were integral parts of the American government's wartime measures against "Japanese alien enemies."[16] His book narrates a legal history of Japanese American incarceration in the War Relocation Authority (WRA) camps, Japanese alien detention in the Justice Department and War Department detention centers, martial law and alien incarceration in Hawaii, and the detention and deportation of Japanese Latin Americans to the United States.[17] Yamakura elucidates the limitations of constitutional and legal protections for civil liberties: lawmakers, bureaucrats, and even court judges can act on racial prejudice, and this sentiment, he argues, influenced all the branches of the U.S. government.

Like Yamakura, I view Japanese American wartime incarceration in relation to U.S. efforts to control enemy aliens. But while his book attempts to provide the comprehensive legal history of ethnic Japanese in the Americas during World War II, mine focuses on the removal of Japanese Americans from the West Coast and their incarceration in the WRA camps. Also, instead of concentrating on the experiences of Japanese and Japanese Americans and emphasizing how racial prejudice prevailed, this book contextualizes internment as a response to other major dilemmas: maintaining the nation's safety and preventing governmental abuse of power in an emergency.

Through discourse analysis, this chapter shows how, in the beginning of the Pacific War, Japanese Americans as a racial group were collectively *alienated* from discursive American citizenship. This allowed for a shift in the usual wartime procedures for the administrative control of civilians and the treatment of enemy aliens. The chapter also explains how, in the war's later years, the ostensibly antiracist language used both to affirm *and* to condemn such a discriminatory policy opened up a path for the passage of a "concentration camp law" after World War II.

Although most literature on Japanese American incarceration looks at how racial prejudice existed before, during, and after the war, scholars such as Izumi Hirobe and Lon Kurashige have illuminated antiracist opposition to America's discriminatory immigration and domestic policies, even during the exclusion era.[18] These studies complicate the history of Asian exclusion. Similarly, this book critically examines the discourses both *for* and *against* mass exclusion/incarceration and shows that many antiracist discourses emerged from the wartime treatment of Japanese Americans. It also examines how the boundary of citizenship was manipulated—first to exclude Japanese Americans from American citizenry and later to include them as legitimate, even "model," citizens. Although this chapter treats racism as the key element that caused the wartime mass incarceration, it emphasizes the shifts in, rather than the consistency of, the way race was perceived by policymakers and legal experts during World War II.

Civil Liberties in Times of Internal Security Crisis before World War II

The question of how to balance individual freedom and internal security has been discussed in the United States since the nation's inception.[19] The 1798 Alien and Sedition Acts granted the president power to deport dangerous aliens and restrict domestic criticism of the government, constituting the first major test of civil liberties. Many Republicans critical of the Federalist administration and journalists sympathetic to the Republicans were arrested before the law expired two years later, and this period left a bitter memory among many Americans about the political repression of their freedom of speech.

The Aaron Burr case of 1807 became the first legal test of treason, which the Constitution defined as "levying war" against the United States or "in adhering to their [the nation's] enemies, giving them aid and comfort."[20] Burr was charged with assembling an armed force and instigating the separation of the trans-Appalachian states from the Union. The Supreme Court ordered his acquittal, despite the Jefferson administration's pressure to sustain a conviction, because the prosecution lacked the two witnesses required for proving an act of treason. This precedent prevented the government from applying a loose definition of treason that included a variety of political acts against the state.

The Civil War introduced the next grave internal security crisis. The existing treason law could not be used, because millions of southerners were "levying war" against the United States and many in the border states were, "in adhering to their enemies, giving them aid and comfort." Instead of officially charging people with treason, the government adopted military and summary arrests to deal with citizens suspected of disloyalty. President Abraham Lincoln insisted on the Union government's right to maintain its own existence by restricting the constitutional liberties of the discontented minority who tried to destroy the union. Congress passed the Habeas Corpus Suspension Act of 1863, making it difficult for an imprisoned individual to challenge detainment by demanding a legal examination of evidence.

The emergency measures during the Civil War led to a landmark Supreme Court decision soon after the war. Lambdin P. Milligan, a civilian resident of Indiana and a Confederacy supporter, was arrested and sentenced to death by hanging by a military commission. The Supreme Court unanimously ruled that the defendant should be released because he should not have been tried by the military tribunal when the civil court was functioning. The Supreme Court ruled in *Ex Parte Milligan* (1866) that only Congress could suspend the writ of habeas corpus and that no military action could be taken to control civilians except under martial law conditions, which could exist only where the courts and civil administration could not function. The Court insisted that military control of civilians was allowed only during "actual and present" invasion, and this principle was maintained until World War II.[21]

The next major challenge to American civil liberties arose in 1917 with U.S. participation in World War I and the outbreak of the Russian Revolution. Before World War I, issues relating to civil liberties were treated almost exclusively as state concerns. The Fifth Amendment restricted only the federal government, and even though the Fourteenth Amendment restricted the states, its application had been limited to the protection of property rights against state interference. Civil liberties in state or local communities were generally considered by the majoritarian rule, and the rights of dissenting or alienated minorities were often given low priority. The notion of freedom of speech was also interpreted differently before World War I than it is today. The traditional interpretation was that the government could not censor or stop publication—a principle called the "rule of no prior restraint."[22] After publication, however, the government could arrest and try a writer or speaker if it decided the writing or the speech was injurious to the public interest.

In 1917, Congress passed the Espionage Act, which banned statements interfering with the draft or promoting military insubordination. In the following year, by passing the Sedition Act, the government made it unlawful to "incite mutiny or insubordination in the ranks of the armed forces"; to use "disloyal, profane, scurrilous, or abusive" language to describe the government, the Constitution, the flag, or the military uniform; or "by word or act [to] oppose the cause of the United States." These laws severely restricted civil liberties in wartime, and in practice the Espionage Act introduced political censorship, restricting many publications—not only radical and dissenting newspapers but also major periodicals such as the *Saturday Evening Post* and the *New York Times*—from being delivered to subscribers.[23]

The constitutionality of the Espionage Act was tested in the trial of a socialist who delivered antiwar leaflets urging people not to enlist. In 1919, in *Schenck v. United States*, the Supreme Court upheld the act, ruling that free speech could be limited if the words were "of such a nature as to create a clear and present danger that they will bring about . . . substantial evils."[24] In *Abrams v. United States* that same year, the Supreme Court upheld the Sedition Act by affirming the convictions of five plaintiffs who had published pamphlets criticizing the government's military expedition to Russia and inciting a general strike of workers in ammunition factories.[25]

Between 1917 and 1920, the government launched a large-scale antiradical campaign. Attorney General A. Mitchell Palmer strengthened the Bureau of Investigation, which later came to be known as the Federal Bureau of Investigation.[26] The bureau blacklisted labor organizers, socialists, communists, and war critics, and government agents broke into homes and meeting halls without search warrants. More than four thousand people were arrested and six hundred aliens deported as the result of these "Red Scare" raids.[27]

Palmer's repressive approach drew criticism from liberals in political and legal realms. In 1920, a group of liberal lawyers established the American Civil Liberties Union (ACLU) to protect the rights of conscientious objectors, leftists, and radical labor activists. In the 1920s, however, radicals and anarchists could not expect much protection from the courts. Numerous states passed criminal syndicalism and sedition laws, and the Supreme Court in most cases upheld them.[28] The Supreme Court maintained its affirmation of the Espionage Act, while Congress in the 1920s passed stricter immigration laws in an attempt to keep radical immigrants out of the United States.

It was during the 1920s and 1930s that an important standard developed to measure the balance between national security and civil liberties. In the 1919 Supreme Court decision in *Schenck v. United States*, Justice Oliver Wendell Holmes Jr. presented the "clear and present danger" doctrine, which claimed that freedom of speech should be restricted only when the words would "bring about the substantive evils" that Congress had a right to prevent. This doctrine gradually became a measuring rod in cases that involved the balance between freedom of speech and national or internal security.

In the years leading up to U.S. involvement in World War II, Congress passed a set of laws restricting civil liberties to control the domestic influence of totalitarian regimes, including the Foreign Agents Registration Act (McCormack Act) in 1938, the Voorhis Act in 1940, and the Alien Registration Act in 1940. The Alien Registration Act required all aliens to register with the government and get fingerprinted, and it stipulated deportation as the penalty for those who had in the past belonged to subversive organizations. Title I of the Alien Registration Act, known as the Smith Act, was the first general peacetime sedition statute since 1798, making it a crime to advocate the overthrow of the government by force or violence. The Smith Act was designed to deal with communists as well as supporters of totalitarian regimes within the United States. However, after Nazi Germany invaded the USSR, the Soviets became part of the Allied Forces. Communists in the United States, therefore, supported the war, and the Smith Act did not become a key weapon against communists until after World War II.

The historical analysis of civil liberties in the United States elucidates the long history of antiradicalism in American political culture, which, on the other side of the coin, shows the existence of a vibrant history of radicalism.[29] In recent years, historians have studied radicalism among immigrant communities because antiradical laws have often been coupled with anti-immigration statutes.[30] The United States repeatedly made laws that restricted freedom of speech and the press when it felt the necessity to control domestic radicalism, communism, and other activities that were perceived to threaten its polity. After the critical situations—such as a war or major social unrest—had subsided, liberal ideas prevailed again, reflecting Americans' general attachment to the idea of freedom.

It should be noted that with the exception of during the Civil War, when hundreds of arrests were made to prevent violence or interference with the military, prior to World War II—even in national security crises—the American government never officially resorted to preventive detention for internal security purposes. Denaturalization and deportation were important administrative devices for dealing with radical immigrants, but Congress never granted the government the power to arrest and detain citizens on the basis of the possibility of future subversive conduct. This precedent, however, was broken in the early months of 1942, when Japanese Americans were suspected of constituting a collective threat to national security.

The Alienation of Japanese American Citizens and Their Forced Removal from the Pacific Coast

Historian Norman Naimark, in *Fires of Hatred: Ethnic Cleansing in Twentieth-Century Europe* (2002), analyzes five European cases of large-scale forced removal of citizens, concluding that "ethnic cleansing" was a violent expression of twentieth-century nationalism as modern states organized themselves by ethnic criteria.[31] One of Naimark's examples is the Turkish removal and genocide of Armenians during World War I. In 1915, the Turkish government designated the eastern regions of the Ottoman Empire as war zones and removed Armenians on the basis of the claim that they were disloyal to Turkey and sympathetic to Russians as fellow Christians. An estimated 1.5 million Armenians died during this removal.[32]

Through his analysis, Naimark explains how war provides excuses for ethnic violence even though each historical case has its own particularity and contingency. Armenian ethnic cleansing shows similarity to Japanese American exclusion—not in its scale or the extent of its brutality but in the discursive structure through which the total removal of an ethnic minority was justified. This section elucidates how war and national insecurity led to the racial removal of Japanese Americans from the U.S. West Coast, explaining this development in relation to the changing nature of war and the altering relationships among nationalism, ethnicity, and citizenship.

Beginning on December 7, 1941, the fate of Japanese Americans fell in the hands of two government agencies: the Department of Justice, which was in charge of internal security, and the Department of War, which was in charge of national security. On the same day as the attack on Pearl Harbor, President Franklin D. Roosevelt signed, along with the declaration of war, Proclamations 2525, 2526, and 2527. These declared that the nationals of Japan, Germany, and Italy, respectively, who were within the United States were "alien enemies." The proclamations permitted the summary apprehension of any such aliens "deemed dangerous to the public health or safety of the United States."[33]

In fact, the American government had already launched a study of the loyalty of Japanese Americans toward the United States before the war started. This occurred through the joined efforts of three intelligence agencies. The Military Intelligence Division (G-2) was in charge of army intelligence activities. The Office of Naval Intelligence (ONI) started its investigation of the possible existence of espionage rings on the West Coast in the mid-1930s.[34] In 1939, President Roosevelt ordered that the activities of the three agencies—the ONI, G-2, and the FBI—be coordinated.[35] They compiled what was called the "ABC list" of subversive and dangerous aliens who might be arrested in the event of war. The names of Japanese persons on the list grew to over two thousand by early 1941.

In a study commissioned by the ONI, Lieutenant Commander K. D. Ringle of the U.S. Navy estimated that the number of persons who could act as saboteurs and espionage agents was 3 percent, or "3,500 in the entire United States who were identifiable individually."[36] In June 1941, a Japanese spy ring was uncovered around Itaru Tachibana, a Japanese naval officer, as a result of a raid on the Japanese Consulate in Los Angeles. On the basis of the investigations into the spy ring, Ringle concluded that the Japanese American community was loyal to the United States and that the Japanese government's effort to recruit Nisei for its espionage operations was unsuccessful.[37] Anticipating a war with Japan, President Roosevelt also set up an independent intelligence organization, supervised by journalist John Franklin Carter.[38] Carter assigned Curtis B. Munson to investigate the ethnic Japanese community on the West Coast and in Hawaii. Munson reported that there was no evidence of disloyalty.[39]

Within a few days of the Pearl Harbor attack, however, the Justice Department arrested over one thousand Japanese nationals.[40] Those arrested included Japanese American community leaders, fishers, Buddhist and Shinto priests, and Japanese language-school teachers, along with those who had expressed sympathy for Japanese military activity in Asia.[41] On December 22, 1941, Attorney General Francis Biddle created the Alien Enemy Control Unit, with Assistant Attorney General Edward J. Ennis in charge as director. Under Ennis's direction, arrests of Japanese aliens continued, and by February 16, 1942, the number rose to 2,192.

The arrested Issei, first-generation Japanese Americans, were held in temporary detention stations and later sent to Justice Department detention camps in Santa Fe, New Mexico; Missoula, Montana; Bismarck, North Dakota; Fort Sill, Oklahoma; and Crystal City, Texas. The Tuna Canyon Civilian Conservation Corps camp was turned into a temporary detention center for enemy aliens arrested by the FBI in Southern California. Tuna Canyon Detention Station, located in Tujunga, a northern suburb of Los Angeles, held in total over two thousand Japanese, German, and Italian aliens, of whom the vast majority were Japanese, between December 16, 1941, and October 1, 1943.[42]

Presidential proclamations also ordered the confiscation of cameras, weapons, short-wave radio sets and transmitters, and other instruments of possible espionage and sabotage belonging to enemy aliens.[43] On December 29, 1941, all enemy aliens were ordered to deposit prohibited articles with the local police. On January 1, 1942, Attorney General Biddle authorized the issuance of search warrants on reasonable cause for believing that aliens possessed contraband. The FBI, with help from the local police, searched the houses of Japanese Americans and confiscated forbidden items.

The War Department had to decide how to deal with possible domestic security threats. Of the five thousand Nisei serving in the military, six hundred were discharged by late 1941, while others were transferred to menial tasks. The Selective Service stopped accepting Nisei since they were categorized as 4-C, a class "not acceptable to the armed forces because of nationality or ancestry."[44] General John L. DeWitt, who headed the Western Defense Command, ordered continuous surveillance of the Japanese American community. DeWitt demanded that the Justice Department conduct mass raids of citizens as well as aliens without search warrants, and that it should exclude enemy aliens from the "restricted zones" designated by the military.[45] At this point, the restricted zones were limited to areas around the airports, dams, power plants, fuel pumping stations, harbor areas, and military installations.

After the publication of the Roberts Commission Report on January 24, 1942, which investigated the Pearl Harbor incident and pointed out the military's unpreparedness for foreign attacks, public agitation for the removal of the entire Japanese population from the West Coast quickly became rampant.[46] The FBI and local police forces proceeded with large-scale search-and-seizure raids of houses and fishing boats owned by Japanese Americans. Japanese American households, in most cases, included both Japanese nationals (Issei) and U.S. citizens (Nisei and Sansei), and even though the Justice Department was aware of these differences in status, it proceeded to allow the constitutional rights of citizens to be violated. What harmed Japanese Americans even further was that these raids attracted attention from the press, which sensationalized the danger of espionage and sabotage and fueled public suspicion.

Provost Marshal Allen W. Gullion and his assistant, Karl R. Bendetsen, who liaised between the Western Defense Command and the War Department, pushed General DeWitt toward mass removal.[47] California attorney general Earl Warren publicly supported the total removal of Japanese Americans.[48] Warren tapped into the public's anxiety about fifth-column activities in a total war and successfully connected it with the conventional distrust against the "Asiatic race" on the West Coast.[49]

Attorney General Biddle, in an effort to stop mass removal, sent a delegate to California as a liaison between the Justice Department and the Western Defense Command to implement the limited exclusion policy DeWitt had demanded.[50] The liaison officer, lawyer Thomas C. Clark, was assigned to administer the exclusion of enemy aliens from the prohibited zones and restricted areas.[51] Clark, however, failed to control the growing sentiment in favor of mass exclusion. Contrary to the attorney general's intention, Clark, who after the war became a conservative attorney general and a Supreme Court justice, believed that the military should be given full authority in the matter.

Seeking legal advice, Biddle asked three lawyers outside the Justice Department, Benjamin V. Cohen, Oscar Cox, and Joseph Rauh, to assess the constitutionality of the mass relocation policy. The report in response, "The Japanese Situation on the West Coast," carefully balanced the constitutional protection of individual liberties with national security. It concluded, "So long as a classification of persons or citizens is reasonably related to a genuine war need and does not under the guise of national defense discriminate against any class of citizens for a purpose unrelated to the national defense, no constitutional guaranty is infringed."[52] The authors did not favor the mass incarceration of Japanese Americans, but their report supported the policy by underlining the constitutionality of such measures as long as they were necessary for the war effort.

Although high military officials initially expressed reservations about the mass removal on both constitutional and practical grounds, it was ultimately the military that demanded the authority to conduct it. On February 11, 1942, Secretary of War Henry L. Stimson asked the president if he agreed to the mass removal of Japanese American citizens as well as Japanese aliens from the restricted areas designated by the military. The president's reaction to the plan was "very vigorous."[53] Stimson told Assistant Secretary of War John McCloy that the constitutional repercussions could be overridden by dictating the policy under "military necessity."[54] On the other hand, Brigadier General Mark Clark at the General Headquarters of the U.S. Army, who had been assigned to make the official military report on the advisability of mass removal, reported around February 12 that such a measure could not be recommended because Japanese invasion on the Pacific Coast was highly unlikely.[55]

On February 14, General DeWitt sent the Secretary of War his final recommendation on the "Evacuation of Japanese and Other Subversive Persons from the Pacific Coast." He explained that mass exclusion was necessary to protect the West Coast, which was vital in military communication as well as in the industrial production of military supplies, particularly aircraft. This report emphasized Japanese Americans' racial unassimilability:

> The Japanese race is an enemy race and while many second and third generation Japanese born on United States soil, possessed of United States citizenship, have become "Americanized," the racial strains are undiluted. . . . That Japan is allied with Germany and Italy in this struggle is not ground for assuming that any Japanese, barred from assimilation by convention as he is, though born and raised in the United States, will not turn against this nation, when the final test of loyalty comes.[56]

On February 19, President Roosevelt signed Executive Order 9066, which authorized the Secretary of War and the designated military commanders to prescribe military areas within U.S. territory "from which any and all persons may be excluded" whenever and wherever such commanders deemed it necessary.[57]

Thus, the mass removal of ethnic Japanese civilians from the Pacific Coast was made possible by transferring the governance of domestic enemy aliens and potentially dangerous citizens from the Department of Justice to the Department of War. The policy-making process shows that the mass removal of Japanese Americans from the West Coast was the result of the failure on the side of the military to distinguish between Japanese aliens and Japanese American citizens in regard to their constitutional rights. The military had little interest in making such a distinction because its primary concern was to protect American territory from foreign aggressors and insidious domestic foes.

Emerging studies on the military decisions leading to mass removal indicate that those decisions might have had more to do with tactical concerns than with racial hatred. For example, historian Brian Hayashi discovered documents suggesting that the mass removal was intended to secure the coordination of military operations among the United States, Canada, and Mexico.[58] Although General DeWitt's descriptions of Japanese Americans clearly reveal his racial prejudice, the conventional interpretation that he was persuaded by West Coast racists might need to be revised when more military documents are examined. In any case, it is clear that the military refused to distinguish Japanese American citizens from Japanese aliens despite the Justice Department's plea to make such distinctions. Since the military is an institution primarily concerned with national security, it would be reasonable to think that its leaders made a conscious decision rather than a careless one based solely on racial prejudice or cultural misunderstandings.

The decision to incarcerate Japanese Americans as a group, regardless of citizenship status, exemplifies the fact that the boundaries of citizenship are unfixed, and also that such boundaries tend to blur when the safety of the state is at stake. Political scientist David Campbell, in *Writing Security: United States Foreign Policy and the Politics of Identity* (1998), points out that "for the state, identity can be understood as the outcome of exclusionary practices in which resistant elements to a secure identity on the 'inside' are linked through a discourse of 'danger' through threats identified and located on the 'outside.'"[59] Campbell argues that American identity is "performatively constituted" through the inscription of boundaries that "demarcate an 'inside' from an 'outside,' a 'self' from an 'other,' a 'domestic' from a 'foreign.'"[60] The language that explained the military exclusion of Japanese Americans placed the Nisei outside the discursive national boundary of citizenship, as they were branded "enemy non-aliens" and categorized as unfit for military service because of their ancestry. They were considered a threat on the West Coast regardless of their individual actions, and even the lack of evidence of disloyalty was considered suspicious. As Earl Warren warned the House

Select Committee Investigating National Defense Migration (Tolan Committee), the fact that no reports of sabotage and espionage had been made was evidence that fifth-column activities were "timed just like Pearl Harbor was timed."[61]

Originally intended as a policy of removal, the government's plan soon developed into one of incarceration, as General DeWitt prohibited Japanese aliens and Japanese American citizens from leaving military areas and ordered them to report to gathering stations with only what they could personally carry. The Western Defense Command created the Wartime Civil Control Administration (WCCA), whose responsibility was the administration of living conditions as well as the transportation of Japanese Americans herded into temporary detention sites called assembly centers. The assembly centers detained Japanese Americans until the military transferred them to more permanent camps in the interior. To administer these permanent camps, the War Relocation Authority (WRA) was established within the executive branch on March 18, 1942.[62]

After Executive Order 9066 was issued, Congress passed Public Law 503, making the violation of military orders a misdemeanor.[63] Only three representatives outside the Pacific region showed substantial interest when the law was passed.[64] Congressman Martin Dies (D-Texas), Congressman John E. Rankin (D-Mississippi), and Senator Tom Stewart (D-Tennessee), all southerners, joined the Western delegates who passionately supported mass removal. John Rankin proclaimed, "Once a Jap, always a Jap!" He demanded that the internees be separated by sex to prevent them from reproducing. It is noteworthy that Rankin's racial view of the Japanese paralleled his view of African Americans. He believed that granting citizenship to people of color would "mongrelize America." He insisted that the Pacific side of the war was a "race war," in which the "White man's civilization" had come into conflict with "Japanese barbarism."[65]

Before Public Law 503 was passed, only one member of Congress made a comment criticizing the bill. Senator Robert Taft (R-Ohio) stated:

> I think this is probably the "sloppiest" criminal law I have ever read or seen anywhere.... It does not say who shall prescribe the restrictions. It does not say how anyone shall know that the restrictions are applicable to that particular zone.... I have no doubt that an act of that kind would be enforced in wartime. I have no doubt that in peacetime no man could ever be convicted under it, because the court would find that it was so indefinite and so uncertain that it could not be enforced under the Constitution.[66]

Taft, however, voted in support of the bill because he understood "the pressing character of this kind of legislation for the Pacific Coast" at the time.[67] Like the Department of Justice, Congress also deferred to the decision of the Department of War without any careful review of the policy plans or military necessity that the army claimed to exist. Although the decision-making process was characterized by a lack of agreement, in the end a consensus was built on the point that the War Department should have its way in wartime.

Supreme Court Decisions and the Alienability of Citizenship

Securing his authority over enemy alien control on the West Coast, General John L. DeWitt ordered that all persons of Japanese ancestry should stay at home between 8:00 P.M. and 6:00 A.M. DeWitt also issued proclamations that designated the zone along the entire Pacific Coast and one hundred miles inland as the "Military Area" and ordered the exclusion of all persons of Japanese ancestry from this region. Some Japanese Americans violated the military orders and were arrested pursuant to Public Law 503. Among them, three Nisei—Minoru Yasui, a lawyer in Portland, Oregon; Gordon Kiyoshi Hirabayashi, a college student in Seattle, Washington; and Fred Toyosaburo Korematsu, a welder in San Leandro, California—became famous because their convictions were reviewed by the U.S. Supreme Court.[68] In addition, the Supreme Court reviewed a habeas corpus petition by Mitsuye Endo filed from inside a WRA camp.[69] *Yasui v. United States* and *Hirabayashi v. United States* were brought together to the Supreme Court, which announced its opinions on June 21, 1943.[70] *Korematsu v. United States* and *Ex Parte Endo* were both decided on December 18, 1944, one day after the exclusion orders were lifted.

Because these cases have been closely and critically reviewed in legal studies, such as Peter Irons's *Justice at War* (1984) and Eric K. Yamamoto et al.'s *Race, Rights and Reparation* (2001), this chapter does not describe the decisions in detail.[71] However, it pays special attention to the manipulative language that the Court adopted to avoid ruling on the constitutionality of mass incarceration, examining how this manipulation discursively placed American citizens, such as Hirabayashi and Korematsu, outside the national boundary and thus rendered them unprotected by constitutional assurances. Close analysis reveals how the carefully crafted logic of the Japanese American Supreme Court cases, which at first utilized racial and cultural discourses but in the end resorted to the discourse of loyalty, undermined the "inalienability" of civil rights and liberties.

The Military and the Civilian Court at War: *Hirabayashi v. United States* (1943)

Gordon Hirabayashi, a senior at the University of Washington in Seattle, was working for a Quaker relief group helping Japanese American families who were forced to relocate. On May 16, 1942, he defied his own relocation order and turned himself in to the FBI office, accompanied by his ACLU lawyer.[72] He explained his action as a citizen's "duty to maintain the democratic standards" of his country.[73] Minoru Yasui requested to be arrested by the police because he believed that the exclusion order violated his right to equal protection under the law. Hirabayashi was tried in the federal District Court on October 20, 1942, and was found guilty of violating both the curfew and the exclusion orders. He was sentenced to imprisonment for ninety days for each count but allowed to serve the sentences concurrently. Yasui was also convicted for violation of the curfew and travel ban as he moved without permission from Portland to Hood River, where his family lived. Hirabayashi and Yasui's cases were heard in the Supreme Court on May 10 and 11, 1943, and on June 21, the Court affirmed their convictions unanimously. Chief Justice Harlan F. Stone wrote the opinion of the Court. Justice William O. Douglas, Justice Frank Murphy, and Justice Wiley Rutledge wrote concurring opinions, although they were critical of the majority opinion.[74]

Hirabayashi's attorneys argued that Congress had unconstitutionally delegated its legislative power to the military commander by authorizing him to impose the curfew, exclusion, and other military orders. They also contended that, even if the military regulations were lawfully authorized, the Fifth Amendment prohibited discrimination between citizens of Japanese descent and those of other ancestry.[75] Another claim was that the wording of the law was too vague, and DeWitt's orders violated the guarantees of due process and equal protection. A. L. Wirin, defense attorney on behalf of Minoru Yasui, argued that General DeWitt was influenced by hatred against people of the Japanese race. Wirin quoted the 1932 Supreme Court decision *Sterling v. Constantin*, which held that decisions made by military authorities were subject to judicial review even under martial law.[76]

Acting on behalf of the government, Solicitor General Charles Fahy argued in both *Hirabayashi* and *Yasui* that wartime emergency shifted the balance between the protection of individual freedom and the protection of the nation from espionage and sabotage. During wartime, he went on, "reasonable discretion" by the military in exercising the government's war power should be given more weight than the due process clause, although in peacetime a descendant of one nationality could not be convicted for an act that would not be a crime for a descendant of another nationality.[77]

The Supreme Court upheld separate treatment of Japanese Americans under the government's war power, which Chief Justice Harlan Stone defined as "the power to wage war successfully." The Court limited the ruling to the curfew order while contending that the war power extended to every matter and activity related to war and was "not restricted to the winning of victories in the field."[78] The military commander had the authority to decide what was necessary to protect war resources from espionage and sabotage, and General DeWitt had decided that the curfew order was an appropriate means to minimize the danger. Hirabayashi and Yasui, who knowingly violated the military order, were therefore punishable, the Court concluded.

Another important question asked in *Hirabayashi* was whether government policies or military orders discriminated against citizens of Japanese ancestry. Legislative classification or separate treatment based on race alone had often been held to be a denial of equal protection, and in these cases the Court was obliged to review the substantial effects of the law in question, not merely its wording.[79] Therefore, even though neither Executive Order 9066 nor Public Law 503 mentioned Japanese or Japanese Americans, the Court would have to strike them down as unconstitutional if the orders issued under them proved discriminatory in substance against a particular racial group. In *Schneider v. State* (1939), the Supreme Court ruled that the Court must "weigh the circumstances and . . . appraise the substantiality of the reasons advanced in support" when the "rights so vital to the maintenance of democratic institutions" were regulated for public convenience.[80] In *Hirabayashi*, because the curfew order applied only to enemy aliens and citizens of Japanese ancestry, its enforcement had to be proven to be reasonably related to the purpose of preventing espionage and sabotage.

The military explained that there were an unknown number of disloyal persons among ethnic Japanese residents, and "no ready means existed for determining the loyal and the disloyal with any degree of safety."[81] The Court accepted the government's argument and decided that, even though racial discrimination was prohibited in most circumstances, separate treatment of Japanese Americans was justified because the "fact alone that [the] attack on our shores was threatened by Japan rather than another enemy power set these citizens apart from others who have no particular associations with Japan."[82]

Justices Douglas, Murphy, and Rutledge wrote concurring opinions that were critical of the majority opinion. The Court showed deference to the military decision, but not everyone was willing to give the military unlimited power over citizens' treatment, even in wartime. Justice Douglas devoted a large part of his opinion to expounding the gravity and imminence of the threat of Japanese invasion on the West Coast and the difficulty of reviewing military decisions in such a critical situation. He sounded almost resigned about the Court's powerlessness over the military's actions at war: "Since we cannot override the military judgment which lay behind these orders, it seems to me necessary to concede that the army had the power to deal temporarily with these people on a group basis."[83]

Justice Murphy also wrote a concurring opinion, in which he conceded that modern war did not always wait for the governmental observance of procedural requirements. However, he expressed his grave concern about the implication of *Hirabayashi* for civil liberties:

> Under the curfew order here challenged no less than 70,000 American citizens have been placed under a special ban and deprived of their liberty because of their particular racial inheritance. In this sense it bears a melancholy resemblance to the treatment accorded to members of the Jewish race in Germany and in other parts of Europe. The result is the creation in this country of two classes of citizens for the purposes of a critical and perilous hour—to sanction discrimination between groups of United States citizens on the basis of ancestry. In my opinion this goes to the very brink of constitutional power.[84]

Justice Rutledge, in his short concurring opinion, wrote that a military officer was not granted unrestricted power even though he or she "must have wide discretion and room for its operation."[85] By this he implied that the Court should have the capacity to protect civilians if the officer overstepped certain bounds.

Was Public Law 503 an unlawful delegation of legislative power to the military commander? One problem was that this power transfer occurred in a political struggle between the Department of Justice and the Department of War over the control of enemy aliens. Concessions made by the Justice Department were not only devastating for Japanese Americans but also a threat to U.S. civil liberties, as they granted virtually unlimited power over civilian lives to the military—a sector seemingly less concerned about civil liberties or constitutional restrictions on governmental actions.

The other question was whether the military commander issued orders in the way that Congress had intended. When Congress passed Public Law 503, there was little debate or clarification about the possibility of the law affecting American citizens. Members of Congress clearly understood that the military was planning to remove only the ethnic Japanese population, and there was little discussion on the status of American citizens of Japanese ancestry, particularly those without Japanese citizenship. Colonel B. M. Bryan, representing Provost Marshal Gullion, referred to "American citizens of Japanese extraction" in the Senate Military Affairs Committee, explaining they had dual citizenship and "thus fell in the alien category."[86] Congress did not discuss the treatment of Nisei citizens without Japanese citizenship, like Hirabayashi and Korematsu, when it gave the military the authority to relocate any persons, citizen or alien, from the military zones.

In a total war, if the government's war power is the power to wage war effectively and successfully, this power affects a wide range of activities, from actual combat on battlefields to the enhancement of morale among ordinary citizens on the home front. It could mean that civilian lives are entirely subject to governmental intervention. Since the military is not an elected institution, delegation of the government's war power to it should be done with extreme caution, particularly when the power involves restrictions on civil liberties in noncombat areas. It becomes crucial to verify the appropriateness of military decisions so that the abuse of delegated power can be prevented. The role of the Court, therefore, becomes critical in such assessment.

One consolation for anyone who cared about civil liberties was that the Court's opinion was limited to the constitutionality of the military curfew order in the *Hirabayashi* decision. The Court accepted that military findings about the danger that enemy aliens posed to the nation at war provided enough support for concluding that the curfew order imposed on Japanese Americans, including Nisei while not including Italian or German Americans, was an appropriate means of protecting war resources on the West Coast from espionage and sabotage. Therefore, the Court contended, it was unnecessary to consider whether or to what extent such findings would support other orders that General DeWitt had issued. The Court thus gained some time before it had to address the constitutionality of the mass exclusion of Japanese Americans from the West Coast.

Differentialist Racism and the Failure of Rigid Scrutiny: *Korematsu v. United States* (1944)

Fred Toyosaburo Korematsu, who stayed in the prohibited area by disguising himself with plastic surgery and a false identity, was arrested in San Leandro, California, on May 30, 1942, about two weeks after the rest of the area's Japanese Americans were removed.[87] Korematsu was tried in the federal court in San Francisco and sentenced to five years of probation. As soon as his sentence was announced, the military police grabbed him at gunpoint and brought him to Tanforan Assembly Center, in accordance with General DeWitt's exclusion and incarceration orders.[88] Korematsu appealed, and upon another sentence of conviction in the Court of Appeals, he asked the Supreme Court to review his case. The Supreme Court handed down its judgment on December 18, 1944. Six justices affirmed Korematsu's conviction, while three dissented: Justices Owen J. Roberts, Frank Murphy, and Robert H. Jackson.

The *Korematsu* decision, written by Justice Hugo L. Black, adopted the same logic used in *Hirabayashi*, thus making the distinction between the curfew and the exclusion orders irrelevant. Black wrote that in light of the principles announced in the *Hirabayashi* case, the Court was "unable to conclude that it was beyond the war power of Congress and the Executive to exclude those of Japanese ancestry from the West Coast war area." Black acknowledged that, like curfew, the exclusion of those of Japanese origin was deemed necessary because of the assumed presence of an unascertained number of disloyal members of the group. The Supreme Court ruled that it was within the military's authority "to say who should, and who should not, remain in the threatened areas."[89]

The crucial issue in these cases was whether the Supreme Court performed adequate scrutiny of government and military actions. Justice Black's ruling opinion in *Korematsu* conveyed a clear principle:

> It should be noted, to begin with, that all legal restrictions which curtail the civil rights of a single racial group are immediately suspect. That is not to say that all such restrictions are unconstitutional. It is to say that courts must subject them to the most rigid scrutiny. Pressing public necessity may sometimes justify the existence of such restrictions; racial antagonism never can.[90]

The standard for "pressing public necessity" to justify a restriction of individual liberties was that the action of the accused constituted a "clear and present danger." The Supreme Court heard the military's contention that the ethnic Japanese population on the West Coast posed a potential threat to national security and therefore mass exclusion was necessary to remove danger from the military area. The Court neither assessed whether this contention was substantiated by factual evidence nor heeded the arguments that concluded otherwise.

Forty years after the case was closed, Aiko Herzig-Yoshinaga, a researcher for the Commission on Wartime Relocation and Internment of Civilians (CWRIC), discovered a document proving that the military report had been altered.[91] The report, authored by General DeWitt, contained unsubstantiated information on espionage and sabotage allegedly conducted by Japanese Americans. The Justice Department officials, Edward Ennis and John Burling, attempted to add a footnote to refute these findings, contending that the FBI and other intelligence agencies had found no proof of such acts within the Japanese American community.[92] The footnote was omitted from the final version of the report. Furthermore, DeWitt's ultimate policy recommendation revealed overt racial prejudice. He claimed that the military could not distinguish the loyal from the disloyal among Japanese Americans because of their inscrutablility, deriving inherently from their race. Knowing that such reasoning would oblige the Supreme Court to strike down the exclusion order as discriminatory, John McCloy altered the wording to say that the distinction between the loyal and the disloyal could not have been made within the necessary time limit. The original drafts were destroyed.

The discovery in the 1980s that the War Department had intentionally misinformed the Court led to the *coram nobis* cases, which vacated the convictions of Hirabayashi, Korematsu, and Yasui.[93] This discovery was also instrumental for the achievement of Redress, through which Japanese Americans received a governmental apology and monetary compensation for their treatment during wartime. *Korematsu v. United States* came to mark a serious blot in the constitutional history of the United States, but it was not until 2018 that the decision was officially repudiated by the Supreme Court.[94]

The *Korematsu* decision was problematic in the way the Supreme Court defined the case. The Court's majority opinion separated the military exclusion order from the incarceration of Japanese Americans in the assembly and relocation centers.[95] Justice Black wrote, "Had [the] petitioner here left the prohibited area and gone to an assembly center we cannot say either as a matter of fact or law that his presence in that center would have resulted in his detention in a relocation center."[96] This was false: the military had prohibited voluntary migration outside the prohibited area after March 29, 1942. There was no way Korematsu could avoid detention except by staying in the prohibited area and going into hiding. However, the Court separated exclusion and detention, and upheld Korematsu's conviction, by judging him only on the fact that he had remained in the prohibited area in violation of the military order, "regardless of the true nature of the assembly or relocation centers."[97]

This decision was refuted by four Supreme Court justices: one wrote a concurring opinion, and three expressed straightforward dissent.[98] Justice Roberts wrote:

> This is not a case of keeping people off the streets at night . . . nor a case of temporary exclusion of a citizen from an area for his own safety or that of the community. . . . On the contrary, it is the case of convicting a citizen as a punishment for not submitting to imprisonment in a concentration camp, based on his ancestry, and solely because of his ancestry, without evidence or inquiry concerning his loyalty and good disposition towards the United States.[99]

Another dissenter, Justice Murphy, argued that the military orders had "no reasonable relation to an 'immediate, imminent, and impending' public danger." Murphy contended that the mass exclusion policy against only Japanese Americans did not pass the rigid-scrutiny or substantial-basis tests. He rather blatantly criticized the military for not acting in good faith and declared that Korematsu's conviction "goes over 'the very brink of constitutional power' and falls into the ugly abyss of racism."[100]

Regarding the doctrine of rigid scrutiny, Justice Jackson in his dissenting opinion described the impossibility of judging the legitimacy of military orders for civilians at war. The Court could not examine evidence to decide whether or not the orders of General DeWitt were reasonably expedient military precautions, and even if they were, they might not be constitutional. Jackson did not offer any solution for the tension between the Court and the military at wartime, but he declared that he "would [prefer to] reverse the judgment and discharge the prisoner."[101]

Historically, a conventional way of resolving conflicts between internal security and civil liberties has been reversing the judgment after the crisis. When Abraham Lincoln ordered the suspension of habeas corpus during the Civil War, military and summary detentions were conducted as preventive measures. Most of the prisoners were discharged after loyalty screening or the termination of the emergency, and the *Milligan* decision, announced after the war, provided strict restraints on military control over civilian lives. Because the *Korematsu* decision was handed down in December 1944, when the military threat of Japanese invasion was already minimal, reversing the lower court's decision might have been one way for the Court to avoid validating "the principle of racial discrimination in criminal procedure and of transplanting American citizens."[102] Instead, the historically established balance between the military and the civil was "shifted dangerously to the side of the military by the known and unknown terrors of total war and by a quiescent and irresolute judiciary."[103]

Although many studies on the Japanese American cases point to the problems of the Supreme Court decisions, it is useful to further analyze how the *Hirabayashi* and *Korematsu* rulings marked a watershed in American constitutional history involving race, loyalty, and civil liberties. It needs to be emphasized that the Supreme Court declared that racial antagonism could never justify curtailing the civil rights of a single racial group. If one read the decisions carefully, one could not fail to notice that the opinions of the Court utilized cultural arguments for treating Japanese Americans differently from other Americans. In *Hirabayashi,* Justice Stone listed numerous cultural traits of Japanese Americans—the prevalence of Japanese language schools, a common custom of sending children to Japan for education, and the retention of close-knit communities—as justification for the military decision. Even religious and social activities were used as factors that legitimized the military's suspicion of Japanese Americans' loyalty toward the United States.

These findings in *Hirabayashi* were then adopted in *Korematsu* to legitimize mass exclusion. The traits mentioned, however, were commonly found in any ethnic communities in the United States and not unique to Japanese Americans. As Justice Douglas pointed out in his concurring opinion for *Hirabayashi*, loyalty is not determined by blood or race but is "a matter of mind and of heart."[104] Similarly, the extent of assimilation should not be the basis for treating a particular race or ethnic group differently. Emotional attachment to another country is a separate issue from subversive activities in one's country of residence. In the end, however, cultural arguments presenting Japanese Americans as alien supported the constitutionality of their mass exclusion.

This is an example of what French philosopher Etienne Balibar calls "differentialist racism."[105] The difference of an ethnic group from the dominant ethnic or racial group itself substantiates separate, discriminatory treatment. Racism does not necessarily involve the overt idea that one race is superior or inferior to another; arguments premised on the incompatibility of different cultural groups suffice to justify discrimination against certain ethnic minorities and their exclusion from the mainstream social structure. Differentialist racism, a cultural apparatus of "othering," had been continuously used in demands for the exclusion and segregation of racial minorities, and it was also adopted when the loyalty of Japanese Americans toward the United States was assessed within the camps.

By pointing out cultural differences, supporters of mass exclusion and the Supreme Court constructed Japanese Americans as the cultural other. This otherness was then translated into danger, which legitimized their exclusion based on military orders. Therefore, the military did not have to prove that Japanese Americans were disloyal or dangerous. It was enough to say that the Japanese American community contained a small but unknown number of *potentially* disloyal persons whose identity could not be determined because of the group's cultural differences from mainstream Americans. Legal and birthright citizen status did not protect people of Japanese ancestry from being discursively excluded from cultural citizenship. They were constructed as enemies of the state, or "un-Americans," while their ancestral land was at war with the United States. Thus, under the military logic of national security, the Supreme Court upheld a racist policy while verbally rejecting racism as a constitutional principle.

A similar contradiction can be found in the enigmatic behavior of Justice Department official Edward Ennis in the *Hirabayashi* hearing. All existing literature agrees that Ennis opposed the mass exclusion of Japanese Americans, including Japanese aliens. He almost resigned in protest when the decision was made, and he filed complaints about the military's misrepresentation of facts in the *Korematsu* case. However, Ennis presented a judicial notice for *Hirabayashi* in defense of the government, observing that the military's decision to impose curfew on all alien enemies *and* citizens of Japanese ancestry was justifiable considering the threat of Japanese invasion on the Pacific Coast. Eric Muller speculates that Ennis might not have seen his own actions as inconsistent when he vigilantly acknowledged the illegality of the military's separate treatment of one racial group while simultaneously remaining complicit with the military's insistence on the imminent danger of invasion, even though he knew the top military officials did not believe such a threat existed.[106] Instead, Muller suggests, he was likely influenced by the long-term "racial schema" built up for several decades in the United States that depicted the Japanese as "inscrutable, untrustworthy," and "inherently suspicious."[107] Muller argues that many officials conscious of the constitutional principle of civil liberties—including Ennis, Secretary of War Stimson, and others—were susceptible to the resulting image of waves of Orientals invading the nation and threatening its "very integrity," a typical discourse of the "Yellow Peril."[108] Conversely, historian Roger Lotchin repudiates such long-term racism as the cause of the executive and military decisions to exclude the ethnic Japanese, emphasizing that these decisions were made when Americans felt most vulnerable to a foreign attack.[109] And even then, Lotchin adds, many officials, military and civil, had problems with the notion of racial exclusion. However, in my study, careful discourse analysis of primary sources, such as the government and military reports and court decisions, reveals that it was ultimately race that tipped the balance between the constitutional protection of liberties and military necessity, in favor of the latter, at the crucial moment of decision making and during the judicial review of that decision.

Legal experts in the school of critical race theory analyze how law, "itself a cultural process that both reflects and reinforces the racial categories defined initially outside of law," contributes to perpetuating racial stereotypes and assumptions prevalent in the larger society.[110] Accordingly, critical race theory scholar Jerry Kang dismisses the idea that the Supreme Court justices were misguided by the government into affirming the convictions of Hirabayashi and Korematsu. Perceiving the Court as a part of, not above, the general cultural episteme, Kang argues that it "willfully" went along with the lies of the military and the government in regard to the likelihood of Japanese Americans getting involved in subversive activities and the alleged impossibility of distinguishing loyal citizens of the "Oriental" races from disloyal ones.[111]

Perhaps to balance out the grim implication of the *Korematsu* case for the court's ability to protect the civil liberties of minorities in wartime, a habeas corpus petition from inside a camp was taken up by the high bench on the same day.

The Reintegration of Japanese Americans through the Discourse of Loyalty: *Ex Parte Endo* (1944)

Mitsuye Endo never appeared in court but was at work in an office in the WRA camp in Topaz, Utah, when her case was heard by the Supreme Court. Endo was selected as the "perfect type" of plaintiff for a habeas corpus petition from inside a camp, representing the entire incarcerated population of Japanese ancestry.[112] She was a twenty-two-year-old woman (the gender generally considered less likely to be a military threat), had worked before the war in the California Department of Motor Vehicles in Sacramento, neither spoke nor read Japanese, had never been to Japan, and was a Methodist. Moreover, the fact that her brother was serving in the U.S. Army made her an ideal subject for the test case.

In short, Mitsuye Endo was a "model minority," a prototype of Asian immigrants that made the entire group acceptable in the cultural pluralist concept of the American nation.[113] Historian Ellen D. Wu in *The Color of Success: Asian Americans and the Origin of the Model Minority* (2014) elucidates how World War II "fostered the advent of racial liberalism."[114] Wu points out that, to counter Japanese propaganda during World War II and Soviet propaganda during the Cold War, mainstream representations of Asian Americans shifted from unassimilable aliens to the model minority, and this process was part of the larger machinery of intellectual "race making" in mid-twentieth-century America.[115] Racial liberalism was the belief that racial integration could be managed through the assimilation of nonwhites; it was based on the American idea of social engineering, which promoted individual engagement in state affairs through patriotism and active citizenship regardless of race. The induction of Nisei into the military was a scheme based on a shared contention among the WRA, the U.S. Army, and the Japanese American Citizens League (JACL) that military service—the ultimate self-sacrificial devotion to one's state and hence the fulfillment of "the highest obligation of citizenship"—would restore the collective public image of Japanese Americans and help their reintegration into the larger society.[116] Accordingly, it was through Endo's case that the Supreme Court was forced to directly face the issue of mass incarceration.

In *Ex Parte Endo*, the Supreme Court unanimously ordered that Endo should be freed unconditionally. In contrast to *Hirabayashi* and *Korematsu*, the *Endo* case revealed the Court's intention to reintegrate Japanese Americans into mainstream society, and for this purpose, the Court stressed Japanese American loyalty instead of potential disloyalty.

While granting freedom to Endo and the rest of the Japanese Americans still in camps, the Court dealt with the case by taking up the narrowest issue possible—the authority and responsibility of the War Relocation Authority, the civilian agency administering Endo's incarceration. The Court ruled that the WRA had three main responsibilities: (1) the maintenance of relocation centers as interim places of residence for the internees; (2) the segregation of loyal evacuees from disloyal ones; and (3) the continued detention of the disloyal and, as far as possible, the relocation of the loyal in selected communities.[117] This did not include the authority to continue detaining those who were proven loyal. By holding the WRA responsible for Endo's detention, the Court avoided discussing the military order that caused her detention in the first place. The Court assumed that the original exclusion was justified but determined that the continuous detention of loyal Japanese American citizens was unconstitutional, thus managing to maintain consistency throughout the four legal cases.

Two justices who wrote concurring opinions challenged the Court's evasion of interpreting the original military orders. Justice Murphy insisted that detaining people of Japanese ancestry in relocation centers regardless of their loyalty was "another example of the unconstitutional resort to racism inherent in the entire evacuation program." Justice Roberts claimed that the Court was avoiding the constitutional issues that were necessarily involved. Asserting that the government was aware of what was being done, he wrote that the Court was "squarely faced with a serious constitutional question"—whether Endo's detention violated the Bill of Rights, especially the guarantee of due process.[118]

Even Justice William O. Douglas, who wrote the majority opinion, problematized the weakened position of the judiciary vis-à-vis the executive branch during wartime. He opined that the Court "must assume that the Chief Executive and members of Congress, as well as the courts, are sensitive to and respectful of the liberties of the citizen," and it "must assume that their purpose was to allow for the greatest possible accommodation between those liberties and the exigencies of war" in its interpretation of a war measure.[119] The Court's reliance on these assumptions, however, contradicted the "rigid scrutiny" doctrine proposed in the *Korematsu* decision, which was handed down on the same day.

Even though *Ex Parte Endo* marked the end of exclusion for Japanese Americans from the West Coast, the decision left a sinister legacy for civil liberties. It changed civil liberties from an inalienable right to a reward for citizens' allegiance to the state through the disciplining language of "loyalty." By shifting the discourse from race to culture and then to loyalty, the Court avoided delivering an opinion on the constitutionality of Japanese American mass incarceration. By using the detainees' loyalty to assess the constitutionality of citizens' mass detention, the Court adopted loyalty, or the potential lack thereof, as a factor that could legitimize governmental restrictions on civil liberties. This move paved the way for a new scheme of governmental restrictions on the freedom of citizens in the postwar period, which is discussed in the next chapter.

The Termination of Exclusion

The exclusion order from the West Coast was lifted on December 17, 1944, one day before the *Korematsu* and *Endo* decisions were delivered. Ending the detention, however, was a longer process. Removing a certain segment of the population from a society is a relatively simple process, particularly when the removal is conducted under military authority. Reintegrating the segregated population into mainstream society is far more complicated.

The military was the first governmental sector to engage in the reintegration project. In January 1943, Secretary of War Stimson and Assistant Secretary of War McCloy met with representatives of the JACL and agreed to create a segregated regiment for Nisei as "the best method [for Nisei] to prove their loyalty to the public."[120] More than ten thousand men volunteered from Hawaii, along with a few thousand from the War Relocation Centers, albeit only after a rigorous recruiting campaign by the JACL. The 442nd Regimental Combat Team became one of the most decorated units in the history of the U.S. Army, with 18,143 individual decorations and 9,486 casualties.[121] In January 1944, the military recategorized Nisei from 4-C (enemy aliens) to 1-A (eligible for immediate induction), making them eligible for conscription. The conscription met with serious resistance among the Nisei, of whom 315 refused compliance, resulting in 263 convictions and jail sentences.[122]

Ellen Wu contends that public relations efforts to advertise the tremendous accomplishments of Nisei troops were enthusiastically promoted by the federal government as part of its scheme of racial liberalism. Wu also points out that the JACL's public memorialization of Nisei soldiers and its denouncement of resisters, including both those who answered "no" to the loyalty questions and those who resisted the draft, were efforts by racialized elites to ensure Japanese Americans' inclusion in the American national polity.[123]

In the meantime, the War Relocation Authority was in charge of resettling the internees. When the loyalty of an internee was affirmed through the questionnaire, he or she could sign the "Application for Leave Clearance" and leave the camp to go to school or work in the resettled community. Numerous religious and civic organizations helped with this process. A great number of Nisei resettled in the Midwest and eastern states before the exclusion order was lifted.[124]

The loyalty questionnaire also produced a group of Japanese Americans who were branded as disloyal. Those who did not answer yes to both questions were gathered in the Tule Lake Segregation Center, while those who gave the desired responses were shipped to other War Relocation Centers. The people incarcerated in Tule Lake were placed outside the discursive regime of U.S. citizenship. There was an assumption that they would be repatriated to Japan after the war, and in July 1944, Congress passed a denationalization law that enabled Nisei to voluntarily denounce their citizenship, opening a legal avenue to place American citizens outside the realm of American citizenry.

After the plan to close the camps was announced, the WRA had to resettle the remaining population. This was a challenging task, because those who remained in the camps were less inclined to adjust to mainstream American culture for economic, cultural, social, or psychological reasons. Over 5,500 internees in the Tule Lake Segregation Center renounced their American citizenship and applied for deportation to Japan.[125] Similarly, some incarcerees in the WRA camps were reluctant to leave and requested to continue living as free farmers on the land they cultivated within the camps.[126]

The resettlement project required a complete shift in the government's portrayal of Japanese Americans. Military and civilian agencies made concerted efforts to portray Japanese Americans as loyal, productive citizens and courageous soldiers. Along with the rise of racial liberalism in the mid-1940s United States, the push for Japanese American resettlement necessitated a governmental effort to represent Japanese Americans as bona fide immigrants and/or a "model minority."[127]

Political developments and experiences during World War II forced Americans to reconsider race relations within as well as outside the country after the war. The horrific genocide in Europe at the hands of the Nazis shocked the entire world. The mobilization of racial minorities in combat services gave the opportunity for minority communities to push for "double victory"—an overseas victory against fascism and a domestic victory against racism.[128]

After the war was over, public images of Japanese Americans turned positive. Politicians and military officers made public speeches and announcements highlighting the loyalty of Japanese Americans. On July 15, 1946,

President Harry S. Truman received the 442nd Combat Team at the White House. The president congratulated Nisei veterans as follows:

> You are to be congratulated on what you have done for this great country of yours. I think it was my predecessor who said that Americanism is not a matter of race or creed, it is a matter of heart. . . . You fought not only the enemy, but you fought prejudice—and you have won. Keep up that fight, and we will continue to win—to make this great republic stand for just what the constitution says it stands for: the welfare of all people all the time.[129]

Municipal officials made statements to urge the public to accept the relocated Japanese Americans in their communities. In early 1947, Mayor Hubert H. Humphrey of Minneapolis stated:

> During the war we came to know the Nisei well in connection with the fine patriotic service they performed at Fort Snelling and Camp Savage. It is a pleasure to note that many of them have chosen to make Minneapolis their permanent home, and that they are becoming a part of our social community. . . . I would like to urge that every Nisei participate to the fullest possible extent in the numerous civic activities. We need to know each other better and to build strong bridges of understanding between us so that we all recognize that we are a part of a single democratic tradition in which the dignity of every individual is placed uppermost.[130]

These public expressions of gratitude toward Japanese Americans revealed the contradictions in their treatment during wartime. The more the government emphasized the loyalty of Japanese Americans, the clearer it became that their incarceration had been unjust. In 1946, Truman established the President's Committee on Civil Rights to review the current state of civil liberties and race relations in the United States.[131] The presidential committee conducted research on lynching, segregation in the army and navy, suffrage in poll tax states, job discrimination, segregation in the South, and other issues surrounding civil rights and liberties. In its report, *To Secure these Rights*, the committee commented that the removal and incarceration of Japanese Americans constituted the "most striking mass interference since slavery with the right to physical freedom."[132] While refraining from reviewing the entire military relocation program or directly criticizing the government's policy, the committee expressed doubt over the legitimacy of the harsh treatment Japanese Americans faced during World War II and declared that it was "disturbed by the implications of this episode so far as the future of American civil rights is concerned."[133] Noting that the WRA's final report had recommended compensation for those who experienced property and business losses, the committee also expressed support for this idea.

On July 2, 1948, Truman signed the Japanese Evacuation Claims Act. The law allowed Japanese Americans to file claims against the government "for damages to or loss of real or personal property . . . that is a reasonable and natural consequence of the relocation or exclusion from a military area in Arizona, Washington, Oregon, or California."[134] Before the deadline of January 3, 1950, 23,689 claims were filed with the attorney general's office, and in the end the government paid approximately $38 million, which was less than ten cents for every dollar lost.[135] The amount was far from adequate, from both economic and moral points of view. The reparation, however, suggests that the government acknowledged that the internees' property rights, if not civil rights, were violated. Yet as Cindy I-Fen Cheng elucidates in *Citizens of Asian America: Democracy and Race during the Cold War* (2013), the main impetus for the federal government to remove overt discriminatory practices against racial minorities was the Cold War imperative to demonstrate to the world the superiority of American democracy over communism.

Conclusion

The relocation and incarceration of Japanese Americans during World War II were products of a total and technological war. Fear of espionage and sabotage gave legitimacy to the military argument that the incarceration of the entire ethnic Japanese population was necessary because of the lack of time to distinguish between loyal and disloyal individuals. The racist purge of an ethnic minority that had been a target of marginalization and discrimination for several decades easily gained public support during the war, when the state demanded loyalty and conformity from every individual in the country to secure its war effort. The recognition that the country was involved in a modern, total war caused all three government branches—executive, legislative, and judiciary—to defer to military authority, even though many individuals in the government had serious doubts about the constitutionality of the military's decisions.

From economic, military, political, and civil rights points of view, the internment was a "disaster."[136] The estimated overall cost of mass removal and incarceration was nearly a quarter of a billion dollars.[137] The policy cost the Western Defense Command personnel and resources that could have been used for national defense, and it weakened the labor force by incarcerating those who could have been more efficiently mobilized for the war effort.

The War Relocation Authority, the agency the government had created to administer confinement and resettlement, ended up accused by the Supreme Court of exercising unauthorized powers of detention. The four Supreme Court cases discussed in this chapter revealed the weakening of the constitutional guarantee of liberty and equality for civilians. Last but not least, the forced exclusion, relocation, and incarceration caused Japanese Americans a tremendous amount of suffering through the deprivation of physical liberty, the disruption of community and family structures, economic and property losses, and psychological trauma.

The damage of mass removal and incarceration, furthermore, did not end when the military order was lifted. The affirmation of Hirabayashi's, Yasui's, and Korematsu's convictions greatly shifted the balance between civil liberties and national security and severely weakened the principle of equal protection under the Fifth and Fourteenth Amendments. The Supreme Court interpretations in these cases extended the government's war power to affect all aspects of life. The military's discretion expanded to an almost unlimited control over civilians, even though, as Jacobs tenBroek warns, "the need for the increased participation of the military in the regulation and administration of wide areas of national life" in a total war "increases rather than decreases the necessity to retain normal judicial safeguards in the management of war and preparations for war."[138]

Did the Court sanction the military's use of this power to restrain civilian lives all over the United States during World War II? Not when the exclusion did not involve a racial minority. During 1942 and 1943, several naturalized American citizens of German descent were excluded from the Eastern Seaboard by various military orders, issued by commanders who were granted the authority to exclude any person from military areas by Executive Order 9066 and Public Law 503.[139] In these cases, federal court judges unanimously ruled that exclusion orders directed against Americans of German descent were invalid.[140] In *Schueller v. Drum* (1943), the decision contended:

> The normal civilian life of the area was being pursued; commercial and industrial activities, their tempo heightened by a demand for greater production, were in private ownership; the courts both federal and state were open and functioning as well as all the administrative and executive departments of government, and it could not be honestly said that ordinary law did not adequately secure public safety and private rights.[141]

On the West Coast in 1942, the "normal civilian life of the area was being pursued"; the federal and state courts were open, and administrative and executive government departments were functioning normally. However, Japanese Americans were not only excluded from military areas; they were also confined in desert detention camps for years. This suggests that race did matter, after all.

Constitutional historian Bernard Schwartz points out that the *Endo* case "graphically demonstrates the limitations of judicial power as a practical check on military arbitrariness."[142] Even though the court can correct abuses arising from improper use of authority, it cannot prevent them. In Endo's case, it took two and a half years after the petition was first filed to grant her the liberty that should not have been taken away from her in the first place.

Schwartz contends that judicial control not only corrects but also serves to restrain the improper exercise of authority and suggests that this restraining aspect might be more significant for protecting civil liberties. However, it is also true that judicial precedent often validates a principle and expands it for new purposes. After the end of World War II, the *Hirabayashi*, *Korematsu*, and *Endo* cases were used to expand rather than restrain the government's arbitrary power to detain American citizens during the intensification of national insecurity in the Cold War.

The Japanese American cases created a breach in the Constitution that would adversely affect Americans when the distinction between wartime and peacetime virtually disappeared in the 1950s. The ominous implication of these cases was already predicted in the dissenting opinion in *Korematsu*. Justice Jackson pointed out that the upholding of Korematsu's conviction would have a far more significant effect on American civil liberties than on the fate of people of Japanese ancestry:

> Much is said of the danger to liberty from the Army program for deporting and detaining these citizens of Japanese extraction. But a judicial construction of the due process clause that will sustain this order is a far more subtle blow to liberty than the promulgation of the order itself. A military order, however unconstitutional, is not apt to last longer than the military emergency. . . . But once a judicial opinion rationalizes such an order to show that it conforms to the Constitution, or rather rationalizes the Constitution to show that the Constitution sanctions such an order, the Court for all time has validated the principle of racial discrimination in criminal procedure and of transplanting American citizens. The principle then lies about like a loaded weapon ready for the hand of any authority that can bring forward a plausible claim of an urgent need. . . . A military commander may overstep the bounds of constitutionality, and it is an incident. But if we review and approve, that passing incident becomes

the doctrine of the Constitution. There it has a generative power of its own.[143]

Michel Foucault once warned, "People know what they do; they frequently know why they do what they do; but what they don't know is what what they do does."[144] The American government removed and incarcerated Japanese American citizens and aliens by branding them potentially disloyal. Reasons for supporting the mass removal were diverse. Some were genuinely concerned by the military threat on the West Coast, while others had additional motives—economic, racial, political, and cultural—to oust Japanese Americans from their neighborhoods. When the president issued Executive Order 9066 and when Congress passed Public Law 503, everybody knew that the orders affected only Americans of Japanese ancestry. What they did not know was that by stripping the constitutional guarantee of civil liberties from their fellow citizens, they weakened the Constitution itself and stripped themselves of their own civil liberties protection. As Justice Jackson predicted, American citizenship lost its protective power after the incarceration of Japanese American citizens was upheld: the mere branding of disloyalty could now strip a citizen of his or her civil liberties, notwithstanding constitutional protections. In the Cold War period, when the difference between the battlefield and home ceased to exist, the hunt for the disloyal would rampage through the home front. In a few years, Americans were to learn what what they had done during the war would do to them.

2

Legalizing Preventive Detention

*The Passage of the
Emergency Detention Act of 1950*

The mass removal of Japanese Americans broadened the government's war power. Bernard Schwartz points out that the Supreme Court, in judging the *Korematsu* case, did not give "a judicial seal of approval on the manner in which Korematsu had been treated" but determined only that there was a "reasonable basis" for the military's action.[1] However, the very fact that the Court upheld Korematsu's conviction in effect affirmed the breadth of the government's or military's power to impinge on personal liberty through exclusion orders. Moreover, in choosing not to rule directly on the constitutional questions regarding Korematsu's and Endo's incarceration, the judicial branch failed to deny to the executive the power of preventive detention. The questions of whether the government and military had the power to detain citizens without due process but through an emergency measure, and whether Congress should allow such governmental interference with individual freedom, were left for lawmakers in the postwar period to decide.[2]

After the end of World War II, the rising tension between the United States and the USSR, particularly over the development of nuclear technology, intensified domestic fear of espionage and sabotage in aid of foreign regimes. Post–World War II anticommunism shared some characteristics with the Red Scare following World War I. In both periods, the government strengthened its apparatus of domestic surveillance. As anticommunism aroused deep nativist suspicion among ordinary Americans, immigration and naturalization laws were tightened in both the early 1920s and the 1950s. Hundreds of aliens were deported from the United States for their political beliefs, and many more were denied entry.[3]

Suspicion against political radicalism came hand in hand with heightened antagonism against racial minorities and civil rights activists. As a Spanish flu pandemic swept through the United States in 1919, a surge of racial violence took place in Charleston; Washington, D.C.; Chicago; Omaha; and Elaine, Arkansas, among other places. Leftist labor unions became targets of intense investigatory raids when they advocated the racial integration of labor movements and supported the "long civil rights movement."[4] In the late 1940s and 1950s, southern segregationists took advantage of anticommunist anxieties for their political ends by associating the Civil Rights Movement with international communist conspiracy.[5]

On the other hand, the anticommunist fervor during the early Cold War period had new characteristics that were not part of the post–World War I Red Scare, now that America faced the threat of nuclear mass destruction. Only two atomic bombs had killed over two hundred thousand civilians in Hiroshima and Nagasaki within a couple of months, many within days. Scientifically it was only a matter of time before other nations obtained this technology. Now, a whole city could be wiped out completely and thousands of lives could be lost instantly, even when the United States was not officially at war.[6]

This fear gave the conservatives leverage to create laws more restrictive of civil liberties. The same fear also made it easier for them to demonize activists fighting for civil and human rights as well as supporters of anticolonial movements. In parts of Asia and Africa, much of the anticolonial critique of colonialism and imperialism relied on communist social and economic theories. This theorization of the connection between racism and capitalist colonial exploitation led to the emergence of the notion of what would a few years later be called the "Third World."[7] Even though American liberals supported the independence of former British colonies in the Indian continent and the Middle East, radical antiracist anticolonialism proved threatening. The birth of the People's Republic of China and the start of the Korean War gave Americans the impression that there was a well-organized world communist movement led by Moscow.[8]

The Cold War against the USSR and the hot wars in Asia gave an opportunity to the Republicans and segregationist Southern Democrats to utilize anticommunist discourses to block the Truman administration's progressive domestic social and economic policies.[9] Such was the political atmosphere in which Congress discussed the Internal Security Act of 1950.

Passing the Internal Security Act of 1950: The Legislative Process

The Internal Security Act, passed on September 23, 1950, is popularly known as the McCarran Act, named after its sponsor, Senator Patrick McCarran (D-Nevada).[10] The law had two parts: Title I, the Subversive Activities Control Act, and Title II, the Emergency Detention Act. Title I required communist organizations to register with the attorney general and contained other provisions that tightened immigration and naturalization laws. Title II, the Emergency Detention Act, authorized the attorney general during an internal security emergency to apprehend and detain any person who the government suspected would "probably engage in espionage or sabotage."[11]

The origin of the Internal Security Act was the mandatory communist registration bill introduced by Karl E. Mundt (R-South Dakota) and Richard M. Nixon (R-California) in the House of Representatives in 1948. This bill emerged from the investigation conducted by the House Un-American Activities Committee (HUAC) on communist activities in the United States. While admitting that such laws involved grave constitutional questions, HUAC determined that the Constitution should not hamper the power of Congress to enact laws that would "defend the Nation from those who would use liberties guaranteed by the Constitution to destroy it."[12] In 1948, HUAC held public hearings on this bill, which was passed by the House on May 19, 319 to 58. The Senate Judiciary Committee, however, did not discuss the bill. President Truman did not comment on it but expressed his opposition to any bill that outlawed political parties.[13]

The overwhelming support for the Mundt-Nixon Communist Registration Bill in the House reflected a widespread fear of communist threat, perceived to be coming from both inside and outside the United States. The Gallup Poll showed that 77 percent of voters favored the bill, while 12 percent opposed it and 11 percent had no opinion.[14] The arrest of Alger Hiss in the same year further raised suspicion about espionage related to nuclear technology. The popular fear of communism gave conservative Republicans the opportunity to attack liberals for being "soft" on communism.[15] It was not until February 1950 that Senator Joseph McCarthy (R-Wisconsin) became famous for his speech on communists within the administration, but the phenomenon later named "McCarthyism" had already begun in the late 1940s and was to continue long after the personal influence of the senator had waned.[16]

In 1949, Mundt, now a senator, introduced a new communist registration bill in the Senate (S2311). S595, sponsored by McCarran (D-Nevada), tightened safeguards against espionage and sabotage. HR10, sponsored by

Representative Sam Hobbs (D-Alabama), tightened control of aliens in custody pending deportation. S1694 and S1832, both sponsored by McCarran, tightened immigration law provisions for the deportation of subversive aliens and the denial of admission to the United States. Despite the efforts of conservatives, however, none of these subversive activities control bills became law until the summer of 1950, when a war broke out in the Korean Peninsula.

In March of that year, the Senate Committee on the Judiciary reported on the Mundt bill, S2311. The Senate report was accompanied by a constitutional analysis by the American Bar Association, whose Standing Committee on the Bill of Rights had reported that S2311 was constitutional "in its entirety," as the First Amendment did not "entitle any individual or group of individuals to engage in conspiracies to perform acts aimed at the destruction of the very freedoms" that the amendment guaranteed.[17] Upon the North Korean army's invasion into the South, the proposed antisubversive legislation began to gain momentum. In the House, Richard Nixon's Communist Registration Bill (HR7595) and HUAC Chairman John Wood's (D-Georgia) bill barring communists from government and defense jobs (HR3903) were combined and introduced as the Wood Bill (HR9490). In mid-July, pressure on the Senate to pass Mundt's communist control bill "skyrocketed," and conservative pressure groups such as the Chamber of Commerce, the American Legion, and other organizations were "reported to be 'blanketing' the Senate with communications demanding passage of S2311."[18]

The Truman administration was put on the defensive in finding a way to project an image of being tough on communism. On August 8, 1950, President Truman sent a special message to Congress making recommendations related to internal security legislation. He urged Congress to pass a bill that preserved "basic liberties" and protected internal security at the same time. He recommended that Congress remedy defects in the existing laws concerning espionage, the registration of foreign agents, and the security of national-defense installations, and that it should enact legislation permitting the attorney general to exercise supervision over aliens subject to deportation. On the other hand, Truman opposed laws that would seriously damage the right of free speech and silence the voice of opposition, which, he insisted, would lead to the construction of a police state. He cautioned Congress not to be "swept away by a wave of hysteria."[19]

Despite the president's plea for moderation, an anti-administration coalition of nationalist Republicans and Southern Democrats supported a severe anticommunist bill.[20] Two days after Truman's special congressional address, Patrick McCarran, chairman of the Senate Judiciary Committee, introduced S4037, combining the Communist Registration Bill with the restrictive im-

Herb Block cartoon, "I Asked You To Send Over A Rat-Trap," *Washington Post*, August 31, 1950. (A 1950 Herblock Cartoon, © The Herb Block Foundation.)

migration and naturalization bills.[21] Other senators from the southern states, such as Senator James O. Eastland (D-Mississippi), who opposed Hawaiian statehood, also advocated the early passage of the anticommunist bills to delay discussion on the statehood bills.[22] Three senators in the Committee on the Judiciary—Harley M. Kilgore (D-West Virginia), Frank P. Graham (D-North Carolina), and William Langer (R-North Dakota)—expressed opposition to S4037 by submitting minority views in the Senate report.[23]

While conservative politicians formed an effective coalition against the Truman administration, the pro-administration liberals were poorly organized.²⁴ To counter the congressional demand for communist registration bills, the White House and pro-administration senators were pressured into drafting an alternative anticommunist statute.

White House assistant Stephen J. Spingarn took charge of designing a bill that would strengthen the government's power to prevent espionage and sabotage. Spingarn—whose father, Joel Elias Spingarn, was a longtime civil rights activist and a prominent Jewish leader of the National Association for the Advancement of Colored People (NAACP)—was a strong believer in racial equality and the need to protect civil liberties.²⁵ During World War II, Spingarn served as a counterintelligence officer and handled a number of espionage and sabotage cases by the Axis agents. As an expert on wartime espionage and sabotage, he knew well the threat those actions could bring to national security and the need for effective legislation against espionage and sabotage.²⁶ On the other hand, he was conscious of the possibility of the government abusing its war power and thus saw the need to prevent such abuse through legislation. Spingarn became the key figure in the administration working on measures to combat subversive activities.

The Truman administration's first attempt to form an anti-espionage bill happened around 1947 in the Interdepartmental Intelligence Committee, comprising the director of the FBI and the heads of the intelligence branches of the army, navy, and air force, with the Loyalty Review Board and the Department of Justice.²⁷ Spingarn, at the time working in the Department of the Treasury, suggested that the proposed bill required substantial changes in order to provide stronger protection for civil liberties.²⁸

In May 1950, Spingarn and another White House assistant, Charles S. Murphy, sent a memorandum to Truman on the basic policy formulation in the field of internal security legislation. Spingarn and Murphy suggested that the president should advise the Justice Department to consider such laws and that all internal security proposals should be carefully scrutinized by its civil rights branch as well as by its security branches to confirm that the policy was well balanced in protecting both internal security and individual rights.²⁹ Taking in these suggestions, the administration designed an alternative bill that tightened the Espionage Act and the Foreign Agents Registration Act.

The administration's bill was then introduced in the House and the Senate on August 16 and 17, respectively. In the Senate, liberals Kilgore, Graham, Warren G. Magnuson (D-Washington), Scott W. Lucas (D-Illinois), Francis J. Myers (D-Pennsylvania), C. Estes Kefauver (D-Tennessee), Theodore Francis Green (D-Rhode Island), Paul H. Douglas (D-Illinois), Hubert H. Humphrey (D-Minnesota), and Herbert H. Lehman (D-New York) sponsored the administration bill (S4061). In the House, Representative Emanuel Celler (D-New York), chairman of the House Judiciary Committee, introduced an identical bill (HR9502). Liberal newspapers such as the *New York Times* and the *Washington Post*, liberal intellectuals and organizations such as the ACLU and Americans for Democratic Action (ADA), and major labor unions supported the administration bill. Within Congress, however, it did not gain much support. The House passed the Wood Bill (HR9490) on August 29, by a majority of 354 to 20.[30] With Senator Eastland's persistent request for Senate debate on the McCarran bill, the administration and liberals had no choice but to devise an even stronger way to counter conservatives' demands.

It was at this political moment that the Emergency Detention Bill appeared in Congress. Historical materials provide various accounts on the origin of the bill. According to a memorandum by Spingarn, he talked on July 10, 1950, with Irv Hoff, administrative assistant to Senator Magnuson, chairman of the Senate Judiciary Subcommittee.[31] Magnuson considered the immediate introduction of a bill "to authorize the President to have the FBI arrest any individual known to advocate, or to be a member of an organization advocating, the overthrow of the government by force, and to hold such individual in custody as long as the national security may demand."[32] Such arrests were to happen when the president with the concurrence of the majority and minority leaders of both houses of Congress declared a national emergency to exist by reason of an actual or threatened war or invasion or a disturbance or threatened disturbance of international relations.

On the other hand, multiple historical accounts suggest that the idea of emergency detention originated in Senator Douglas's office. Senator Lehman recalled two years after the event that Douglas's staff prepared the preliminary draft of the proposal, although it might "have come to Senator Douglas from an outside source."[33] The *New Republic* reported that Senator Douglas "spent a weekend studying the problem and decided that the emergency detention system by the British during the last war might be the answer."[34] Cornelius Cotter and Malcolm Smith explained the origin of the detention bill in an article published in 1957:

> The detention provisions which were embodied in the second part of S.4130 reflected a week-end effort to produce an American counterpart to *Defense Regulation 18B*, under which the British, during the Second World War, arrested and preventively detained persons whose freedom was deemed by a high officer of state to endanger the national security. The bill's framers had a copy of the Regulation before them, and also drew upon the advice of Justice Department officials who had something to do with the detention of Japanese-Americans in the last war.[35]

Cotter and Smith do not reveal the source of this information, so the identities of these Justice Department officials are unknown. However, in Senator Douglas's memoir he mentions two individuals who were involved in the drafting process of the bill, which suggests the connection between Japanese American incarceration and Title II:

> Our progressive group immediately asked Joe Rauh and Frank McCulloch to draft an alternative [to the Communist Registration Bill]. We did not want to take a purely negative position when some real danger to the nation was involved. The alternative we devised was a compulsory-detention law based on the system adopted by Great Britain in World War II.[36]

"Joe Rauh" was Joseph L. Rauh Jr., a former student of and later a law clerk for Justice Felix Frankfurter. Rauh had also worked for the Federal Communications Commission until he was assigned to work in the Office of Emergency Management, established in May 1940 to mobilize the government and industry for entering the war. Frankfurter and Rauh, both Jewish, shared a feeling that the United States should enter the war to stop Hitler's aggression in Europe.[37]

In February 1942, Rauh, along with two other lawyers, had advised Attorney General Francis Biddle about the constitutionality of Japanese American incarceration. About this incident, Rauh recollected in the 1980s that "the memorandum was the final effort by the three of us to prevent evacuation and internment."[38] In actuality, Rauh, Benjamin V. Cohen, and Oliver Cox had collectively advised the attorney general shortly before Executive Order 9066 was issued that military necessity might uphold the constitutionality of mass exclusion. However, Rauh's statement in a 1989 interview that Cohen was in tears after seeing a picture of Japanese American children being incarcerated in camps demonstrates that the episode distressed those lawyers, at least after the fact. After the war, Rauh became involved in civil rights and politics pertaining to civil liberties. He was one of the founders of ADA with Arthur Schlesinger Jr. and James Loeb, among others, in 1947.[39] By 1950, Rauh was an active civil liberties lawyer in Washington, D.C. If he was indeed involved in the drafting of the Emergency Detention Bill, it is most likely that he had done so with a clear memory of what happened to Japanese Americans during World War II.

On September 4, 1950, Senator Kilgore called Senators Douglas, Graham, Kefauver, and Lehman into an informal caucus to decide on a strategy to amend S4061.[40] Their proposal added the emergency detention clause to the administration's bill.⁴¹ Paul Douglas's memoir gives three reasons for drafting the emergency detention legislation. First, an affirmative substitute was necessary to "derail" the Mundt-Nixon-McCarran bills. Second, he hoped to "change the focus of public attention from Communist speech and association to the genuine problems of sabotage and espionage."⁴² The third reason was to set a legal procedure for the detention process and to secure procedures for the detainees' release when there was no danger of sabotage or espionage. Douglas thought this was necessary, particularly when J. Edgar Hoover had announced that the FBI was prepared to arrest twelve thousand alleged communists once a war started with the USSR.⁴³

Liberal senators agreed to collectively sponsor the bill "as the only possible way of beating the McCarran bill."⁴⁴ They consulted the president on September 6. Truman told them to "go ahead" but said he would reserve judgment on the proposal until the bill reached him.⁴⁵ On the same day, Senator Kilgore introduced S4130 on the Senate floor, incorporating the administration's bill as Title I and the Emergency Detention Bill as Title II. Senators Douglas, Humphrey, Lehman, Graham, Kefauver, and William Benton (D-Connecticut) cosponsored the bill.⁴⁶ Humphrey had been mayor of Minneapolis during World War II and helped the relocated Japanese Americans settle in his city. It is likely that his involvement in Japanese American resettlement had affected his thoughts about human rights protection even in wartime.

Truman hoped to kill the Communist Registration Bill by inaction, but with the Korean War progressing and anticommunist sentiment gaining momentum in Congress, it was impossible for the administration and liberal senators to halt the passage of an anticommunist bill.⁴⁷ On September 12, the Senate took a series of votes on the internal security bills. First, a proposal by Senate Majority Leader Scott Lucas (D-Illinois) to substitute the emergency detention plan for the registration provision was voted down.⁴⁸ Lucas, to the surprise of other Democratic senators, then offered to add the Emergency Detention Bill to the Communist Registration Bill. This idea was rejected, but by a close margin of 37 to 35. Then, Senator Kilgore suggested substituting his Emergency Detention Bill for the Communist Registration Bill while adding the president's program to tighten sabotage and espionage laws. This proposal was rejected 50 to 23. Kefauver, another pro-administration senator, offered a series of amendments that would restrict the provisions of the original McCarran bill, but these were mostly rejected.

After an amendment was approved that deleted a section setting up a new, semi-independent passport and visa section in the State Department, Senator Millard E. Tydings (D-Maryland) moved to reconsider Lucas's proposal to add the emergency detention clause to the Communist Registration Bill. When this happened, Senators McCarran and Homer Ferguson (R-Michigan), so far opposed to the emergency detention plan, suddenly expressed their support for this idea. Thus, the McCarran Internal Security Bill came to contain both the communist registration and the emergency detention provisions. The amended bill passed the Senate 70 to 7.

After the Internal Security Bill passed in the Senate, Kefauver submitted S4163 as an attempt to delete the provisions for communist registration. The Kefauver bill contained clauses from the administration's bill that strengthened laws against sabotage and espionage and also "provided for the internment of saboteurs, dangerous Communists and 5th Columnists in the event of war, invasion or grave national security."[49] The emergency detention provisions of the Kefauver bill allowed the government to declare an internal security emergency automatically when the U.S. Armed Forces were in combat with another nation's army. The bill provided that in such situations, all laws applicable to wartime treason, sabotage, and espionage would go immediately into effect. The passage of the Kefauver bill would have invoked Title II immediately, since the U.S. Armed Forces were already fighting in Korea. However, even this final attempt to act tough on Communists and fifth columnists failed to change the current of debate.

In the meantime, McCarran took the Senate version of his Internal Security Bill back to the Internal Security Subcommittee and added further amendments. The House agreed to confer with the Senate over the differences in their respective internal security bills, and the resulting Conference Report was filed on September 19. The Senate and House Internal Security Subcommittee members "gave serious consideration to the constitutional questions" and concluded that "the precedents afforded by court decisions sustaining the validity of the Japanese relocation program in effect during World War II provide[d] ample authority" for the enactment of the emergency detention clause included in the bill.[50]

Even at this late stage, liberals could not produce a concerted strategy. Senator Lucas's proposal to add the Emergency Detention Bill to the Internal Security Bill put the president as well as the sponsors of the Kilgore bill "on the spot."[51] Senators were now forced to choose either to endorse the entire Internal Security Bill or to discard it, in which case they would face the embarrassing situation of voting against their own propositions. This led to a division among the pro-administration senators. Most of the liberal senators went along with Democratic leader Lucas and voted in support, while seven senators opposed it: Frank Graham, Theodore Green, Edward Leahy, Estes Kefauver, James E. Murray (D-Montana), Glen Taylor (D-Idaho), and Herbert Lehman. Senators Kilgore, Douglas, Humphrey, Magnuson, and Myers, on the other hand, contributed their votes to passing the Communist Registration Bill they had struggled so hard to defeat. The final bill passed in the Senate 51 to 7, and in the House 313 to 20. Paul Douglas recollected his sense of defeat and regret concerning his vote in his memoir:

> That evening I found my sons, John and Paul, dispirited by what I had done. I somehow felt, despite my excuses, that I had failed morally. For the next two nights I could not sleep as I pictured the persecution of the innocent that might come at the hands of the new Subversive Activities Control Board, and of a new reign of terror settling over the country.[52]

After the Senate vote, the Democratic Party leaders in the Senate had a conference with President Truman, urging him to sign the bill. Truman did not agree to this request.[53] However, he agreed that he would not pocket veto the bill.[54] In the meantime, Senators Kilgore, Lehman, Murray, and Kefauver wrote to Truman urging him to veto it and to send another special message to Congress.[55] On September 22, President Truman sent the second special message, written mostly by Spingarn, explaining his veto.[56] The House voted shortly after the message had been read, overriding the veto 286 to 48.[57]

When the veto message was taken to the Senate, the White House asked pro-administration senators to prolong the discussion so that the veto would get more media coverage. Senators Hubert Humphrey, Paul Douglas, Etes Kefauver, Herbert Lehman, James Murray, and William Langer made long speeches so that the discussion lasted until the following morning.

The Senate battle over the internal security legislation closed dramatically: Senator Langer suddenly collapsed on the podium and was carried away to the hospital. In the afternoon, the vote was taken. This time, several senators who had voted for the bill—namely Douglas, Murray, Dennis Chavez (D-New Mexico), Kefauver, Kilgore, and Humphrey—voted to sustain the veto.[58] Conservatives, however, marked an overwhelming victory. The omnibus bill passed 57 to 10, overriding Truman's veto, to become Public Law 831, the Internal Security Act of 1950.[59]

The Internal Security Act: The Law

To understand Title II and why liberals created it, it is important to analyze the actual wording of the Internal Security Act, both Title I and Title II. The Subversive Activities Control Act (hereafter Title I), or Title I of the Internal Security Act, explains the necessity of this law on the basis of the investigation conducted by the House Committee on Un-American Activities (HUAC). Section 2.1 mentions the existence of a "world communist movement" whose purpose is to establish a totalitarian dictatorship. The law defines communism as a conspiratory movement controlled by a foreign state, namely the Soviet Union, and overtly negates the idea of its being a political ideology.[60] Section 2.9 states that those individuals in the United States "who knowingly and willfully participate in the world communist movement . . . in effect repudiate their allegiance to the United States." Defining the followers and supporters of communism as foreign agents, Title I places communists, regardless of their citizenship status, outside the constitutional protection of freedom of thought.

Title I warned that a large number of aliens had used their citizenship as a "badge for admission into the fabric of [American] society" and that HUAC had found many of them to be deportable. These clauses legitimized the stricter immigration and naturalization regulations included in Title I. Historically in the United States, anti-immigrant pressure groups have constantly advocated similar types of suspicion against aliens, and those who pushed for the mass exclusion of Japanese Americans during World War II also relied on rhetoric emphasizing the threat of foreign invasion.

The last clause of Section 2 of Title I concluded that the communist organization within the United States presented "a clear and present danger" to the security of the United States and to the "existence of free American institutions." By using phrases such as "a clear and present danger" and "provide for the common defense," the law invoked the Constitution to justify the restrictions it imposed on individuals' basic rights to freedom.[61]

Section 4 listed certain acts prohibited under this law. Section 4a made it unlawful to "combine, conspire, or agree with any other person to perform any act which would substantially contribute to the establishment within the United States of a totalitarian dictatorship." Section 4b prohibited all government employees from communicating to an agent of foreign governments or an officer or member of any communist organization any information related to national security. Section 4c prohibited all foreign agents from obtaining or attempting to obtain such information. Section 4d stated that the violators of these regulations would be punished by a fine not exceeding $10,000, imprisonment not exceeding ten years, or both.

The criminalization of actions such as passing information affecting national security to a foreign agent was originally written in the administration's bill. These sections were designed by governmental and military experts on intelligence activities. On the other hand, the administration and liberals disagreed with the clause in Title I that criminalized actions "which would substantially contribute to the establishment within the United States of a totalitarian dictatorship." Unlike the Smith Act, which made it a crime to teach or advocate the "overthrow of the government by force or violence,"

Title I did not specify what kind of actions would "substantially contribute" to establishing a dictatorship. If broadly interpreted, such a provision could make advocating an economic doctrine of communism, an action conventionally protected by the freedom of speech, punishable.

The act's restriction of personal freedom extended much further than its classification of criminal activities. Section 12 established the Subversive Activities Control Board (SACB), composed of five members appointed by the president with the consent of the Senate. The duty of the SACB was to determine whether an organization was a "communist-action organization" or a "communist-front organization," and also to determine whether any individual was a member of a communist-action organization. Those groups labeled communist-action or communist-front organizations were ordered to register as such with the attorney general. If an organization failed to register, individuals were held responsible for registering themselves as members. At the time of registration, each organization was to give its name and the address of the principal office, the names and addresses of its officers, a financial statement, and in the case of a communist-action organization, the names and addresses of all its members. All of this information had to be renewed every year by an annual report to the attorney general.

Members of registered communist organizations were banned from holding government employment, and the members of communist-action organizations were forbidden to work in any defense facility, defined by the Secretary of Defense. Moreover, communist organizations were denied tax deductions and exemptions, and their members were denied the right to apply for or renew passports. Any letters or parcels mailed by these organizations were to be marked as "Disseminated by ——, a Communist organization," and any radio or television broadcasts were to be preceded by the statement "The following program is sponsored by ——, a Communist organization." The information on the registration and annual reports was to be available for public inspection, and the attorney general was to submit an annual report to the president and Congress listing the names and addresses of the registered organizations as well as the names and addresses of the individuals listed as members of such organizations. Failure to register or to file an annual report was punishable. Organizations that failed to register within thirty days after the final order from the SACB were to be punished by a fine not exceeding $10,000, and each individual who failed to register was subject to a fine not exceeding $10,000, imprisonment not exceeding five years, or both.

Title I also carried sections amending espionage policy that reflected the administration's bill. Section 18 tightened the restriction on gathering, transmitting, or losing defense information, and this was broadened to include "instruments" and "alliances" in the category of items that were unlawful to transmit under certain circumstances. It also banned the oral transmission of any documents and writings related to defense information. Section 20 amended the Foreign Agents Registration Act by requiring the registration of persons who had knowledge of, or had received instructions or assignment in, the espionage, counterespionage, or sabotage services or tactics of a foreign government or a foreign political party.

Title I brought about numerous amendments to the immigration and naturalization laws. It substantially widened the classes of aliens denied entry to the United States by excluding those "who seek entry to engage in activities which would be prejudicial to the public interest or would endanger the welfare or safety of the United States," a rather ambiguous category, in addition to anarchists and members of a communist organization or any totalitarian party. It also excluded those "who advocate world communism or totalitarianism" or "who advocate or teach unconstitutional overthrow of the government of the United States." Aliens "who write or publish material advocating unconstitutional overthrow of the government of the United States; who are affiliated with any organization that writes or distributes material advocating unconstitutional overthrow of the government; or who would likely engage in espionage and sabotage" were also to be denied entry.

Section 25 stated that any country that refused to accept a returned alien was to be barred from sending any immigrants to the United States, and if a person naturalized after January 1, 1950, engaged in any of the activities listed in the category of deportable aliens, his or her citizenship was to be revoked.

Section 31 amended Title 18 of the U.S. Codes so that picketing federal courts or the homes of federal judges, jurors, witnesses, or court officers was to result in a $5,000 fine and/or one-year imprisonment.

In short, Title I was not concerned as much with subversive activities per se as with communist registration and the exclusion and deportation of undesirable aliens. On the contrary, Title II, at least in theory, addressed the issues of espionage and sabotage directly. Section 101 explains the purpose of Title II. The first nine clauses of Section 101 were almost identical to Section 2 of Title I, explaining the existence of a communist threat. Sections 101.10 to 101.14 referred to the threat that espionage and sabotage posed to the internal and national security of the United States.

Section 101.10 indicated that the law was heavily influenced by historical memories of World War II. It stated that "the experience of many countries in World War II and thereafter with so-called 'fifth columns' . . . to weaken the internal security and defense of nations resisting totalitarian dictatorships" demonstrated the dangerous efficacy of "internal" espionage and sabotage. Consequently, Section 101.11 adopted a broad definition of war power:

> The security and safety of the territory and Constitution of the United States, and the successful prosecution of the common defense, especially in time of invasion, war, or insurrection in aid of a foreign enemy, require every reasonable and lawful protection against espionage, and against sabotage to national-defense material, premises, forces and utilities, including related facilities for mining, manufacturing, transportation, research, training, military and civilian supply, and other activities essential to national defense.

This clause indicates that the government's war power and the war-related sectors controlled under it expanded even further than during World War II. General DeWitt's final recommendation on the "Evacuation of Japanese and Other Subversive Persons from the Pacific Coast" had stated that the defense of the West Coast was essential not only because the lines of communication and supply to the Pacific theater passed through it but also because the region housed war-related industrial plants, particularly those of the aircraft industry.[62] In *Hirabayashi v. United States*, the Supreme Court had defined the war power of the government as "the power to wage war successfully," which extended to "every matter and activity so related to war as substantially to affect its conduct and progress."[63] In 1950, the power was broadened to include any activities "essential to national defense."

Section 101.12 of Title II emphasized the difficulty of national defense in modern technological warfare. It insisted that "the free and unrestrained movement" of members or agents of subversive organizations made "adequate surveillance to prevent espionage and sabotage impossible." Thus, as concluded in Section 101.14, the detention of persons suspected of potentially committing espionage and sabotage in a time of emergency was "essential to the common defense and to the safety and security of the territory, the people and the Constitution of the United States."

Unlike Title I, however, Title II emphasized the necessity of finding a balance between internal security and civil liberties:

> It is also essential that such detention in an emergency involving the internal security of the Nation shall be so authorized, executed, restricted and reviewed as to prevent any interference with the constitutional rights and privileges of any persons, and at the same time shall be sufficiently effective to permit the performance by the Congress and the President of their constitutional duties to provide for the common defense, to wage war, and to preserve, protect and defend the Constitution, the Government and the people of the United States.[64]

This clause reflected the ambivalence shared by the liberals who authored the law and echoed the pleas for balance President Truman made during the law's legislative process. Its wording served two functions. On the one hand, the clause reflected the bill's designers' call for the government to exercise prudence in carrying out the emergency detention program so as not to unreasonably deprive individuals of civil liberties guaranteed in the Constitution. At the same time, by adding this sentence to the law, the politicians defined the emergency detention program as within the government's power to defend the nation and thus implied that such a program was constitutional.

Sections 102 and 103 were the core of Title II. In the event of an "invasion of the territory of the United States or its possessions," a "declaration of war by Congress," or an "insurrection within the United States in aid of a foreign enemy," the president was authorized to make a public proclamation of the existence of an "Internal Security Emergency." Upon such a declaration, the president, acting through the attorney general, was authorized to apprehend and detain "each person as to whom there is reasonable ground to believe that such person probably will engage in, or probably will conspire with others to engage in, acts of espionage or of sabotage."

Section 104 specified the procedure for apprehension and detention. The attorney general had to issue a warrant before any arrests were made, and such warrants had to be issued "only upon probable cause, supported by oath or affirmation," and to "particularly describe the person to be apprehended or detained." With this clause, the law forbade the government to incarcerate a class of citizens or aliens of a particular racial or ethnic category, such as Japanese Americans. Detention had to be conducted on an individual basis. Moreover, Title II stated that only officers of the Department of Justice, designated by the attorney general, could conduct arrests and that the apprehended persons were to be confined in places of detention prescribed by the attorney general. This clause ensured that the Justice Department controlled the detention procedure, preventing the military from taking over such actions. Each apprehended person had to be brought before a preliminary hearing officer, who would hear evidence and decide whether there was reasonable justification for his or her detention. In contrast, during World War II, assessment of Japanese Americans' individual loyalty to the United States was conducted *after* their mass removal and incarceration.[65]

Section 105 established the Detention Review Board, consisting of nine members appointed by the president with the consent of the Senate. The board was authorized to review an individual's detention order, upon petition by the detainee, to determine whether the detention was reasonable and to revoke the order if it decided that there was no reasonable ground for detention. It was also authorized to hear claims for loss of income resulting from groundless detention and to order the attorney general to compensate claimants. Section 111 provided judicial review for detainee petitions that were rejected by the Detention Review Board. These clauses were intended as safeguards for the law, granting detainees multiple chances to appeal their detentions and seek their freedom.

It should be noted that a provision in Section 107 was altered from the original draft. Kilgore's proposed bill had stated that when the Detention Review Board reviewed a detention order, the board was to require the attorney general to inform the detainee of the grounds for detention and the evidence supporting it, including the identity of any informants. However, Section 107 of Title II allowed the attorney general to refrain from disclosing the evidence or informant identities if he or she believed "it would be dangerous to national safety and security to divulge." It was the Senate Internal Security Subcommittee (SISS), chaired by Patrick McCarran, that made this change to the bill.

Sections 112 and 113 delineated provisions for criminals. Persons who resisted, knowingly disregarded, or evaded apprehension, or escaped or attempted to escape from confinement or detention were to be fined up to $10,000, imprisoned for up to ten years, or both. Those who advised, aided, assisted, or procured resistance, disregard, or evasion of apprehension, or escape from confinement or detention were liable to the same penalty.

These penalties had also been adjusted by the SISS. The original Kilgore bill had stated that the penalty for resisting, disregarding, or evading apprehension or escaping was a fine not exceeding $1,000 or one year of imprisonment. McCarran's subcommittee made the punishment much heavier.

The SISS made another important alteration to the Emergency Detention Bill. The original draft contained a provision that the law would cease to be effective three years after enactment unless extended by a joint resolution of Congress. This indicates that the senators who originally supported the bill envisioned it as a temporary wartime expedient to deal with the Korean War. The SISS, however, removed the time limit.

Examining the original bill alongside Title II confirms its drafters' claim that the bill was based on a historical precedent of preventive detention as a means to control enemy aliens (i.e., Japanese American exclusion and incarceration). Liberal senators attempted to write a law that improved the government's emergency detention power by preventing the human rights violations that befell Japanese Americans. The final version of Title II demonstrates, however, that some of the human rights protections the drafters provided were removed by the SISS. Yet at least when it was conceived by the pro-administration senators, Title II was designed to provide legal protection of civil liberties in case the government conducted preventive detention of potential subversives during war, invasion, or insurrection.

Debates on Title II: The Contest over Toughness on Communism and Respect for the American Liberal Tradition

The congressional debates that took place during the legislative process of Title II show why different politicians advocated or criticized the communist registration or preventive detention measures as useful means of securing the safety of the United States from internal threats. Despite the overwhelming support for the Internal Security Act at the time of final voting, the debates indicate that it was an extremely controversial law. The debates reveal the conflicts between the pro-administration and anti-administration factions in Congress, including their contradicting definitions of communism and diverse perceptions about the nature of the internal security threat America was facing. At the same time, ironic though it may seem, the congressional debate on internal security demonstrates politicians' complex but consistent use of liberal language, upholding freedom as a fundamental American value. Through discussing the pros and cons of various internal security bills, lawmakers in 1950 negotiated diverse notions of civil liberties and ended up writing two laws that granted the government greater power to restrain civil liberties than at any other time in American history.

Conservatives who advocated communist registration argued that it was the fear of espionage and sabotage that drove them to introduce such bills. Yet xenophobic sentiments appear in their anticommunist statements as well. McCarran, the primary sponsor of Title I, quoted FBI Director J. Edgar Hoover's testimony that there were a total of 54,174 members of the Communist Party in the United States and even argued that the strength of the communist fifth column could be larger than the number of party members, because each member was "a nerve center exercising a deadly influence over a much larger number of persons."[66] McCarran likened the communist network in the United States to "a weed . . . deliberately transplanted in this country by foreign agents."[67] For him, the existence of communists and a large number of immigrants constituted an internal security threat that justified restrictive immigration laws and the constriction of individual liberties.

McCarran also referred to the contemporary international crisis as justification for the bill he sponsored. He likened the situation to "fighting a war for independence today" and emphasized that the war against communism was "on two fronts"—against both the enemy in open warfare and the enemy who attacked "from within, with lies, half truths, slander, misstatement of facts, and seeds of discord, and stealthy sabotage, with a smile to the face and a knife in the back."[68] This image of domestic espionage as conducted by "insidious foes" was a direct heir of the images that emerged during World War II of the Nazi fifth columnists and the Japanese as well as Japanese Americans.[69]

Congressman Wood, sponsor of the House internal security bill, used a medical metaphor for the crisis, describing communist infiltration as a "cancerous growth on [the] body politic of the American people." He insisted that the bill offered the "nearest approach to the question without infringing upon the liberties and the freedom of thought and freedom of speech."[70] As a cancer, communism and communists should be removed from the American "body," Wood claimed. Unlike McCarran's xenophobia, Wood's metaphor evokes an image of internal disease, composed of malicious cells growing in number and influence inside the nation.

If McCarran and Wood represented the conservative view of the communist threat, Senator Lehman expressed the liberal view:

> As fascism represents the denial of truth communism represents the utter corruption of truth. Because Communists in the United States are stooges of Moscow and are at the beck and call of Soviet imperialism with its aggressive designs, I consider American Communists capable of any kind of subversive activity. I believe that we must check and punish all subversive activities.[71]

Lehman's statement shows that liberals shared with conservatives a view of communists as foreign agents and potential fifth columnists. However, their interpretation of what was threatening internal security differed slightly from that of conservatives. Regarding the communists, liberals believed that the United States "face[d] no real danger from their views, but rather from their subversive activities."[72] Liberals differentiated communism as political thought from communism as a world revolutionary movement. They insisted that an individual should not be punished for holding certain views, unpopular though they might be, but that subversive actions such as espionage and sabotage must be punished and, more importantly, prevented.

Liberals' concern for political repression did not derive from only their fundamental belief in civil liberties and freedom of thought. They criticized the Communist Registration Bill because the definition of a "communist organization," particularly a "communist-front organization," was vague and could be applied to noncommunist organizations that happened to advocate the same policies that communist organizations did.[73] Similarly, the definition of "any act which would substantially contribute to the establishment within the United States of a totalitarian dictatorship," an act punishable under the bill, was very broad. Considering the opposition from conservatives against the civil rights bills that President Truman was pushing forward as well as against his Fair Deal policies, noncommunist social reformers had good reasons to be anxious of the bill being used against them.[74] For this reason, liberal and leftist social reform organizations, labor unions, and immigrant and minority organizations opposed the Communist Registration Bill.[75] Senator Lehman pointed out that conservatives had been criticizing Truman administration policies such as public housing, rent control, federal social security, and compulsory health insurance as "substantial contributions to the establishment of a totalitarian dictatorship in the United States."[76]

The debate involved issues of not only class but race as well. In advocating the Communist Registration Bill, John Rankin (R-Mississippi), one of the most powerful members of HUAC, listed the names of suspected communists and spies, including Julius and Ethel Rosenberg, stating:

> Communism is out not only to destroy our form of government but also to destroy the Christian religion—the Christian civilization. . . . There is not a single Christian or a single white gentile among these Communists which I have just named, who have been plotting the overthrow of this Government and the destruction of our Christian civilization.[77]

The anti-Semitism and racism of Rankin and others did not go unnoticed. Congressman Abraham J. Multer (D-New York) criticized the supporters of Title I for attempting to insinuate that Jewish and African Americans were "not good Americans."[78] The debate indicates that there were a wide variety of opinions among the members of Congress regarding where the boundary between loyal and disloyal Americans should be drawn. Congressman Rankin, who had vehemently supported the wartime incarceration of Japanese Americans on the grounds of protecting white Christian America, agitated in 1950 about the danger of communist espionage with the same racist and anti-Semitic language.[79]

While no member of Congress protested the exclusion of American citizens of Japanese ancestry in 1942, Rankin's racialization of suspected communists and spies immediately drew criticism from Jewish representatives, who not only expressed concerns about alienating Jewish people but also condemned a definition of disloyalty based on skin color, religious belief, and place of origin. Congressman Vito A. Marcantonio, an American Labor Party member and representative from New York, warned about the extension of repression to other targets once communist registration was legalized. He pointed out that

Hitler and Mussolini made similar speeches to deny the constitutional rights of not only the communists and Jews but also trade unions and eventually "all the people destroyed all the way down the line."[80] Dismissing conservatives' argument that the Subversive Activities Control Bill did not infringe on the liberty and freedom of the American people, Marcantonio asked his fellow members of Congress:

> What freedom? The Taft-Hartley freedom that you who promote this legislation have imposed on American labor? The Jim Crow freedom that you leaders in this drive to impose this tyranny on America have imposed upon 15,000,000 Negro people in this Nation? What freedom? You are destroying the freedom of the founders of this country of ours laid down in this Constitution; you are destroying the 10 amendments written in there with the blood of Americans who fought a revolution to win them.[81]

The debate on communist registration reveals that the conflict was about not only the appropriate measures to protect internal security but also the schism between pro-administration and anti-administration politicians on a wide range of contemporary issues—civil rights, social reforms, race relations, labor relations, and treatment of political and religious minorities. This rhetorical overflow indicates that the fear of communism in the early Cold War era was not only about communism; it was a metaphoric language through which Americans discussed various social tensions. Lawmakers contested and negotiated the border between the "truly American" and the "un-American," reflecting contemporary political divisions over issues concerning race, class, religion, ideology, and so on.

President Truman, defending his social and security policies, insisted on the necessity of strengthening the domestic security system and the protection of civil liberties at the same time. He emphasized that it was the freedom inscribed in the Constitution that was making the United States stronger than totalitarian nations: in Truman's logic, democracy was the weapon with which Americans should fight against communism. He shared liberals' views that communism as an idea should be tested within the democratic institution and that the best defense against the communist threat was "a vigorous, functioning democracy" that succeeded in "meeting the needs of its people."[82] On the other hand, Truman warned that the nation needed protection from subversive actions such as espionage and sabotage. He suggested that the internal security agencies authorized by the government should be granted greater power and more resources to deal with those covert activities.[83]

Truman's message reflected the viewpoint of the government's internal security agencies. Two years earlier, the Justice Department had criticized the communist registration measures proposed by conservative members of Congress. In 1948, responding to a request from the Senate Committee on the Judiciary, Attorney General Thomas C. Clark—who, back in 1942, mediated between the military and the Justice Department when the mass exclusion of Japanese Americans was discussed—analyzed the Communist Registration Bill and reported that the registration provision that would penalize the registrant might be held to deny freedom of speech and thought and constitute self-incrimination.[84] He also suspected that the vague definition of "criminal act" might not meet the requirements of due process under the Fifth Amendment. The largest concern of the attorney general, however, came from a practical viewpoint that this law might drive communists "underground" where surveillance of their activities would become "increasingly difficult."[85]

In 1950, the White House and pro-administration liberals criticized the Subversive Activities Control Bill on the same grounds. Senator Humphrey insisted that the investigation of communists should be left to the FBI.[86] Liberal newspapers also warned that communists were ready to go underground if the registration bill was passed.[87] During a hearing by the Subversive Activities Control Board, the FBI and other intelligence agencies were likely to be obliged to publicize the information they had gathered on communists or other subversive persons. The administration argued that this might in fact jeopardize national security.

The above debate reveals that there was another source of conflict between the pro- and anti-administration members of Congress. Anti-administration factions sought to investigate and control communists and subversive persons in Congress, primarily through HUAC and the SISS. The administration and pro-administration liberals advocated fortifying the internal security and domestic intelligence agencies in the executive branch.

In the political culture of 1950, it was political suicide to oppose any anticommunist bills.[88] When it became clear that the administration's bill did not have a strong enough impact to swing public opinion to oppose the Wood and McCarran bills, liberals decided to introduce the Emergency Detention Bill. This transformed the nature of debate, because now two different countermeasures to communism were juxtaposed. The debate between conservatives and liberals turned into a peculiar competition over which side was more anticommunist—and whether each side was "truly American" or "un-American."

While conservatives defined true Americanism as consisting of patriotism and anticommunism, liberals also appealed to nationalist enthusiasm to legitimize their political positions. Emanuel Celler, a pro-administration Democratic congressman, quoted Truman's words in a speech expressing his opposition to the Wood Bill:

> Today we can agree that all good Americans are anti-Communist, but we must never assume that the degree of a man's anticommunism is a test of his American patriotism or his devotion to the things in which we believe. Hitler was an all-out anti-Communist; so was Mussolini. The real test of a man's genuine Americanism today is not merely that he is anti-Communist but also that he is devoted to the ideals and traditions which have made this country great—our concepts of democracy, of individual rights, and of equal opportunity for all.[89]

According to Truman, liberalism, democracy, and devotion to constitutional ideals indicated Americanism. Using the same logic, Celler criticized his opponents as being "un-American." He argued that the Communist Registration Bill was legislation not against communism but against the Bill of Rights, as it disregarded the First and Fifth Amendments and embraced guilt by association. Celler concluded that the bill was un-American because it made punishable "what a man thinks and not . . . what a man does."[90]

Liberals tried to counter the accusation of being soft on communism by shifting the definition of Americanism. For conservatives, the repression of communists was intrinsically a patriotic political action, because communism was un-American and communists and their sympathizers were disloyal simply as such. On the other hand, liberals argued that preserving the constitutional principles of freedom of thought and speech was an American behavior, and therefore the repression of political thought was an un-American way to deal with communism. They suggested that rather than forcing communists and those labeled communist sympathizers to register during peacetime, detaining potential saboteurs before they could engage in any acts of espionage and sabotage once the nation faced an emergency would be more effective in preventing damage to internal security. Senator Douglas explained the merit of emergency detention measures over the registration measures as follows:

> The operation of the substitute bill, namely the Kilgore bill, is more like that of the rifle, while the McCarran bill resembles the blunderbuss, which shoots off in so many directions at once that it is hard to tell whether it will hit real or only imaginary enemies. And when it

does hit them, it is not clear whether it will hurt them more than it does the government that fires the gun and feels the recoil.[91]

The idea of preventive detention was based on the premise that the FBI already had a list of approximately twelve thousand "dangerous" communists. Title II provided legal sanction for the FBI to arrest them immediately. This, according to liberals, showed their own toughness on communism while providing a less un-American way to control subversive activities. Congressional committees such as HUAC were smearing particular classes of citizens by labeling them as communists and virtually destroying their social lives by publicizing their names. This, liberals argued, would degrade some Americans as second-class citizens on the basis of their political beliefs. As an alternative, liberals attempted to "put the control of Communism outside the reach of McCarthyite congressional committees."[92] If the responsibility for internal security was placed on the attorney general and the FBI, professionals could handle the situation. Professionals could deal with the problem of subversive citizens and aliens as part of an administrative routine and thus keep the problem out of politics. Liberal politicians also believed that preventive detention measures effectively prevented subversive activities but did not punish subversive thoughts and therefore were closer to the constitutional ideal of freedom of speech.

When liberals challenged conservatives with the Emergency Detention Bill, which would strengthen governmental power to counter subversive activities, the positions between liberals and conservatives were reversed. Now it was liberal senators who were pushing for more restrictive measures, while conservatives appealed to the traditional libertarian ideals.

The supporters of the Communist Registration Bill attacked the Emergency Detention Bill as being offensive to civil liberties because it equipped the government with the power to detain people who had not committed a crime. Senator Ferguson, a major sponsor of the Communist Registration Bill, expressed his opposition to the Emergency Detention Bill. Ferguson argued that legalizing emergency detention or internment would allow the government to build "concentration camps," which he believed would be a great deviation from the American concept of freedom. He contended that, while statutes had been made to prohibit a person from committing a crime "where one is in position to do it, intending to do it, and is intercepted," Congress had "never gone as far as to go down into the recesses of a man's mind, into his thoughts," to make it a crime to have a thought of committing a crime, and to subject the thinker to "punishment—whether it is called imprisonment, detention, or anything else."[93]

While liberal politicians branded the Communist Registration Bill as a "thought control bill," conservative politicians mocked the Emergency Detention Bill as a "concentration camp bill." Senator Mundt argued that the Detention Review Board would create "a swarm of Gestapo agents in this country, a whole swarm of unknown politicians, to travel around the country locking up in concentration camps, without charges and without a trial, anyone whom they may dislike or who, they may think, is contemplating sabotage." He joked that perhaps the review would be conducted by an "obscure political agent" who would deny release by "saying, in Gestapo language, 'Nein, nein,' or as a Communist agent would say, 'Nyet, nyet.'" [94]

The conservative politicians' usage of libertarian rhetoric, however, lasted for only a short while during the debate on the internal security bills. On September 12, four days after the above statements were made, Senators McCarran, Ferguson, and Mundt all switched their positions and supported the addition of the emergency detention provisions to the Internal Security Act.

The debate before the passage of the Internal Security Act shows that neither conservatives nor liberals wholeheartedly endorsed it. It was, rather, a product of political rivalry and manipulation of the legislative process that turned out to be a clear victory for anti-administration conservatives. Title II was a byproduct of a muscle-flexing contest between liberal and conservative politicians showing who was more tough or "hard" on communism. At the same time, liberals and conservatives advocated their respective positions using similar rhetoric, both appealing to the American democratic tradition. In the end, liberals, to their own distress, voted for a law they considered a violation of the American liberal tradition and constitutional principles.

Both liberal and conservative politicians agreed that communists were a threat to internal and national security, but they disagreed on who the communists were, what the nature of the threat was, and how the government could curtail the communist threat most effectively without infringing on the civil liberties of loyal Americans. In contrast to the smooth ratification of Public Law 503, which endorsed Executive Order 9066, Title II's passage induced heated discussion in Congress. In 1942, everybody in Congress understood that Executive Order 9066 would affect only people of Japanese ancestry, while in 1950 the potential targets of Title II were contested. In the case of the Japanese American removal, the rhetorical national boundary was drawn on a clear-cut ethnic category. In 1950 the boundary between "Americans" and "un-Americans" was vague. Contested as it was, Title II legalized the detention and incarceration of potentially disloyal citizens, a drastic power of domestic enemy control that the government had granted itself through the removal of Japanese Americans during World War II.

Japanese American Wartime Incarceration in the Debate on the Emergency Detention Bill

In the historiography of Japanese American incarceration, many works refer to historical amnesia after the war.[95] The evolution and final text of Title II, however, indicate that the removal and incarceration of Japanese Americans were very much alive in the minds of politicians when they contemplated internal security issues. The wartime experiences of politicians and bureaucrats generated ambivalent attitudes toward this legal precedent while they drafted the Emergency Detention Bill and debated internal security legislation in Congress.

The drafters of the Emergency Detention Bill stressed that it was designed to be an improvement over the wartime mass removal of Japanese Americans. On September 8, 1950, when Senator Douglas explained the idea of emergency detention, he insisted that his bill gave the president and the attorney general "the positive assistance of statutory authority" with "procedures clearly understood and to a lesser degree previously employed, in alien enemy internment and war relocation cases."[96] He argued that if the executive branch became empowered to institute a detention program, it was better to give it explicit authority to act and provide the concrete and essential safeguards for individual freedom.

Refuting Senator Ferguson's argument that the law gave a criminal punishment to those who had not committed a crime, Douglas pointed out that Japanese Americans were detained without being accused of any crime but merely on the basis of race and nationality, whereas the detention based on his bill would be carried out "not on the basis of race or nationality but on the basis of demonstrated actions likely to lead to acts of espionage or sabotage."[97] In Douglas's logic, the wartime incarceration of Japanese Americans raised constitutional problems because Japanese aliens were detained solely on the basis of nationality and Japanese American citizens on the basis of race. At the same time, liberal senators defending the Emergency Detention Bill downplayed the harshness of Japanese Americans' wartime treatment. Douglas stated that the camps in which Japanese Americans were confined had "not been the same as Alcatraz" and that the imprisonment of criminals involved "defamation and a stigma upon the character" while detention did not. However, historical evidence later showed that wartime detention left a great psychological stigma on Japanese Americans, both as individuals and as a community, for many decades afterward.[98]

Attacking the Emergency Detention Bill, Senator Ferguson defined Japanese American incarceration as a special wartime measure. He argued that the government had attempted to "follow a legally fictitious procedure of barring people from certain areas but allowing them to go up into camps voluntarily" when it implemented Japanese American removal and incarceration.[99] To contrast Japanese American incarceration to preventive detention, Ferguson emphasized that in the *Endo* case, a writ of habeas corpus was granted while the war was still continuing.

Neither Ferguson nor Douglas openly criticized the mass incarceration of Japanese Americans as a mistake, let alone an injustice, but their ambivalence about the measures was clear in their descriptions of them. On one hand, Douglas described emergency detention as equivalent to the detention of enemy aliens. Ferguson, on the other, said that alien enemies were "an entirely different category" from citizens. Douglas then pointed out that citizens of a particular ancestry had been a target of preventive detention in the past by citing the example of Japanese Americans.[100] This rhetorical confusion was not caused by a limited understanding of this historical precedent; rather, it was a direct reflection of the abnormal administrative procedure through which these policies had been enacted and the perplexing rhetoric with which the Supreme Court upheld them. Lawmakers in 1950 carried ambivalent historical memories of the Japanese Americans' wartime removal and incarceration because in 1942 the rules for enemy aliens had been applied to a class of citizens on the basis of ethnic ancestry. This loophole in the constitutional protection of civil liberties opened an avenue for the postwar Congress to pass a law that allowed the detention of citizens at the discretion of the government.

The historical memory of Japanese American incarceration also provided ideas concerning the category of citizens the government could or should detain. To distinguish between Japanese American incarceration and emergency detention, Senator Douglas reiterated that loyalty was the key element that should determine if a person could be detained or not:

> Is the Senator aware of the fact that in the case to which he refers [*Endo*], involving a Japanese woman, she was freed because it was found that she was loyal? Because it was found that she was loyal a writ of habeas corpus was granted. If there had been a finding that she was not loyal, the writ would not have been granted. I believe such an inference may well be drawn from the opinion of Justice Douglas in that case.[101]

Ferguson agreed that the detainee's loyalty was the Supreme Court's reason for ordering Endo's freedom, but he refuted the idea that the Court sanctioned the detention of disloyal citizens. He correctly pointed out that the two Supreme Court decisions were limited to narrow grounds: the *Korematsu* decision dealt with only the exclusion order and avoided making a judgment on the detention order; in the *Endo* case, the Court ordered Endo to be freed but did not discuss disloyal citizens or aliens among the Japanese American community. As Ferguson argued, these rulings did not sanction the imprisonment or detention of aliens or citizens on the basis of disloyalty, let alone suspected disloyalty. However, because the Supreme Court did not rule on this grey zone between civil liberties and internal security, supporters of the Emergency Detention Bill were able to use the Japanese American cases to justify it. The eventual passage of Title II meant that the American legal system sanctioned the detention of citizens on the basis of suspected disloyalty.

Another problem concerning Japanese American incarceration came up during the debate. Senator Ferguson refuted Douglas by arguing that what Japanese Americans experienced was the wartime removal of citizens from a particular military area and that their incarceration in "special centers" should not be compared to the peacetime detention of enemy aliens.[102] The Emergency Detention Bill, in contrast, was not restricted to military areas but applied to the entire territory of the United States. On this point, Ferguson was only partly correct. The military zones designated by the Western Defense Command involved only the areas one hundred miles from the Pacific Coast, later expanded to include the entire state of California. However, Executive Order 9066 authorized the secretary of war to designate *any* areas within the United States and its territories as military zones. In principle, the Japanese American exclusion as a historical precedent allowed the government to remove any citizens from any areas within the United States; it was not as limited as Ferguson implied.

Senator Douglas's reply to Ferguson's challenge had even larger implications for postwar governmental control over American civil liberties. He went as far as to say that in the current struggle with communism, virtually the whole United States had become a military area. Under Cold War conditions, the boundary between military and nonmilitary areas disappeared, and the nation might be "faced with a period of seriously threatened espionage and sabotage prior to a formal declaration of war."[103] Given that an actual war was going on in Korea, Senator Douglas even suggested that the internal security emergency should be declared as soon as Congress passed the bill.

Ferguson rejected the idea that the historical precedent of Japanese American incarceration granted the government unconditional authority to conduct preventive detention. He reminded his opponents that the Japanese American cases were tried before a jury of peers. Douglas reiterated his previous argument that the actions covered by the Emergency Detention Bill did not involve crime and therefore did not require a trial by jury. To this, Ferguson countered:

That then involves the protections of due process under the fifth amendment. The Senator and I differ with respect to what is a criminal prosecution. If I am put in prison by fiat and kept there for a day or a year or until Congress, by passing an act, lets me out, or the President of the United States lets me out, I should certainly feel that I was wrongfully kept in prison.[104]

Conservatives did not accept liberals' argument that preventive detention was milder than imprisonment. By calling detention centers "concentration camps," they criticized the Emergency Detention Bill as far more repressive than Japanese American incarceration.

The debate indicates that the historical memory of the Japanese American removal and incarceration was an ambivalent one for both liberal and conservative politicians in 1950. Liberal politicians did not criticize the mistreatment of Japanese Americans directly, but by offering improved procedures for detention, they implied that the previous procedure was constitutionally suspect. Rather than leaving this power to an executive order or to the military, liberals insisted that Congress should legalize the procedure for preventive detention and provide avenues for appealing detention. Thus, they aimed to prevent the arbitrary detention of innocent citizens and to protect citizens from being detained on the basis of race, nationality, or certain political beliefs that do not involve subversive actions.

Conservatives, on the other hand, discursively constructed Japanese American incarceration as a wartime exclusion of enemy aliens. They also did not criticize the policy itself, but in their criticism of Title II, they expressed reservations about constructing "concentration camps," which they labeled "un-American." In the debate over Title II, two interpretations of the wartime treatment of Japanese Americans—incarceration of citizens based merely on race and nationality and wartime exclusion of enemy aliens for national security—coexisted.

It is important to note that both liberals and conservatives discussed the Japanese American mass removal and incarceration in the context of how to control the repressive power of the government during an emergency. In both liberal and conservative minds, notions such as internment, preventive detention, and concentration camps generated discomfort. The wartime mass incarceration of Japanese Americans was a problematic precedent for postwar America in considering the balance between civil liberties and internal security. Lawmakers in 1950 were aware of the problems the precedent created: the expansion of the government's war power, the application of enemy alien policy to American citizens, and the weakening of constitutional guarantees of due process and equal protection.

Conclusion

Fear of espionage and sabotage escalated as Americans felt increasingly insecure about national defense, mainly because of the possibility that the Soviet Union would create weapons of mass destruction. The fear heightened existing tensions even on domestic issues such as public policy and civil rights, and the hunt for the "enemy within" intensified on the home front. The two components of the Internal Security Act of 1950 were products of this fear. The law embodied two different responses—communist registration and emergency detention—to the perceived threat.

Mainstream commercial and veterans' associations such as the U.S. Chamber of Commerce, the Veterans of Foreign Wars, and the American Legion supported the act. Opposition was expressed by numerous liberal and labor organizations such as the Communist Party, the Socialist Party, and the American Labor Party. Organizations such as the NAACP and the Women's International League for Peace and Freedom also pronounced strong disagreement with the law.

Conservative politicians aimed to alienate whoever they branded as communists and communist sympathizers. Liberal politicians and organizations, as well as minority organizations, were threatened by this measure because the brand-and-alienate scheme targeted activists and even government officials who advocated social reforms that would improve race relations, labor relations, and social welfare. Liberals wanted to make only subversive actions punishable and preserve the freedom of thought. The measure they adopted authorized the government's internal security agencies in case of war, invasion, or insurrection to detain potential saboteurs before they had a chance to commit espionage and sabotage.

The passage of the Internal Security Act was an ironic political event. Both liberals and conservatives showed their concerns about the constitutional guarantees of civil liberties when they criticized the bills sponsored by their political foes. In the end, they collectively passed both Title I and Title II, which they had all branded during the congressional debates as totalitarian and un-American. The passage of the law was particularly ironic for liberal Democrats, who tried to stop the passage of the Communist Registration Bill and then turned around and drafted a law that would be remembered as a "concentration camp law." Title II tragically contradicted their own beliefs in individual freedom and constitutional democracy.

Liberals' introduction of Title II also showed a paradox within liberalism itself. On the one hand, the Truman administration and the sponsors of the Emergency Detention Bill repeatedly emphasized their respect for civil liberties and individual freedoms, particularly of speech and thought. Liberals, at the same time, advocated executive control as they opposed the McCarthyite congressional inquisitions by HUAC and the SISS. They stressed the importance of professionals in the governmental internal security agencies taking charge to ensure accuracy and institutional efficiency.[105]

Some liberals were wary of the government's growing power over civil liberties. Senator Douglas's memoir suggests that liberal politicians considered it necessary to regulate the FBI's activities. J. Edgar Hoover had announced that his bureau was "ready to seize some 12,000 dangerous persons in case of war with Russia," and he gave even larger numbers of potentially disloyal people when he announced there were approximately 55,000 Communists and "a half million fellow travelers and sympathizers ready to do the Communist bidding."[106] Liberals were concerned about a large-scale raid and detention in case of war. Douglas thought there should be procedures for the detainees' release where there was no danger of sabotage or espionage.[107] Liberals, while advocating the allocation of stronger power to professionals in government agencies to curb subversive activities, felt uncomfortable granting uncontrolled authority to those agencies. Their wariness was in fact reasonable. Perhaps the biggest irony in this episode was that Senator Paul Douglas himself was on the FBI's blacklist of people to be detained under Title II.[108]

The drafting and passage of Title II also show that the relationship between race and citizenship had shifted after World War II. Ellen Wu and Cindy Cheng have elucidated how the Cold War promoted racial liberalism toward Asian Americans while racial exclusion continued via various structural economic, social, and diplomatic apparatuses. Similarly, congressional debates over Title II reveal how Cold War politics induced the delegitimation of overt racial exclusion. The drafters of Title II clearly remembered the Japanese American incarceration and used it as a historical precedent for wartime preventive detention. The Supreme Court had sanctioned the government's discriminatory application of curfew and exclusion orders to a "potentially disloyal" racial group, while also ruling that the detention of a citizen "proven to be loyal" was constitutionally unacceptable. Particularly important was the notion of loyalty, which the Court had discursively used to mark the border between those who could be detained and those who should not. The discursive boundary for constitutional protection now stood on the ambiguous and easily manipulated notion of loyalty to the state. When the Cold War erased the separation between military zones and the home front, Congress gave the government power to detain anybody, alien or citizen, from any part of the country, and allowed this without checking whether there was an appropriate "relationship between the exercise of the detention power and the gravity of the actual emergency."[109]

The passage of Title II legally confirmed the hole in the U.S. Constitution that the Japanese American incarceration had de facto made. The internment, however, did not merely provide justification for preventive detention in a national emergency. Both liberals and conservatives agreed that detention based on race and nationality was discriminatory. Moreover, liberals emphasized that the Emergency Detention Bill contained clauses for appealing one's detention through a preliminary hearing, a hearing in front of the Detention Review Board, and judicial review. Also, the law was to be applied only on an individual basis, not to an entire class of citizens. By adding these clauses to protect civil liberties, lawmakers in 1950 indirectly pointed to the injustice done to Japanese Americans during World War II.

Even though wartime mass removal was affirmed and supported, politicians and legal experts expressed ambivalence and reservations—mass detention as a national security measure was acceptable, but mass detention based on racism was not. In the discussion of Title II, memory gradually shifted from the former to the latter. This ambivalence lingered until Title II attracted popular attention again in the late 1960s.

3

The Shifting Ground of Civil Liberties

McCarthyism, the FBI, and the Supreme Court in the Age of Concentration Camps

The passage of the Internal Security Act neither settled the political rivalry between the administration and Congress nor lulled public fervor to persecute the "Reds." On the contrary, the hunt for domestic enemies intensified. After the summer of 1950, McCarthyism led to a full-fledged assault on civil liberties at every level of American society.

Anticommunist rhetoric gave the anti-administration politicians a strong verbal weapon to attack the administration and the members of Congress who supported it. In particular, a sensational offensive by Joe McCarthy on the government, in which he claimed that he had obtained a list of communists who worked for the State Department, demonstrated that labels such as "communist" or "disloyal" could effectively undermine the authority of most powerful politicians in the nation.[1] McCarthy's attack, in fact, was deliberately targeted at high government officials who represented the growing "anonymous power [that] alienated many Americans grounded in individualist and anti-statist traditions."[2]

Popular anti-elite, anti-statist sentiment, however, cannot fully explain McCarthyism. First, popular support is rarely the source of a politician's strong influence in the government. Second, McCarthy was removed from a position of influence when the administration changed from Democrat to Republican, implying that Republicans had used him as a political pawn to attack the Democratic administration. Third, and most importantly, high-ranking officials in the government were by no means the primary victims of the McCarthyite purge. A far larger number of political liberals and leftists, former New Dealers, labor unionists, civil rights activists, sexual minorities, and nonconformist academics, journalists, and artists fell victim to red-baiting.[3]

The attorney general of the Truman administration, J. Howard McGrath, repeatedly emphasized the intensification of the domestic communist threat. He warned that communists were "everywhere—in factories, offices, butcher stores, on street corners, in private business."[4] The fear that communists were everywhere justified the government's search for them everywhere.

In the 1950s, categories such as race and nationality could no longer be used to distinguish the loyal from the disloyal. Everyone was potentially disloyal, and on the basis of mere suspicion, anyone's civil liberties could be restricted in the name of national and internal security. The Internal Security Act, equipped with communist registration and emergency detention, provided concrete measures with which the individuals suspected of being subversive could be labeled as such and incarcerated if the government considered it necessary.

Reactions to the Internal Security Act

The passage of the Internal Security Act was a marked victory for the conservative faction in Congress. But while they had been defeated in the battle over this legislation, groups opposed to the Internal Security Act made efforts to repeal the law. Some senators prepared repeal bills, while liberal organizations continued to study the law and express their opposition to it. The White House tried to regain control over the internal security legislation by appointing a new commission. None of these efforts, however, led to the repeal of either Title I or Title II.

Executive and Congressional Attempts to Repeal or Revise the Internal Security Act

Soon after the passage of the Internal Security Act, Senators Douglas, Lehman, Kilgore, Kefauver, Humphrey, Murray, Graham, Green, and Chavez declared their intention to work for the repeal or drastic moderation of the law at the following session. The declaration, meanwhile, warned other repeal advocates to refrain from "any association with communist-sponsored attacks on the new law" and called for "loyal compliance" with the act.[5]

Liberal senators' attempts to repeal the Internal Security Act bore no fruit, even though they continued to receive letters from their constituents asking them to repeal it.[6] With Patrick McCarran serving as the chairman of the Senate Committee on the Judiciary, there was no hope for repeal. In the

House, sporadic repeal attempts occurred, but these bills neither obtained enough support for passage nor survived the conservative HUAC.

After the embarrassing defeat of the veto in Congress, the White House tried to regain control of internal security policies. Democrats were having difficulty shedding the image of being soft on communism, especially after Senator McCarthy made an allegation that the State Department was infiltrated by communists. To counter McCarthy's attack, the Senate created the Tydings Committee to review the federal loyalty program, which was launched through Truman's executive order back in March 1947. The loyalty program centered on investigation, relying on the surveillance conducted by the FBI, to check on the ideological and other traits of every federal employee. The Tydings Committee, chaired by Millard Tydings (D-Maryland), concluded that the State Department had an effective security program and no communist worked for the department, but its findings neither swept away popular suspicion of governmental elites nor caused McCarthy to stop his smear campaign. Tydings felt the need for an additional President's Commission on Internal Security and Individual Rights.[7] Stephen Spingarn, until his sudden transfer to the Federal Trade Commission, struggled to establish the subcommittee.[8]

In January 1951, Truman issued an executive order to establish the President's Commission on Internal Security and Individual Rights, also known as the Nimitz Commission since Fleet Admiral Chester W. Nimitz served as chair. The commission's tasks were to examine the internal security laws, to review the federal loyalty program, and to make recommendations for legislative and administrative actions to seek a balance between security and freedom.[9] The Nimitz Commission, however, stalled even before it started its investigations because Patrick McCarran, chair of the Senate Committee on the Judiciary, refused to introduce a bill to exempt the commission personnel from the operation of conflict-of-interest statutes, which hampered them from taking investigatory actions.[10] Despite a personal appeal from the president to McCarran to pass the bill, the Judiciary Committee continued to block the process.[11] On November 14, 1951, Truman issued an executive order to revoke the Nimitz Commission. The battle over control of the internal security field again ended in the administration's defeat.

Civil Organizations' Reactions to the Internal Security Act

Among liberal nongovernmental groups and individuals, the opposition to the Internal Security Act was even stronger than among politicians. Immediately after its passage, liberal bishops and academics, as well as journalists such as Cary McWilliams, formed the National Committee to Repeal the

McCarran Act.[12] McWilliams was a well-known journalist who criticized the removal of Japanese Americans during World War II. Liberal newspapers condemned the Internal Security Act and praised President Truman's veto.[13] Telegraphs urging repeal flooded into the White House and the offices of liberal senators.[14]

A number of minority organizations expressed concerns about the Internal Security Act. The American Jewish Congress published an evaluation reporting that the Internal Security Act combined five separate pieces of legislation and therefore was causing "a great deal of confusion and misunderstanding as to its actual provisions and content."[15] Discussing the registration provisions of Title I, the report warned about the possibility of liberal organizations becoming classified as communist-front organizations. It also criticized the manner in which the alien exclusion provision was implemented. For example, Title I denied entry to all aliens who at any time had been members of totalitarian parties. This, if carried out literally, denied entry to most immigrants from Eastern Europe and former Axis nations. The attorney general had permitted the entry of immigrants from former Axis nations as "nominal" Nazis and Fascists, while excluding all "communists." The report's analysis complained that this law implied that ex-Nazis and ex-Fascists were less repugnant to democratic institutions than communists.

Jewish organizations generally took critical stances toward Title II, but they recognized the merit of regulating the government's power to enact preventive detention. Their reports show that they saw a clear connection between Title II and the wartime incarceration of Japanese Americans. The American Jewish Congress report pointed out that the detention of Japanese Americans, "including some 70,000 American citizens," was conducted "without any hearing or the right of effective judicial review."[16] The report contended that Title II would have provided a salutary limitation on the arbitrary abuse of executive authority and could function as "some protection against a repetition of the Japanese evacuation" as long as the requirements for a fair hearing were completely honored.[17]

The report also pointed out crucial shortcomings of Title II. The attorney general was allowed to withhold information for national security reasons, yet the Detention Review Board was allowed to consider such undisclosed information as evidence. This denied the accused a fair hearing. Thus the American Jewish Congress's overall evaluation of Title II was negative: the report argued that the existence of an emergency could under no circumstances justify detaining thousands of people without informing them of the evidence against them or the identity of their accusers.

Similarly, the American Jewish Committee and the Anti-Defamation League of B'nai B'rith issued a joint memorandum summarizing and analyzing the Internal Security Act.[18] The memorandum called for an outright repeal of Title I. As for Title II, the joint analysis noted that the detention provisions had been criticized as providing for the indefinite imprisonment of individuals merely suspected of being likely to commit sabotage or espionage. It concluded that the law was parallel to the policy enacting the detention of West Coast Japanese Americans—which, the memorandum insisted, was an action of which Americans had become "deeply ashamed."[19]

The National Lawyers Guild also analyzed the Internal Security Act and concluded that the law should be repealed, or else the guarantees of the Bill of Rights would be "reduced to a mere shadow."[20] The organization condemned the fact that Congress "for the first time in history provided for the indefinite imprisonment of thousands of people merely on suspicion."[21] It further criticized the law for potentially imprisoning people not on suspicion that they have committed a crime but rather on suspicion that they might do so at some unknown future date. Such suspicion could be based on no more than the possession of information, and the detained person might never be advised of either the accuser's identity or the evidence against him or her. This, the analysis criticized, was "the pattern associated with fascism."[22]

Within African American communities, concerns about the Internal Security Act, particularly Title II, was strong. The *Pittsburgh Courier* carried an article titled "The U.S. Is Set to Fill Its Concentration Camps Now—or Did You Know It?" The article reported that the FBI had gathered some fourteen thousand names of people who would certainly be picked up once an emergency was declared. It also reported that HUAC listed many well-known artists, academics, and writers, including Langston Hughes, Paul Robeson, and W.E.B. DuBois, as affiliated with communist-front organizations. The article warned that many readers could be on the list without knowing it if they had "placed their weight behind movements for social and political progress in the last couple of decades."[23] Some civil rights organizations attempted to take direct actions to strike down the Internal Security Act. For example, the Civil Rights Congress advocated launching a suit before the Federal Court in Washington, D.C., to call for a court declaration that the act was unconstitutional.[24] Shortly after the passage of the Internal Security Act, the ACLU announced its willingness to aid in court tests of some of the act's provisions it considered unconstitutional.[25]

The Japanese American Citizens League (JACL) took a keen interest in the McCarran Act. The JACL Anti-Discrimination Committee, of which Edward Ennis was a legal counsel, studied both Title I and Title II. The JACL was mainly concerned with the immigration and naturalization clauses within Title I, because Representative Francis Walter (D-Pennsylvania) was moving to pass a resolution attached to this law that lifted the ban on Asian immigrants' naturalization.[26] As much as the JACL hoped for the passage of the Walter Resolution, which would have granted Issei access to citizenship, the JACL was disturbed by the repressive nature of McCarran's immigration and naturalization bill. The resolution that granted Asians the right to naturalization was passed as part of the Immigration and Nationality Act of 1952, popularly known as the McCarran-Walter Act.[27]

Japanese Americans also saw problems in the emergency detention provisions of Title II. Around the passage of the McCarran Act, *Pacific Citizen*, the JACL newspaper, carried editorials comparing the wartime incarceration of Japanese Americans to the possible detention of those branded as "disloyal" under the Emergency Detention Act. One titled "The Accuser and the Accused" perceived an "uncomfortable resemblance" between the summary dismissal of Nisei from employment in 1942 and what was happening "to numerous artists because of alleged connections with subversive ideas." The similarity lay in the fact that "there was no opportunity (for the persecuted artists) to face the accuser or deny the charge."[28] Larry Tajiri wrote in his regular editorial column, "Nisei USA":

> The Nisei are the only Americans who can speak with experience regarding any proposal which provides for wartime concentration camps. There are differences, of course, since the mass evacuation of 1942 was carried out along racial lines and Nisei of all political beliefs were lumped together and detained in the relocation camps. The Kilgore amendment applies to political subversives and provides for the internment of potential subversives by the Attorney General with a procedure for individual hearings, the right of appeal to a board of detention review and a right of petition to an appellate court. The proposal will legalize a form of selective internment not dissimilar to that which was carried out during World War II regarding Japanese and other "enemy aliens."[29]

As the Chinese military intervened in the Korean War, tension arose around Chinese communities throughout the United States. Surveillance of Chinese Americans intensified, and Chinese American organizations in major cities performed "mass avowals of loyalty" to the United States.[30] However, many Chinese Americans "compared their situation to the predicament of persons of Japanese descent on the Pacific coast after Pearl Harbor," and "there were rumors of impending mass evacuation and internment" in Chinatowns.[31] *Pacific Citizen* also reported on the civic movements that supported minority communities. For example, the Council for Civil Unity of San Francisco adopted a resolution that condemned the rising anti-Chinese sentiments directed against Americans of Chinese ancestry, vowing that it would "take all essential steps to ensure that neither they nor any other group shall suffer because of race or ancestry as Japanese Americans did in World War II."[32]

Mainstream liberal organizations, such as Americans for Democratic Action (ADA) and the ACLU, maintained a critical stance toward Title I. To Title II, on the other hand, they gave mixed responses. Their ambivalent attitudes echoed those of the liberal senators who had introduced the law.

In November 1950, ADA published a legal analysis of the Internal Security Act that criticized most of the provisions in Title I. ADA found problems particularly in the registration requirements and the directives to the Subversive Activities Control Board, which, in their view, authorized Congress to "institute and enforce thought control."[33] The analysis reiterated liberal critiques that the enforcement of the provisions would be cumbersome and virtually impossible and that the law would make the FBI's surveillance of communist activities more difficult. It also criticized the law's alien, immigration, and naturalization sections, which ADA believed were "ill-considered, unworkable and dangerous" and would bring about "a thoroughly undemocratic treatment of those entering or seeking to enter the United States."[34]

The ADA analysis of Title II saw problems in two aspects: the writ of habeas corpus and the desirability of the law. First, ADA noted that detaining a person not charged with a crime raised serious constitutional questions unless the writ of habeas corpus was suspended. The analysis, however, argued that in view of the Supreme Court decisions in the Japanese American cases, Title II might be effective even though the writ of habeas corpus was not suspended. ADA adopted a position similar to that of the liberal senators on the significance of the *Hirabayashi*, *Korematsu*, and *Endo* decisions:

> Although the question of detention has never been adjudicated as such, it was implied from the language of Mr. Justice Douglas in Ex Parte Endo that he would consider constitutional the power to detain so long as it is derived from the power to protect the war effort against espionage and sabotage. And in the Korematsu case, the Japanese exclusion case, Mr. Justice Frankfurter indicated that the power to wage war is the power to wage war successfully and that an action cannot be stigmatized as lawless in wartime solely because it is considered to be lawless in times of peace.[35]

The question that interested ADA most was the extent to which the failure to have such legislation as Title II could permit an executive order or legislative action resulting in detention without the safeguards implicit in the law. The analysis refers to the Japanese American incarceration as an example of such an executive order. Considering the human rights violations inflicted on Japanese Americans, ADA concluded that it would be better for the "detention legislation with adequate legal safeguards [to] be provided" than for such emergency measures to be left to ad hoc executive orders in the event of war, invasion, or insurrection.[36]

In short, ADA took a position on Title II virtually identical to that of the bill's drafters. This was not only because the organization's ideological standpoint was similar to that of those senators but also because its members included people directly involved in the drafting process of Title II as well as the implementation of Japanese American removal. For example, Joseph L. Rauh Jr., a founder and leader of ADA, was one of the original drafters of Title II.[37] Francis Biddle, attorney general during World War II, was one of the most prominent ADA members. The ADA analysis, written in November 1950, reveals the dilemma liberals faced in balancing civil liberties and internal security; furthermore, it shows that the legal legacy of Japanese American exclusion and incarceration was still haunting the liberal concept of internal security even after Title II was passed.

Edward J. Ennis and the ACLU's Analysis of Title II

Another important person involved in the wartime removal of Japanese Americans analyzed Title II after its passage. Edward J. Ennis, director of the Alien Enemy Control Unit in the Justice Department during World War II, conducted a study on Title II for the ACLU. The ACLU immediately announced its opposition to the Mundt-Ferguson-Johnston Communist Registration Bill (S2311) in 1950, and after the introduction of the administration bill that fortified the governmental intelligence capacity, the organization preferred it to the McCarran and Mundt-Ferguson proposals.[38] When the Emergency Detention Bill was introduced in the Senate, the ACLU sent detailed comments and suggestions to Frank W. McCulloch, one of its drafters.[39] The ACLU initially expressed its opposition but suggested that a more detailed study should be done.[40] It sent its analysis of the Emergency Detention Bill to the National Civil Liberties Clearing House, a coalition of noncommunist civil liberties organizations that opposed the McCarran and Mundt-Ferguson-Johnston bills.[41]

After the law's passage, however, the ACLU withheld opposition to Title II.[42] In November 1950, the ACLU board of directors appointed a special committee, consisting of Jonathan Bingham, Edward J. Ennis, Morris L. Ernst, and Arthur Garfield Hays, to study Title II.[43] A month later, the Committee on Emergency Detention Provisions of McCarran Act recommended through a majority opinion that the ACLU should *not* oppose the emergency provisions.⁴⁴ Hays, however, wrote a separate minority statement urging a repeal of the law in its entirety.⁴⁵

The majority statement of the committee, authored by Ennis, Bingham, and Ernst, consisted of three sections. The first discussed the principle of emergency detention, analyzing Title II against historical precedents and comparing it with related laws. The second section explained why the ACLU should change its position from opposition to support. The committee then suggested some modifications to strengthen the procedure for reviewing detentions and granting compensation for wrongful accusation in order to prevent the arbitrary confinement of innocent individuals.

The text of the majority report indicates that the committee considered Title II in light of the history of American civil liberties and preventive detention. While the text never directly refers to Japanese Americans, a close reading of its logic and wording implies that the committee members were clearly conscious of Japanese American removal and incarceration as a comparable precedent.

Section 1 of the committee report explained why the ACLU should not oppose Title II. The subsection titled "Historical Analogy" declared that there was "ample historical authority" for the emergency detention of enemy aliens. It argued that the persons who posed the greatest threats to national security were likely not aliens but citizens. Title II declared that such persons were "virtually alien enemies" because they owed their allegiance to a foreign power.⁴⁶

There was not in fact "ample" historical authority for the preventive detention of citizens, which had been traditionally considered in the United States a serious breach of the due process guaranteed by the Fifth Amendment. However, a recent and significant historical precedent confirmed the government's authority to detain citizens on suspicion of foreign allegiance by obscuring the distinct citizenship statuses defining aliens and citizens. Thus the ACLU committee report adopted the same logic that was used to justify Nisei detention during World War II.

The report also discussed the possibility of using martial law as an alternative in case of an emergency but denounced it on the grounds that martial law could be imposed only where the civil courts were closed; it also asserted that without Title II the temptation would be stronger to declare martial law when it was unnecessary. The committee argued that "martial law would result in the deprivation of almost all civil liberties for all of us, whereas emergency detention would result in deprivation of most civil liberties only for a relatively few."⁴⁷ It concluded that emergency detention was therefore the lesser of two evils.

These phrases indicate that even the ACLU, a highly influential civil liberties organization, adopted the "balancing test" approach rather than "preferred freedoms" doctrine in 1950.[48] It is doubtful, however, that the ACLU would have approved a law that secured general convenience for the majority at the severe expense of restricting civil liberties for certain minority citizens had it not been for the logic adopted in the "historical analogy" subsection, which equated subversive citizens with enemy aliens. The ACLU was, after all, an organization that was created to protect the rights of persecuted minorities. The wording in the statement ("martial law would result in the deprivation of almost all civil liberties for all of *us*" [emphasis added]) inadvertently betrayed the othering of such citizens as could be detained—in other words, citizens who could be detained were discursively constructed as "virtual alien enemies" or "un-Americans." It is important to note that Japanese American incarceration was upheld with the same logic that allowed citizens who had allegiance to a foreign power (or were suspected of such) to be removed without due process. The logic that placed Japanese Americans outside discursive American citizenship played a crucial role in the ACLU's affirmation of preventive detention in the 1950s.

Comparing emergency detention to the Selective Service, the committee argued that the drafting of men to risk their lives was a greater infringement on civil liberties than the detention of individuals likely to commit espionage or sabotage. While this might be true, it is a rather peculiar comparison. There is no doubt that the civil liberties of loyal citizens may be restricted or violated in times of war, but this issue is not related to the emergency detention of disloyal citizens. Moreover, questions of civil liberties and equality surround both the freedom to be drafted and the freedom not to be drafted. Although those branded as loyal citizens may wish not to be drafted, those whom the state brands as potentially disloyal for one reason or another may wish to serve the nation to prove their loyalty. Such was the case for Japanese American Nisei. The relationship between citizenship and the right (and/or duty) to serve in the military involves a great range of obligation and privilege and is much more complex than the ACLU's comparison.[49]

The report argued that the exclusion of potentially disloyal persons from some areas without their detention was impractical because this would require continuous surveillance of such persons. The unsupervised exclusion of enemy aliens from restricted areas had proven to be impossible during World War II, and in 1942 Ennis, as the director of the Alien Enemy Control Unit in the Justice Department, was in a position to know this better than anybody.

The ACLU report also discussed the inadequacy of existing criminal law. Criminal law cannot deal with a crime that has not yet been committed. The text repeated its previous claim that "the Union cannot object, because this invasion of civil liberties is practiced in order to protect civil liberties for us all."[50] Again, those who would be subject to preventive detention, which the committee assumed were people "trained in espionage or sabotage," were rhetorically separated from loyal citizens. The problem still remained, however, of how to draw the line between potentially loyal citizens and potentially disloyal citizens, and the report did not answer this question.

The committee criticized the idea that law enforcement authorities in times of war or emergency should be allowed, without legal foundation, to take actions necessary for the safety of the nation. The report declared that the ACLU should not advocate or support "such a flagrant violation of due process of law."[51] The problematic precedent referred to in the "historical analogy" subsection is clearly Executive Order 9066, which gave the military carte blanche to do what they wanted.[52] The later sections that discussed the suggestions for improving the law make this point even clearer.

The committee noted that Great Britain had legislation permitting emergency detention "even without a requirement that the persons charged be advised of the charges against [them]."[53] The British government detained and deported a large number of aliens and citizens who were associated, by blood or by ideology, to the Axis nations. As a matter of fact, Defence Regulation 18B provided:

> If the Secretary of State has reasonable cause to believe any person to be of *hostile origin or associations* or to have been recently concerned in acts prejudicial to the public safety or the defence of the realm or in the preparation or instigation of such acts and that by reason thereof it is necessary to exercise control over him, he may make an order against that person directing that he be detained.[54]

The drafters of Title II studied this British statute, but it should be noted that Title II did not contain the term "hostile origin." Given the ambiguity of "origin," the phrase could cause serious problems comparable to the Japanese American incarceration in countries with sizable populations of immigrants and their descendants. In any case, the ACLU special committee argued that even Britain, a country that had a respect for civil liberties, authorized the detention of citizens in times of war.

The last subsection of Section 1 compared the current situation with World War II, asserting that "the argument that we had no espionage in the last world war from domestic advocates of fascism is irrelevant."[55] The committee emphasized that in the conflict with communism, domestic espionage or subversion would happen.

Section 2 of the report, titled "The Provisions of the Act," started with the argument that the ACLU should switch from opposing Title II to endorsing it. The committee, however, called for hearings to consider the amendments the

ACLU was suggesting. Referring to the introduction of martial law to Hawaii during World War II as an undesirable historical precedent, the committee again used the "lesser of two evils" logic:

> It has been argued that the presence of the law at this time on the statute books inevitably results in restrictions of freedom of speech, thought, and association. This is undoubtedly true. But there is no reason to believe that its absence on the statute books with a threat of even more stringent detention laws to follow would not result in an even greater effect on those freedoms.[56]

Section 3 of the report suggested some "procedural improvements." The committee insisted that the attorney general should be required to apply to a court for arrest warrants. It further suggested that such warrants should be examined by proctors, appointed by the chief justice of the Supreme Court. If the proctors determined that probable cause for suspicion existed, then the warrants would be issued.[57] The government did not apply for individual warrants when it mass-incarcerated Japanese Americans. The military raided Nisei households for contraband without search warrants, although Ennis at the Justice Department opposed searches without warrants.

Section 3 provided ideas for securing the detainees' right to counsel. It pointed out that although Title II protected the detainees' right to be represented by counsel in the event of a round-up, this right might be violated in practice because of the possibility that communist lawyers would be apprehended as well: few attorneys would be courageous enough to defend the civil liberties of communists. The committee also warned that it might be impossible to have the court appoint sufficient counsels to defend all the detainees. The report therefore suggested that a "detained persons defender" should be appointed for each detention site. The defender should be "selected from civil liberties committees of bar associations, from legal counsel to organizations active in the fight for civil liberties, and not from persons who have within the past three years been associated with any prosecution agency of any state, federal, or local government."[58] The section also suggested that Title II should expressly provide that all members of the Emergency Detention Review Board must be civilians, emphasizing that the military must not be allowed to exercise judgment over civilians. Considering the conflicts Ennis experienced with the military over the control of civilians during World War II, it is understandable that the committee's statement strongly advocated maintaining civilians in positions of control.

The report shows that the committee attempted to use lessons from history to improve preventive detention measures:

The act provides that detention without reasonable grounds is to be indemnified, the amount to be determined presumably by the income lost as a result of detention. It should go further. *All* detainees should be indemnified. If we single out these individuals, require them to give up their livelihoods on suspicion that they may be security risks, the least we can do is to indemnify them for the period of their detention which they are serving for the security of the rest of us. It is suggested that such indemnification be paid to all detainees at the rate paid to persons serving in the Army of the rank of private, those detained without reasonable ground to receive the additional compensation already provided for.[59]

This is a rather radical suggestion, given the fact that the committee assumed in earlier sections that those detained would be potentially disloyal aliens and citizens and would most likely be communists. The detainees, who had been described as equivalent to aliens in Section 1, were now described like martyrs "serving for the security of the rest of us." The committee's recommendation seems incredibly generous, suggesting that potentially disloyal citizens should get, without sacrificing their lives, the same amount of compensation that loyal citizens drafted in the military would receive.

The committee recommended the creation of special courts to handle the intermediate review of all detention cases to ensure against undue and unfair delays. It also proposed standards of evidence that would permit detentions to be affirmed. The statement referred to the suggestion made by some organizations that the Internal Security Act should be amended from the current provision that evidence should be "reliable, substantial, and probative" to require proof "beyond a reasonable doubt." The committee rejected this idea since it was impossible to prove beyond a reasonable doubt the "*likelihood* of a person committing a crime."[60] However, it did not offer any suggestions for improving the standards of proof.

In contrast to the majority opinion, the minority statement prepared by Arthur Garfield Hays expressed clear opposition to Title II, which he considered to allow "the State to hold men under suspicion in concentration camps."[61] Hays agreed to the procedural improvements suggested by the majority and recommended that the ACLU should work informally to realize them, but he insisted that the ACLU should announce its opposition to the principle of the law and work for the repeal of the entire McCarran Act.

The ACLU committee's split response to Title II reflected the dilemma Americans who endorsed civil liberties carried in the 1950s. Liberals were fighting political struggles on two fronts. On the one hand, the communist threat to American internal security could not be taken lightly in the early

1950s, and liberals had to answer the public demand for strong measures against nuclear espionage. On the other hand, McCarthyism was impeding American civil liberties to an unprecedented degree. Liberals perceived Title II both as a legislative device to achieve balance between civil liberties and internal security and as a weapon with which they could counter the attacks from the right. Furthermore, Title II was modeled after historical precedents during World War II in both Britain and the United States. Given the unsettling memories of this recent war, the ACLU special committee, especially Ennis, could not denounce Title II unequivocally.

The fact that the ACLU report did not mention Japanese Americans is suggestive, since most of the analyses made by other organizations and all of the legal analyses refer to the wartime treatment of this group when discussing Title II. The omission may be one example of what Caroline Chung Simpson calls an "absent presence." Simpson argues that the Japanese American internment "existed everywhere in the immediate postwar as a vacated history" because it was "too disruptive to be borne by conventional historical accounts of the nation."[62] Ennis, as the Justice Department official directly in charge of the administration of aliens and citizens, had gone through severe psychological distress during World War II. For him, perhaps, it was too disruptive a memory to be borne. The peculiar absence of any reference to Japanese Americans suggests that Ennis had not resolved in himself the ethical problems and constitutional contradictions that their incarceration had posed.

The committee report demonstrates that the Japanese American wartime incarceration provided the ACLU with justification to support Title II both in positive and negative ways. On the one hand, the Supreme Court cases affirmed the government's war power to detain potentially disloyal citizens as well as aliens, and this gave Congress the rationale for passing a law that officially granted such power to the government. At the same time, particularly for Edward Ennis, who was aware of the government's wartime misconduct—actions that induced the Supreme Court to affirm that innocent citizens had been wrongfully incarcerated—it was a tragic historical precedent whose recurrence needed to be prevented. The report reveals the committee's mistrust of the military in civil liberties issues, and this mistrust, paradoxically, resulted in the decision to support Title II.

Reactions from Legal Scholars

During the 1950s and 1960s, Title II became the subject of a number of legal studies, which, without exception, referred to the Japanese American removal as a historical precedent. Legal scholars concurred that, in principle, emergency detention as an internal security measure contravened the civil liberties guaranteed in the Bill of Rights. At the same time, they agreed that the nation's war power included taking actions to prevent sabotage and espionage that could threaten the survival of the nation or the Constitution. The Supreme Court decisions in the Japanese American cases, which in effect placed the detention of potentially disloyal citizens within the government's war power, gave these scholars a strong basis to conclude that the Supreme Court would not strike down Title II on constitutional grounds.

Arnold Brecht's analysis of the concept of "concentration camp" was published in June 1950, when Congress was still debating the internal security bills.[63] Comparing preventive detention legislation in Britain, Germany, France, the USSR, and the United States, he pointed out that even in democratic countries, there remained a "twilight sphere of police power" regarding persons not charged with penal offenses but considered dangerous to public safety.[64] Studying both the British and the American experiences during World War II, Brecht suggested that in these two nations, the principle of habeas corpus did not protect persons perceived as dangerous by the executive branch of the government during wartime. Furthermore, he warned that despite the public's confidence that such detention would be limited to times of war, it was legally possible to expand the scope of war powers "to provide justification for a similar exercise of police power at any time when public safety was thought to demand it."[65] Brecht suggested that governments should fortify human rights guarantees such as adequate treatment and living conditions for the detainees, and provisions should be made to ensure that their detention would be limited to the shortest possible time. He argued that the United States should champion such a cause as protecting human rights and civil liberties, since the country occupied "a better position in the eyes of the people of the entire globe, including those under totalitarian rule."[66]

Arthur E. Sutherland Jr., a prominent Harvard law professor, discussed the nation's dilemma between guaranteeing freedom and ensuring internal security from a liberal point of view.[67] Particularly in the early Cold War period, which he described as "war and half-war," the nation and its people had to make choices affecting liberties on the basis of guesses about the unpredictable future. He lamented, "Sooner or later to all who study the law comes the sobering realization that no freedom can be absolute."[68] Sutherland took the middle ground between the left and the right on the communist issue—he rejected the leftists' argument that the threat of a world communist movement had no substance but also emphasized that there was no connection between American liberalism and Russian expansion, thus denying an idea espoused by conservative politicians. He predicted that the Internal Security Act would be brought to the Supreme Court and would "not be found beyond the constitutional power of the Federal Government," especially since Congress had already made the legislative judgment that communism in the United States constituted a "clear and present danger."[69]

In May 1951, *Columbia Law Review* published an article on the Internal Security Act.[70] It reviewed in detail both Title I and Title II and concluded that overall the act was constitutional. On Title II, the article shared the view with other legal studies that even in democratic countries, governments in wartime had detained potential spies and saboteurs regardless of whether specific legislation authorized such detention, and therefore the preventive detention of persons likely to commit espionage and sabotage could be considered an essential wartime safeguard. It studied the *Hirabayashi, Korematsu,* and *Endo* cases as "the closest American precedents" and, on the basis of these Supreme Court decisions, concluded that the preventive detention of both aliens and citizens was within the scope of the government's war powers. Agreeing with the drafters of Title II that the *Endo* decision implied that detaining disloyal citizens was constitutional, the author gave that part of the law a particularly positive evaluation:

> By Title II of the Internal Security Act, Congress has sought to avoid such an indiscriminate round-up of persons as occurred during World War II. . . . The provisions are important . . . because they enact safeguards for those who may be detained. The Act guarantees that detention will not be arbitrary, that treatment will be decent, and most important, that the persons detained, because they will have access to the courts, will not disappear on some government official's say-so into the unknown void which has become the equivalent of preventive detention in totalitarian countries.[71]

The article concluded that Title II provided a satisfactory resolution of the conflict between the requirements of national security and preservation of civil liberties.

An article focused only on Title II appeared in the *University of Pittsburgh Law Review* in late 1952.[72] Leslie W. Dunbar compared the law with the Japanese American exclusion cases in close detail. Though adopting a critical tone, Dunbar concluded it was unlikely that the Supreme Court would strike down the Internal Security Act: both Title I and Title II contained congressional findings about the menace of the communist movement, and it was unlikely that "any court would be willing to say that the findings of the congress were wholly unwarranted."[73] On Title II, he stated that the Supreme Court "gave ample illustration of its reluctance to controvert authoritative estimations of danger."[74] Dunbar emphasized the fact that during World War

II, neither presidential order nor congressional legislation directly authorized the relocation program: the Supreme Court had upheld the curfew and exclusion orders on the basis of merely *"a military commander's interpretation as to what was necessary in the face of security requirements."*[75] He argued that the congressional findings included in the Internal Security Act were "deserving of at least as much respect."[76] Dunbar thus pointed out that the Japanese American internment and the subsequent passage of Title II confirmed judicial and congressional deference to the executive branch in times of war.

Dunbar's analysis contained some critical interpretations of the Japanese American incarceration. By comparing Title II to the *Endo* decision, Dunbar emphasized the fact that the former was specifically based on the congressional finding that "those individuals who knowingly and willfully participate in the world Communist movement, when they so participate, in effect repudiate their allegiance to the United States." This, according to Dunbar, was "a more respectable and solemn basis for action than the vague and fragmentary discoveries of General DeWitt regarding the disloyalty of the Nisei."[77] He also valued the fact that the law made provisions for releasing persons whose loyalty was confirmed. On the "equal protection" issue, however, the article soberly stated that "it is hard to suppose that the Court of the 1950's will gag at discrimination against Communists, when the Court of 1943 and 1944 tolerated it against Japanese Americans."[78]

Charles Fairman, a lawyer who had defended the constitutionality of the removal of Japanese Americans during World War II, argued for an expanded interpretation of the government's war power.[79] Writing in 1956, Fairman contended that because the postwar world faced the possible outbreak of nuclear conflict, the government needed even greater authority to react quickly to prevent espionage and sabotage.

Thomas C. Mack analyzed the historical relationship between the government's right to protect itself against subversive elements and the individual's rights to freedom, concluding that the Japanese American cases clearly indicated "a judicial policy of non-interference with the legislative-executive judgment with respect to dangers to national security."[80] Mack admitted that Title II contained many problematic provisions as a criminal statute. For example, a detention was to be based on evidence of what might be done rather than of an act already taken, and the attorney general could withhold some evidence in the interest of national security. Moreover, the law de facto assigned the burden of establishing innocence to the detainee. The vagueness of the conduct that could lead to detention also caused some constitutional problems. Ultimately, however, Mack set aside all these concerns and contended that the detention of suspected security risks was "an established method of governmental self-defense during wartime."[81] He concluded that Title II might be "shocking to the conscience of a democratically-oriented people," but in light of "the precedent of the Japanese American cases," it seemed "a valid exercise of the war power, as a self-protective, national defense measure."[82] For Mack as well as many other legal experts, the state of world affairs at the time—the Cold War and the threat of nuclear espionage—made it appropriate to impose detention measures when urgency demanded it.

Legal scholars agreed that in principle preventive detention, when perceived as criminal punishment, violated constitutional rights. On the other hand, they agreed that strong security measures were necessary to counter espionage and sabotage during a national emergency. All these legal analyses considered the Japanese American Supreme Court cases and realized that the Court would most likely uphold Title II after affirming the *Hirabayashi* and *Korematsu* rulings. Many of them considered it better to have legislation that would regulate executive measures in times of emergency than to allow the government to grant itself emergency powers after a pressing situation had already arisen. The wartime incarceration of Japanese American citizens demonstrated the kind of injustice that could happen to innocent citizens if emergency measures were left to the government's discretion.

Ironically, the problematic memories of Japanese American incarceration led lawyers to support rather than denounce Title II because it provided some civil liberties protections not granted to Japanese Americans during World War II. Legal scholars, along with civil liberties organizations and liberal politicians, thus supported Title II despite their clear recognition that preventive detention violated civil liberties that they conventionally considered paramount in the American constitutional system.

The Implementation of Title II

Title II gave the government power to detain people when the president declared the existence of an "internal security emergency" in case of war, invasion, or insurrection in aid of a foreign enemy. Thus it granted only the *potential* power to conduct preventive detention, and the law was never invoked before it was repealed in 1971. This explains the lack of interest in this law in past studies. However, Title II had serious consequences for the civil liberties protections of the American people through the physical construction of detention camps and the expansion of the governmental surveillance agency.

The Construction of Detention Camps

After the passage of Title II, Attorney General J. Howard McGrath stated it would take him about two years to implement its detention camp provisions.

In December 1951, McGrath announced that he had ordered the camps to be set up on a "stand-by basis" at six locations: Florence and Wickenburg, Arizona; Avon Park, Florida; Allenwood, Pennsylvania; El Reno, Oklahoma; and Tule Lake, California. None of the camps were newly built: rather, already existing facilities were designated by the Bureau of Prisons as potential sites that might be used to detain possible subversives.[83] Tule Lake was one of the War Relocation Centers, later turned into a segregation center that detained Japanese Americans considered to be disloyal. The site in Florence, Arizona, was a federal prison and detention center for undocumented immigrants. This prison was close to the former Gila River War Relocation Center and had held Japanese Americans who were arrested in the camp during World War II.[84]

After the attorney general's announcement, many ordinary citizens as well as those belonging to liberal and labor organizations sent letters and telegrams to President Truman or members of Congress urging the repeal of the Internal Security Act, particularly its detention provisions. In May 1952, public concern shifted to the McCarran-Walter immigration bill, which restricted immigration but also opened citizenship to Asian immigrants. But letters continued to arrive opposing the construction of what many of them called "concentration camps."[85]

After the camps became available, some members of Congress attempted to make use of them by activating Title II. On January 16, 1952, James Eastland, a Democratic senator from Mississippi, introduced a joint resolution "declaring the existence of a state of internal security emergency and placing in full force and effect the provisions of the Emergency Detention Act of 1950."[86] He also insisted as a member of the Senate Internal Security Subcommittee that he had "reliable" information that fifty thousand communists were ready to overthrow the government of the United States. He urged the Senate to "promptly seize and detain" treacherous domestic communists while American soldiers were fighting in Korea.[87] Eastland rhetorically conflated North Korean communists with communists residing within the United States, even though there was no evidence that persecuting domestic dissidents would help America's war effort in the Korean peninsula. He is also known for alleging that civil rights activists were agents controlled by the Kremlin.[88] The joint resolution was referred to the Committee on the Judiciary, but no further actions were taken. Nonetheless, Charles R. Allen Jr., a freelance journalist who reported on the detention camps, identified no fewer than twenty-four separate occasions during the 1950s in which the members of the House of Representatives and the Senate urged the president to declare a state of internal security emergency that would put Title II into effect.[89]

In 1952, Allen visited the detention site in Pennsylvania. He talked with its superintendent, a retired colonel named Guy C. Rexroad, who admitted that the basic nature of his mission there was to rehabilitate the place "for use as a detention camp under provisions of the 1950 Internal Security Act."[90] Rexroad remembered the wartime treatment of Japanese Americans. Asked whether the camp was for males only, he answered that the uniforms he had received so far were for males, but he assumed that there would be women as well and that the camp would be filled with whole families, because that was "what they did with the Japanese." He considered this to be "more humane than breaking up the families."[91] The place could hold four thousand to seven thousand people, and it got very hot in summer and cold in winter. "Oh, it won't be any picnic. Probably won't be any better—if as good—as the Japanese camps," he confided to Allen.[92]

In June 1952, James V. Bennett, director of the Federal Bureau of Prisons, testified during hearings before the Senate Appropriations Subcommittee that the Department of Justice was spending $750,000 per year to prepare and maintain wartime internment camps for the purpose of housing up to fifteen thousand subversives.[93] The camps were maintained in "stand-by" status until 1957 under the supervision of the Bureau of Prisons.

In 1955, the *New York Times* carried a full-page article on the current statuses of the detention camps.[94] Its reporter, Luther A. Huston, visited three of the six camps: El Reno, Florence, and Wickenburg. Florence was a federal penitentiary, housing about 150 prisoners, two-thirds of whom were undocumented immigrants. El Reno, a World War II prisoner-of-war camp, had been unoccupied since German POWs were moved out in 1945. Wickenburg was built as an air force glider training school during World War II, and after the detention camp program was set up, it housed some federal prisoners. It was closed by the time Huston visited the camp in 1955. Huston reported that none of the camps had anything resembling the "concentration camps" that horrified the world right after World War II. All three camps had recreational facilities, and none of them had barbed-wire fences. Yet Huston wrote they were no "luxury camps, where prisoners might loll on beds of ease and grow fat on rich food." He was particularly concerned that the places would be "mighty uncomfortable" when they were filled or overcrowded. He also recounted a bleak story claiming that the desert area around the Florence camp had been cleared so that the tracks of fugitives would be visible, with bloodhounds available to follow them.

The article goes on to describe the camps Huston did not visit. Referring to Tule Lake, Huston reported that after the Japanese Americans left, the camp had not been maintained; most of the buildings were torn down, leaving about fifteen structures that could be used to house spies or saboteurs. Avon Park, another camp originally built as a federal prison, no longer housed any prisoners. Nevertheless, Huston wrote, the camp was kept in good repair by the Bureau of Prisons and could house eight hundred to nine hundred detainees if a national emergency arose.

In 1957, Congress terminated the funding for the camps. Some of them faded into disuse while others were leased, sold, or turned into ordinary prisons.[95] According to a Justice Department report in 1962, the Allenwood and Florence camps were at that point being used as minimum-security federal prisons, confining about 550 people.[96] The Wickenburg camp was turned into a school, and Avon Park was converted into a state prison camp. The camp at El Reno was in the process of being razed, and Tule Lake was housing migrant workers. The government made no budget allocations for the camps after 1957.

The FBI's Internal Security Index

While no actual detention ever happened under Title II, the law legally sanctioned expanding the government's surveillance power over citizens' political activities. Title II assumed that intelligence investigations on potentially subversive persons were to be conducted routinely, so that once an internal security emergency was declared, the FBI could "pick them up" immediately.[97] The supporters of the Emergency Detention Bill had emphasized this point. As Hubert Humphrey asserted during the debate on the Internal Security Act:

> The FBI knows who these people are. J. Edgar Hoover came before the Appropriations Committee and said he needed $6,000,000 more to hire agents so as to keep track of 12,000 really dangerous Communists. And he said, "I can pick them up like that"—snapping his fingers. We provide our substitute [the Emergency Detention Bill] as the way to pick them up.[98]

The significance of Title II, therefore, was not limited to authorizing the government to apprehend and detain people on suspicion of potential disloyalty. The emergency detention measures were based on the premise that government agencies could conduct surveillance of citizens and aliens *in peacetime* to determine who potential saboteurs and spies might be. Such surveillance was different from a criminal investigation. The latter was limited in duration and target; was conducted on probable cause; resulted, if charges were filed, in a court trial; and was subject to due process and other constitutional guarantees.[99] Surveillance and investigations to gather intelligence were not subject to such restrictions.

Moreover, due to the lack of accountability and the wide discretion granted to their administrators, internal security investigations tended to allow excessive, illegal, or improper actions, such as wiretapping, breaking and entering, opening letters, using secret informers, and distorting information.[100] Through Title II, Congress indirectly sanctioned—while trying to control—the development of a domestic intelligence agency, the FBI.[101]

In fact, the FBI did not even have to start listing subversive citizens and groups after the passage of Title II, since such a list already existed. As early as 1936, President Franklin Roosevelt authorized the FBI to initiate an "extensive domestic intelligence system to investigate subversive activities in the United States, particularly Fascism and Communism."[102] The FBI conducted confidential investigations to identify individuals "on whom there is information available to indicate that their presence at liberty in this country in times of war or national emergency would be dangerous to the public peace and safety," compiling what was called the Custodial Detention List.[103]

In 1943, Attorney General Francis Biddle ordered the FBI to terminate the Custodial Detention List on the grounds that there was neither statutory authorization nor justification for keeping such a list.[104] Instead of complying with the order, FBI director J. Edgar Hoover integrated the names into a new list, the Security Index. Hoover instructed that the existence of the Security Index should be kept strictly confidential, withholding the information from the liberal attorney general.[105]

The FBI director developed a closer relationship with Biddle's more conservative successor, Thomas C. Clark, who became attorney general in June 1945.[106] In March 1946, Hoover informed Clark that the FBI had been "taking steps to list all members of the Communist Party and any others who would be dangerous in the event of a break in diplomatic relations with the Soviet Union." Hoover suggested to the new attorney general that in such a situation, it might become necessary to "immediately detain a large number of American citizens."[107]

Hoover repeatedly requested statutory backing for the FBI detention programs between 1946 and 1948.[108] In August 1948, Clark instituted a secret emergency detention program known as "Attorney General's Portfolio."[109] In February 1949, he and Secretary of Defense James Forrestal formalized the procedures for the preventive detention program.[110] The FBI meanwhile compiled the Communist Index, which was more extensive than the Security Index, but kept it a secret from Justice Department officials.

When Title II was passed in September 1950, the FBI faced the need to adjust the preexisting detention program to conform to the mandates of the new law. Title II, while formally authorizing the attorney general to detain potential subversives, provided for more liberal detention programs than Attorney General Clark and the FBI had envisioned.[111] For example, the Attorney General's Portfolio allowed the suspension of habeas corpus, while Title II did not.[112] The portfolio provided a master arrest warrant, while Title II mandated that individual warrants be issued "only upon probable cause."[113] Furthermore, Title II provided many procedures for detainees to appeal their detentions. Clark's successor, Attorney General J. Howard McGrath, instructed Hoover to disregard the provisions of Title II and "proceed with the program as previously outlined."[114] Deputy Attorney General Peyton Ford formally advised the FBI that in case of an emergency, "all persons now or hereafter included by the Bureau on the Security Index should be considered subjects for immediate apprehension."[115] Given the administration's sanction to circumvent the protective provisions of Title II, the FBI continued its investigation on the alleged communists, their sympathizers, and other subversives.

Although Title II was never invoked, the Internal Security Index, a confidential list of potential subversives detainable in the event of war or other emergencies, substantially contributed to McCarthyite purges of federal and state employees as well as the political smearing and defamation of many American citizens in the 1950s. The information gathered by the FBI was leaked to sympathetic members of Congress and utilized in the congressional investigations conducted by HUAC and the federal employee loyalty program of the executive branch.

Though less well-known than HUAC in the history of McCarthyism, the Senate also played an important role in attacking alleged communists and other subversives, not only in government agencies but also in the academic and entertainment sectors and in the labor and civil rights movements. Senator McCarran, who became the first chairman of the Senate Internal Security Subcommittee established in December 1950 under the Committee on the Judiciary, had a close relationship with J. Edgar Hoover. From March 1951, the FBI and the SISS shared information obtained from their respective investigations on communists and subversives, whom both the FBI director and the members of the SISS (McCarran, Eastland, Ferguson, and so on) sought to purge.[116] The SISS played a major role in investigating the Institute of Pacific Relations and became one of the Truman administration's most formidable congressional foes. The SISS became a stronghold of anticommunism and hampered civil rights reforms under the leadership of McCarran and Eastland, a powerful Mississippi Democrat who most firmly defended racial segregation in the South.[117]

The FBI also provided information from the Security Index to state authorities through its Responsibility Program in the internal security field. Initiated by J. Edgar Hoover in February 1951, the Responsibility Program secretly supplied state governors and high-level municipal authorities with information on "possible Communist subversives employed in government and public utilities."[118] The information was provided on the condition that it could not be attributed to the FBI. When governors requested information on specific persons who were not on the Security Index, the FBI officials added those names, with some exceptions, to the list.[119] Thus the Security Index grew with cooperation from state governors and other public officers. The scope of the Responsibility Program was extended from the employees of public offices and organizations to private businesses, and later to college and university faculty as well as public school teachers and employees.[120] The program resulted in the dismissals of a large number of people suspected of being communist, pro-communist, or potentially subversive for other reasons.

With its expansion, however, the Responsibility Program became difficult to control by the mid-1950s. By this time, the public was becoming weary of the McCarthyite persecutions of alleged communists. From September 19 to October 7, 1954, the *Denver Post* published a series of articles titled "Faceless Informers and Our Schools," reporting on the FBI's surveillance of local schoolteachers and the leakage of intelligence information to school administrators.[121] The media exposure of this covert program started to give the FBI a negative reputation among the public. Hoover terminated the Responsibility Program in March 1955.[122]

Title II provided the statutory justification for the FBI's listing of potentially subversive persons, but the procedural protections that Congress provided for the emergency detention program did not have much effect in the face of a domestic intelligence agency led by a director who refused intervention from any political or administrative offices. The Department of Justice continued its equivocal directions on whether the FBI should conform to the provisions of Title II or to the looser Attorney General's Portfolio. By November 1952, the number of individuals listed in the Security Index increased to 19,577, and by December 1954 it had grown to 26,174.[123] Beginning in 1956, the FBI expanded its activities even further, moving from purely investigatory activities to more aggressive counterintelligence programs (COINTELPRO) intended to disrupt and neutralize any activities that the FBI considered potential threats to the internal security of the United States.

The Eisenhower Administration and the Communist Control Act of 1954

During the first term of the Eisenhower administration (1953–1957), America saw both the height of McCarthyism and the rapidly waning political influence of the Wisconsin senator who propelled it. On April 27, 1953, Dwight D.

Eisenhower issued Executive Order 10450, which reformed the federal employee loyalty programs to be far more stringent than the Truman administration's loyalty program. All new applicants for federal employment had to undergo a full field investigation of their personal backgrounds and associates. Even those whom the Truman administration had cleared had to go through the investigation again. By January 1954, more than 2,200 employees had been "separated" from the federal government under the new security program.[124] In his 1954 State of the Union address, Dwight Eisenhower recommended that Congress should pass a law that would deprive subversive citizens of their American citizenship.[125] This measure, however, would have required a constitutional amendment, which the administration never moved to enact.

In 1954, Congress passed a bill that expanded the provisions of the Internal Security Act. The Communist Control Act of 1954 outlawed the Communist Party, required "communist-infiltrated organizations" to register with the attorney general, and denied to members of the Communist Party of the United States (CPUSA) the "rights, privileges, and immunities attendant upon legal bodies." It prohibited party members from running for elective office and deprived any labor union labeled a "communist-infiltrated organization" of governmental protection for organizing and collective bargaining.[126]

The origin of this anti-labor/anticommunist legislation was a bill proposed by John M. Butler, a Republican senator from Maryland, and supported by Republicans and conservative Democrats. The bill removed governmental protections for organizing and collective bargaining from "communist-infiltrated" labor unions. To defeat Butler's proposal, Senator Hubert H. Humphrey introduced a bill that penalized members of the Communist Party by subjecting them to fines of up to $10,000, imprisonment for five years, or both. The bill declared the CPUSA an "agency of a hostile foreign power" that constituted a "clear and present danger to the security of the United States."[127] The bill's nineteen cosponsors were liberal Democrats, including Paul H. Douglas, Herbert H. Lehman, Warren G. Magnuson, and John F. Kennedy.

Humphrey's bill, like the Emergency Detention Bill, was drafted and introduced as a substitute for Butler's bill, which liberals and organized labor strongly opposed. With this alternate proposal, liberal politicians also attempted to show a tough image of striking "a really effective blow against Communism."[128] Liberals at the same time intended to make communist registration a matter for the court to decide. By making party membership a criminal act, the bill would ensure that individuals suspected of being communists would be subject to the protections provided in the Bill of Rights, including the right to counsel, the right to face their accusers, and the right to be informed of the evidence against them.[129] Neither the federal loyalty program nor the congressional investigations provided the accused with such protections. Moreover, if membership in the Communist Party were made illegal, the registration provisions of the Internal Security Act would become unenforceable: the admission of party membership would constitute self-incrimination, which was forbidden by the Fifth Amendment.

As had happened in 1950, however, liberals were outmaneuvered by conservatives. The two bills were joined, and a severability clause was added so that if the Humphrey bill were struck down as unconstitutional, the Butler bill would remain intact. Furthermore, the penalty provisions of the bill were removed during the House-Senate conference, which was dominated by Patrick McCarran.[130] The Senate passed the amended bill unanimously (79–0), and the House approved it by an overwhelming majority with only two opposing votes (265–2).[131] When the Communist Control Act of 1954 became law, liberals had once again contributed to passing legislation that they were "not . . . proudest of."[132]

The Communist Control Act, however, had little effect as an anticommunist measure. Its applications were limited to some minor state cases. The law's constitutionality was never tried in court. Preceding legislation such as the Smith Act and Title I of the Internal Security Act proved sufficient to prosecute leaders of the CPUSA, whose membership had dwindled after World War II.

Nonetheless, one of the intentions of the liberal Democrats who sponsored the Communist Control Bill—to make the handling of subversive citizens a matter for the court—became actualized in a series of trials when Communist Party members were charged with violating the Smith Act. The court cases, which pitted the Communist Party against the Subversive Activities Control Board, questioned the constitutionality and enforceability of the Internal Security Act until the Supreme Court ultimately decided its fate. The Court also played a crucial role in shifting the balance between civil liberties and internal security in the 1950s and 1960s. The change, however, came slowly, requiring fifteen years of legal battles between the government's internal security agencies and the American citizens branded by the government as subversives.

Supreme Court Decisions on Internal Security in the 1950s and 1960s

On November 22, 1950, the attorney general filed with the Subversive Activities Control Board a petition under Title I, charging the CPUSA with being a communist-action organization. The SACB commenced hearings in April 1951; two years later, the SACB designated the CPUSA as a communist-action organization and ordered it to register as such. Instead of complying, the CPUSA filed a motion with the Court of Appeals for leave to introduce additional evidence before the board, alleging that certain witnesses on whose testimony the board had relied had perjured themselves in other cases of a similar nature. It was the start of a series of judicial battles between the party and the board.

Before the Supreme Court contemplated the constitutionality of Title I, anticommunist legislation had been tested in criminal trials. *Dennis v. United States* (1951) and *Yates v. United States* (1957) were two landmark cases that tested the constitutionality of the Smith Act as applied to Communist Party leaders. The *Dennis* decision marked, according to constitutional scholar Morton J. Horwitz, "the low ebb of Supreme Court protection of free speech," while the opposite ruling in the *Yates* case portended a shift in the Supreme Court's positions on internal security and civil liberties.[133]

Dennis v. United States (1951)

The *Dennis* case went to the Supreme Court after twelve officers of the CPUSA, including its general secretary, Eugene Dennis, were arrested and convicted for violating the provisions of the Smith Act directed at conspiracies to teach or advocate the overthrow of the government by force or violence. With one exception, the defendants had been sentenced to imprisonment for five years as well as fines of $10,000 each. On June 4, 1951, the Supreme Court upheld the convictions by a 6–2 vote. Chief Justice Fred Vinson read the majority opinion, while Justices Hugo Black and William O. Douglas dissented. Justice Thomas Clark did not participate in the case because he had been the attorney general at the time of the original indictments in 1948. Chief Justice Vinson stated that organizing the Communist Party, a political party that in his view was designed to overthrow the government by force or violence "as speedily as the circumstances would permit," constituted "a clear and present danger" that Congress had a right to prevent.[134]

Justice Black wrote that the convicted CPUSA leaders were charged neither with attempting to overthrow the government nor with overt acts designed to overthrow the government but merely with having "conspired to organize the Communist Party and to use speech or newspapers and other publications in the future to teach and advocate the forcible overthrow of the Government." He contended that indictment on such charges was "a virulent form of prior censorship of speech and press" and thus forbidden by the First Amendment. Black also argued that the petitioners had not been granted a fair trial because the record showed a discriminatory selection of the jury panel and one member of the trial jury had been violently hostile to the petitioners before and during the proceedings. Justice Douglas wrote that restrictions on freedom of speech should not be allowed "except in the extreme case of peril from the speech itself" and argued that the threat of the CPUSA did not even constitute an "imminent" danger, a looser standard than a "clear and present" danger. His dissent emphasized the necessity of preserving freedom—which, he contended, held the diverse nation together—and underlined the aversion to political censorship in the American constitutional tradition.[135]

In his concurring opinion, Justice Felix Frankfurter dismissed the application of the "clear and present danger" test to such charges of conspiracy, insisting that it did not matter whether the CPUSA had the power to *actually* overthrow the government by violence.[136] Frankfurter, a prominent Jewish justice, played an ironic role in determining American civil liberties during the Cold War. As politicians exploited anticommunist rhetoric to advocate conformity, McCarthyite attacks on dissenting groups and individuals, ranging from labor unionists to civil rights workers, as well as the persecution of Hollywood and the media disclosed not only white supremacy but also anti-Semitism. Justice Douglas's multiculturalist view of an American society where diverse religious, political, economic, and racial groups live together under the constitutional protection of their individual freedoms was still a minority opinion at this time.

On the other hand, Douglas's opinion was also a product of the early Cold War era. Referring to emergency detention, he pointed out that the followers of Soviet-style communism were known to the FBI so that in case of war they would be "picked up overnight as were all prospective saboteurs at the commencement of World War II."[137] His dissent thus echoed the liberal lawmakers' logic when they introduced the Emergency Detention Act—potential saboteurs should be left free in peacetime but blacklisted so that they could be locked up in wartime.

Yates v. United States (1957)

The conviction of Dennis and other top leaders of the Communist Party encouraged further arrests of CPUSA members.[138] In 1951, fourteen party members were arrested and convicted for violations of the Smith Act, and their case was reviewed by the Supreme Court in June 1957. Written by Justice John Marshall Harlan, the majority opinion overturned the ruling of the lower court, reversing the convictions of five of the petitioners and ordering new trials for the other nine. Chief Justice Earl Warren and Justices Frankfurter and Burton agreed with Harlan, while Justices Black and Douglas wrote opinions concurring in part and dissenting in part. Only Justice Tom Clark dissented, approving the trial court's rulings.

The *Yates* case reversed *Dennis v. United States*. Two main arguments provided the basis for overturning the lower court's decision. The second-string communist leaders had been convicted of conspiring to (1) advocate and teach the forcible overthrow of the government of the United States and (2) organize, as the CPUSA, a society of persons who so advocated and taught. On the second point, Justice Harlan contended that the term "organize," as used in the Smith Act, referred to the creation of a new organization; consequently, since the Communist Party was founded before 1945 and the indictment was not returned until 1951, prosecution on this charge was barred by the three-year statute of limitations.[139] On the first point, the Supreme Court adopted a narrower interpretation of "advocacy" than it did in ruling on *Dennis*, thus restricting the application of the Smith Act:

> The legislative history of the Smith Act and related bills shows beyond all question that Congress was aware of the distinction between the advocacy or teaching of abstract doctrine and the advocacy or teaching of action, and that it did not intend to disregard it. The statute was aimed at the advocacy and teaching of concrete action for the forcible overthrow of the Government, and not of principles divorced from action.[140]

The majority opinion ruled that for five of the petitioners, the evidence against the *Yates* defendants was insufficient to prove either that they had had specific intent to accomplish a forcible overthrow of the government or that they had advocated overtly illegal acts. The Court ruled that a retrial was necessary for the others.

Justices Black and Douglas opined that all the defendants should be acquitted on the basis that the First Amendment forbade Congress to punish people for "talking about public affairs, whether or not such discussion incites to action, legal or illegal."[141] Conversely, Justice Clark's dissent criticized the majority's interpretation of "organize" as used in the Smith Act, arguing that it might prevent the prosecution of Communist Party members with the "organizing" provision in the future. Clark also wrote that it was inappropriate for the Court to hand down the opposite conclusion from *Dennis*, which covered essentially the same charges.[142]

On the same day it ruled on *Yates*, the Supreme Court also reversed the contempt conviction of a witness who pleaded the Fifth Amendment and refused to answer questions in a HUAC investigation. Chief Justice Warren wrote the majority opinion in *Watkins v. United States*, ruling that congressional investigative power was not unlimited but should meet an equivalent standard of due process required in the criminal court.[143] Also on the same day, in *Sweezy v. New Hampshire*, the Supreme Court ruled that a state legislative investigation, in which a university lecturer refused to testify about the content of his lecture and his knowledge of Progressive Party members, had violated the plaintiff's First Amendment rights.[144] Conservatives denounced June 17, 1957, as "Red Monday," criticizing the Warren Court for being sympathetic to communists, subversive citizens, and convicts. The "Red Monday" decisions were a portent of the liberal Warren Court, which, starting with the famous civil rights case of *Brown v. Board of Education* in 1954, handed down many decisions that expanded civil rights and liberties in America. Because of its active interventions in contested political issues such as desegregation and law enforcement, the Warren Court is described as the most powerful embodiment of judicial activism.[145]

Nevertheless, any who rejoiced that convictions would no longer happen under the Smith Act were to be disappointed, since the Court retreated into the position of repeatedly rubber-stamping McCarthyite legislation for the next five years.[146] In 1959, in *Barenblatt v. United States*, the Supreme Court's 5–4 majority opinion reversed its decision in *Watkins* and upheld a contempt conviction against a university instructor who refused to answer HUAC questions about his past political beliefs.[147] In *Scales v. United States* (1961), the Court upheld the conviction of the chairman of the North and South Carolina Communist Party under the Smith Act.[148]

In 1962, Justice Felix Frankfurter retired. The resulting change in the liberal-conservative lineup of justices critically affected the Supreme Court's rulings on internal security legislation. A series of trials on the Internal Security Act clearly reflected this shift. Over time, clause by clause, the Supreme Court gradually made the Internal Security Act unenforceable.

Communist Party v. Subversive Activities Control Board (1961)

In 1953, when the Subversive Activities Control Board designated the CPUSA a "communist-action organization" and ordered it to register as such, the party argued to the federal Court of Appeals that three of the witnesses, professional informers hired by the Department of Justice, had made perjurious testimonies during the SACB review. The appeal was rejected. But in 1956, six members of the Supreme Court, in an opinion by Justice Frankfurter, held that the Court of Appeals had erred in denying the motion to introduce additional evidence; reversing the judgment of the appellate court, it remanded the case to the SACB.[149]

In 1961, however, the Supreme Court upheld the registration provision of the Internal Security Act in *Communist Party v. Subversive Activities Control Board*.[150] The CPUSA argued that compulsory registration restricted the freedom of speech and association guaranteed by the First Amendment and constituted self-incrimination banned by the Fifth Amendment. In a 5–4 decision, Justice Frankfurter opined that the freedom-of-speech protection was to be weighed against the public interest and that the Fifth Amendment right against self-incrimination should be applied only to individuals and not to a political party. Chief Justice Warren, along with Justices Douglas and Black, dissented, advocating the "clear and present danger" doctrine over the "balancing test," while Justice William J. Brennan Jr. wrote a partly concurring, partly dissenting opinion. However, the five-man conservative bloc led by Justice Frankfurter affirmed the Subversive Activities Control Act, Title I of the Internal Security Act.

Albertson v. Subversive Activities Control Board (1965)

Even after the Supreme Court's decision in *Communist Party v. Subversive Activities Control Board*, the CPUSA refused to comply with the board's order to register. The SACB, in turn, ordered individual party members to register on request from the attorney general. While the case had ended in the board's victory, the question of whether the compulsory registration of individuals constituted self-incrimination in violation of the Fifth Amendment remained unsolved. The question was answered finally in 1965, when William Albertson and other members of the Communist Party appealed to the Supreme Court after the Court of Appeals affirmed the SACB's order to register with the attorney general and submit the list of party members.

The Supreme Court reversed the Court of Appeals' ruling that the constitutional issues raised by the petitioners were "not ripe for adjudication and would be ripe only in a prosecution for failure to register if the petitioners did not register."[151] It ruled, as the petitioners had argued, that compulsory registration would force the claimants to choose between incriminating themselves and risking serious punishments for refusing to do so. This, Justice Brennan wrote, in effect denied to the petitioners the protection of the Fifth Amendment.[152]

The *Albertson* decision overruled Frankfurter's majority opinion in *Communist Party v. Subversive Activities Control Board*. Without striking down Title I's registration provisions as unconstitutional, *Albertson* made it virtually impossible to force members of any communist or subversive groups to register. Moreover, a year before the *Albertson* decision was handed down, the Supreme Court ruled that the provision in Title I that denied passports to

Communist Party members was a violation of the right to travel.[153] In 1967, the Supreme Court struck down the provision of Title I that barred members of communist-action organizations from employment in defense facilities.[154]

This series of decisions on the Internal Security Act reflected a shift in the political makeup of the Supreme Court. In 1962, the balance of justices tipped in favor of liberals with the replacement of Felix Frankfurter by Arthur J. Goldberg. After 1962, the "clear and present danger" doctrine regained its status as the constitutional standard for protecting freedom of speech. By the late 1960s, the Warren Court made Title I of the Internal Security Act impossible to enforce. And in 1968, three years after the *Albertson* decision, Congress finally repealed the sections of Title I requiring the registration of communist-action and communist-front organizations and their members.[155]

Conclusion

During the 1950s and 1960s, opposition to the Internal Security Act never ceased to exist. Yet despite the continuing demands for its repeal, the conservative bloc in Congress, particularly those in HUAC and the SISS, ensured that the law stayed intact and was used against those whom they branded disloyal. The Truman administration tried to regain control of the issue by reviewing legislation on internal security. Nevertheless, during the first half of the 1950s, the coalition among Republicans, Southern Democrats, and conservative Western Democrats, backed by strong anticommunist sentiment among the public, seemed invincible. HUAC and the SISS conducted investigations on subversive ideas and actions among people in defense facilities, government agencies, academia, public education, and even cultural production. McCarthyism severely hampered American civil liberties in the 1950s.

The ambivalent reactions from civil liberties organizations and liberal individuals to Title II indicate that even liberals at the time were complicit with the McCarthyite anticommunist fervor. While criticizing conservatives for defamation and thought-control tactics, liberal organizations such as the ACLU and ADA did not renounce Title II but instead approved emergency detention as a measure to deal with subversion. Liberals, including many who were directly involved in implementing the wartime incarceration of Japanese Americans, supported Title II because the law was designed to prevent the arbitrary detention of innocent citizens on the basis of race or nationality. Title II, they maintained, also provided human rights protection for the detainees. Liberals also believed that allowing the preventive detention of truly dangerous persons during an emergency situation would protect civil liberties for the rest of the society in peacetime.

These rationales imply that there was an element of scapegoating in the notion of preventive detention. Liberals upheld the preventive detention of a minority as a necessary means to protect security and civil liberties of the majority—exemplified in the statements by Edward Ennis and Justice Douglas. During World War II, government leaders mass-incarcerated Japanese Americans even though they knew that few, if any, Japanese Americans constituted threats to national security. The potential existence of an unknown number of people who might cause danger was enough to justify the detention of the entire group. Early in the Cold War, when people came to feel that singling out dissenters or disloyal persons was vital for the survival of the nation, liberals, morally disturbed by the ongoing persecution of individuals on the basis of their ideological or political inclinations, chose to advocate emergency detention (i.e., preventive detention in times of emergency). Liberals were conscious of the constitutional problems inherent in detaining a person who was yet to conduct any illegal actions, but they reasoned that it was an appropriate way to balance internal security and civil liberties. They used the precedent of Japanese American wartime incarceration to justify their compromise.

Liberals, however, failed to perceive that emergency detention necessitated the constant surveillance of citizens and aliens in peacetime so that once an emergency arose, persons listed as potentially disloyal could be arrested and detained immediately. As a result, the FBI gained great power and influence as a domestic internal security agency during the 1950s and 1960s. Even though Title II was never invoked, it provided a statutory justification for the FBI's surveillance power over citizens. The FBI's Internal Security Index was used for McCarthyite investigations, contributing to serious violations of individual freedoms for a great number of citizens and aliens.

It was the Supreme Court that reversed this tide. By adopting the "preferred freedoms" doctrine over the "balancing test" approach and assuming judicial activism as opposed to judicial restraint, the Warren Court strove to alleviate the political and legal harassment of individuals and groups who did not conform to the mainstream as well as activists who pursued social and civil rights reforms. However, except in a few occasions such as the "Red Monday" decisions in 1957, the Court went along with the executive and legislative branches in allowing the McCarthyite persecutions well into the 1960s.

The voting patterns in the Warren Court demonstrate an ironic switching between two politicians' positions vis-à-vis internal security issues. Earl Warren, as California's attorney general in 1942, vocally endorsed the mass removal of Japanese Americans from the West Coast. As chief justice of the Supreme Court in the 1950s and 1960s, Warren became its most prominent supporter of civil rights and liberties. Tom Clark, on the other hand, was sent to California by Attorney General Francis Biddle in 1942 to alleviate the anti-Japanese sentiment in California and announce the Justice Department's position that Japanese Americans on the West Coast should be treated fairly and legally. Clark, however, failed the mission as he demonstrated deference to the military. As the attorney general in the late 1940s, he granted wide discretion to the FBI when it compiled a list of potentially subversive citizens. Warren and Clark, on the Supreme Court bench in the 1950s and 1960s, almost always cast opposite votes when it came to internal security cases—Warren stood on the liberal side and Clark on the conservative. The fact that Warren had advocated the Japanese American removal, however, would haunt him in the late 1960s, as illustrated in the next chapter.

The Subversive Activities Control Act, Title I of the Internal Security Act, was used as a legal weapon—though with limited effectiveness—to prosecute communists and groups deemed sympathetic to communists. The direct victims of such prosecution, members of the Communist Party, appealed in court, and by the late 1960s the Supreme Court's decisions had made the act practically unenforceable. Title II, on the contrary, was never activated as a law. Even though the emergency detention measures had substantial effects on civil liberties, Title II was never officially invoked and therefore was never tested in court. The law remained in the statute books throughout the 1950s and 1960s, but its potential seemed to wane as Cold War anticommunism lost its fervor. Title II could have stayed on as a dead law, like other obsolete and ineffectual legislation, had it not attracted public attention again in the late 1960s.

4

Quiet Americans No More

*The Expansion of Political Dissent and the
Grassroots Campaign to Repeal Title II*

On January 20, 1961, when John F. Kennedy took the oath of office, America was filled with aspirations for a new decade of progress and hope. The conservative political atmosphere caused by widespread fear of domestic subversion was finally, and quickly, fading away. The new president was young and handsome, and he spoke with confidence about sharing America's prosperity with the rest of the world.

Kennedy's inauguration speech was a great departure from the conformist political culture of the 1950s. Instead of emphasizing the importance of fighting treacherous enemies within the country, he urged people to fight all forms of poverty and oppression in both domestic and international arenas. Furthermore, he claimed that new prosperity would be built through the communal efforts of the American people rather than individual aspirations for personal success. Kennedy reminded Americans that they were the heirs of the "revolution," a term associated in the previous decade with dangerous conspiracy and a threatening worldwide movement led by Moscow.

"Ask not what your country can do for you—ask what you can do for your country," Kennedy exhorted the people. Urging individual Americans to get involved in social changes, he shifted the discursive relationship between citizenship and loyalty. In the 1950s, expressing dissent to government policies made citizens vulnerable to criminalization for being "un-American." In the new era of social reforms, particularly through the televising of the Civil Rights Movement and the Vietnam War, many Americans, particularly of younger generations, started to think that citizens had the obligation to dissent when the government perpetuated injustice. Simultaneously, minorities demanded recognition of their contributions to building the nation. It became harder for conservatives to ostracize dissenters by placing them outside the discursive boundary of citizenship: simply branding them as disloyal and "un-American" would no longer have the same effect.

Swearing in the new president was Earl Warren, chief justice of the Supreme Court. Warren had repeatedly voted to support civil liberties and civil rights over internal security. *Yates* and the other "Red Monday" decisions prompted President Eisenhower to say that his appointment of Warren as chief justice was "the biggest damn fool thing" he ever did, even though in most cases during the 1950s Warren sided with the minority opinion.[1] The Warren Court profoundly changed the scope of police and government action in criminal and internal security investigations; Morton J. Horwitz argues that it redefined the concepts of democracy and freedom.[2] Democracy carries an inherent tension between majority rule and the protection of minority rights. Concepts such as the balancing test and judicial restraint underscore the former aspect, while preferred-freedoms libertarianism and judicial activism emphasize the Constitution's protective functions. The Warren Court embodied the latter ideology. Furthermore, the Court adopted the idea of positive liberty, which contended that the government was obligated to promote the conditions for maximum individual self-fulfillment. "Equal protection" and "due process" meant not only equal political access, such as through voting rights, and freedom from arbitrary governmental intervention but also relative social and economic equality. The Warren Court based its decisions on the notion that the protection of minority rights and substantive equality of treatment were necessary preconditions for democracy.

The war in Vietnam brought about a great shift in American notions of democracy and race relations. In a way, war integrated people of different races, because bullets and shells did not distinguish between whites and nonwhites on the battlefields. However, war also made clear the contradiction between the notion of democracy the government promoted in the international arena and the racial discrimination rampant in the domestic sphere. In 1967, when President Lyndon B. Johnson sent observers to Vietnam to ensure free and democratic elections, civil rights activists remarked scornfully that "it would mean much more to send observers to Mississippi" to make certain that African Americans were "assured justice and fair play in all elections."[3] Similar observations had been made during World War II, but in the 1960s, this kind of criticism received support from a wide segment of society, not just from a handful of social reformers predominantly from minority communities.

If World War II was a "Good War" and its veterans were heroes, veterans of the Vietnam War were called "baby-killers."[4] Although the government justified the war in Vietnam using anticommunist rhetoric, extreme anticommunism itself was a tainted cause after the McCarthy era. National leaders failed to provide a clear rationale for the conflict, which continued to escalate and took the lives of tens of thousands of young Americans.[5] The Vietnam War thus alienated people from the government. With the rising tide of civil disobedience and widespread social protest, and with the desperate backlash against radical social changes, Americans in the late 1960s saw increasing violence in the public arena. This was the time when public opposition to Title II reemerged.

The 1960s: Changing Race Relations and the Question of Internal Security

The Kennedy administration brought an important change to the Supreme Court as Arthur J. Goldberg was appointed to replace Felix Frankfurter in 1962. When Frankfurter, the champion of judicial restraint, left the bench, the tide of its decisions turned: the Warren Court launched into active judicial intervention and pushed freedom and equality forward in many key cases involving criminal, social, and civil rights issues.

The Warren Court played a crucial role in reforming criminal procedures at the state level. Traditionally, the provisions of the Bill of Rights dealing with these issues had restrained only the federal government but not the state governments. In *Betts v. Brady* (1942), the Supreme Court upheld the robbery conviction of a man who appealed the lower court ruling on the grounds that he had been denied a fair trial, being deprived of the right to the assistance of counsel.[6] In *Wolf v. Colorado* (1949), the Supreme Court's majority opinion, written by Justice Frankfurter, upheld the conviction affirmed by the state Supreme Court on the basis of evidence obtained by an unreasonable search and seizure, which was not allowed by the federal rule.[7]

In 1961 the Supreme Court reversed its position from the earlier *Wolf* decision and in *Mapp v. Ohio* overturned the conviction of a defendant indicted for the illegal possession of obscene materials.[8] The *Mapp* decision, written by Justice Tom Clark, ruled that the Fourth Amendment applied to the states; consequently, evidence obtained by searches and seizures in violation of the Constitution was inadmissible in a criminal trial in a state court.[9] In *Gideon v. Wainwright* (1963), the Supreme Court unanimously ruled that the Sixth Amendment right to counsel in criminal cases was applicable to state trials under the due process clause of the Fourteenth Amendment.[10] In *Escobedo v. Illinois* (1964), the accused had been denied a chance to consult his lawyer and had not been informed of his right to remain silent during the police investigation. The Court declared that the police violated the plaintiff's rights, on the basis of the Sixth Amendment, which prohibited self-incrimination.[11] In *Miranda v. Arizona* (1966), Warren established the standard procedures that should be followed prior to any police questioning: "The person must be warned that he has a right to remain silent, that any statement he does make may be used as evidence against him, and that he has a right to the presence of an attorney, either retained or appointed."[12]

Since its groundbreaking decision in *Brown v. Board of Education of Topeka* (1954), which renounced school segregation as "inherently unequal," the Warren Court had given great hope to those struggling to end institutionalized racial discrimination, and it had been severely criticized by conservatives for the same reason.[13] After the *Brown* decision, the Civil Rights Movement gained momentum. The battle to end racial segregation and oppression expanded well beyond the courts and legislative institutions. Starting with the 1955 Montgomery Bus Boycott led by Martin Luther King Jr., civil rights activists persistently fought segregation wherever it was found: on the street, on public transportation, and at schools, lunch counters, and voting stations.

Issues of criminal justice and internal security came to be associated with racial concerns as the Civil Rights Movement became widespread and gained attention from a large segment of American society. After Justice Goldberg replaced Frankfurter in September 1962, the Warren Court frustrated the opponents of desegregation in the southern states who continually used anti-communist rhetoric to legally harass civil rights organizations. Goldberg was directly responsible for overturning two cases that dealt with state harassment of the NAACP.[14] In *Gibson v. Florida Legislative Investigation Committee* (1963), the Florida Legislative Investigation Committee had ordered the Miami branch of the NAACP to submit its membership list on the grounds that the organization had been infiltrated by communists.[15] One month after Goldberg's appointment, the case was reargued, and in March 1963 the Supreme Court overturned in a 5–4 decision what had been a 5–4 affirmation when Frankfurter was on the bench. Similarly, in *NAACP v. Button* (1963), the Court protected the NAACP when the state of Virginia tried to ban the organization under a Virginia law that forbade the improper solicitation of legal business.[16] On the basis of the argument conducted on November 8, 1961, Frankfurter drafted a majority opinion upholding the constitutionality of the Virginia law. But after Frankfurter retired, the case was reargued on October 9, 1962, and the Court handed down a 5–4 decision, in January 1963, favoring the NAACP on First Amendment grounds.

As the Civil Rights Movement progressed, however, the problem of internal security intensified. While Kennedy was alive, there was a general sense that if some white men, like Birmingham Commissioner of Public Safety Bull Connor and Alabama governor George C. Wallace, stood for America's racial oppression, there were others fighting against them. After the passage of the Civil Rights Act and the Voting Rights Act, however, African Americans and other minorities faced a frustrating lack of improvement in their housing, employment, and economic opportunities. The desperation arising from deteriorating conditions in urban communities and the increasing violence inflicted on racial minorities radicalized the antiracist movement.

In 1966, Stokely Carmichael, a leader of the Student Non-violent Coordinating Committee (SNCC), proclaimed that what was needed for African Americans was not integration but "Black Power." Militant groups asserted that social justice for African Americans could be achieved only through a revolution and the decolonization of people of color.[17] In 1966 in Oakland, California, Huey P. Newton and Bobby Seale formed the Black Panther Party for Self Defense (BPP). The BPP influenced contemporary movements by many other minorities, such as Asian Americans and Latinos, and also had a long-lasting legacy through its theorization of the structure of both American and global racial oppression.[18]

The polarization of American society intensified with the escalation of the Vietnam War. New Left organizations vocally opposed the war. Students for a Democratic Society (SDS), the largest antiwar student organization, sponsored the first large-scale antiwar protest in Washington, D.C., in April 1965. Antiwar activism grew, and by 1968, almost every university campus across the nation witnessed protest activities such as sit-ins, teach-ins, rallies, marches, and picketing. Protests in front of the Pentagon against military escalation resulted in over six hundred arrests and fifty hospitalizations from teargassing and beating. Both antiwar and antiracist protests grew more militant as government authorities increasingly resorted to violence.

As President Kennedy had urged, Americans in the 1960s asked what they could do for their country. Countless organizations were built to make collective efforts to change the social structure and improve domestic race relations as well as to help the poor abroad. The people, however, also asked what their country could do for them. Civil rights activists demanded equal voting rights and employment opportunities, as well as the minimum standard of living to maintain human dignity. They also demanded the enforcement of the laws to stop hideous hate crimes against them and other minority citizens. Some protested against police brutality. Many demanded peace at home and abroad.

Furthermore, people started to assess what their country could *not* do for them. Thousands of students burned their draft cards to resist the government's claim to their lives, and students were also angered by the government's attempts to repress antiwar protests. After 1965, when protesters started to clash with police in inner cities and college campuses, the tension between social dissent and internal security resurfaced as an urgent political question, although in a context different from that of the 1950s. If the personified images of domestic threat during McCarthyism were insidious traitors and stealth ideological agents whose affiliations with the United States were suspect, internal security disturbances in the 1960s were direct and visible. They were clashes between the establishment and the minorities who demanded more expansive definitions of American citizenry in legal, social, and conceptual senses. Thus, Americans had to collectively tackle both new and old questions: Was it legitimate for the government to use violence against its own people to repress dissent if the protesters resorted to violence? What sort of repressive power could the government use to maintain law and order? Could the government conduct surveillance of the people by illegal means? To prevent civil disturbances, could the government detain people before they committed unlawful acts? These concerns resurrected the "concentration camp" law as a topic of public political debate.

Rising Public Awareness of "Concentration Camp" Issues

As America went through a social upheaval within, its people also became interested in "concentration camp" issues because of events occurring outside the country. As the trial of Adolf Eichmann, a former Nazi officer and the main facilitator of the Holocaust, was televised from Jerusalem to the whole world, and as the outbreak of the Six-Day War aroused keen interest in Zionist causes among the world's Jewish population, Jewish scholars and journalists started to widely publicize the Holocaust. Also, a diplomatic shift toward détente with the Soviet Union and the publication of Aleksandr Solzhenitsyn's novels in the Western world disclosed information about the camps used in Siberia for political repression during the Stalin regime.[19] The tumultuous social and political atmosphere and profound changes in international relations made the notion of concentration camps appear more relevant to people in the United States. Among those who became interested in the issue were a few Japanese Americans.

The Spread of the "Concentration Camp" Rumor

In July 1967, Raymond Okamura, a Nisei from Berkeley, California, sent a letter of inquiry concerning Title II to the headquarters of the Japanese American Citizens League (JACL). Okamura was disquieted by a rumor spreading in minority communities that the government was preparing concentration camps for those who resisted government policies. In his letter, Okamura called for action by the JACL to repeal Title II, arguing that "the American

Japanese, as the historic victims, have a public duty to prevent a revival of these camps."[20] This letter started a four-year political campaign that would lead to the repeal of the Emergency Detention Act.

The rumor Okamura referred to started around 1966 after a booklet titled *Concentration Camps, U.S.A.* came out. Its author, Charles R. Allen Jr., was a freelance journalist commissioned to do research on the emergency detention camps by the Citizens Committee for Civil Liberties (CCCL), a leftist organization founded in 1961. CCCL's primary goal was the nullification and repeal of the Internal Security Act, which it considered to be "the extension and legal arm of mccarthyism [sic]."[21] The booklet was the report of Allen's research.

Concentration Camps, U.S.A. contained accounts from Allen's trips to the detention camps in the 1950s and 1960s. In 1952, he visited Allenwood, Pennsylvania, and conversed with officers from the Bureau of Prisons who were renovating the prison buildings in preparation for detaining subversive citizens in case Title II was activated. In 1966, Allen toured five of the six camps. He reported that the Allenwood, El Reno, and Florence camps were in a state of "immediate stand-by." Allenwood had an estimated capacity of 3,000 to 8,000 inmates, and El Reno and Florence could detain 1,500 inmates and 3,500 inmates respectively. Wickenburg and Tule Lake, according to the booklet, had changed ownership but were maintained as detention campsites. Wickenburg had an estimated capacity of 3,500, and Tule Lake could hold 8,000 to 10,000. Allen recorded other locations in Mill Point, West Virginia; Greenville, South Carolina; Montgomery, Alabama; Tucson, Arizona; Safford, Arizona; McNeil Island, Washington; and Elmendorf, Alaska, as available detention sites. *Concentration Camps, U.S.A.* concluded that the total known estimated capacity of detention centers in the United States was 26,500.

Allen emphasized the imminence of the government's possible use of the detention camps. He insisted that there had been twenty-four separate occasions in which members of Congress had tried to force the White House to declare a state of internal security emergency, "which would put Title II of the McCarran Act into action as quickly as one could switch on a TV set."[22] He also quoted a radio interview with a former FBI agent, Jack Levine:

> Oh, yes, the FBI has got a very carefully laid out and detailed plan of action. . . . This plan has been set up under the authority of the Emergency Detention Act (Title II of the McCarran Act). . . . [T]he FBI has labeled it Operation Dragnet. . . . [T]he FBI estimates that within a matter of hours every potential saboteur in the United States will be safely interned.[23]

Allen also pointed out that Title II could be used to deal with inner-city uprisings and radical social protests. He asserted that African Americans organizing resistance and "those bearing arms in self-defense against the force and violence of the bigot mobs, the police and national guard" could provide "the pretext for the White House to declare that such resistance was in actuality an 'insurrection from within,'" an action with which Title II could be activated.[24]

The booklet generated genuine fear among African American communities and activists in radical organizations.[25] African American congressman Louis Stokes (D-Ohio) reported that one of his African American interns witnessed copies of Allen's report being sold within a black community for as much as $50 each.[26] Representative Abner J. Mikva (D-Illinois) also encountered students at a predominantly African American high school who had heard the concentration camp rumors. He recalled that his assertions "that the law was not intended for blacks and other minority groups were to no avail."[27]

Several members of Congress, along with some private citizens, made inquiries about the current status of the detention camps to the Department of Justice. Assistant Attorney General J. Walter Yeagley replied that the detention camp project had been discontinued and the camps abandoned. Yeagley also said that Allen's booklet was "replete with inaccuracies."[28] Nevertheless, the rumor survived, even after the Justice Department made a public announcement that there were no concentration camps in the United States.

The media both reflected and exacerbated public anxiety about concentration camps. As early as 1966 an article that made a mockery of the rumor appeared in *Saturday Review*:

> An unconfirmed rumor has come to my attention that our FBI is well prepared for a World War III in which our major enemy will be China. Detention camps have been secretly prepared in which will be "relocated" all the Chinese in the United States so that they may be screened, and prevented from sabotaging the war effort and from signaling Peking with short-wave radios.[29]

The article went on to advise people how to distinguish between the Japanese ("our friends") and the Chinese ("our enemies").

In March 1968, the *Washington Post* published an article much more serious in its tone. According to staff writer Paul W. Valentine, the *Post* had conducted a survey over several months and found that the fear of concentration camps among inner-city African American communities was deep and widespread. Valentine himself visited Allenwood and received confirmation from Superintendent P. A. Schuer that the Bureau of Prisons was not preparing to convert the prison into a detention camp. He also interviewed Yeagley, who assured him that there were no plans to reactivate any detention camps. He reported, however, that African American leaders such as Stokely Carmichael and H. Rap Brown made speeches about ten to twenty-four camps being under construction, and that Martin Luther King Jr. said publicly that he feared "some form of detention system" was being devised as a part of the white reaction to African Americans' demands for equality. The article also quoted a boxing promoter saying, "The kids I see coming in off the street have all heard there's going to be some kind of mass camps." Roy J. Jones, director of Howard University's Center for Community Studies, commented in the article that belief in the existence of the camps was so strong because of what African Americans felt was "an increasingly belligerent mood of the white establishment." The rumor also existed among some New Left whites who saw themselves as "potential tenants" of the camps.[30]

Immediately after the assassination of Martin Luther King Jr. in April 1968, Attorney General Ramsey Clark appeared on the TV program *Meet the Press*. He tried to calm public fears by saying emphatically, "There never had been concentration camps in the United States; [t]here are no concentration camps in the United States today; [a]nd there never will be concentration camps in the United States in the future."[31]

Nevertheless, a report by HUAC fanned the flames of public anxiety. Released on May 6, 1968, *Guerrilla Warfare Advocates in the United States* declared that there were "mixed Communist and black nationalist elements" that were "planning and organizing guerrilla-type operations against the United States."[32] It concluded:

> Acts of overt violence by the guerrillas would mean that they had declared a "state of war" within the country and, therefore, would forfeit their rights as in wartime. The McCarran Act provides for various detention centers to be operated throughout the country and these might well be utilized for the temporary imprisonment of warring guerrillas.[33]

The HUAC report, which patently recommended the detention of radical leftist students and African American activists, generated an immediate reaction from mainstream as well as ethnic media. The *Pittsburgh Post-Gazette*, *Evening Star* (Washington, D.C.), *Courier-Journal* (Louisville, Kentucky), *UCLA Daily Bruin*, *Los Angeles Times*, *Milwaukee Journal*, and *San Francisco Chronicle*, among other newspapers, criticized it for exacerbating the tension among racial minorities.[34]

The day after the report was released, *Washington Afro-American* featured an article titled "Concentration Camps for Ghetto? Is Rap Brown Right?" The article condemned the HUAC report for giving evidence for the concentration camp rumors, since "responsible colored leadership has been telling ghetto dwellers that such proposals were only rumors conjured up by political radicals like H. Rap Brown and Stokely Carmichael." It also asked why HUAC never thought of detaining the Ku Klux Klan and other vigilant groups, and "why in the case of poverty-stricken slum-dwellers in a land that preaches equality before the law the idea of individual guilt and punishment could be so quickly recommended into limbo and replaced by one of mass guilt and mass punishment." The article carried a cartoon titled "Most Never Thought It'd Happen," with a mass of African Americans herded into a space between walls as white soldiers aimed machine guns at them.[35]

In its May 28, 1968, issue, *Look* magazine carried a six-page article titled "America's Concentration Camps: The Rumor and the Realities."[36] Besides providing a detailed report on Title II, writer William Hedgepeth vividly portrayed the kind of agitation that was seen on the streets:

> "What do you mean, am I serious?" The Negro gave a querulous, squinting look. He cocked his head like a cross-examining attorney. "Only way this system know how to put people down is by hitting 'em with clubs, Mace, tear gas. And them twenty-four concentration camps ain't sitting out there for nothing. The blacks can't fill up twenty-four camps. It's me *an'* you, man, me *an'* you!" A small group of young men and women, five or six little boys, two dogs and a hen had gathered around us on the street. "A-men," one said. Others nodded.[37]

Hedgepeth reported that Martin Luther King Jr. had said to him six days before his death, "I see a ghetto perhaps cordoned off into a concentration camp."[38] King had been distressed by the collapse of the civil rights coalition between African Americans and liberal whites. In his book *Why We Can't Wait*, published in 1964, he criticized the white backlash as a cause of deteriorating race relations in the urban areas.[39] He might not have believed in the rumor himself but felt there was a possibility. He warned Hedgepeth, "The more there are riots, the more repression will take place, and the more we face the danger of a right-wing take-over, and eventually a Fascist society."[40] The article also mentioned the Internal Security Act of 1968, a bill sponsored by Senator James Eastland of Mississippi that attempted to apply the wartime definition of treasonable conduct to peacetime activities.[41] Although the bill never passed, it nevertheless showed that some politicians were pushing for stricter laws to deal with civil disturbances.

The fear of concentration camps spread across class lines. The *Chicago Daily News* carried an article titled "When Black Professional People Start Talking like Rap Brown (and They Are) . . . " Written by L. F. Palmer Jr., it reported that in the South Side of Chicago, middle-class professionals were talking about a rumor that a concentration camp was being built in Algonquin, Illinois, to incarcerate African Americans.[42]

On June 3, 1968, *The Nation* carried a column on the government's response to the concentration camp rumor. It reported an interview with Attorney General Clark in which he reassured Americans that the government had no plans to build concentration camps and that Title II did not pose a threat. The columnist, however, argued that Title II should be repealed, since as long as the law was on the statute books, "rumors of the kind now afloat [would] add to the current tension and uneasiness." He welcomed the ACLU's preparations to file an action that would seek an injunction against the enforcement of Title II on the grounds that it was unconstitutional.[43]

The *Hokubei Mainichi*, a Japanese American newspaper, reported that Stokely Carmichael had made a speech on concentration camps at a rally. According to the article, current interest in the subject of camps had led many popular radio talk shows to discuss "the Evacuation of Japanese Americans from the West Coast" during World War II. Japanese Americans, however, were disturbed by many "erroneous" statements being broadcast. The article gave as an example Ray Taliaferro's statement during a program on the station KNEW "that Chief Justice Earl Warren has publicly apologized many, many times for his role in the Evacuation."[44] In fact, although pressured by Japanese Americans such as activist Edison Uno, Warren had persistently refused to apologize for supporting the mass removal of Japanese Americans.[45]

Black Panther Party members were most interested in the concentration camp debate since they perceived themselves to be the major target of incarceration. They sponsored rallies with Japanese American students on the issue. Their newspaper *Black Panther* stated:

> On September 22, 18 years ago Congress, by a two-thirds vote, made an official public law 831. Now it is known as the Internal Security Act of 1950. . . . Thus giving the pigs the power to arrest and jail anyone they think will engage in or probably conspire against the government of the United States. You can be snatched off the streets or from your home and never be heard from again. . . . Anyone considered as a ghetto dweller can be a threat because the manner of life you are forced to live warrants change, not to mention, revenge.[46]

Thus the rumor about concentration camps attracted attention across multiple forms of news media, with diverse readerships.[47] Moreover, coverage was not limited to a particular region in the United States. Stories on concentration camps appeared in newspapers in not only Washington, D.C., and New York City but also Los Angeles, San Francisco, Chicago, St. Louis, and Honolulu, among other places.[48] The topic also appeared in various nationally circulated magazines such as *Newsweek*, *The Nation*, *Look*, *Time*, and *Atlantic Monthly*.[49]

Social Contexts for the Spread of the "Concentration Camp" Rumor

The fear of concentration camps that emerged in the late 1960s was widespread and increasingly gained credibility—particularly, though not exclusively, among African American communities and radical antiwar groups. It certainly reflected changes in the nature of social protest between the early and late 1960s. The Civil Rights Movement was based on a fundamental trust in the U.S. Constitution. Martin Luther King's "I have a dream" speech showed a vision of hope that could be shared by many Americans. Protests in the late 1960s, however, were narrated in more critical tones and by more disparate voices. The major antiwar group SDS, whose membership exceeded seventy thousand at its peak, believed that the Vietnam War indicated the American government's moral illegitimacy. SDS's ideology was part of a larger New Left body of criticism refuting the liberal theses offered by the "consensus historians" who had reigned over the American intellectual world in the previous decade.[50] While in the 1950s terms such as "imperialism" or "totalitarianism" had been used only to emphasize the difference between the free America and the Stalinist USSR or Nazi Germany, New Left writings often used them to refer to the U.S. regime.

For the radicals among racial minority groups, such as the Black Panther Party, the American government was nothing but racist and imperialist. The BPP platform showed no faith in liberal political institutions or American democratic ideals:

> We want an end to the robbery by the white man of our Black Community. We believe that this racist government has robbed us and now we are demanding the overdue debt of forty acres and two mules. . . . The Germans are now aiding Jews in Israel for the genocide of the Jewish people. The Germans murdered six million Jews. The American racist has taken part in the slaughter of over fifty million

black people; therefore, we feel that this is a modest demand that we make.[51]

Clearly revealing party members' mistrust of the government, the platform compared the history of African Americans to the history of Jewish people, and the American government to the Nazis. A bulletin from the BPP's Ministry of Information also referred to the Japanese American wartime experience:

> Japanese Americans were defined as a political threat after Pearl Harbor was bombed—but these very same Japanese who were taken to concentration camps owned lots of rice land and controlled the rice trade at that time. The white racist businessmen ordered them to sell their property to them for next to nothing before it was confiscated, and then took away all their capital while they were in the camps. . . . Now, Japan itself is virtually a colony of the U.S.; its government is controlled by U.S. businessmen, and its territory is still occupied by the U.S. Army today—23 years after these racist pigs dropped an atomic bomb on Hiroshima. . . . We can all see that black people are now, as we move to unite and organize our community, becoming a so-called "political threat" to major U.S. cities. We can take a lesson from the Japanese as to what Alioto has up his sleeve for black people, and check out how he is operating now.[52]

Even the general public was starting to lose trust in the government. This was largely because of its failure to solve the problem of poverty, which seemed to be creating "two societies, one black, one white—separate and unequal," and its inability to stop the deteriorating military operation in Vietnam or restore law and order within the United States.[53] In this political culture, the idea of American concentration camps did not sound so incredible.

Another factor that contributed to the spread of the concentration camp rumor was the close surveillance—and frequent violence—imposed on protest groups by government authorities. Civil rights activists became targets of widespread acts of terrorism from right-wing organizations, such as the Ku Klux Klan, that resisted desegregation.[54] Violence against activists and racial minorities was rarely punished or prevented, because the perpetrators of crimes were often closely related to, if not members of, law enforcement agencies, particularly in the southern states.[55] Initially, the FBI's intervention in the crimes against civil rights organizers remained minimal, which frustrated the activists and sometimes led to severe tension between them and the bureau.⁵⁶ However, the FBI was not in direct confrontation with the civil rights activists.

In the late 1960s, the FBI adopted complex and forceful methods to counter protesters and activists.⁵⁷ J. Edgar Hoover, director of the FBI, believed that social protesters were causing major civil disorder and therefore were a threat to internal security. Moreover, Black Nationalists and the New Left groups were dedicated to social revolution, which, in Hoover's mind, equaled communism. During the 1960s, the FBI developed massive counterintelligence programs to conduct surveillance on, disrupt, and sometimes destroy the organizational activities of the protesters. These counterintelligence programs, or COINTELPRO, were designed "to create an elite informant squad and send it around the country and the world in pursuit of 'domestic subversive, black militant, or New Left movements.'"⁵⁸ The informants not only gathered information about the protest groups but also directly disrupted their activities, conducted media campaigns against them, and arrested and convicted many of their leaders. In the case of COINTELPRO-BPP (the counterintelligence program against the Black Panther Party), the informants and police officers even participated in the assassination of group members.⁵⁹

Although the FBI had, to a large extent, autonomy over internal security matters, the Department of Justice also created new agencies for the surveillance of groups that might cause civil disturbances. In 1967, the attorney general established the Interdivision Information Unit to keep an eye on protest groups throughout the United States.⁶⁰ The unit collected information on campus and community protest activities from all over the country, including detailed weekly reports from the FBI. It lasted until 1976.

The tension between the public and the government escalated to the point of social crisis in 1968 and 1969. It was at this time that the concentration camp rumor had the greatest credibility among activists and minority communities. The surveillance, disruptions, and actual clashes between social protesters and law enforcement officers seemed to substantiate their fears. One logical explanation for the spread of this rumor is that anxiety fueled the belief in concentration camps, which in turn caused further emotional distress.

At the same time, however, evidence shows that knowledge of the Japanese American wartime incarceration started to circulate around this period, providing a historical precedent that added reality to the rumor. Newspapers reported that the concept of concentration camps for African Americans was "often compared with the Japanese [American] relocation program in World War II."⁶¹ The previously quoted *Look* magazine article referred to the Japanese American wartime experience as "a grisly precedent for this type of mass imprisonment."⁶² The publication that had the greatest impact on popularizing the memory of Japanese American mass incarceration was Allan Bosworth's *America's Concentration Camps*, published in 1967.[63] It was the first book that referred to the War Relocation Authority camps as "concentration camps" rather than "relocation centers" or "internment camps" in its title.[64]

Japanese American newspapers started to carry articles on the camps. For example, a December 1967 issue of *Pacific Citizen*, the JACL newspaper, devoted thirteen pages to the wartime incarceration of Japanese Americans.[65] Bill Hosokawa wrote a biography of Earl Warren, exploring the question, "Is Warren's legal philosophy of today a consequence of Evacuation?" The paper reprinted an article by Warren titled "The Bill of Rights and the Military," which was the first public comment he had made on the wartime treatment of Japanese Americans after being appointed to the U.S. Supreme Court.[66] A review of the three Supreme Court cases—*Hirabayashi*, *Yasui*, and *Korematsu*—also appeared in the issue. From this time on, Japanese Americans started to refute the official justification for their wartime removal and incarceration—military necessity—and began to openly argue that the policy was shaped more by racism than by military concerns.

Another notable shift in the cultural and political meaning of the term "concentration camps" occurred with Americans' increasing interest in the Holocaust. According to historian Peter Novick, the Holocaust did not become particularly important to American culture until the late 1960s. In the 1940s and 1950s, the mass murder of Jewish people in Europe was considered just one of many atrocities Nazis conducted during World War II. Americans were generally not interested in listening to the survivors' stories, particularly after West Germany became an important ally of the United States. The "DPs" (displaced persons) who immigrated to the United States were encouraged to forget about the past and assimilate into American culture.[67]

That situation changed in the 1960s. In April 1961, Adolf Eichmann's trial started in Jerusalem. The world was shocked to see a balding man sitting behind bulletproof glass who looked more "like a middle-aged accountant than a mass murderer."[68] The banality of the accused contrasted sharply with the gravity of the crime he committed. The trial, however, was not so much about the man who claimed he was "just following orders" as about the comprehensive history of the Holocaust and, moreover, the entire world history of anti-Semitism.[69] Witnesses testified to the brutality enacted by the perpetrators of the Nazi concentration camps and the acts of resistance performed by the victims, while the Israeli attorney general Gideon Hausner positioned the Holocaust as the "culmination of several thousand years of anti-Semitism."[70] The trial provided an opportunity for the world to learn about the Holocaust and remember it in a particular way—the Holocaust became an almost exclusively Jewish experience and also an experience shared by the entire Jewish population in the world, including American Jews who had no direct relationship to the event.

The publication of *Eichmann in Jerusalem* by Hannah Arendt in 1963 intensified the discussion.[71] Arendt's criticism of the explicit Zionist propaganda in the Eichmann trial, and her emphasis on the banality of the Nazi's crimes, infuriated some Jewish leaders in the United States. Questions about the meaning of the Holocaust, whether it was the culmination of anti-Semitism or the culmination of modernity, generated debates among Americans. Some Zionist spokespeople became very vocal about the Holocaust and started a campaign to claim its history as a uniquely Jewish possession.[72]

The outbreak of the Six-Day War in the Middle East in 1967 drove the American Jewish community to use the Holocaust as a cultural metaphor to win the U.S. government's support for Israel.[73] As Novick points out, ethnic relations in American society were changing from an "integrationist" to a "particularist" ethos.[74] Ethnic groups started to emphasize their differences from one another rather than their similarities. The political meanings of historical victimhood for an ethnic group also shifted. The voicing of pain and outrage started to be considered empowering as well as therapeutic. Against this background, Novick observes, the "market" for Holocaust memories grew in the late 1960s. There was more demand for survivors' stories, hence an increased supply.[75] The fact that "concentration camps" became a culturally loaded term to not just Holocaust survivors but American people in general made the allegation of American concentration camps a strong metaphor that pointed to the historical oppression and exclusion of minorities in the United States.

The Grassroots Campaign to Repeal Title II

Despite the keen attention to the concentration camp issue among some minority communities and radical leftist organizations, few civil liberties and civil rights organizations, including Jewish, African American, and labor groups, showed much interest in Title II.[76] The organized demand for repeal came from "an unexpected non-left source": the former residents of the "American concentration camps" and their descendants.[77]

The Rising Japanese American Interest in Title II

When Raymond Okamura wrote to the JACL on July 20, 1967, urging the organization to act on Title II repeal, its reaction was far from friendly. Mike Masaoka, a Washington representative of the JACL, sent a harsh reply condemning Okamura for confusing the Internal Security Act of 1950 and the

Walter-McCarran Immigration Act of 1952. Masaoka also urged him to become a JACL member before telling the organization what to do.[78] The JACL took the position that no action was necessary regarding Title II since government officials were denying both the existence of concentration camps and any possibility that they would use the law or the camps. The organization took no action on this issue for the following eight months.

In the meantime, the rumor of concentration camps lingered. Concerned by the worsening race relations after the assassination of Martin Luther King Jr. five days earlier, Isao Fujimoto, assistant professor at the University of California, Davis, sent a letter to Senator Thomas Kuchel (R-California) concerning the camps.[79] Fujimoto had spent four years in the Heart Mountain War Relocation Center as a child. He asked Senator Kuchel to what extent the provisions of the Internal Security Act had been implemented and which congressional committee was most directly concerned with the matter of civil liberties in times of crisis. He also asked if there had been a recent appropriation made for the maintenance or upkeep of the detention facilities or sites, having heard a rumor that $400,000 had been allocated for the purpose. Kuchel, a member of the Senate Committee on Appropriations, answered that extensive inquiry had failed to show "any expenditures or appropriations for any 'sites and/or facilities' relative to Administration of the McCarran Act" in the previous decade.[80] The senator had himself asked the Justice Department about the current status of detention camps a year earlier, so his statement is likely to have been sincere.[81]

A month later, on May 6, 1968, HUAC published *Guerrilla Warfare Advocates in the United States.* Authored by HUAC chairman Edwin E. Willis (D-Louisiana), the report recommended that African American militants should be placed in detention camps, and this fact was widely publicized. On May 10, Okamura sent a letter to Masaoka for the first time after their disputatious exchange the previous year. He repeated his conviction that the JACL and individual Americans of Japanese ancestry should do everything possible to prevent a recurrence of the incarceration of innocent citizens in the name of national security:

> We Americans of Asian ancestry are in a uniquely impartial position in America's racial conflict. I believe it is our obligation and duty to work for the liberation of black Americans, and at the same time, educate and console the white Americans. But I am saddened by the tendency of my ethnic colleagues to remain "neutral" and stay aloof from the conflict that may destroy us all. The future of America is at stake and we must do our part.[82]

Okamura also wrote to his representatives in the House and the Senate, Congressman Jeffery Cohelan (D-California) and Senator Kuchel.[83] In these letters, he disputed Attorney General Clark's statement that there had been no "concentration camps" in the United States.[84] He asked them to recall that Japanese Americans were "imprisoned in concentration camps without due-process-of-law." Okamura personally remembered "the armed guards, barbed wire and guard towers." In the letter to the senator, he also wrote, "When white Americans feel sufficiently threatened, Americans can and have resorted to concentration camps."[85] While admitting that "America did not go as far as Germany," he pointed out that the American public did not care any more than the Germans about "the rights of a helpless minority." He warned that "concentration camps" were a threat to each and every American, including African Americans, Chinese Americans, and young Americans who protested the Vietnam War and shared their fear about "American concentration camps." Okamura asked his congressional representatives to send him a copy of Title II.

As Okamura had lamented in his letter to Masaoka, few Nisei initially showed interest in the concentration camp issue. Perhaps for many of them the term resurrected a trauma so deep that they did not want to become publicly involved. However, younger Japanese Americans became vocally concerned. Coming of age during the Civil Rights Movement, young people of Asian descent, mainly third-generation Japanese Americans and Chinese Americans, had become politically mobilized. Their activities developed primarily, though not exclusively, in local ethnic communities and on college campuses on the West Coast. As college students started to engage with community services and ethnic cultural events, the movement generated a new pan-ethnic identity under the newly coined term "Asian Americans."[86]

The best-organized activities took place in the San Francisco area. Inspired by the militant Black Power movement, Asian American students started to associate American military aggression in Asia with the historical oppression of Asians and Asian Americans within the United States. Following the logic developed by both Black Power and the New Left student movement, radical Asian American students traced the atrocities inflicted by American soldiers on the people in Vietnam and the discrimination against Asian Americans at home to the same source: American imperialism and racism. They became part of the Third World Liberation Front, an interethnic/interracial coalition of student organizations on university and college campuses on the West Coast.[87]

Among the Asian American student organizations, the Asian American Political Alliance (AAPA) was the most radical and also advocated the most pan-ethnic perspective.[88] The first AAPA was founded at the University of California, Berkeley, in May 1968, after Yuji Ichioka called for an Asian Caucus among the Asian American members of the Peace and Freedom Party, a coalition of anti–Vietnam War activists and Black Panthers.[89] Although the main purpose of the AAPA was to address political issues concerning Asian Americans, its ultimate goal was "to bring about the kind of social and political change in America that would result in self-determination for people of color."[90] AAPA members participated in antiwar rallies and supported protests to free Huey P. Newton, cofounder of the Black Panther Party, who had been arrested for manslaughter.

It was at the second meeting of AAPA, according to a former member, that the issue of concentration camps came up.[91] A Chinese American member, Larry Jack Wong, asked the Japanese American members why they were not protesting about the camps. After a long discussion, another member, George Woo, said, "Hell, the way things are going now, they might do that to us. So you're not doing this just for the Japanese, but for all other people."[92] The wartime mass incarceration, a previously a "taboo" topic in the Japanese American community, became "*the* issue among Japanese American activists" after this.[93] From this moment, also, repealing Title II—the so-called "concentration camp law"—became one of the main items on the AAPA agenda.

Tension existed between the mainstream Nisei of the JACL and the younger Japanese American activists involved in the Asian American movement.[94] Since World War II, JACL leaders had maintained the position that Japanese Americans must prove their loyalty as Americans by integrating into the larger society. Moreover, this assimilationist stance had been praised by the mainstream white community. With the passage of the Hart-Celler Act of 1965, which removed the quota based on national origin that discriminated against non-European immigrants, Asian Americans were entitled to full citizenship. In 1966, the *New York Times Magazine* carried an article written by William Petersen called "Success Story: Japanese American Style."[95] It praised Japanese Americans because, it said, they did not depend on welfare, did not rebel or start riots, worked diligently, and achieved a respectable status economically and socially in postwar America as middle-class citizens. Japanese Americans had been accepted into the mainstream society as a "model minority"—as opposed to some other minorities that seemed to be less inclined to assimilate both culturally and socially, had a harder time lifting themselves out of poverty, and expressed stronger complaints about the status quo of American social and economic structures.

Ellen D. Wu describes how Asian American communities went through a self-screening process, in which conservative ethnic elites denounced any kind of actions that could be considered deviations from a middle-class American value system.⁹⁶ Targets of condemnation ranged from juvenile delinquency to involvement in the African American freedom movement. At the same time, Japanese Americans and Chinese Americans who got into politics worked actively to gain influence by utilizing the image of the model minority and distancing themselves from other racial minorities.⁹⁷ On the other hand, Robert G. Lee points out that the pressure for silence in immigrant communities came through the large-scale surveillance and infiltration into Chinese American communities conducted by the FBI and the Immigration and Naturalization Service (INS) after the establishment of the People's Republic of China (PRC).⁹⁸ Ethnic elites cooperated with the FBI and INS agents, giving out information about dissidents and left-leaning activists within the community. As a result, leftists were branded as subversive PRC sympathizers, and many faced deportation or other kinds of severe harassment from both within and outside the ethnic community.

Despite the lingering community pressure for silence, there were a few Nisei who supported the issues Sansei were addressing in the Asian American movement. Edison Uno, community activist and lecturer at San Francisco State College, was among them. Uno joined Raymond Okamura to criticize the Nisei conservatism and denounce the "model minority" image of Japanese Americans. Instead of seeking inclusion into the mainstream community, Sansei activists and their Nisei supporters identified with the oppressed minorities in the United States.

On June 2, 1968, Raymond Okamura, now a JACL member, and Mary Ann Takagi from Oakland formed a volunteer committee focused on Title II repeal. The first actions by the Ad Hoc Committee were to conduct research about the act and also to bring JACL's local chapters to pass resolutions to get involved in a campaign to repeal Title II. Upon the committee's request, the Berkeley, Oakland, Contra Costa County, and San Francisco chapters passed such a resolution.⁹⁹ The resolution was then presented to the Northern California–Western Nevada District Council of the JACL, which passed it unanimously.¹⁰⁰ The District Council delegates submitted the resolution to the national convention of the JACL.

Masaoka, a veteran JACL lobbyist in Washington, D.C., opposed the repeal campaign, expressing reservations about its practicality. He insisted that the climate in Congress was not favorable for repealing Title II and thus the effort would be costly and futile. He also feared that such a campaign would encourage "extremists and the arch-conservatives" to update Title II and use it to "really take care" of the dissenters.¹⁰¹ Masaoka's opinion represented the conservative mainstream of the JACL Nisei. Events in the summer of 1968, however, proved that this perspective could not monopolize the representation of Japanese American ethnic organizations any longer.¹⁰²

The Twentieth JACL National Convention in San Jose, California, held August 21–24, 1968, provided an opportunity to bring together the separate efforts to repeal Title II by different groups of Japanese Americans, as well as to move the national headquarters. While the JACL leaders showed reluctance to become involved in the repeal campaign, AAPA members and other Japanese American civil rights activists took drastic measures that shocked the moderate participants. The supporters of the repeal campaign posted replicas of the 1942 Evacuation Order at the conference site.[103] The posters were titled "Instruction to All Persons of Japanese Ancestry" and signed by Lieutenant General J. L. DeWitt of the Western Defense Command. For a community that had kept silence about their wartime experiences for the past two decades, it was an astounding but awakening sight.

The young activists' political stance was a total departure from the model-minority paradigm that the JACL had adhered to from the time of what conservatives called "the Evacuation."[104] A pamphlet titled "Are You Going to Be a Typical YELLOW-WHITE AMERICAN?" demonstrated the position of these radical Sansei:

> The McCarran act is only one step in the pattern followed by the Establishment to make dissent equal to treason . . . to snuff out individual self-respect, self-determination, and free choice. The Black Liberation movement is a direct outgrowth of what the government has done to suppress, abuse, exploit, people to make them ashamed of what they are and where they came from. The Chicano and American Indian Liberation movements are also examples of the people finally re-awakening . . . becoming proud of themselves. . . . We as yellow people have also been made to feel ashamed of our color. . . . [W]e don't have to become white. We have so much to be proud of . . . a culture, a heritage, a way of life. . . . Time to stop shuffling and bowing till our heads are scraping the pavement! YELLOW IS BEAUTIFUL!ced[105]

As this pamphlet shows, grassroots activists of what became known as the Yellow Power movement perceived Title II as a government apparatus to repress dissent and deprive ethnic minorities of their rights to self-respect and self-determination. The Title II repeal campaign was for them part of a larger endeavor to reawaken their ethnic pride, dignity, and heritage. It was a way of resisting the assimilation into mainstream society that had been advocated by JACL leaders for a quarter of a century.

The pamphlet also demonstrated that the activists in the Title II repeal movement took an interracial and/or pan-ethnic position. At the JACL convention in San Jose, delegates from other racial and ethnic groups presented on the concentration camp issue. In the discussion of Title II and political dissent, psychiatrist Price M. Cobbs spoke for African Americans, and Joe P. Maldonado, coordinator of the Economics and Youth Opportunities programs for the western states, represented Mexican Americans.[106] Caucasian youth also participated in the five-hour discussion, which was moderated by national chairperson K. Patrick Okura of the JACL. From the Japanese American community, leaders from Seattle, Cleveland, Los Angeles, Philadelphia, and Washington, D.C., exchanged ideas with local representatives from Santa Clara County. At the recommendation of the delegates, the JACL adopted a resolution to work toward the repeal or amendment of Title II.[107] Not only did the JACL resolve to oppose Title II; it also decided that its National Board would establish an ad hoc committee to develop and coordinate an active program to repeal or amend Title II.

National Ad Hoc Committee for the Repeal of the Emergency Detention Act

After the National Convention, Jerry Enomoto, national president of the JACL, appointed Raymond Okamura and Paul Yamamoto as co-chairs to launch the JACL campaign to repeal Title II.[108] Based in the San Francisco Bay area, the steering committee contacted all chapters of the JACL across the country and instructed them to choose district representatives, who would be in charge of organizing local operation units to work on the repeal campaign at the local level. Taking advantage of the well-organized national structure and highly motivated members, the National Ad Hoc Committee launched the first political campaign since the end of World War II that involved a large segment of the Japanese American community.

Its primary purpose was to inform people both inside and outside the Japanese American community about Title II and what it meant.[109] Local chapters were instructed to implement a five-part campaign strategy:

> 1) a drive to seek support of other civil rights, minority, and civic organizations for repeal, 2) campaign to educate the general public about the dangers of the Detention Act through local general newspapers and other media, 3) petition campaign, 4) letter campaign to elected representatives of all levels, and 5) leaflet and book campaign (perhaps Allan Bosworth's paperback edition) to educate the public and at the same time raise funds.[110]

As Title II repeal became a JACL goal, Masaoka agreed to take part in the repeal campaign. As part of the activities of the Washington office, he proposed to make a presentation on Title II at the National Leadership Conference on Civil Rights, a coalition of 160 civil rights organizations, and persuade its member groups to support the campaign.¹¹¹

Masaoka's relationship with the National Ad Hoc Committee, however, was tense, at best, from the start. He sought to control the campaign by demanding that the committee submit all the campaign plans to him in advance for his comment, particularly plans concerning efforts to secure the cooperation of local chapters of the various national civil rights organizations.¹¹² The committee rejected this demand, contending that Masaoka should be under its command, not the other way around, since it was the official JACL representative in the repeal campaign.¹¹³

Furthermore, Masaoka did not agree with the committee's suggested publicity campaign. As a Washington lobbyist, he had over the past two decades built close ties with prominent politicians on Capitol Hill, preferring to negotiate privately with influential members of Congress or other figures. Since early in 1942, Masaoka had acted as the sole spokesperson for the entire Japanese American community, at least in the perception of mainstream policymakers.¹¹⁴ His assimilationist stance, however, by no means received support from the whole community during or after the war. The fact that the JACL passed the repeal resolution in 1968 was an indication that the period when Masaoka's was *the voice* of the Japanese American community was quickly drawing to a close. Contrary to Masaoka's intention, the JACL repeal campaign retained its character as a grassroots movement.

Notwithstanding Masaoka's advice, the National Ad Hoc Committee went ahead with its education and publicity campaigns. Japanese American activists realized that the existing anxiety about concentration camps would help the public become aware of the issues surrounding the government's power to remove undesirable citizens from the society. Even before the campaign officially started, San Francisco–based civil rights leader Ron Nakayama stated at the JACL National Convention that "the fact that there is a public controversy gives a lot of free publicity to the issue, which will otherwise be very difficult to get the American public interested [in]."¹¹⁵ The Title II repeal movement provided a golden opportunity for Japanese American activists to educate the general public about their wartime experiences.

The National Ad Hoc Committee made its first public appearance on November 20, 1968, at the First Unitarian Church in San Francisco.¹¹⁶ An all-Nisei panel, composed of Raymond Okamura, Mary Ann Takagi, JACL national director Mas Satow, and Edison Uno, discussed Japanese American wartime incarceration and Title II. Eighty-five people attended, mostly Nisei along with fifteen to twenty Caucasian church members.¹¹⁷ To Uno's disappointment, no African Americans were in the audience. The panelists distributed copies of the 1942 Evacuation Order to the audience and spoke of their own experiences in the camps.[118] In addition to the panelists' personal accounts of wartime incarceration, Satow explained the history of the JACL and Edison Uno traced the anti-Asian movements and policies in the United States. He compared the social and political situation in early 1942 to that of 1968, focusing on racial tensions, fears and rumors of concentration camps, and the government's denial of such rumors. After that, Okamura explained Title II to the audience. The Japanese American wartime experiences provided historical evidence that detention of innocent citizens could happen again, since "it did happen once before."[119] Action-oriented leaflets on Title II repeal were distributed, and copies of Bosworth's *America's Concentration Camps* were sold. As an answer to the question "What can we do?" the audience was told to spread the word about Title II. From then on, hundreds of such rallies were held across the country to raise awareness and support for Title II's repeal.[120]

Japanese Americans evoked memories of historical injustice beyond their own experiences. At Glide Methodist Church in San Francisco, Paul Yamamoto spoke to the racially diverse audience on the implications of Title II. Besides explaining Japanese American incarceration, he quoted from the section of Bosworth's book on the removal of Native Americans. Yamamoto said to the audience, "In the 111 years since 1831 (when the Government moved the American Indians out of their homes for the purpose of benefiting a few profiteers and land-hungry entrepreneurs), the Government acquired a little more sophistry and employed a little more finess[e]. We were neither handcuffed nor chained (like the Indians)."[121] The comparison between Japanese American and Native American experiences was repeated many times during the campaign.

There were attempts to associate the mass incarceration of Japanese Americans with the Jewish experience in World War II as well. In the article "The Failure of Democracy in a Time of Crisis: The War-Time Internment of the Japanese Americans and Its Relevance Today," Isao Fujimoto quoted the famous words of German pastor Martin Niemöller, "First they came for the Socialists," to warn against silence and inaction in the face of injustice.[122] The article also referred to contemporary social problems:

> Every generation is held accountable for its abstentions or stand on moral issues. The spectre of Eichmann prompts Germans to be asked, "You were alive and free when Hitler began his genocide campaigns, so what did you do?" Subsequent generations can ask of this group, "What were you doing when the police dogs lunged at Negro school children at Birmingham?; What were you doing when people were

napalmed in Vietnam?" . . . Those of us here were alive and aware at a time in American history when democracy faced another crucial moral test. I refer to the war-time concentration of Americans summoned by orders such as the one shown on the next page [1942 Evacuation Order]. Such discriminatory selection was a very real experience to more than 110,000 American residents whose sole crime was their Japanese parentage.[123]

Japanese Americans at the grassroots level shaped the repeal effort into a moral campaign that could be shared by many people regardless of their race, ethnicity, class, and political affiliations. Instead of claiming wartime incarceration as an exclusively Japanese American experience, campaign activists tried to persuade people of the importance of personal involvement in political causes to stop social injustices affecting many different peoples in the world. They specifically called for individual actions to repeal the law the government might use to repress dissenting opinions.

On July 13, 1969, the *San Francisco Chronicle* reported that J. Edgar Hoover testified before the House Appropriations Subcommittee on April 17, 1969, about the threat of "Red Chinese infiltration" into the United States and the "300,000 Chinese in the United States, some of whom could be susceptible to recruitment through ethnic ties or hostage situations because of relatives in Communist China."[124] Jerry Enomoto, JACL national president, wrote an open letter to Hoover: "The spectre of detention of American citizens again, this time the Chinese Americans, cannot be easily ignored when respected public officials make such statements."[125] In the same letter he mentioned the Title II repeal campaign. This shows that the repeal campaign gave an opportunity for Japanese Americans to publicly express their opinions concerning the possibility of other ethnic minorities becoming subject to similar governmental persecution in the name of national or internal security. The Title II repeal campaign was an important historical turning point for Japanese Americans because it politically empowered them as publicly acknowledged former wartime incarcerees and their descendants.

The National Ad Hoc Committee promoted media coverage of Title II. The earliest action toward this end took place on November 24, 1968, when Frank Chuman, a lawyer and former national president of the JACL, discussed Title II as a guest on a KLAC radio talk show.[126] Audience members called in to the program to ask questions and make comments. Fujimoto also presented his aforementioned article on the radio.[127]

On January 8, 1969, Phil Nakamura, chairman of the Civil Rights Committee of the San Francisco JACL, and Chiz Iiyama, a member of the Civil Rights Committee of the Contra Costa JACL, appeared on a one-hour "calling-in" TV show hosted by Jim Dunbar. The station, according to *Pacific Citizen*, was "flooded with calls." Nearly all the callers expressed their beliefs that the wartime incarceration of Japanese Americans had been "a mistake." Most expressed their objection to Title II, but some were concerned about militant African Americans and felt there should be "some means to control them." To this, Iiyama responded by pointing out that the general public was "equally, if not more, suspicious of the Japanese Americans in 1941." The article reports that one Black Panther Party member stated that if anyone tried to put him in a concentration camp, it would have to be done forcibly. A representative of the National Committee to Abolish HUAC (NCAHUAC) also called in to say that they too had been campaigning for Title II's repeal. Some callers suggested that members of Congress should be contacted on the issue.[128] By March 13, 1969, two public forums, one television appearance, and one radio broadcast sponsored by the National Ad Hoc Committee had been made in the San Francisco area, and two public forums and one radio broadcast had been made in the Los Angeles area.[129]

In the meantime, the campaign to obtain support from various civil rights and other civic organizations proceeded. The Palo Alto and San Jose chapters of the ACLU had passed resolutions to support the JACL's repeal campaign. The Los Angeles County Commission on Human Relations (LACCHR) also passed a resolution supporting Title II's repeal, and the Community Relations Conference of Southern California concurred in the LACCHR's resolution and called for support and action toward this end from its member organizations. The LACCHR resolution stated that American citizens of all nationalities "regret" the incarceration of Japanese Americans.[130] Such statements were repeated in numerous resolutions adopted by organizations participating in the repeal movement. This indicates that the Title II repeal movement was providing opportunities for civic organizations on the West Coast to publicly express remorse for the harsh wartime treatment of their Japanese American neighbors.

In addition to assisting with the JACL repeal campaign, the Sansei activists continued their own grassroots campaign to repeal Title II. In an AAPA meeting at the University of Southern California, militant members of African American and Asian American student organizations participated in a "heated emotional exchange."[131] An African American representative expressed "his disgust with talking, meeting, and electing," and insisted that the money raised to send delegates to Washington should be used to buy guns. Some Yellow Power group members echoed this and insisted on "action." The meeting, however, was not attended by only militants. The AAPA had invited David Miura, chairman of the JACL's Ad Hoc Committee on Ethnic Concern; Frank Wilkinson, director of the NCAHUAC; and Mary

Schacter, legislative director of the local chapter of the ACLU. This indicates that the Title II repeal campaign provided sites where liberal civil rights activists gathered with radicals and the Old Left met with the New Left.

During the campus strikes at San Francisco State University and the University of California, Berkeley, the AAPA adapted the 1942 Evacuation Order into a campaign document. Instead of 1942, the date was shown as 1969, and "Instructions to all persons of Japanese Ancestry" was changed to "Instructions to all persons of Asian Ancestry."[132] The leaflet urged Asian American students to participate in the strike because, regardless of their social or economic positions, their future could not be "separated from the struggle of all COLORFUL people."[133] The AAPA's poster created from the 1942 Evacuation Order carried the headline "*YOU* have a vested interest in SELF-DETERMINATION for *ALL!*"[134] This poster was a chilling reminder that all persons of Asian ancestry could be the target of removal, just as all persons of Japanese ancestry had been in 1942. By using this historical document, the AAPA tried to remind or inform Asian American students of the United States' past racism and the necessity of getting involved in the movement to fight racism in the present. This focus on the mass incarceration of Japanese Americans attracted people's attention to the issue of race relations on college campuses.

In its May 15, 1969, issue, the *California Aggie*, a student newspaper at the University of California, Davis (UCD), devoted two full pages to the concentration camp issue, with seven pictures of the former War Relocation Centers. One of the photos was of two Sansei at Tule Lake, where their parents had once been detained. The newspaper also reported that the Asian American history class at UCD sponsored a panel discussion on the wartime experiences of Japanese Americans. Speakers included JACL president Jerry Enomoto, Japanese American faculty members at UCD including Isao Fujimoto, and Japanese American students who edited the newspaper's coverage of the concentration camp debate.

As evidenced by the participants of these grassroots meetings, the repeal campaign involved liberal organizations as well as radical leftist groups. Incidentally, the Citizens Committee for Constitutional Liberties (CCCL), a New York organization that published the booklet *Concentration Camps U.S.A.*, and the Law Center for Constitutional Rights, based in Newark, New Jersey, filed a suit to prevent the attorney general from enforcing Title II.[135] Most of the sixteen plaintiffs were leaders of leftist groups who had been persecuted through the HUAC investigations or prosecuted with punitive jail sentences or court charges.[136] The only nonpolitical plaintiff was a Japanese American woman, Gail Unno, who entered the case as a person "who was raised in a U.S. concentration camp." The JACL decided against entering the case, both because of the political stance of the CCCL and because of the possibility that the case would be dismissed for lack of "justifiable controversy," since none of the plaintiffs were actually being detained.¹³⁷ The JACL, however, offered moral support to Unno, who was no political activist but joined the case from her deep personal conviction that Title II should be repealed.¹³⁸

While mainstream JACL leaders were cautious about cooperating with left-wing organizations, activists in the National Ad Hoc Committee did not hesitate to work with them. Despite Masaoka's recommendation against associating with organizations he thought were too far left, the committee worked in coalition with the NCAHUAC and the CCCL, exchanging information and campaign literature.¹³⁹ The coalition helped the National Ad Hoc Committee members, generally inexperienced in politics, to learn how to make impressive campaign literature and conduct an effective political movement.¹⁴⁰ On the other hand, the Japanese American campaign activists provided information on Japanese American wartime experiences for organizations opposing Title II. For example, Edison Uno sent a letter to Robert S. Morris, treasurer of the NCAHUAC, to express his concern that the group's brochure failed to mention "the historic evacuation of all persons of Japanese ancestry during World War II in American-style concentration camps."¹⁴¹ This letter sparked further correspondence between the two organizations. By invoking the historical precedent of Japanese American incarceration in their campaign literature, leftist organizations strengthened their demands for the repeal of Title II.

Uno emphasized the importance of building coalitions with numerous ethnic, political, and civil rights organizations.¹⁴² Okamura appeared on television in the Joe Dolan Show on KBHK in San Francisco with William Kunster of the Law Center for Constitutional Liberties in April 1969. Kunster was one of the attorneys representing the sixteen plaintiffs challenging the constitutionality of Title II in the District Court of Washington, D.C.¹⁴³

The National Ad Hoc Committee also formed an alliance with the California Farmer-Consumer Information Committee, which suggested that the JACL committee should contact Earl Warren Jr., a Sacramento municipal court judge and the son of Chief Justice Earl Warren. The reason for this suggestion was that Uno, one of the main activists in the National Ad Hoc Committee, had also been involved in a campaign to demand an apology from Earl Warren Sr. for his role in the mass removal of Japanese Americans. Grace McDonald, executive secretary of the Farmer-Consumer Information Committee, wrote to Okamura that criticism of the liberal chief justice should be conducted with caution given the current national attack on civil liberties. Since Judge Warren Jr. had indicated sympathy to liberal causes and was very close to his father, McDonald thought it would be a good idea for the committee to "talk tactic[s]" with the judge.[144]

The relationship between Chief Justice Warren and the Japanese American activists had not been amicable. Japanese Americans never forgot his words to the Tolan Committee, one of the crucial statements in the decision-making process leading to mass exclusion. Victims of the policy, however, were not the only people who remembered Warren's role. Constitutional scholar Bernard Schwartz recounts an episode revealing the wider American historical memory of Warren's involvement in the forced removal:

> Years later, when he was chief justice, Warren was having lunch with his law clerks. He began teasing one of them about the way voting rights were being violated in his southern state. The clerk, not feeling at all responsible for the violations, thought the Chief was riding him too hard. "Wait a minute," he retorted. "What was the name of the guy in California who put all the Japanese in concentration camps during World War II?"
>
> At this there was a dead silence at the table. The other two clerks looked on in horror, as though they expected the offending clerk to be fired on the spot. Instead, Warren soon began to laugh and said, "Well, I get your point. But that was a clear and present danger. We really thought their fleets were going to land in California and I didn't think I had any choice."[145]

For Japanese Americans in the late 1960s, the question was not whether the community should forget what Warren said but whether they should forgive him. In 1967, Bill Hosokawa wrote in *Pacific Citizen* an article titled "Is Warren's Legal Philosophy of Today a Consequence of Evacuation?" He concluded that it seemed "likely that the experience [during World War II] had a profound effect on [Warren's] thinking, his moral and legal philosophy, and certainly had an influence on his career as Chief Justice of the United States," even though he might never "bring himself to an open admission."[146]

Not all Japanese Americans shared the forgiving tones of mainstream JACL writers like Hosokawa. Uno had written to Earl Warren in the early 1968 to ask him to publicly acknowledge his role in the historic injustice. Warren did not answer, but his executive secretary wrote back saying that "it would serve no good purpose to dredge it up at this time."[147] Uno wrote another letter on April 9, 1969, that read, "I have the highest respect and admiration for your contribution to the civil and human rights of all Americans; however I believe that your greatness and stature as a Statesman, Libertarian, and Humanitarian would be complete by one admission or apology that you can easily make before your retirement."[148] His plea went unanswered.

On April 11, 1969, Warren made a speech titled "Observations on Human Rights and Racial Discrimination" at the University of California, Berkeley, Boalt School of Law Conference on International Human Rights. A delegation of twenty-five Japanese American students, mostly AAPA members, sat in the front of the auditorium directly facing him. After his speech, the student spokesperson made a request to ask questions, which was refused. Outside, on the patio of the Earl Warren Legal Center, a number of Sansei and African American students stopped Warren to demand an explanation and apology for his role in incarcerating Japanese Americans. Warren refused and told the students to ask the federal government about it. He said to them, "I never apologize for a past act. Besides, that is just a matter of history now." Other Asian American, African American, and white students joined the heated discussion by asking Warren about Title II. Warren refused to comment, telling the students to ask members of Congress about it.[149] In total, Warren was stopped on three occasions by different clusters of angry Sansei students.

Mainstream JACL members were not pleased with the confrontational approach these radical Sansei students adopted. Mike Masaoka wrote to the JACL headquarters that such a public confrontation might harden the chief justice's attitude so that he would turn down any invitations to future meetings with the JACL involving Title II repeal.[150] He cautioned the National Ad Hoc Committee not to take another chance but rather to wait until he could secure the proper timing and connection. In *Pacific Citizen*, an editorial appeared saying, "Let's Forgive Earl Warren."[151] However, this hostility did not discourage Japanese Americans from approaching Warren to ask him to recognize his role in the wartime incarceration. Edison Uno, the sole activist to demand Warren's apology during the previous year, was joined by other JACL members in his effort to get Warren's support for repealing Title II.

Taking the advice from the California Farmer-Consumer Information Committee, the National Ad Hoc Committee approached Judge Earl Warren Jr. The JACL committee had obtained information that Warren Jr. would attend a dinner held in San Francisco featuring Senator Daniel Inouye on September 26, 1969.[152] Raymond Okamura, Edison Uno, and Mary Ann Takagi consulted Jerry Enomoto on the best approach for meeting with him. The plan was made among only these four participants in strict confidence, and Okamura specifically asked Enomoto not to consult with his "usual" JACL advisors, implying Mike Masaoka. At the dinner, Uno sat next to Warren Jr. and informed him of his father's role in the forced removal of Japanese Americans from the West Coast. The judge, not aware of his father's involvement, showed great interest in the subject. The discussion went very cordially, and at the end of the meeting, Warren Jr. offered to "help in any way he could."[153] He and his wife promised that they would speak to the retired chief justice and asked Uno to send copies of the materials on Japanese American wartime experiences Uno had compiled. The dinner meeting was a great success.

Earl Warren Jr. later informed the JACL that his father "might be willing to come out."[154] The former chief justice sent a letter to Enomoto on May 18, 1970, expressing support for repealing Title II. He wrote:

> Title II is not in the American tradition. It was passed in the most turbulent days of the Cold War. Although in all probability it would never be used except in times of public hysteria, still the danger of its use is always present. Only repeal of the act will remove that danger.

He concluded by saying, "I express these views as the experience of one who as a state officer became involved in the harsh removal of the Japanese from the Pacific Coast in World War II, almost 30 years ago."[155] The letter was reprinted in *Pacific Citizen* and was also publicized at the congressional hearing on Title II that later took place. Warren refers to this letter in his memoir, crediting himself with contributing to Title II's repeal by writing it.[156] Many Japanese Americans accepted Warren's letter as his apology to their community.[157]

Another important repeal campaign tactic was to gain support from the state legislative assemblies. Bob Suzuki, chairman of the Legislative Committee of the JACL Pacific Southwest District Council, contacted Charles Warren, member of the California State Assembly, with a request to pass a resolution through the California State Legislature to support Title II's repeal.[158] The Assembly passed a resolution to support the cause.

A JACL progress report dated June 15, 1969, recorded nine governmental bodies, eleven public media outlets, and twelve organizations that had passed resolutions or favorably commented on repealing Title II.[159] While the National Ad Hoc Committee geared up its successful publicity and educational campaign locally, activities were limited to the San Francisco area and Los Angeles at the initial stage. By mid-June, however, JACL's Chicago chapter was developing an effective activist committee. The National Ad Hoc Committee repeatedly emphasized that it was essential that JACL chapters across the nation become actively involved in the grassroots campaign.[160] It continued to instruct all chapters to (1) get resolutions supporting the repeal campaign passed by local civil groups, city councils, county boards of supervisors, human relations commissions, and state legislatures; (2) get their local members of Congress to read the resolutions into the *Congressional Record*; (3)

contact local newspapers and ask them to publicize the repeal campaign or write editorials supporting repeal; and (4) contact local chapters of national civil rights organizations such as the NAACP, ACLU, and Anti-Defamation League, as well as churches, labor unions, other ethnic organizations, and professional organizations.[161] The committee made the campaign literature, such as copies of the 1942 Exclusion Order and Evacuation Order as well as a JACL position paper titled "Arguments for the Repeal of Title II of the Internal Security Act of 1950" and reprints of relevant pages from the *Congressional Record*. These materials were made available to the JACL chapters so that they could be used for the local repeal campaigns.

In the latter half of 1969, the Title II repeal campaign brought together Asian American activists in various parts of the United States. Particularly important was the fact that, in July 1969, the National Ad Hoc Committee connected with Asian American activists in New York City. Mary (Yuri) Kochiyama, a Nisei activist, spoke before the American Committee for Protection of Foreign Born, which had been actively opposing the McCarran Act and the Walter-McCarran Immigration Law since the 1950s. The American Committee for Protection of Foreign Born published a booklet titled *Concentration Camps USA* featuring the life story of Kochiyama, who had spent the war years in the Jerome War Relocation Center in Arkansas.[162] Upon reading the booklet, Raymond Okamura sent Kochiyama some campaign literature and materials related to Title II repeal that the JACL committee had prepared. Kochiyama in return sent materials related to the newly formed Asian Americans for Action (AAA), a radical group of activists in New York. She noticed that Asian American political activism, which started on the West Coast, was inspiring people on the East Coast, and she encouraged Asian American students in New York to organize.

Kochiyama wrote to the National Ad Hoc Committee:

We feel that the days of the "quiet hyphenated-Americans" are over. The docile, cooperative acceptable Orientals—just for the sake of making the mainstream and becom[ing] assimilable—must be passé. We must stand up, question, disagree, and challenge when necessary; and further than that, extricate ourselves from 'things American' when they are detrimental to the welfare and freedom of humanity. Up until recently, we did not think that a group could be organized on the East Coast. . . . Now we are finding, here and there in some unexpected places, Asian-Americans who not only wish political participation in effecting changes for a better society, but [are] willing to do so through radical politics. It is all very exciting.[163]

Kochiyama's participation in the Title II repeal campaign brought in diverse community activists from African American and Asian American communities on the East Coast.

The committee's efforts to nationalize the repeal movement gradually bore fruit. By November, the JACL campaign had spread well beyond California and Chicago. JACL members in Seattle, Portland, Salt Lake City, Denver, Philadelphia, Omaha, Minneapolis, and Tiffin (Ohio) brought the Title II issue to their communities and succeeded in generating some interest and support. A few non-JACL groups outside California also worked actively on Title II repeal. Asian Coalition for Equality, based in Seattle, and AAA in New York City were among those groups.[164]

On November 9, 1969, some eighty Native Americans occupied Alcatraz Island in San Francisco Bay to call attention to the plight of the indigenous peoples in the United States. They were soon joined by several hundred indigenous activists, including members of the American Indian Movement (AIM). On December 14, the National Ad Hoc Committee decided to aid the occupation to show support for Native Americans as one of the "two racial groups who have a common bond of the experience of incarceration in American concentration camps and the U.S. government reservations."[165] Within one week, nearly three tons of supplies—"fresh meat, crates of produce, boxed of canned foods, sacks of rice and bundles of warm clothing"— and about $500 were donated.[166] The support event also served as a commemoration of the twenty-fifth anniversary of the *Korematsu* decision.[167] On December 21, the supplies were taken to the island by boats owned by some Nisei in San Francisco.

Different segments of the Japanese American community in San Francisco responded to the National Ad Hoc Committee's plea to support the Native Americans. Donations came from Japanese American produce wholesalers, importers, and business owners, as well as concerned individual citizens. Christ United Presbyterian Church in Nihonmachi (Japantown in San Francisco) opened its facilities to be used as sleeping quarters by the indigenous activists joining the occupation of Alcatraz.[168] Students, staff, and faculty of the Asian American Studies Department at San Francisco State College also expressed support, and fundraising received a boost when Watsonville Buddhist Church expressed support for the cause.[169] The aid from Japanese Americans was received with much gratitude from the Native Americans on the Rock.[170]

While interethnic and interorganizational cooperation developed at local levels, the JACL's efforts to solicit support from national civil rights and labor organizations by contacting their Washington representatives were unsuccessful until mid-1969.[171] While Okamura called for greater grassroots efforts to get the necessary backing from the local chapters and membership, which would eventually pressure the national organizations, Mike Masaoka and other JACL leaders pursued the other phase of the repeal campaign—to raise enough sympathy to obtain support in Congress. To actually have the law repealed, the National Ad Hoc Committee had to get involved in the congressional campaign to repeal Title II. To achieve this the clout of the conservative JACL cohort was essential, as they had the expertise maneuvering in politics on Capitol Hill.

Conclusion

When a handful of progressive Nisei started a campaign to repeal Title II, the mainstream Japanese American organizations did not approve of the cause. Most Japanese Americans had kept silent about their wartime experiences, striving for reintegration into mainstream society. They were not only busy rebuilding their disrupted lives; they were living with trauma. Nisei taught Sansei not to stand out as an ethnic group. Children were pressured to excel in school and grow up to be law-abiding citizens with stable white-collar jobs. Nisei emphasized the importance of education, and by the time Sansei came of age, a higher percentage of Japanese Americans had received post-secondary education than the white population. By the mid-1960s, Japanese Americans were praised by the mainstream media for "outwhiting the whites."[172]

After the ebb of McCarthyism, Cold War racial liberalism gained a greater hold in the mainstream racial consciousness. The advancement and success of Asian Americans, seemingly overcoming racial prejudice and exclusion, constituted a convenient piece of proof for the legitimacy of the American polity. Asian American ethnic elites had utilized their favorable image to gain political influence and differentiate themselves from further disadvantaged groups such as African Americans, Native Americans, and Latinos/as, and especially from those who sought more fundamental equality and civil rights by radical or militant means. Asian American elites maintained an accommodationist stance and often actively silenced dissent within their ethnic communities.

It was a remarkable change, then, when in the late 1960s Japanese Americans broke their silence and started talking about their own wartime incarceration in light of social and historical injustice. General interest in concentration camps provided Japanese Americans with an opportunity to publicly discuss their wartime experiences and thus helped their experience to become part of the shared American historical memory. An even greater part of the American public became aware of the term "concentration camps" around the same time because the rumor of new camps happened, coincidentally, just as the Jewish Holocaust became an important part of Americans' shared public knowledge.

The concerns regarding American concentration camps led social activists to form coalitions with each other. Those who felt threatened by the looming images of preventive detention and possible incarceration held rallies and shared the history of political and racial oppressions they had experienced in the past or were currently experiencing. The rumor brought people together to think about issues such as law and order, civil liberties, and the appropriate relationship between the government and its critics. Unsubstantiated as it was, the rumor provided a concrete image of concentration camps, a metaphor that could be shared by many people, minority and mainstream, who were concerned about political repression conducted against the people.

The wartime incarceration of Japanese Americans provided a concrete historical precedent of preventive detention in American public memory, and by doing so it gave people a sense that "it can happen in America." Furthermore, some Japanese Americans strongly believed in the necessity of making their wartime experiences known to the American public and taking action to prevent other Americans from suffering from similar kinds of injustice. Because the mass incarceration of innocent citizens on the basis of race seemed unjust and totalitarian, people generally came to support the repeal of Title II, even though those same people might have considered the preventive detention of militant activists justifiable. The very presence of Japanese Americans in the campaign to repeal Title II left Americans little choice but to take the fear of concentration camps seriously.

5

Recommitting to Civil Liberties

The Repeal of Title II and the Passage of the Non-Detention Act

The intensification of the Vietnam War and the escalation of domestic turmoil forced the U.S. government to make national and internal security the top priority in its policy making. American troops needed to find a way to get out of Vietnam without totally losing face. President Nixon admitted there was "no way to win the war," but instead he pledged to "win the peace."[1] In the international arena, Western Europe and Japan had largely recovered from the war; people there started to enjoy material prosperity and consumer culture, while divisions among communist nations were growing. America's competition with the Communist Bloc no longer had to depend on sheer military force. Without retreating from the arms race against the USSR, Nixon pursued further détente with Moscow and, at the same time, schemed to open a diplomatic relationship with the People's Republic of China.[2] His Cold War strategy shifted its emphasis from military competition toward ideological and moral competition. Between 1969 and 1973, America's defense budgets "declined sharply (about one-third) when adjusted for inflation and in terms of share of GNP."[3] At the same time, its military technology and power had become so highly developed that espionage and sabotage by ordinary civilians had long ceased to be of much importance.

To win the ideological war against communism, the rhetoric of American moral superiority over the communist regimes became even more important than in the 1950s. In the late 1960s, rather than defending national security from espionage and sabotage, the American government had a bigger stake in defending its own credibility and legitimacy, particularly in the midst of accusations from domestic dissidents that political systems in the United States were as imperialistic and totalitarian as in communist societies, if not more so. Against this background, concentration camps for the purpose of repressing domestic criticism became increasingly feared as one of the symbols of the American government's totalitarian nature. The symbol became a concrete target to fight against as the grassroots campaigners worked to repeal the "concentration camp law." The elites in the Japanese American community successfully brought the issue to Congress, and again it turned out that the presence of the former incarcerees of American concentration camps was essential for the law's repeal.

Introducing Bills to Repeal Title II

On April 6, 1969, the JACL's National Ad Hoc Committee sent a confidential memorandum to all the JACL chapters stating that Senator Daniel K. Inouye (D-Hawaii) was planning to introduce a bill to repeal Title II. Inouye, who had expressed his support for the JACL resolution on Title II repeal, was privately asking other senators to join him in cosponsoring the bill.[4] The committee instructed all JACL chapters to immediately send letters and telegrams to their senators urging them to join Senator Inouye. It also asked them to instruct individual members to write personal letters to their senators. The committee emphasized the urgency of the letter-writing campaign so that Senator Inouye and Mike Masaoka could effectively persuade as many senators as possible to cosponsor the bill.[5]

Inouye introduced S1872, a bill to repeal Title II, on April 18, 1969. Nineteen senators cosponsored the bill, which simply read, "Be it enacted by the Senate and the House of Representatives of the United States of America in Congress assembled, that the Emergency Detention Act of 1950 (50 U.S.C. 811–826) is repealed."

The National Ad Hoc Committee asked the JACL chapters to thank those senators who had become cosponsors and write to others asking for their support.[6] It also instructed the chapters to ask for several copies of S1872 when they wrote to their senators. Requests for reprints indicated the amount of interest and support a particular bill had. This kind of instruction shows that the committee was well informed in its tactics for acquiring congressional support. A JACL memorandum reported that the response to the letter-writing campaign was generally good.[7]

However, support for repealing Title II did not come only from the senators who were interested in protecting civil liberties. In fact, there was another bill in the Senate, S12, sponsored by James Eastland (D-Mississippi), chairman of both the Senate Internal Security Subcommittee and the Senate

Judiciary Committee.[8] Eastland was recommending the repeal of Title II through S12, also known as the Internal Security Act of 1969. S12, introduced on January 15, 1969, was an attempt to relegislate the Internal Security Act provisions that had been struck down by the Warren Court. It was a ninety-four-page bill that included clauses to control wartime sabotage, espionage, treason, sedition, and subversive activities. Sixteen senators cosponsored the bill. Three of them—George Murphy of California, Len Jordan from Nebraska, and Karl Mundt from South Dakota—were also cosponsors of S1872.

After the introduction of S1872, the National Ad Hoc Committee started to prepare a program to introduce repeal bills in the House of Representatives. The JACL-sponsored bill was not the first Title II repeal bill introduced in the House. On September 10, 1968, California congressman Charles G. Gubser had introduced HR19646 for that purpose. The same bill was reintroduced on January 3, 1969, as HR1157 and had been referred to HUAC.[9] The National Ad Hoc Committee was suspicious of Gubser's motives for supporting the repeal because he had not consulted the JACL before he introduced his bill.[10] Moreover, Gubser was running in the congressional election against Grayson S. Taketa, a young San Jose lawyer and a former Gila River camp detainee.[11] Taketa had made an issue out of Title II during his campaign.[12] In addition to Gubser, at least fourteen members of Congress had already introduced their own bills to repeal Title II. The National Ad Hoc Committee instructed the JACL chapters not to contact any members of Congress until it asked them to do so.

The committee selected Spark M. Matsunaga (D-Hawaii) and Chet Holifield (D-California) to be the principal authors of the JACL-sponsored repeal bill.[13] Matsunaga was not only the senior Japanese American politician in the House of Representatives but also a member of the House Rules Committee. He also had influence within the Democratic Party as the secretary of its steering committee. Congressman Holifield was a senior member of the California delegation and one of the most influential representatives from the West. More importantly, he was one of the few members of Congress who had been sympathetic to Japanese Americans since World War II, and he had voted against the Internal Security Act in 1950. The Matsunaga-Holifield bill, HR11825, was introduced in the House of Representatives on June 3, 1969.

Another letter-writing campaign started on June 1. The JACL chapters and concerned individuals sent letters and telegrams to members of Congress, urging them to join Matsunaga and Holifield in cosponsoring the repeal bill. Representatives who had introduced their own bills were encouraged to cooperate with Matsunaga and Holifield.

In mid-June, the National Ad Hoc Committee ratcheted up both the congressional and the grassroots campaigns. It urged not only the JACL chapters but also individual JACL members to write, wire, telephone, or personally visit members of Congress to seek their support for S1872 and HR11825. The National Ad Hoc Committee also geared up for their efforts to get resolutions passed at the local level of civic and human rights organizations and state, county, and municipal governments. When a resolution was passed, the committee asked supportive members of Congress to read it into the *Congressional Record*, since this indicated that the repeal movement had strong public support.

After the first round of letter writing, the JACL got twenty-six senators and thirty-nine representatives to cosponsor bills to repeal Title II.[14] In addition to this support for the cause, which resulted directly from the JACL campaign, some fifteen other members of Congress had introduced independent repeal bills due to the public interest. S1872, the Inouye bill, which now had twenty-six cosponsors, was referred to the Senate Judiciary Committee; HR11825, the Matsunaga-Holifield bill, was referred to the House Internal Security Committee (HISC) along with eight related bills (HR1157, HR10396, HR10727, HR11575, HR12220, HR12221, HR12282, and HR12609); and HR11373, introduced by Representative Abner Mikva (D-Illinois), was referred to the House Committee on the Judiciary along with five related bills. Three of the companion bills to the Matsunaga-Holifield bill were initiated by the JACL.

The Mikva bill provided for the repeal of Title II, but it also contained a clause "to prohibit the establishment of emergency detention camps and to provide that no citizen of the United States shall be committed for detention or imprisoned in any facility of the United States except in conformity with the provisions of Title 18."[15] This wording was added to HR11373 to make sure that the bill would be referred to the House Judiciary Committee in case the Matsunaga-Holifield bill got blocked in the HISC, a newly created committee whose predecessor was HUAC. A few members of the House had shown clear opposition to the repeal based on their concerns about internal security. The spearhead of the opposition was Representative Richard H. Ichord (D-Missouri), chairman of the HISC.[16] To prevent the HISC from killing all the repeal bills, the supporters of the repeal effort had decided to fight the issue on two fronts: the HISC and the House Judiciary Committee.

Some members of Congress overtly connected the Title II issue with historical events during World War II. For example, one of the cosponsors of S1872 was Alan Cranston (D-California), who had served in Germany as a reporter for the Internal News Service during the 1930s, when the Nazi party was gaining power. Cranston had published Hitler's *Mein Kampf*, with anti-Nazi explanatory notes, and sold them for ten cents until Hitler's literary agents filed suit in 1939. In supporting the repeal of Title II, Cranston said: "Most of us have the attitude that concentration camps would never be used in this country, but few realize that right now we have a law on the books that would allow the attorney general to round up and detain in a crisis those whose political views seem to him to be threatening or dangerous."[17] April 30, the day he expressed his sponsorship, was the anniversary of Adolf Hitler's suicide.

Some ethnic minority members of Congress, particularly Asian Americans, supported Title II's repeal. For example, Hiram Fong, who in 1959 had become the first Asian American to be elected senator, added his support to the Inouye bill.[18]

After the May 1969 issue of *Atlantic Monthly* reported that Deputy Attorney General Richard Kleindienst had suggested using Title II against disruptive students, shock and criticism rose like a tidal wave.[19] Senator Inouye publicly expressed his dismay at Kleindienst's anti-activist message, declaring to the Senate:

> This statement will further fuel the fires of these dissidents in America who fear that concentration camps are being readied for those who hold unpopular views and beliefs. While it is expected that reason will prevail over this approach to America's problems, there is no question that statements of this sort erect barriers of trust between our Government and some of our citizens. I recently introduced S1872, a bill to repeal Title II of the Internal Security Act of 1950.... I may add that the Department of Justice has denied that the Deputy Attorney General Kleindienst made such a statement; however, the mere fact that it has been reported is, in my opinion, further reason for speedy action.[20]

The Department of Justice claimed that the deputy attorney general had been misquoted, but the *Atlantic* report spread the rumor of concentration camps to a wider segment of society. This accelerated the growing public support for Title II repeal as well as the support from the media and members of Congress.

In May and June, the grassroots repeal movement succeeded in getting support from local public media, which issued editorials advocating the repeal of Title II.[21] National media also promoted the JACL-led campaign to repeal Title II. For example, *The Nation*, which a year before had covered the rumors of concentration camps among radicals and African American communities while stating that "the public and the Congress have been apathetic in this matter," now commented that the current movement for repeal was "under correct auspices," as the Japanese Americans were "the first group in the U.S. to have concentration camp experience."[22]

On June 24, CBS aired an episode of *60 Minutes* featuring the growing public interest in Title II. The JACL office in Washington cooperated in making this program by providing information about members' wartime experiences. The program also covered the history of Title II and its "past, present, and future implications for all Americans."[23] Inouye explained the law and the case for its repeal. During the show, the anchor, Mike Wallace, interviewed Senator Eastland, who said he supported repeal on the grounds that the law was unnecessary for internal security. Representative Albert W. Watson (R-South Carolina), a member of the HISC, appeared in the show as the only "out-and-out champion" of retaining Title II. Watson insisted that "Title II was needed in case of guerrilla warfare by those who would destroy the government by violent and revolutionary means."[24] An officer from the Department of Justice insisted that no emergency detention camps were being constructed, nor would Title II be used against students, war protesters, or demonstrators who had American citizenship. The same officer, however, implied the possibility of the law being helpful against foreign subversion and said that the administration would defend Title II if it were challenged in the courts.[25]

Mike Masaoka was disappointed that the show did not mention Representatives Matsunaga and Holifield as the principal cosponsors of the repeal bill in Congress. However, it did cover the wartime treatment of Japanese Americans, which may have provided millions of Americans with an opportunity to learn for the first time about their removal and incarceration.[26] The evidence it presented clearly favored the effort to repeal Title II.

As Title II attracted greater attention from the public and the media, the number of cosponsors of the Matsunaga-Holifield bill (HR12220) rapidly increased. By June 17, forty-four representatives had joined as cosponsors of this repeal bill, which required that Matsunaga and Holifield sponsor an identical bill (HR12221) since the rules of the House allowed only twenty-five names to be included as cosponsors of a single bill.[27] The number of repeal bills increased from then on as the number of cosponsors increased.

Local chapters of national civil rights groups started to pass resolutions to support Title II repeal and to pressure their national organizations to support the cause as well. For example, the Berkeley NAACP voted unanimously on June 12, 1969, to support the repeal campaign after Raymond Okamura made a presentation to its executive board. Mary Jane Johnson, the chapter's president, stated that it would prepare a resolution for adoption by the district and national NAACP.[28] In Seattle, the Federated Auxiliaries of the International

Longshoremen's and Warehousemen's Union called for Title's II repeal by supporting the Inouye and Matsunaga-Holifield bills at its biennial convention.[29] The repeal movement, which had been initially limited to the West Coast, spread into the Midwest, the Southwest, and the Mountain States.[30] Even on Capitol Hill, Representative Phillip Burton (D-California), who added his name to the cosponsors of the Matsunaga-Holifield bill, noted that "the sentiment in Congress seems to be growing for repeal of this unfair law."[31]

In mid-July, Matsunaga asked Ichord to request the necessary executive department and agency reports on Title II repeal and to schedule public hearings.[32] The Washington office of the JACL requested an opportunity to testify on the repeal bills to Eastland, chairman of the Senate Judiciary Committee; Ichord, chairman of the HISC; and Emanuel Celler, chairman of the House Judiciary Committee. The Nixon administration thus far had not commented on the issue of Title II repeal. Matsunaga urged the House to act early on the repeal bills.

By late October, the number of cosponsors of repeal bills grew to twenty-six senators and one hundred and twenty-seven representatives. Now that it had obtained sufficient congressional supporters, the National Ad Hoc Committee strengthened its demand for public hearings. To pressure Congress to act, it instructed the JACL local chapters to generate as much support as possible from other organizations by making them actively involved in the repeal campaign.[33] The committee also heightened its scrutiny of conservatives in Congress. Senator Eastland, who had introduced S12, the Internal Security Act of 1969, was likely to move to add the repeal of Title II as an amendment to S12. The committee decided that if this happened, the JACL would oppose the Eastland bill because it included such provisions as creating a new crime of "peacetime treason" and enacting a sweeping loyalty program for employees of so-called "defense facilities," which could have included "virtually all industrial, commercial and educational facilities."[34]

On December 3, 1969, Kleindienst announced that the Justice Department supported Title II repeal. This was a reversal of its earlier position. The National Ad Hoc Committee claimed that the reversal of the Justice Department's position on the Title II repeal issue was due to the fact that many hundreds of individuals and groups sent statements and resolutions urging repeal.[35] However, this view might be naïve, because the Department of Justice had been conducting close surveillance of groups that might cause civil disturbances through the newly established Interdivision Information Unit, and it might have decided that through this unit and the FBI's COINTELPRO it could control domestic dissenting movements without resorting to the emergency detention authority.[36] Furthermore, as discussed in Chapter 3 of this book, the FBI had been compiling a confidential list of subversives since the 1930s and had not been abiding by the legislative restrictions provided by Title II. In 1969, the Bureau of Prisons in the Department of Justice issued *The Emergency Detention Manual*, which does not attribute the authority for detention to any legislation in the past or present.[37] This implies that the Department of Justice was preparing a detention program for an emergency with or without the legal authorization for such actions.

Upon hearing the Justice Department's support for Title II's repeal, the Senate passed a repeal bill—but only after an important revision was made to S1872, the Inouye bill. The preamble of Title II, which was titled "Findings of Necessity" and included the HUAC findings concerning the existence of the world communist movement, was excluded from the repeal bill. The new Inouye bill also retained a phrase in Title II's preamble: "[T]hose individuals who knowingly and willfully participate in the world communist movement in effect repudiate their allegiance to the United States, and in effect transfer their allegiance to the foreign country."[38] After making these amendments, conservatives agreed to pass the Inouye bill that repealed Title II. Inouye discussed the situation with Mike Masaoka, who consented to the change, and then agreed to the revision in the Senate. S1872 was then passed without any delay.

The National Ad Hoc Committee members were infuriated by this compromise. Raymond Okamura, Edison Uno, and Paul Yamamoto insisted that retaining Title II's preamble defeated the purpose of Title II repeal. It meant that the government could still violate the rights of those whom it suspected of being communists and deny the allegedly disloyal citizens the constitutional protection of civil rights and liberties by placing them outside the discursive American citizenry. Okamura also worried that the retained preamble might give the justification and philosophical basis to enact the quick implementation of S12, the Internal Security Act of 1969, which legislated notions such as peacetime treason, or to conduct emergency detention under presidential executive orders. He pointed out that as long as the JACL accepted the principle of a "presumption of guilt" and allowed the laws that utilized such a notion to pass, various groups would be charged with "probable disloyalty."[39]

Okamura wrote to Masaoka:

> The whole purpose of JACL involvement in the Title II repeal project is to prevent any repetition of [the] emergency detention that Japanese Americans experienced. The "Findings of Necessity" sounds chillingly close to the "Military Necessity" arguments used in the Korematsu decision. The finger is clearly pointed at so-called Communists, and

we have already witnessed attempts to label militant Blacks (by former Congressman Willis) and Chinese Americans (by J. Edgar Hoover) as "Communists."[40]

The National Ad Hoc Committee members were also displeased that Masaoka had agreed to the compromise without consulting them.

A few weeks later, however, the National Ad Hoc Committee modified its position to "restrained approval."[41] The priority was to pass the repeal law, even if that meant participating in shrewd congressional politics. The committee decided that the best course of action was to obtain a commitment from Ichord, the HISC chairman, that the HISC would move the repeal bills out of committee on the condition that the HISC would add only the Inouye amendments. If the first priority was not achieved, the JACL committee would seriously consider shifting its support to the House Judiciary Committee. The worst-case scenario was that the conservative members would attach undesirable rider bills in the HISC or the conference committee. Among those possible outcomes, outright repeal with the Inouye amendment to retain the preamble seemed at the time an acceptable compromise.

In late January 1970, the HISC announced its plan to hold public hearings on bills to repeal Title II, beginning on March 16. The National Ad Hoc Committee started to recruit witnesses to testify in front of the HISC, and Representative Matsunaga informed all 127 cosponsors of the repeal bill about the hearing date, suggesting they either testify in person or submit a written statement to be incorporated into the hearing records.[42]

At the same time, the JACL committee initiated its third letter-writing campaign. It had compiled a key mailing list of seven hundred addresses, including the offices of over two hundred members of Congress. The committee asked its supporters to write letters both to their own congressional representatives and to Richard Ichord himself. It also encouraged people to send statements to the HISC or participate as witnesses in the public hearings.

In February 1970, the State of California passed a resolution asking Congress to repeal Title II. It was the first state legislature to express support of the repeal. George Matsuoka, chairman of the Sacramento JACL Committee to Repeal the Emergency Detention Act, coordinated the efforts to get the state legislature to pass the resolution, obtaining crucial support from Assemblyman Charles Warren of Los Angeles.[43]

By the time the HISC hearings started, the list of organizations and public media supporting repeal included forty-two governmental bodies (including the state legislative assemblies of California and Hawaii), eighty-five civic organizations, four student organizations, thirty-one churches, and thirty-nine public media outlets.⁴⁴ Although the majority of the supportive organizations still came from the West Coast, the repeal movement by this time was by no means confined to that region. By June 1970, most of the JACL chapters across the country had participated in the letter-writing campaign to members of Congress. In addition to the support expressed by the state legislatures of California and Hawaii, some state politicians had made public statements, including Calvin Rampton, governor of Utah; Ronald Reagan, governor of California; and Paul Simon, lieutenant governor of Illinois.⁴⁵ In March 1970, the HISC hearings started. This became the primary site of public discussion on Title II repeal.

The House Internal Security Committee Hearings on Bills to Repeal the Emergency Detention Act

On March 16, 1970, HISC chairman Richard Ichord declared the opening of public hearings on the bills to repeal Title II.⁴⁶ Numerous members of Congress either appeared in person or sent statements to the hearings. A number of noncongressional government officials and prominent political figures testified, including former Supreme Court justice Arthur J. Goldberg and Ronald Reagan, governor of California. Present and former officials of government internal security agencies were also invited to testify. These included Herbert A. Philbrick, a confidential informant for the FBI (1940–1949); Edward Hunter, a World War II propaganda specialist for the Office of Strategic Services; and J. Walter Yeagley, assistant attorney general from the Justice Department. Ethnic, political, and religious organizations sent witnesses, including Clarence Mitchell of the NAACP, Miriam Friedlander of the CCCL, Lawrence Speiser of the ACLU, and Ross Wilber of the American Friends Service Committee. People who were directly involved in the removal and incarceration of Japanese Americans were also invited to testify. These witnesses included not only the delegates of the JACL but also people like Philip M. Glick, a former general counsel for the War Relocation Authority; and Dorothy Swaine Thomas, a sociologist who led the Japanese American Evacuation and Resettlement Study (JERS).⁴⁷ Earl Warren and Milton Eisenhower, the first director of the WRA, sent letters to support the repeal.

Mainstream Narratives on Title II Repeal

Despite the witnesses' diverse backgrounds and political stances, virtually every statement at the hearings referred to the wartime mass incarceration of Japanese Americans. Ichord opened the hearing by branding the incident "a black page in American history," and a wide array of those testifying reiterated this point.[48] Some of those who acknowledged the injustice of mass exclusion viewed the wartime tragedy as a lesson or sacrifice so that America could become a more democratic nation. The former Supreme Court justice Arthur Goldberg, for instance, stated that what happened to Japanese Americans during World War II was a "colossal injustice." He argued that it was inconceivable that the Supreme Court would sustain such an act, and that it was a learning experience for the nation.[49]

While most admitted the injustice, few mainstream witnesses questioned the goodwill of the administrators who implemented and sustained the mass removal and incarceration. Some were apologetic for those who made what they called the wartime mistake. Ichord emphasized that the policy was "proposed by the Army, authorized by President Roosevelt, ratified by the Congress . . . [and] upheld and confirmed by the Supreme Court." He stated that no one could say that the president or any of the Supreme Court justices were "evil men."[50] Interestingly, members of Congress from the West Coast openly admitted that the wartime treatment of Japanese Americans was a product of racism, which was a clear diversion from the conventional explanation that the policy was based on military necessity. Harold T. Johnson, a representative from California, stated that the greater tragedy "lay in the acceptance of the totalitarian concept of judging one's guilt or inferring one's disloyalty because of race, creed, color, class or national origin."[51]

For some, the repeal effort functioned as a way to apologize to Japanese Americans. Johnson emphasized that many city and county governments, civic and community organizations, and even the California State Legislature had passed resolutions expressing enthusiastic support for repealing Title II.[52] Earl Warren's letter to the JACL was also presented at the hearing. His message, endorsing repeal as a person "who as a state officer became involved in the harsh removal of the Japanese from the Pacific Coast in World War II," presented a strong tone of regret from a former California politician.[53]

Narratives from mainstream white politicians displayed conflicting historical memories. Charles Gubser, a representative from California, was the first member of Congress to introduce a repeal bill (HR19646), as early as September 1968. Gubser's statements in the hearing record display a modified memory of Californians' involvement in Japanese American mass removal:

> Many of us still retain vivid memories of our close friends and neighbors of Japanese ancestry being stripped of their rights and being relocated in detention centers. . . . I have never known Japanese American to harbor any resentments. . . . America is fortunate that these people have retained their confidence in this Nation.[54]

In describing the incident as the government taking away "close friends and neighbors," Gubser ignored the fact that anti-Japanese public opinion in California was a major factor in the government's decision to oust Japanese Americans from the West Coast.

In contrast, Milton Eisenhower, who also supported repeal, described how strong anti-Japanese hatred was during the war. As the first director of the WRA, Eisenhower had proposed to resettle Japanese Americans further inland, and he called a meeting in Salt Lake City for the governors of the states to which he planned to move the uprooted.[55] At the conference, some governors objected that the evacuees' lives would be in danger if they were to move around freely in their states. In his letter supporting repeal, Eisenhower recalled one governor who exclaimed, with his fist in the WRA director's face, "If you bring the Japanese to my state they will be hanging from every tree!"[56] When juxtaposed with Eisenhower's account, Gubser's statement seems to present a watered-down historical memory concerning anti-Japanese sentiments on the West Coast.

Even the expressions of guilt by white politicians over the nation's racist past proved problematic when contrasted with the actual historical experiences of Japanese Americans. For example, Dante B. Fascell, a representative from Florida, stated:

> When World War II was over, and the story of the terrible mistreatment of the Japanese-American community received national attention, the great mass of the American people was deeply embarrassed. . . . Many speeches of apology were made, and many economic barriers removed from the path of Japanese-Americans at the close of World War II, as a gesture of humility.[57]

Historical records show that there still was rampant anti-Japanese prejudice even after the war. On the West Coast, there were attempts to prevent Japanese Americans from coming back to their former homes.[58] Moreover, the economic barriers imposed on Japanese Americans before World War II were part of the political, economic, and social apparatus of racism, and the postwar removal of these barriers as an "apology" or a "gesture of humility" does not absolve the past injustice inflicted on racial minorities. Fascell's statement is not accurate and in effect not only whitewashes the memories of the wartime removal and incarceration of Japanese Americans but also trivializes the long-term racist policies that targeted them before the war.

Another conspicuous discourse displayed in mainstream accounts was the attempt to include Japanese Americans in the mainstream as a model minority. Again, I quote Charles Gubser:

I personally have never seen a Japanese American in jail. I have never seen one on relief. I have never seen one burning a flag or a draft card or inciting a riot. I do not know of any ethnic group which adheres more rigidly to basic American principles than the Japanese Americans.[59]

This narrative relies on the stereotypical representation of Japanese Americans as an ostensibly desirable ethnic group, implying the existence of others that were undesirable. Gubser's statement is an example of the preferential racialization of "desirable" and "undesirable" citizens among minorities. Moreover, his reasoning was in direct contradiction to the grassroots demand for Title II repeal, which originated from anxiety about the government's political repression of dissenting groups that were "burning a flag or a draft card or inciting a riot." The hearing record reveals the juxtaposition of contradictory narratives even among the supporters of repeal.

Those who were directly involved in policy making or worked closely with Japanese Americans during the war presented more complex memories of the event. Philip M. Glick, who worked as a general counsel for the War Relocation Authority, stated that the WRA always had "grave doubts" about the constitutionality of mass relocation, and its responsibility was "to mediate between the evacuees and the American public opinion."[60] This was not an easy task, because right-wing organizations and individuals had criticized the WRA for being too kind to Japanese Americans placed in camps.[61]

Sociologist Dorothy Swaine Thomas pointed out the government's manipulation of labels used to represent the Japanese American incarcerees. She wrote in an article presented at the hearing that, by calling them "persons of Japanese ancestry" instead of American citizens, "there were disturbing indications that the status of Nisei as descendants of the Japanese enemy might take precedence over their status as American citizens."[62] During the question period, Thomas countered Chairman Ichord's model minority narrative:

> The Chairman: We are all well aware of the fact that the Japanese are among the best of all of many racial groups that we do have in this Nation.
> Mrs. Thomas: You know it is sort of dangerous to talk about one of the best. They were one of the worst when I went to California, in popular mind.[63]

Those who managed the impounded community had to directly face the difficulties emerging from the fundamental contradictions between the rhetoric and the reality of the internment policy. They were in direct contact with the anguished incarcerees and sometimes had to confront those who resisted the camp administrators through violent or nonviolent means. Their historical memories were inevitably more ambivalent than those of the general population and could not be whitewashed as easily.

Minority Narratives on Title II Repeal

The Japanese American witnesses at the hearings included the initiators of the repeal campaign, the leaders of the JACL, and members of Congress. The JACL sent Jerry Enomoto, Mike Masaoka, Raymond Okamura, Edison Uno, Ross Harano, and Robert Takasugi as its delegates. These testimonies reflected multiple voices and perspectives from the Japanese American community.

Okamura stated in front of the hearing committee that there was widespread support for repeal not only in Congress but also among the "city councils, county board[s] of supervisors, newspaper editors, churches, civil veterans, and other organizations."[64] He also presented the resolution passed by the state legislature of California and a statement prepared by Governor Reagan urging repeal. Harano, who was instrumental in the JACL repeal campaign in Chicago, spoke as a person "born in a concentration camp."[65] He brought documents that indicated strong public support for repeal in the Chicago area.[66] Takasugi, a trial attorney, was added to the JACL panel to answer the question, "What will protect our internal security if Title II is repealed?"[67] He effectively explained to the formidable HISC chairman, a known opponent of repeal, that there was enough statutory protection of internal security without Title II.[68]

During the hearings, Japanese Americans narrated their wartime experiences as citizens victimized by racial prejudice. They emphasized Japanese Americans' glorious record of patriotism during World War II. Patsy Mink, a Japanese American representative from Hawaii, stated:

> The mass detention which took place in World War II is the only such tragedy in our nation's history, and the proud fighting record of these Americans during the war along with all other experience with these citizens conclusively demonstrated the error of this detention.[69]

Mink emphasized the uniqueness of the Japanese American experience.[70] Masaoka, a Nisei veteran himself, highlighted the national loyalty of the Japanese Americans "volunteering for combat from concentration camps."[71]

He went as far as to say that "most Japanese Americans came out of that evacuation process without bitterness."[72] These statements use the logic that mass removal was wrong because Japanese Americans were loyal and patriotic. In the late 1960s, however, the primary targets of detention were draft resisters and antiwar activists, as well as African American militants. Arguments rooted in the model-minority myth left open the question of whether the government had the right to detain citizens it deemed *un*patriotic.

It was important that the hearing provided Japanese Americans with an opportunity to present alternative voices from within the ethnic community. In fact, this was the first time that the JACL was represented by someone other than Masaoka at a congressional hearing.[73] Edison Uno, leader of the grassroots repeal movement, refuted the view that Japanese American wartime incarceration was a mere mistake, contextualizing the incident within the nation's historically consistent racism:

> Our experience was no accidental phenomenon—nor is it original in American history, whose only "good" Indians were "dead" Indians. Our experience was carefully planned and deliberately executed by racists, economic and political opportunists, superpatriots, professional militarists, bigoted organizations, and a majority of well-intentioned people who remained silent while some Americans capitalized on a half-century campaign of racial discrimination and prejudice toward Japanese Americans.[74]

In contrast to the mainstream Japanese American narratives, Uno named patriots among those who perpetuated American racism. He insisted that Japanese Americans had an obligation to all Americans to eliminate the statutory provisions that would allow the reoccurrence of their dreadful experience. This attitude was in stark contrast to the generally conservative stance of the JACL establishment, who were reluctant to get involved in non-Japanese issues.

The perspectives presented at the hearing, however, did not represent all that existed in the Japanese American community. Radical voices, in particular, were missing. Although the repeal campaign was initiated and developed by radical groups of students and activists who questioned the "quiet American" stereotype, Chairman Ichord chose not to include them as witnesses, nor did the JACL leaders insist on their inclusion.[75] During the grassroots campaign, the National Ad Hoc Committee worked in liaison with organizations such as the CCCL and the NCAHUAC, which Masaoka considered too far left. Masaoka recommended against associating with those organizations lest it alienate the conservative supporters in Congress.

However, the coalition between the National Ad Hoc Committee grassroots activists and other minorities encouraged many non–Japanese American organizations to participate in the hearings. Witnesses from other groups, particularly African American politicians and organizations, expressed their support for Title II's repeal. Their statements discussed a wide range of issues relating to race, class, and political repression. Many expressed concerns about past and present racism, discrimination, urban poverty, violence, social unrest, and other problems minority communities were facing. They expressed their own experiences in light of historical injustices, and in so doing treated the Japanese American experience as a plight shared by many oppressed minorities. Like Edison Uno, Shirley Chisholm (D-New York), the first female African American member of Congress, described the mass incarceration of Japanese Americans as one of the recurrent tragedies caused by historical racism in the United States. In doing so, she used another loaded metaphor to represent the state of African American lives:

> All black people know what *fascism* means for we have lived with it for over 150 years, and with the advent of the Supreme Court decision to desegregate schools and the civil rights legislation of 1965 we achieved a little "taste of freedom."[76]

Chisholm emphasized that Title II raised special concerns among racial minorities, even though the law was not created to be used on any specific race:

> Although the Emergency Detention Act has not been invoked since its enactment, its mere presence on the books is an offense especially to Americans of color. . . . [I]t was not the Italians and Germans who were rounded up, but the Japanese Americans who were easily identifiable because of the color of their skin. Today it is not the KKK or the syndicate whose doors are being kicked in. It is the Black Panthers. Skin, skin, skin color, gentlemen, that is the criteria. It makes us special targets.[77]

The Title II repeal campaign provided a site where witnesses addressed social problems they were facing and criticized the government for repressing their legitimate right to express dissent. Karl C. Johnson, representing the Church of the Covenant and the Urban League of Cleveland, made one of the most radical statements among the hearing testimonies:

The greatest enemies that the Internal Security Committee faces are poverty, hunger, disease, inadequate housing, unemployment, fractured families, and desperation. Compared to these, the threat of a segment of the international communist conspiracy looks like child's play.[78]

In the late 1960s, all these problems were truly at stake for minority communities, who also worried about having their members thrown into detention camps. Johnson's statement reveals the class issues involved in the Title II repeal movement. It also suggests that the red-scare discourse had lost its hegemonic influence in political scenes by 1970.

Louis Stokes, an African American representative from Ohio and a member of the HISC, described his personal encounters with young African Americans talking about concentration camps.[79] Clarence Mitchell, the Washington representative of the NAACP, argued that removing Title II from the statute books would contribute to easing the minds of those agitated and worried about deteriorating race relations, particularly in urban areas:

I would say, if we went out into the middle of Constitution Avenue and erected a gallows and someone said they have this gallows out there for the purpose of hanging the Negroes in this community, I think we could deny that that would be the purpose, but the more effective way to destroy that rumor would be to remove the gallows.[80]

Even though minorities were most concerned about concentration camps, a large number of Congress members, both mainstream and minority, agreed on the need for alleviating public fear. In fact, the most persuasive rationale in Congress to repeal Title II was that the law created unnecessary alarm. Politicians recognized that the fears were strong, especially on college campuses, in inner cities, and among antiwar protest groups.[81] Many lawmakers felt that the existence of Title II aggravated the division and tension between different racial, ideological, and generational groups, and they saw its repeal as a relatively easy and inexpensive way to alleviate public anxiety.

Opposition to Repealing Title II

The House Internal Security Committee invited specialists on military and security issues to the hearings who opposed repealing Title II. Some military experts defended the mass incarceration of Japanese Americans by emphasizing that it was implemented for military necessity. For example, Frederick Wiener, a lawyer and retired army colonel, reminded those at the hearings that, "after all, Japan had begun a war against the United States." He also stated:

> We would certainly consider it strange if an American born to American parents in, say, Venezuela, were Venezuelan in his loyalties; why then should it have been mere prejudice and racism to believe that some Nisei may have had emotional links to Japan?[82]

The fact that few, mostly military-related witnesses testified to justify the wartime incarceration of an ethnic minority related to an enemy nation indicates that a tension existed in the hearings between the military and civil liberties discourses. The great majority of witnesses, however, considered the policy unjustifiable.

Another kind of opposition came from those who tried to separate Title II from the issue of Japanese American experiences. Ichord repeatedly reminded the witnesses and the HISC members that Title II did not exist when Japanese Americans were incarcerated. He insisted that the act was originally proposed as an attempt to prevent the arbitrary use of the president's executive power, and he warned the committee that its repeal would bring the nation back to 1942, when there was no protection for the detainees.[83]

Some witnesses from military and intelligence institutions used anticommunist rhetoric to oppose the repeal. Edward Hunter, who had served as a propaganda specialist with the Office of Strategic Services during World War II, stated:

> What we really have is a source of agitation . . . and this source of agitation is conspiratorial and communist, exploiting the American citizens of Japanese ancestry, cruelly exploiting the worries of our Negro community . . . and crudely keeping alive the thought of Nazi death camps in Americans of Jewish faith.[84]

Sympathetic as he was to those worried about the concentration camp rumor, Hunter supported the retention of Title II and dismissed public concern by attributing the rumor to a communist conspiracy.

Notwithstanding the testimonies of these military and intelligence experts, the presence of Japanese Americans in the Title II repeal campaign ensured the symbolic connection between Title II and their wartime mass incarceration. Nobody, not even the fiercest anticommunist, antisubversive members of Congress, could contest the unfairness of the mass incarceration of loyal American citizens. The hearings closed on September 10, 1970, after revealing many contradictory accounts of the function of Title II (repression or protection?), the cause of contemporary social unrest (insurrection or rightful dissent?), and the very nature of America's past.

The Final Phase of Title II Repeal

Conservative Attempts to Block the Repeal

Although the overwhelming majority of the witnesses at the HISC hearings supported repeal, Ichord expressed his support for the retention of Title II both within and outside the committee. In August 1970, at the national convention of the Veterans of Foreign Wars, he stated:

> Frankly, I would prefer to see the Congress consider perfecting amendments which would put to rest the fears of those most sincerely critical—namely the Japanese Americans, but I am something less than anxious to grant some of its other critics—such as the Communist Party—the satisfaction of having stripped our country of any appropriate and constitutional means of protecting itself.[85]

Ichord recommended amending the bill, and he invited Mike Masaoka to help the HISC write amendments acceptable to the JACL. The National Ad Hoc Committee instructed Masaoka to refuse cooperation.[86]

Since the HISC was made up of four Republicans and four Democrats, the votes of the Republicans—John Ashbrook of Ohio, Richard Roudebush of Indiana, William Scherle of Iowa, and Albert Watson of South Carolina—were crucial for the HISC decision, since the four Democrats had expressed their support for repealing the act. The National Ad Hoc Committee campaigned to pressure the Republican HISC members to vote for repeal. To the campaigners' advantage, President Nixon was supporting repeal.[87] The National Ad Hoc Committee also instructed each JACL chapter to contact any JACL members with Republican connections to ask them to request Republican members of Congress to urge their party members on the HISC to vote for the repeal bill.

Unsure about the HISC's vote, the National Ad Hoc Committee focused its efforts on passing the outright repeal bill to prevent repressive amendment bills from passing in Congress. The National Ad Hoc Committee decided that if the HISC voted down straight repeal but put forth an amended bill, it would let it pass without comment. In such a case, Matsunaga, a member of the Rules Committee, was to lead the maneuver to amend the HISC bill back to the Inouye version once the former went on the floor. If Matsunaga failed in changing the HISC bill to the Inouye bill, the National Ad Hoc Committee was to urge defeat of the unacceptable HISC repeal bill. In this case, the JACL committee would have to ask all of their congressional supporters to vote against the bill, even risking a chance of the repeal bill never passing Congress. Its members contended that they "would rather face defeat than a compromise version which might be repugnant to civil rights in general."[88]

As the repeal supporters feared, the HISC voted down the Matsunaga-Holifield bill by a 4–4 deadlock on September 23, 1970, and recommended an amended version of Title II (HR19163) instead of all-out repeal. Introduced in the House on September 14, HR19163 was a "last minute scheme designed to defeat the repeal campaign."[89] Its sponsors, Ichord and Ashbrook, insisted that the bill's amendments put public fears concerning wrongful detention to rest while retaining strong protection for the country in cases of emergency.

In recommending the Ichord bill over the Matsunaga-Holifield bill, the HISC House Report proposed four main amendments to Title II. First, the bill required that any determination of the existence of an "insurrection within the United States in aid of a foreign enemy" be made by a concurrent resolution of the Congress instead of by the president. Second, it added a clause stating, "No citizen of the United States shall be apprehended or detained pursuant to the provisions of this title on account of race, color, or ancestry." Third, it provided assurance that detainees would have full opportunity to be represented by counsel, and last, it tightened the criteria that the attorney general and the Detention Review Board were authorized to consider in determining the existence of reasonable grounds to believe that a person would probably engage in espionage or sabotage. Louis Stokes wrote a dissenting view, rejecting the idea that the fears and rumors in communities of color would disappear with these amendments.[90]

The report was met with public ridicule. The *St. Louis Post-Dispatch* carried a cartoon showing a barbed-wire fence and watchtower with Ichord pointing at a sign reading, "U.S. CONCENTRATION CAMP, OPEN TO ALL CITIZENS REGARDLESS OF RACE, CREED, COLOR, ANCESTRY, SHAPE OR LOOKS."[91] The *Honolulu Star-Bulletin* carried an article calling for repeal that included a cartoon depicting Ichord sleeping in bed dreaming about "Detention Act Amendment." In his dream, there is a sign reading "THIS IS AN EQUAL OPPORTUNITY CONCENTRATION CAMP."[92] Even though the public scoffed at the HISC proposal to make "equal opportunity concentration camps," this attempt to repeal Title II failed because the conservative HISC members successfully blocked the process. The Ninety-First Congress adjourned before taking any actions for or against repeal.

Tom Engelhardt cartoon, "There, That Shows Our Sense of Justice," *St. Louis Post-Dispatch*, September 27, 1970. (© 1970 Engelhardt in *The St. Louis Post-Dispatch*; reprinted with permission.)

The Public Hearing by the House Judiciary Committee and the Passage of the Non-Detention Act

Early in the following year, in the first session of the Ninety-Second Congress, a renewed campaign to repeal Title II began. The National Ad Hoc Committee decided that, this time, the public campaign could be "low key," and the committee would shift to a "behind-the-scene approach."[93] The new campaign agenda was to write to senators and representatives and ask them to cosponsor a new bill to repeal Title II.

To avoid the HISC, the new demand for repeal was taken to the House Judiciary Committee. Matsunaga and Holifield joined Abner Mikva and introduced HR234 in the House of Representatives. HR234 was identical to the original Mikva bill, which read, "To amend Title 18, United States Code, to prohibit the establishment of emergency detention camps and to provide that no citizen of the United States shall be committed for detention or imprisoned in any facility of the United States except in conformity with the provisions of Title 18."[94] The bill was worded this way not only to ensure that it was assigned to the Committee on the Judiciary, which was more supportive of repeal, but also to counter Ichord's argument that repealing Title II would remove the legislative safeguard against the arbitrary use of executive power and would not necessarily prevent the future mass detention or incarceration of innocent citizens.

Cosponsors of HR234, "The Legislation to Amend Title 18, U.S. Code, to Prohibit the Establishment of Emergency Detention Camps and to Repeal the Emergency Detention Act," counted 150 representatives. HR234 and its companion bills (HR4237, HR4239, HR4240, HR4241, HR5243, HR5244, and HR5693) were referred to the House Committee on the Judiciary and assigned to Subcommittee No. 3, chaired by Robert W. Kastenmeier (D-Wisconsin). In the Senate, Daniel Inouye reintroduced a repeal bill (S592). Inouye's bill was identical to the bill passed in the Senate the year before that repealed the emergency detention provisions but retained Title II's preamble discussing the danger of a world communist movement.

On March 18, 1971, Subcommittee No. 3 of the House Judiciary Committee held a public hearing on Title II repeal. The National Ad Hoc Committee refrained from testifying in the hearing and also asked all of the supporting organizations to do the same. This strategy was chosen because extensive public hearings had already been held by the HISC in the previous year, and the JACL committee wanted to avoid filibustering its own bills.[95]

Unlike the HISC hearing, the House Judiciary Committee hearing lasted only one day. Five members of Congress testified, including Matsunaga and Holifield. Matsunaga explained that HR234 would not only repeal Title II but actually "prohibit the establishment of concentration camps as a part of the Federal penal and correctional system."[96] All the members of Congress who testified expressed support for repeal. Ten congresspeople who sent statements all supported repeal as well. Five civic organizations—the JACL, the ACLU, the Friends Committee on National Legislation, the Liberty Lobby, and the Los Angeles County Board of Supervisors—also sent statements. Except for the Liberty Lobby, which consistently supported Ichord's argument against repealing Title II, all these groups supported the repeal effort.

The only question raised against HR234 during the hearing came from the Justice Department. Robert C. Mardian, assistant attorney general for the Internal Security Division, expressed the Justice Department's support for repealing Title II but pointed out that not all provisions for the detention of convicted persons were contained in Title 18 of the U.S. Code.[97] Instead of amending all the provisions that would relate to the criminal and penal codes operative under due process, the Judiciary Committee amended the bill to read, "No citizen shall be imprisoned or otherwise detained by the United States except pursuant to an Act of Congress." Section 2 of the bill read, "Title II of the Internal Security Act of 1950 is hereby repealed." The bill was passed by a 9–0 vote and reported out of the House Judiciary Committee.

September 1971 marked the final battle. Representative Ichord, who had reintroduced the Ichord-Ashbrook bill (HR820), attempted to substitute his bill, which amended and strengthened Title II, for the outright repeal bill. During the month of August, the National Ad Hoc Committee instructed the JACL chapters and national officers to write to or personally visit their district members of Congress who were home for recess. By this time, over 170 representatives had openly favored repeal.[98]

On September 14, 1971, the House of Representatives debated Title II for the last time. The Ichord-Ashbrook bill was defeated, while HR234 was passed 356–49. Two days later, Senator Inouye substituted the House version of the repeal bill for the Inouye bill on the Senate floor, and the Senate passed the repeal bill, identical to the House bill, unanimously. On September 25, President Richard Nixon signed the repeal bill, and Title II closed its life after twenty-one years. It was an overwhelming victory for the supporters of repeal, and particularly for the Japanese American leaders of the campaign.

Conclusion

The campaign to repeal Title II took place between 1967 and 1971, when America witnessed an upsurge of radical social criticism and dissent against the government. In retrospect, it seems peculiar that Congress decided to repeal one of the most drastic antisubversive laws at this historical moment. It is also noteworthy that HR234, the Title II repeal bill, contained the "nondetention" clause, which barred the executive branch from detaining American citizens without congressional authorization.[99]

While the executive branch's verbal support for repealing Title II was likely a political gesture to show that it respected the traditional American beliefs in liberty, political scientist Richard Longaker points out that adding the non-detention clause was an active motion by Congress to "assert affirmatively its authority over presidential discretion by outright rejection of the principle of detention and prohibition against its use."[100] He argues that this move reflected a "legislative wariness about presidential power" in the escalation of the Vietnam War.[101] This tension between presidential power and congressional authorization regarding detention gives the study of this legislative episode relevance in the United States today. All three presidents of the twenty-first century have resorted to controversial usage of executive power for the detention of various individuals.[102]

During the public debate on Title II repeal, diverse and conflicting interpretations of the act emerged that directly reflected the social tensions of the late 1960s. For some people, the images of barbed-wire fences and watchtowers symbolized state violence and police brutality against dissenting minorities, while for others they implied potential similarities between America and Nazi Germany or the Stalinist Soviet Union. For conservatives, repealing Title II was a chance to demonstrate America's "abiding respect for the liberty of the individual," thus setting the nation apart from totalitarianism and boosting patriotism, which was necessary given the lingering, unpopular war.[103] Participation in the Title II repeal campaign allowed mainstream figures, particularly on the West Coast, to publicly express regrets, if not apology, for the wartime exclusion and incarceration as well as the prewar racial discrimination inflicted on Japanese Americans.

For mainstream Japanese Americans, Title II repeal gave an opportunity to emphasize their patriotism and model-minority status. Revisiting their wartime experience implied reclaiming their shattered pride and dignity. On the other hand, Japanese American grassroots activists used the repeal campaign to educate the public about their wrongful wartime incarceration and to contribute to American citizens' efforts to fight ongoing oppression in other segments of society.

Furthermore, the repeal campaign stimulated the building of coalitions among minority groups. Minorities got a chance to participate in the legislative process and narrate the particular historical oppression their community had been subjected to. Activists not only talked about emergency or wartime detention but also interrogated the historical and current plights facing many minority communities. For those who pushed for social reforms, Title II's repeal removed another repressive piece of legislation that blocked their demands for justice. By providing a site for the public to narrate their diverse historical memories, the repeal movement contributed to the process of what John R. Gillis calls the "democratization of the past."[104]

How did people build a consensus to repeal Title II despite the variety and incompatibility of their diverse historical memories? A crucial factor was the presence of Japanese Americans. Their wartime experience made it impossible for the opposition to brush aside the possibility of future abuse of the law, since it showed that "such detention of innocent persons, on the basis of mere suspicion, '[could] happen in America.'"[105] During the repeal campaign, Japanese Americans represented themselves and were represented by others as a group of loyal and innocent citizens incarcerated wrongfully solely on the basis of their racial characteristics. In this process, the representation of the camps changed from "relocation centers" to "concentration camps."

Because of the perceived connection between Japanese American incarceration and Title II, the law came to stand for political repression, represented by the image of concentration camps (i.e., an "ugly symbol of totalitarianism").[106] In Edison Uno's words, the repeal was a demonstration of the nation's commitment to a free and democratic society and "the opportunity to enhance the American dream."[107] The majority of witnesses at the congressional hearings branded the law un-American, and this sentiment was conducive to strong congressional support for its repeal. Although some conservatives tried hard to dissociate Title II from the image of concentration camps by contending that the connection was based on false rumor and misinformation, their attempt ultimately failed when challenged by concrete historical evidence presented by the victims of a gross so-called wartime mistake.

Despite the differences in race, class, and ideological affiliation among the people who discussed repealing Title II, all expressed their views and narrated their historical experiences vis-à-vis the shared knowledge of Japanese Americans' wartime incarceration. Minorities developed coalitions among each other, and politicians in their attempt to restore the people's trust in the government seized the opportunity to show sympathy for their "fear and suspicions—unfounded as they may be."[108]

The congressional process of repealing Title II showed that in 1971, being a racial minority or making a public expression of political dissent could not place one outside the discursive boundary of American citizenship. In the age of radical social reforms and the antiwar movement, the meaning of loyalty, or citizens' devotion to their nation, was contested from all different ideological angles, and no particular line of thought could dominate what it meant. Of course, this did not mean that the conservatives stopped their attempts to exclude people whom they marked as undesirable citizens. But the discourse of American citizenship expanded through the 1960s social movements, and a clear-cut identity such as one based on racial or ideological affiliations could no longer separate citizens from constitutional protection.

The need to repeal Title II was a unique issue on which Americans built a consensus even during massive social unrest. Although people had different ideas of what barbed-wire fences and watchtowers stood for, what it meant to be a loyal American, or what a free society was supposed to look like, everyone agreed that concentration camps were incompatible with basic American values. The repeal effort united Americans of diverse racial, ideological, regional, social, and class affiliations. They gathered and built a statutory monument that commemorated the historical injustice of the internment, and through this reaffirmed the American creed by officially prohibiting American concentration camps.

Conclusion

A New Age of Concentration Camps?

Following the political spectacle of Title II repeal, which reconfirmed America's commitment to civil liberties, Japanese Americans were encouraged not just to share their experiences of past maltreatment but to ask for vindication by seeking redress and reparation. As a result of continued grassroots activism and the JACL's continued lobbying, President Gerald R. Ford in 1976 issued Proclamation 4417, in which he confirmed the termination of Executive Order 9066.

The bipartisan Commission on Wartime Relocation and Internment of Civilians (CWRIC), created in 1980, held hearings with over 750 witnesses and also conducted archival research.[1] In 1983, the CWRIC recommended an official apology, monetary compensation of $20,000 to each surviving incarceree, and the establishment of a foundation to educate the public.[2]

Around the same time, in the *coram nobis* cases, the court vacated the convictions of Hirabayashi, Yasui, and Korematsu. On August 10, 1988, President Ronald Reagan signed the Civil Liberties Act, enacting the CWRIC's recommendations. For the entire Japanese American community, redress was a vindication after the wartime shame of being treated like an enemy.[3] Edison Uno, who passed away in 1976, never saw that day, but it was his pioneering activism, joined by many others, that eventually opened the path to "achieve the impossible dream."[4]

While redress marked the government's acknowledgment of its wartime civil liberties violations against Japanese Americans, neither the repeal of Title II nor the redress halted the incarceration or surveillance of aliens or minority citizens within the United States. Two years before the Department of Justice announced its support for repealing Title II, the Nixon administration rearranged internal security institutions to reinforce the nation's domestic surveillance capability. As early as 1967, Attorney General Ramsey Clark had established the Interdivision Information Unit within the Department of Justice to monitor protest groups throughout the United States.[5] Since the mid-1950s, the FBI had expanded its activities from purely investigatory operations to more aggressive counterintelligence programs (COINTELPRO) to disrupt and neutralize any activities that it considered possible threats to internal security.[6] After the radical social movements of the 1960s subsided, the criminalization of young black men continued. Indeed, the "age of concentration camps" was followed by the emergence of what Angela Davis calls the "prison industrial complex."[7]

On September 11, 2001, the suicide attacks on the World Trade Center and the Pentagon by Islamic extremists reminded Americans that national security was still a pressing issue and that national and internal security agencies bear crucial responsibility in protecting the lives of not only Americans but also many other people who live on the nation's soil. At the same time, the aftermath of the 9/11 attack was a sobering reminder of the fragility of civil liberties in a national crisis. Whenever a majority of citizens feel insecure about their country's safety, particular categories of minorities—defined by race, religion, sexual orientation, or political creed—become susceptible to harassment, and serious encroachments on freedom and civil rights occur.

Forty-five days after the terrorist attacks, the federal government passed the first USA PATRIOT Act, which granted the government sweeping powers to conduct surveillance, wiretaps, and secret searches on people, as well as authorizing the indefinite detention of individuals in the name of the "war on terrorism."[8] The newly created Department of Homeland Security strengthened the executive power to control immigration and national borders, resulting in the detention and deportation of an unknown but substantial number of immigrants.[9] Furthermore, military detention facilities held American citizens, and at the Guantanamo Bay Naval Base, civilians captured from foreign countries were incarcerated and tortured during investigation.[10]

The government claimed that the individuals held in those facilities were "enemy combatants."[11] This term originated in the 1942 case of *Ex Parte Quirin*, which involved the habeas corpus petitions of German and American citizens who received military training in Germany and landed on American soil in German submarines carrying explosives. The Supreme Court ruled that the petitioners could be categorized as unlawful belligerents, a term defined as "an enemy combatant who without uniform comes secretly through the lines for the purpose of waging war by destruction of life or property," and as such they were "offenders against the law of war subject to trial and punishment by military tribunals."[12] Crucially, this meant that even civilians with American citizenship could be tried and punished in military tribunals if they were suspected to be "enemy combatants." However, the evidence in this case showed beyond a reasonable doubt that the petitioners were engaged in military operations for an enemy state. In contrast, in the post-9/11 cases, the government refused to present the evidence from which it decided that the detainees were "enemy combatants."[13]

"Enemy combatant" is an ambiguous term that gives the government blanket power to arrest and detain anyone at its discretion. While the label "enemy alien" presumes citizenship of an enemy state, "enemy combatant" could be applied to both citizens and aliens. Although most of the people detained after 9/11 under the war on terrorism were aliens, the government tried to retain the power to detain citizens.[14]

It is telling that the terms "enemy aliens" and "enemy combatants," used during World War II to authorize extralegal detentions, were revived in the present war on terrorism, and it is an interesting academic question to consider which term is more restrictive. From the Japanese American point of view, "enemy combatant" may be fairer, allowing the executive branch stronger control in dealing with domestic espionage or sabotage on the basis of individual behavior rather than a group affiliation such as race, nationality, or ancestry. On the other hand, "enemy combatant" is problematic if the government does not reveal how and why the captured individuals are designated as such, because in such cases their detention becomes unchallengeable.[15] In reality, the detention and interrogation of enemy combatants are conducted less because of investigations into individual behavior than as a result of racial profiling.[16] The ambiguity of these terms continues to allow the government to manipulate the murky boundaries between "citizens" and "aliens," placing certain individuals outside the constitutional protection of civil liberties.

The terrorist attack and its aftermath brought home to Americans that the balance between civil liberties and internal security is still an important but difficult issue. Many think that strong and efficient police power is necessary in a modern society to prevent individuals from violating other people's security and rights. The development of global networks of extremism requires effective intelligence activities. At the same time, it is important that people's civil liberties are not unnecessarily restricted, let alone arbitrarily violated for the interests of those in power. History has shown time and time again that law enforcement power, if abused, becomes the source of oppression, violating people's security and civil rights; moreover, the power is rarely exercised fairly, free of prejudice. The tension between law enforcement officers and African Americans, currently demonstrated in the Black Lives Matter struggle, is another example of the American dilemma in which the entanglement of race and repression results in everyday violence.

The presidential campaign by Donald J. Trump and his eventual victory in 2016 featured a rising tide of racial prejudice and demands for "law and order" at the expense of civil liberties and social justice. Trump not only called for tighter border control and the deportation of all undocumented immigrants but also labeled Mexican immigrants as criminals, rapists, and drug dealers. These discursive tactics, which depict one racial or ethnic group as a menace to the safety of "Americans," resemble the way in which Japanese Americans were branded "enemy aliens" regardless of their citizenship status.

Within a week after his inauguration, President Trump signed two executive orders relating to border protection and immigration. Executive Order 13767, "Border Security and Immigration Enforcement Improvements," signed on January 25, 2017, called for the "immediate construction of a physical wall on the southern border" of the United States and the detention of "individuals apprehended on suspicion of violating Federal or State law including Federal immigration law."[17] Executive Order 13769, "Protecting the Nation from Foreign Terrorist Entry into the United States," signed on January 27, temporarily suspended immigration from seven Muslim-majority countries (Iraq, Syria, Iran, Sudan, Libya, Somalia, and Yemen) for ninety days and halted the admission of refugees from Syria indefinitely. The State of Hawaii legally challenged the order, calling it a "Muslim ban."[18] After the federal Court of Appeals upheld the lower court ruling to suspend this immigration ban, Trump issued another order on March 6 that banned entry into the United States by individuals from six Muslim-majority countries (Iraq was dropped from the list) and suspended refugee programs for 120 days.

As with Trump's allegations that Mexicans are murderers and rapists, his allegations that Muslims are terrorists offended millions of Americans, inducing protests across the nation. An outcry of criticism arose when Trump supporter Carl Higbie cited Japanese American "internment" as a precedent for an immigration registry and when Kris Kobach, Trump's policy advisor and Kansas secretary of state, advocated a federal Muslim registry.[19] When the news came out, wartime photographs of Japanese Americans in the camps appeared in newspapers and television programs on both the right and the left.

Japanese Americans quickly raised their voices. The Japanese American National Museum produced a special exhibit titled "Instruction to All Persons: Reflections on Executive Order 9066" that was open February 18–August 13, 2017. The exhibition included the original pages of Executive Order 9066 as well as Presidential Proclamation 2537, the order requiring aliens from Germany, Italy, and Japan to register with the Department of Justice. One wall of the exhibit was covered with the instructions, mostly reprints but several of them original, ordering all persons of Japanese ancestry in each district within the defense area to appear at the designated sites from which people were shipped to the assembly centers. The exhibit's main title, by omitting "of Japanese Ancestry" from the words of the exclusion order, indicated that the target group for exclusion could shift according to the political atmosphere and be applied to any individuals, including the viewers. In addition to information related to mass exclusion, the exhibit also displayed interview videos of Japanese, German, and Italian men detained in the Justice Department detention centers, such as Tuna Canyon Detention Station.[20]

Actor George Takei, the most famous Japanese American in the entertainment industry and a childhood incarceree of the Rohwer War Relocation Center and Tule Lake Segregation Center, toured the nation with his theatrical production *Allegiance* during the early months of 2018.[21] The musical is based on the story of a Nisei veteran who served in the army while his family was held in the camp, and it features the story of draft resisters along with Nisei soldiers. Takei is one of the most prominent spokespeople for Japanese American experiences as well as LGBT issues in the American mainstream media, and his musical contributed to publicizing and complicating the Japanese American wartime incarceration story.

Seeing media depictions of the Japanese American "internment" in the present, it is noticeable that this historical episode is considered unjust across the board, from conservatives to the left. As divided as opinions on civil liberties are in Trump's America, it is impressive to see a general consensus as far as the historical memory of Japanese American mass incarceration is concerned. This consensus is a contrast to the situation in the immediate post-9/11 era, when Michelle Malkin's book *In Defense of Internment* (2004) appeared in the *New York Times* Best Seller List.[22] At that time, Malkin attracted substantial media attention. Today, while anti-immigrant groups and anti-Muslim sentiment are quite strong within the United States, even conservatives perceive that defending Japanese American internment to argue for Muslim registration or racial profiling is an unwise public relations tactic.[23]

On the other hand, it would be wrong to assume that remembering Japanese Americans' wartime experiences would prevent similar civil liberties restrictions or prejudice-driven civil rights violations from happening now or in the future. On June 26, 2018, in *Trump v. Hawaii*, the Supreme Court reversed the lower court's preliminary injunction that had halted the Muslim travel ban introduced by President Trump's executive order. In a 5–4 split decision, the majority opinion upheld the travel ban as within the president's executive power. Justice Sonia Sotomayor, joined by Justice Ruth Bader Ginsburg in her dissenting opinion, quoted numerous anti-Muslim statements by President Trump to condemn the travel ban as an anti-Muslim policy that "masquerades behind a façade of national security concerns." Sotomayor saw a parallel between *Korematsu v. United States* and *Trump v. Hawaii*, observing that in both cases, the Court deferred to the president's attack on a particular group of minorities in the name of national security at the expense of principles regarding civil liberties and equality. In response to Sotomayor's dissent, Chief Justice John Roberts, who wrote the majority opinion, repudiated *Korematsu*, labeling the decision as "gravely wrong on the day it was decided." Sotomayor objected that the majority opinion "redeploys the dangerous logic underlying *Korematsu* and merely replaces one 'gravely wrong' decision with another."[24] This court decision exemplifies the continuous pattern of how the historical memory of Japanese Americans plays the ironic role of justifying later civil liberties restrictions, even while what happened to Japanese Americans is perceived as unjust.

Since 9/11, and particularly in the Trump era, the Japanese American community continues to be active in sharing their stories with the general American public as well as in reaching out to support other minorities targeted by governmental persecution and its exclusionist supporters. Aiko Herzig-Yoshinaga, a Nisei activist who played a crucial role in the Japanese American Redress movement, believed that there was much more for her community to do as living witnesses of history. When I asked her about the Trump administration's campaign promise to round up Muslims, she replied:

> I think that it just goes to show that the government didn't learn the lesson after having done that to Japanese Americans during World War II, that nobody is paying attention to the fact that the government had to even pay Redress *okane* [monetary compensation] to people for having done that. . . . Since I was a researcher for the Commission on Wartime Relocation, it was my job to dig out as much official documents as possible to make the government apologize to the *Nihonjin* [Japanese, in this case, Japanese Americans] who were affected in the 1940s by the Executive Order 9066. I think it is up to a lot of the *Nihonjin* to speak out. Japanese people don't like to be pointed out. We grew up in an era when we were so discriminated against, you know, when I was young. Now it's a little bit better, but it's still not good enough for minorities, ethnic minorities as well as gender minorities. We still have a lot of work to do.[25]

Numerous Japanese American groups still hold vigil events to remind the nation that concentration camps exist and could expand in America. The current discussions of a Muslim registry, immigration bans, border control, racial profiling, and migrant children's incarceration have led to the reemergence of

Ernie-Jane Masako Nishii and Nancy Kyoko Oda, former child incarcerees in Tule Lake Segregation Center, dressed in judo uniforms in honor of their father, Tatsuo Inouye, at the July 5, 2014, Tule Lake Pilgrimage. (From the collection of Ernie-Jane Masako Nishii. Reprinted with permission.)

Japanese American incarceration in American public memory in even more complex ways than before.[26] This study has shown that the wartime removal and incarceration of Japanese Americans should be considered as more than an example of racial discrimination against American citizens. There is no question that racist and xenophobic paranoia affected the decision making of military and civilian administrative agencies during the months after the attack on Pearl Harbor, or that the mass removal and incarceration of citizens and aliens of Japanese ancestry had an element of "ethnic cleansing," a total removal of a targeted ethnic group for social, economic, and political purposes rather than military necessity or emergency measures.[27] However, this study also shows that Japanese American internment offered an important precedent as a national and internal security measure, particularly in times of war and other emergency situations.

When we see the connections between the mass incarceration of Japanese Americans, the McCarthyite prosecutions, and antisubversive executive measures against domestic dissidents, we start to notice how the boundaries of American citizenship are manipulated through legal and extralegal violence. The genealogy of the Emergency Detention Act demonstrates that exclusion and incarceration based on one category of citizenship can transform to encompass others. In 1942, the government allowed the detention of American citizens in concentration camps by branding Japanese American Nisei as "enemy non-aliens" and placing them outside the discursive national boundary on the basis of race. The Supreme Court, in order to uphold the government's wartime policy, applied the discourse of loyalty instead of race to justify treating Japanese Americans differently from other American citizens. Ironically, this rhetorical manipulation opened an avenue for the government to use disloyalty as a legitimate reason to incarcerate any citizen in detention camps during the Cold War period. The passage of the Emergency Detention Act confirmed this executive power. Title II authorized the government to brand virtually anybody as a potentially disloyal citizen and "track 'em down, round 'em up, put them away."[28]

The judicial affirmation of the mass exclusion of Japanese Americans during World War II weakened the constitutional protection of *all* citizens' rights. However, the relationship between Japanese American incarceration and Title II was more complex than some past studies have assumed. Political ideology (e.g., communism), did not simply replace race as the standard for exclusion or detention. The rise and fall of the concentration camp law shows that it was the tensions and negotiations between racism and antiracism, liberalism and anti–civil rights conservatism, and cultural pluralism and xenophobic nationalism that paved the winding road for the history of American civil liberties and internal security. The wartime removal and incarceration of Japanese Americans, therefore, should be treated not as an experience peculiar to one ethnic group but as a significant part of American history as a whole.

Chronicling the making and unmaking of the Emergency Detention Act, particularly in relation to Japanese American incarceration, illustrates that assuming a clear line between citizens and aliens is not necessarily helpful in assessing whether or not restricting the civil liberties of an individual or group is justifiable. The internment of Japanese Americans was unjust not only because the majority of the internees were U.S. citizens. It was unjust not only because most—some might say all—Japanese Americans were loyal to the United States. The source of the injustice lies in how the very fluidity of these terms—citizenship and loyalty—gives the government or the dominant sector of society the power to draw a line and determine whose constitutional rights should be respected and whose will be excluded from such protection. Without insight about the performative function of these fluid terms in marking the discursive borders of nationality, we would be able to see in hindsight only the injustice done to one group or another. Without such insight, we would fail to recognize and problematize the exclusion, incarceration, and detention happening to the "others" today, even as we review the history of American concentration camps in a critical manner.

Acknowledgments

This project started as my doctoral dissertation research, which I completed and submitted to Doshisha University in 2004 with the title "Japanese American Internment and the Emergency Detention Act (Title II of the Internal Security Act of 1950), 1941–1971: Balancing Internal Security and Civil Liberties in the United States." The world seems to have grown much more volatile since I started my doctoral study in the late 1990s. Even the 9/11 terrorist attacks feel like an occurrence from another time. The political and moral polarization between those who defend civil liberties and those who prioritize national and internal security seems to intensify around the world year after year. We are facing the same dilemma that the protagonists of the story in this book faced. When I started this project, I intended to write about the past. I wish it had remained so.

I am grateful to the members of my doctoral dissertation committee and to those who helped expand and strengthen the project after the completion of my dissertation, particularly through theoretical elaborations on the notions of racism and racialization. Professor Taisuke Kamata, my doctoral supervisor, always inspired me with the humanitarianism he brought to his legal research. Professor Barbara B. Zikmund's constant encouragement enabled me to persevere as I approached the final hurdles of the dissertation program. Professor Ryo Yoshida helped me develop my argument from the perspective of Japanese American history. In the Graduate School of American Studies, Professor Masahiro Hosoya taught me the joy of being a historian and the importance of rigorous archival work in historical research. Professor Takashi Sasaki led me into the discipline of American studies.

I am indebted to many professors and mentors outside Doshisha University for their help over the course of my academic training and my pursuit of historical research in American studies and Asian American studies. For their interest in, comments on, and warm encouragement of my work during and after the completion of my doctoral dissertation, I especially thank Professors Lorraine Bannai, Gavin J. Campbell, Roger Daniels, Taylor E. Dark III, Ruth Wilson Gilmore, Brian M. Hayashi, Yuji Ichioka, Lon Kurashige, Yoko Murakawa, Brian Niiya, Gail M. Nomura, Gary Y. Okihiro, Greg Robinson, David R. Roediger, Patricia E. Roy, Toshiji Sasaki, David W. Stowe, Stephen Sumida, Alan Trachtenberg, K. Scott Wong, Akihiro Yamakura, Eric K. Yamamoto, David K. Yoo, and Henry Yu.

Collecting historical materials constituted most of the research portion of this project. I am grateful to numerous librarians and archivists at the U.S. National Archives; the Library of Congress; Harry S. Truman Library; Herbert H. Lehman Suite and Papers at Columbia University; Seeley G. Mudd Manuscript Library at Princeton University; Bancroft Library at the University of California, Berkeley; and the Department of Special Collections at the University of California, Los Angeles. I also thank librarians at the Manuscript Library at the University of Victoria, the Special Collections Library at the University of Arizona, the Center for Pacific and American Studies Library at the University of Tokyo, and various libraries at Doshisha University.

In the course of my research, I have received a number of scholarships and grants. The Government of Canada Awards allowed me to stay in Canada to complete part of my doctoral research. A grant from the Graduate School of American Studies at Doshisha University enabled me to acquire microfilm from Bancroft Library. Travel grants from Doshisha University funded numerous trips to the United States to complete archival work. I am also grateful to my colleagues at Doshisha University for generously approving my one-year leave from teaching as a Fulbright Scholar between the summers of 2004 and 2005. A Grant-in-Aid for Scientific Research (C 24520847) from the Japan Society for the Promotion of Science helped fund my research on Japanese American incarceration between 2012 and 2015.

Portions of this book previously appeared in academic journals: Part of Chapter 1 and the main body of Chapter 2, which lay out the overall thesis of the book, originally appeared as Masumi Izumi, "Alienable Citizenship: Race, Loyalty and the Law in the Age of 'American Concentration Camps,' 1941–1971," *Asian American Law Journal* 13, no. 1 (2006): 1–30, and are reprinted here by permission of the Regents of the University of California (© 2006 by the Regents of the University of California). Portions of Chapter

4 originally appeared as Masumi Izumi, "Rumors of 'American Concentration Camps': The Emergency Detention Act and the Public Fear of Political Repression, 1966–1971," *Doshisha Studies in Language and Culture* 4 (2002): 737–765. Portions of Chapters 4 and 5 are based on Masumi Izumi, "Prohibiting 'American Concentration Camps': Repeal of the Emergency Detention Act and the Public Historical Memory of the Japanese American Internment," *Pacific Historical Review* 74, no. 2 (2005): 165–194. I am grateful to the anonymous reviewers who provided insightful comments on each of these essays.

Friends and colleagues helped me endure this long journey. I especially acknowledge Fumiko Sakashita, Yusuke Torii, and Wuming Zhao for inspiring me through their exciting work and shared interests in cultural history and cultural studies in the field of American studies. I also owe a great deal of my intellectual development to my dear friends in the History of Racialization Group (HORG) at the University of Victoria. In particular, I thank Mrinalini Greedharry and Pasi Ahonen for founding HORG, which exposed me to critical theories on race and racialization, and Cameron Duder, Meharoona Ghani, and Susan Johnston for providing the warm friendship that I will always treasure. During my professional career, I have come to know many colleagues in the fields of North American history, American studies, and Asian American studies. Although they are simply too many to list here, I hope to thank each one in person when we meet at various conferences and gatherings.

For making the publication of this book come true, I thank Cathy J. Schlund-Vials, Shelley Sang-Hee Lee, and the anonymous manuscript reviewers. Temple University Press editor Sara Jo Cohen has been a tremendous help in guiding me through the long and rigorous process of academic publishing in the United States. I also want to thank Joan S. Vidal and Rose Elfman for their extremely careful copyediting of my manuscript.

Numerous Nikkei elders are the source of my inspiration, and their activism has always driven me to write about Nikkei North American history. I especially acknowledge Aiko Herzig-Yoshinaga, Gordon Hirabayashi, PJ and Roy Hirabayashi, Yuri Kochiyama, the Reverend Masao Kodani, Nobuko Miyamoto, Ernie-Jane Masako Nishii, Nancy Kyoko Oda, Midge Ayukawa, Gordon Kadota, Joy Kogawa, Mayumi Takasaki, Grace Eiko Thomson, and Tamio Wakayama. This is an abbreviated list of people I interviewed, corresponded with, and spent precious time with on my various research projects, and, sadly, some of them have since left us. Soft-spoken, gracious, and physically small by North American standards, to me they are giants who left the great legacy of making our world a better place than the one they were born into. Thinking of them, I have to ask myself, "Are we following their examples to leave a better world for posterity?" I am not sure. We have a lot of work to do.

Finally, I thank my family, Hitoshi and Mana Kamada, for supporting me and bearing with me all these years. They know that when Mom declares that she is "in the mood for writing," some things around the house do not get done. I also acknowledge two people who have shaped how I see the world and world history: Teiko Onda, my maternal grandmother, whose personal stories of loss and survival in and beyond wartime Japan filled the house from the time that I was born, and Dr. Shinzo Izumi, my father, who has taught me that when we see injustice, we must stand up and speak out. My father's own work and actions have demonstrated that we must dedicate ourselves to the kind of deep thinking that leads to the facts and truths that sustain a commitment to social justice.

The world is volatile, but the one thing that I learned through studying the strange trajectory of American concentration camp law is that times change and the pendulum of history swings. Although it may feel like we are swinging away from freedom and the celebration of diversity, every day brings an opportunity to make a difference.

Notes

A NOTE ON TERMINOLOGY

1. As early as 1979, when Senator Daniel K. Inouye proposed the establishment of the Commission on Wartime Relocation and Internment of Civilians (CWRIC), Roger Daniels suggested the need to correct the euphemistic terms currently in use. Roger Daniels, "Words Do Matter: A Note on Inappropriate Terminology and the Incarceration of the Japanese Americans," in *Nikkei in the Pacific Northwest: Japanese Americans and Japanese Canadians in the Twentieth Century,* ed. Louis Fiset and Gail M. Nomura (Seattle: University of Washington Press, 2005), 190–214.

2. National JACL (Japanese American Citizens League) Power of Words II Committee, *Power of Words Handbook: A Guide to Language about Japanese Americans in World War II* (San Francisco: Japanese American Citizens League, 2013), 11, 13, https://jacl.org/wordpress/wp-content/uploads/2015/08/Power-of-Words-Rev.-Term.-Handbook.pdf, accessed September 12, 2018.

3. *Hirabayashi v. United States,* 320 U.S. 81 (1943); *Korematsu v. United States,* 323 U.S. 214 (1944).

INTRODUCTION

1. HR234 was enacted as Public Law 92-128, 85 Stat. 347 (1971). The law is also called the Non-Detention Act, as it contains a provision that reads, "No citizen shall be imprisoned or otherwise detained by the United States except pursuant to an Act of Congress." The law repealed by HR234 was the Emergency Detention Act, 64 Stat. 1019 (1950), which was Title II of the Internal Security Act, 64 Stat. 987 (1950).

2. Richard M. Nixon, "Statement on Signing Bill Repealing the Emergency Detention Act of 1950, September 25, 1971," in *Public Papers of the Presidents of the United States, Richard M. Nixon, 1971* (Washington, D.C.: U.S. Government Printing Office, 1972), 986.

3. The act reads:

Sec. 102. (a) In the event of any one of the following:

(1) Invasion of the territory of the United States or its possessions,
(2) Declaration of war by Congress, or
(3) Insurrection within the United States in aid of a foreign enemy, . . . the President is authorized to make public proclamation of the existence of an "Internal Security Emergency."

Sec. 103 (a) Whenever there shall be in existence such an emergency, the President, acting through the Attorney General, is hereby authorized to apprehend and by order detain, pursuant to the provisions of this title, each person as to whom there is reasonable ground to believe that such person *probably* will engage in, or *probably* will conspire with others to engage in, acts of espionage and sabotage. (Internal Security Act, emphasis added)

4. Nixon, "Statement," 986.

5. There are people who refer to the construction of reservations for Native Americans and the disproportionate rate of incarceration of African Americans in prisons as other examples of American concentration camps. Such arguments have validity, but these topics, while certainly important, are outside the scope of this study because they are more an issue of peacetime social control than of preventive detention as a national security measure. For the same reason, preventive detention for mentally challenged people and those who have past criminal records is not discussed in this book.

6. Allan Wesley Austin, "Loyalty and Concentration Camps in America: The Japanese American Precedent and the Internal Security Act of 1950," in *Last Witnesses: Reflections on the Wartime Internment of Japanese Americans*, ed. Erica Harth (New York: Palgrave, 2001), 253–270; Raymond Y. Okamura, Robert Takasugi, Hiroshi Kanno, and Edison Uno, "Campaign to Repeal the Emergency Detention Act," *Amerasia Journal* 2 (Fall 1974): 70–111; Masumi Izumi, "Rumors of 'American Concentration Camps': The Emergency Detention Act and the Public Fear of Political Repression, 1966–1971," *Doshisha Studies in Language and Culture* 4, no. 4 (2002): 737–765; Masumi Izumi, "Prohibiting 'American Concentration Camps': Repeal of the Emergency Detention Act and the Public Historical Memory of the Japanese American Internment," *Pacific Historical Review* 74, no. 2 (2005): 165–193; Masumi Izumi, "Alienable Citizenship: Race, Loyalty, and the Law in the Age of 'American Concentration Camps,' 1941–1971," *Asian American Law Journal* 13 (November 2006): 1–30.

7. Allan Austin describes the connection between Title II and Japanese American incarceration as follows: "Ideology simply replaced 'race' as the basis for determining group disloyalty." Austin, "Loyalty and Concentration Camps in America," 264.

8. Mary L. Dudziak, *Cold War Civil Rights: Race and the Image of American Democracy* (Princeton, N.J.: Princeton University Press, 2000).

9. Ellen D. Wu, *The Color of Success: Asian Americans and the Origins of the Model Minority* (Princeton, N.J.: Princeton University Press, 2014); Cindy I-fen Cheng, *Citizens of Asian America: Democracy and Race during the Cold War* (New York: New York University Press, 2014).

10. Jeff Woods, *Black Struggle, Red Scare: Segregation and Anti-Communism in the South, 1948–1968* (Baton Rouge: Louisiana State University Press, 2004).

11. Teun A. Van Dijk, "Discourse, Power and Access," in *Texts and Practices: Read-

ings in Critical Discourse Analysis, ed. C. R. Caldas-Coulthard and M. Coulthard (London: Routledge, 1996), 84–106.

12. For details on the Tule Lake Segregation Center and the Citizenship Renunciation Program, see Barbara Takei, "Legalizing Detention: Segregated Japanese Americans and the Justice Department's Renunciation Program," *Journal of the Shaw Historical Library* 19 (2005): 75–105.

13. Eric Schmitt, "U.S. Reroutes Warships toward Korean Peninsula in Show of Force," *New York Times*, April 9, 2017; Gerry Mullany, "Trump Warns that 'Major, Major Conflict' with North Korea Is Possible," *New York Times,* April 27, 2017.

14. Michael S. Sherry, *In the Shadow of War: The United States since the 1930s* (New Haven, Conn.: Yale University Press, 1995).

CHAPTER 1

1. *Newsweek,* December 8, 1941, 51.

2. Michael S. Sherry, *In the Shadow of War: The United States since the 1930s* (New Haven, Conn.: Yale University Press, 1995), fig. 2.

3. *Newsweek,* December 8, 1941, 12.

4. Ibid., 12 (Fleishmann's Enriched Hi-B$_1$), 34 (Coca-Cola), 42 (Bristol Instruments), 51 (Keasbey and Mattison), and 69 (Pacific Mutual Life).

5. Sherry, *In the Shadow of War*, xi.

6. Ibid., x.

7. Ibid., 30.

8. Ibid., 48.

9. Francis MacDonnell, *Insidious Foes: The Axis Fifth Column and the American Home Front* (New York: Oxford University Press, 1995). According to Richard Fried, the term "fifth column" was coined during the Spanish Civil War: "One of Franco's generals was asked which of his four columns advancing on Madrid would take the city; none of them, he replied, but rather the fifth column already inside the gates." Richard M. Fried, *Nightmare in Red: The McCarthy Era in Perspective* (New York: Oxford University Press, 1990), 49.

10. FDR's words quoted in Sherry, *In the Shadow of War*, 33.

11. Ibid., 65.

12. This image of a cunning enemy was attached most often to the Japanese. See John W. Dower, *War without Mercy: Race and Power in the Pacific War* (New York: Pantheon Books, 1986).

13. Brian M. Hayashi, *Democratizing the Enemy: The Japanese American Internment* (Princeton, N.J.: Princeton University Press, 2008), 79–81. Hayashi continues to search declassified military records and other historical and biographical sources on individuals who worked transnationally within or around the American military. He endeavors to contextualize the army's decisions within the wider theater of operations in World War II.

14. Roger W. Lotchin, *Japanese American Relocation in World War II: A Reconsideration* (Cambridge: Cambridge University Press, 2018).

15. Ibid., 54, 203–206. Lotchin has looked extensively at primary sources such as the government reports and camp newspapers as well as the oral history of the former camp residents. However, unlike Hayashi, who examines sources other scholars have

neglected, Lotchin, although sympathetic to Japanese Americans, simply reiterates many of the claims that defenders of the internment policy have conventionally made. His publication, thus, adds little to the factual knowledge about Japanese American removal and incarceration already shared by many scholars.

16. Akihiro Yamakura, *Shimin-teki Jiyu: Amerika Nikkeijin Senji Kyouseishuyo no Rigaru Histori (Civil Liberties: A Legal History of the Wartime Incarceration of the People of Japanese Ancestry in America)* (Tokyo: Sairyu-sha, 2011), 78–79.

17. The War Relocation Authority (WRA) was the federal civilian agency established in February 1942 to care for the Japanese American population excluded from a zone extending one hundred miles from the Pacific Coast. Inland, outside the defense zone, the WRA built ten camps euphemistically called "relocation centers," while the U.S. Army temporarily confined Japanese Americans in the "assembly centers" located in racetracks and fairgrounds within the defense zone. An overwhelming majority among the removed Japanese Americans were confined in the WRA camps during World War II. Many of the Issei men who were picked up by the FBI before the issuance of Executive Order 9066 and some who were deemed dangerous in the WRA camps were locked up in Justice Department detention centers or POW camps. Even though Japanese Americans residing in Hawaii were not interned en masse, the entire territory of Hawaii was controlled under martial law. The government of Peru deported its Japanese residents to the United States in response to President Franklin Roosevelt's request, as the United States considered that it might need more Japanese citizens for its hostage exchange with Japan.

18. Izumi Hirobe, *Japanese Pride, American Prejudice: Modifying the Exclusion Clause of the 1924 Immigration Act* (Stanford, Calif.: Stanford University Press, 2002); Lon Kurashige, *Two Faces of Exclusion: The Untold History of Anti-Asian Racism in the United States* (Chapel Hill: University of North Carolina Press, 2016).

19. To write the brief summary of the balance between civil liberties and internal security, I primarily referred to Alfred H. Kelly, Winfred A. Harbison, and Herman Belz, *The American Constitution: Its Origins and Development*, 7th ed. (New York: W. W. Norton, 1991).

20. Constitution of the United States of America, Article III, Section 3.

21. *Ex Parte Milligan*, 71 U.S. 2, 127 (1866).

22. Kelly, Harbison, and Belz, *The American Constitution*, 511.

23. Ibid., 512.

24. *Schenck v. United States*, 249 U.S. 470 (1919).

25. *Abrams v. United States*, 250 U.S. 616 (1919).

26. The Bureau of Investigation was renamed the Federal Bureau of Investigation (FBI) in 1935.

27. The most notorious case of mass deportation happened in 1919, when 249 political radicals and other aliens were shipped from New York to Hanko, Finland, and then to the Soviet Union. Emma Goldman, a well-known anarchist leader, claimed to have American citizenship but was deported along with the other 248 on the USAT Buford, which was nicknamed the "Soviet Ark."

28. *Gitlow v. New York*, 268 U.S. 652 (1925).

29. For the comprehensive history of anticommunism in the United States, see M. J. Heale, *American Anticommunism: Combating the Enemy Within, 1830–1970* (Baltimore: Johns Hopkins University Press, 1990).

30. Some examples of studies of immigrant radicalism are Marcella Bencivenni, *Italian Immigrant Radical Culture: The Idealism of the Sovversivi in the United States, 1890–1940* (New York: New York University Press, 2011); Tony Michels, *Jewish Radicals: A Documentary History* (New York: New York University Press, 2012); and Seema Sohi, *Echoes of Mutiny: Race, Surveillance, and Indian Anticolonialism in North America* (Oxford: Oxford University Press, 2014).

31. Norman M. Naimark, *Fires of Hatred: Ethnic Cleansing in Twentieth-Century Europe* (Cambridge, Mass.: Harvard University Press, 2002).

32. Ibid., 27–38. The Turkish government has been denying that the decimation of the Armenian population in the Ottoman Empire was a result of a systematic genocide, claiming that the removal was a necessary wartime measure and that the loss of lives was caused by wartime chaos and confusion.

33. Commission on Wartime Relocation and Internment of Civilians (CWRIC), *Personal Justice Denied: Report of the Commission on Wartime Relocation and Internment of Civilians* (Seattle: University of Washington Press, 1997), 54.

34. Greg Robinson, *A Tragedy of Democracy: Japanese Confinement in North America* (New York: Columbia University Press, 2009), 34.

35. Confidential Memorandum from the President to Department Heads, June 26, 1939, quoted in U.S. Senate, Select Committee to Study Governmental Operations with Respect to Intelligence Activities (Church Committee), Senate Report no. 94-755, 94th Congress, 2nd session, Book 2, *Intelligence Activities and the Rights of Americans*, April 26, 1976 (hereafter Church, Book 2), 27.

36. CWRIC, *Personal Justice Denied*, 54.

37. Robinson, *A Tragedy of Democracy*, 55.

38. MacDonnell, *Insidious Foes*, 85.

39. Ibid. Also see Michi Nishiura Weglyn, *Years of Infamy: The Untold Story of America's Concentration Camps*, updated ed. (Seattle: University of Washington Press, 1996), chap. 1.

40. The number of Japanese arrested by the FBI varies between different authors. Frank Chuman writes that the number of enemy aliens arrested within a week on the West Coast was 831, including 595 Japanese and 187 Germans. Frank F. Chuman, *The Bamboo People: The Law and Japanese Americans* (Del Mar, Calif.: Publisher's, 1976), 154. Peter Irons writes that 736 Japanese aliens were picked up by the FBI and military agents. Within four days, he insists, the number of Japanese arrested increased to 1,370. Peter Irons, *Justice at War: The Story of the Japanese American Internment Cases* (Berkeley: University of California Press, 1983), 19.

41. In the late 1930s, some Japanese American organizations worked to explain Japanese overseas military actions in East Asia and appease the American public as sentiment against Japan was growing increasingly critical. Social as well as religious organizations collected monetary donations, clothing, and other materials to send to Japan. These immigrant activities helping the homeland in the prewar period were considered after Pearl Harbor to be evidence for the community's approval of Japanese militarism and disloyalty to the United States. Brian M. Hayashi, *For the Sake of Our Japanese Brethren: Assimilation, Nationalism and Protestantism among the Japanese of Los Angeles, 1895–1942* (Stanford, Calif.: Stanford University Press, 1995); Eiichiro Azuma, *Between Two Empires: Race, History and Transnationalism in Japanese America* (New York: Oxford University Press, 2005); Yuji Ichioka, *Before Internment: Essays in Prewar*

Japanese American History, ed. Gordon H. Chang and Eiichiro Azuma (Stanford, Calif.: Stanford University Press, 2006).

42. The Tuna Canyon Detention Station Coalition was formed around 2013 to memorialize the detention station and gather historical materials related to the facility and those detained in it. In 2013, the City of Los Angeles designated the site as Historic Cultural Monument #1039. See http://www.tunacanyon.org/, accessed September 12, 2018.

43. Presidential Proclamation No. 2525.

44. James C. McNaughton, "Japanese Americans and the U.S. Army," *Army History* 99 (Summer/Fall 2003): 11.

45. CWRIC, *Personal Justice Denied*, 62; Irons, *Justice at War*, 32–36.

46. Lotchin, *Japanese American Relocation in World War II*, chap. 6.

47. Klancy Clark de Nevers studied Karl Bendetsen and illuminated his role in the military's decision to push for the mass removal of Japanese Americans. Klancy Clark de Nevers, *The Colonel and the Pacifist: Karl Bendetsen, Perry Saito, and the Incarceration of Japanese Americans during World War II* (Salt Lake City: University of Utah Press, 2004). The fact that Caucasian agricultural and business groups and chambers of commerce, as well as nativist pressure groups such as the Native Sons and Daughters of the Golden West and the California Department of the American Legion, demanded the total removal of the Japanese and Japanese American population indicates that the public demand for the removal of Japanese Americans was the result of an organized political agitation rather than an impulsive reaction caused by a panic or wartime hysteria induced by the shocking military attack on American territory. Morton Grodzins, *Americans Betrayed: Politics of the Japanese Evacuation* (Chicago: University of Chicago Press, 1949), appendix 1, "The California Press," 377–399; Also see Lloyd Chiasson, "Japanese-American Relocation during World War II: A Study of California Editorial Reactions," *Journalism Quarterly* 68 (Spring/Summer 1991): 263–268. Takeya Mizuno studied the civil libertarian press, including the *New Republic, The Nation,* and *The Crisis,* and found that they tried to balance national security and civil liberties. As a result, they failed to criticize the military decision to exclude Japanese Americans but did become vocal in demanding fair treatment for the internees. Takeya Mizuno, "The Civil Libertarian Press, Japanese American Press, and Japanese American Mass Evacuation" (Ph.D. diss., University of Missouri–Columbia, 2000). In 1982, the bipartisan Congressional Commission that investigated the wartime relocation and incarceration of Japanese American and Aleut civilians concluded that the policy was the result of "race prejudice, war hysteria and a failure of political leadership." CWRIC, *Personal Justice Denied*, 459.

48. Chuman, *The Bamboo People*, 151; Grodzins, *Americans Betrayed*, 98–99. Mike Masaoka, a long-term Washington lobbyist representing the Japanese American Citizens League, contended that "probably more than any single person . . . Earl Warren influenced the Executive decision to authorize and carry out the mass military evacuation and exclusion of all persons of Japanese origin" from the West Coast "without trial or hearing of any kind." Mike M. Masaoka, "Introduction: Some Recollections of, and Reflections on, 1942," *Earl Warren Oral History Project, Japanese American Relocation Reviewed: Volume I, Decision and Exodus,* dir. Amelia R. Fry (Calisphere, University of California, 1976), http://texts.cdlib.org/view?docId=ft667nb2x8&doc.view=entire_text, accessed September 12, 2018.

49. Volumes of studies address the historical anxiety and distrust held by Caucasians toward Asians in America. John Kuo Wei Tchen and Dylan Yates collected writings and images of Asians as the "Yellow Peril," illustrating long-standing racial stereotypes pervasive in Western culture. John Kuo Wei Tchen and Dylan Yates, *Yellow Peril! An Archive of Anti-Asian Fear* (New York: Penguin Random House, 2014). Gary Okihiro has pointed out that the relationship between the positive image of Asians as a "model minority" and the negative image as the "Yellow Peril" is not one of opposition; rather, together they "form a circular relationship that moves in either direction." Gary Y. Okihiro, *Margins and Mainstreams: Asians in American History and Culture* (Seattle; University of Washington Press, 1994), 50–51.

50. Japan-based historian Yoko Murakawa discovered some documents at the U.S. National Archives that illuminated how lower-level Justice Department bureaucrats discussed ways to make it possible for the government to "denaturalize" American citizens of Japanese ancestry, modeling such procedures after those employed for American citizens of German ancestry who had used fraudulent information to become naturalized. Yoko Murakawa, *Kyokaisenjo no Shiminken: Nichibei Senso to Nikkei Amerikajin* [Citizenship on the border: The Japanese Americans during the U.S.-Japanese war] (Tokyo: Ochanomizu Shobo, 2007), 160. Murakawa states that it was unclear whether Attorney General Biddle or other officials such as Edward Ennis and Assistant Attorney General James Rowe knew about such actions, but this shows that one needs to be wary of painting the Justice Department as respectful of the constitutional and civil rights of Japanese Americans during World War II.

51. Grodzins, *Americans Betrayed*, 242–243.

52. Quoted in Irons, *Justice at War,* 54; Grodzins, *Americans Betrayed*, 257.

53. Greg Robinson, *By Order of the President: FDR and the Internment of Japanese Americans* (Cambridge, Mass: Harvard University Press, 2001), 106.

54. Ibid., 106.

55. Ibid., 110. Eric Muller states that in fact General Clark recommended that the designation of the Pacific Coast as the "theater of operations" be rescinded. Eric L. Muller, "Hirabayashi and the Invasion Evasion," *North Carolina Law Review* 88, no. 4 (2010): 1362–1363.

56. Quoted in CWRIC, *Personal Justice Denied*, 82.

57. Executive Order 9066, Authorizing the Secretary of War to Prescribe Military Areas, February 19, 1942.

58. Hayashi, *Democratizing the Enemy*, 79–81.

59. David Campbell, *Writing Security: United States Foreign Policy and the Politics of Identity* (Minneapolis: University of Minnesota Press, 1998), 68.

60. Ibid., 9.

61. U.S. House of Representatives, Select Committee Investigating National Defense Migration, House of Representatives Report no. 1911, *Report of the Select Committee Investigating National Defense Migration,* 77th Congress, 2nd session, February 21 and 23, 1942, 11011.

62. As this chapter focuses on the policy-making process, it discusses the opinions of only those who participated in the decision making. It should be noted, however, that opposition did exist in the liberal and leftist communities. For example, *The Nation* and the *New Republic* published articles opposing mass removal and incarceration in February and March 1942. See Robert Shaffer, "Cracks in the Consensus: Defend-

ing the Rights of Japanese Americans during World War II," *Radical History Review* 72 (Fall 1998): 86–100.

63. Public Law 503, 56 Stat. 173 (1942).
64. Grodzins, *Americans Betrayed*, 328.
65. *Congressional Record,* February 12, 1942.
66. *Congressional Record,* March 19, 1942, 2722–2726.
67. Quoted in Grodzins, *Americans Betrayed*, 344.
68. *Hirabayashi v. United States,* 320 U.S. 81 (1943); *Yasui v. United States,* 320 U.S. 115 (1943); *Korematsu v. United States,* 323 U.S. 214 (1944).
69. *Ex Parte Endo,* 323 U.S. 283 (1944).
70. *Yasui v. United States* (1943) was a companion case to *Hirabayashi v. United States* (1943).
71. Irons, *Justice at War*; Eric K. Yamamoto, Margaret Chon, Carol L. Izumi, Jerry Kang, and Frank H. Wu, *Race, Rights and Reparation: Law and the Japanese American Internment* (New York: Aspen Law and Business, 2001; 2nd ed., 2013).
72. The ACLU initially criticized President Roosevelt for issuing Executive Order 9066, and its lawyers defended Gordon Hirabayashi and Fred Korematsu in the test cases regarding the constitutionality of the military order against Japanese Americans. However, the ACLU National Committee board resolved to accept the president's order in principle while urging that the actions taken under the order "should be based on a classification, having a reasonable relationship to the danger intended to be met." Samuel Walker, *In Defense of American Liberties: A History of the ACLU,* 2nd ed. (Carbondale: Southern Illinois University Press, 1999), 137–142.
73. Quoted in Irons, *Justice at War,* 88.
74. The court decisions are made in the majority rule. When the judges agree with the final decision, they simply join the majority opinion. If any judge agrees with the decision but has different reasons for or reservations about the final decision, he or she writes a concurring opinion.
75. *Hirabayashi v. United States,* 89.
76. Irons, *Justice at War,* 223. During World War II, martial law was placed on the Territory of Hawaii. In *Duncan v. Kahanamoku,* 327 U.S. 304 (1946), the Supreme Court ordered the military tribunals to vacate the convictions of two civilians, both white. The relationship between Japanese American cases and this trial is discussed in detail in Robinson, *A Tragedy of Democracy,* 235–244.
77. Quoted in Irons, *Justice at War,* 225.
78. *Hirabayashi v. United States,* 93.
79. *Yick Wo v. Hopkins,* 118 U.S. 356 (1886).
80. *Schneider v. State (Town of Irvington),* 308 U.S. 147 (1939).
81. U.S. Department of War, *Final Report: Japanese Evacuation from the West Coast, 1942* (Washington, D.C.: U.S. Government Printing Office, 1943; repr., New York: Arno Press, 1978), 9.
82. *Hirabayashi v. United States,* 101.
83. Ibid., 107.
84. Ibid., 111.
85. Ibid., 114.
86. Irons, *Justice at War,* 66.
87. For details of Korematsu's life, see Lorraine K. Bannai, *Enduring Conviction:*

Fred Korematsu and His Quest for Justice (Seattle: University of Washington Press, 2015).

88. Irons, *Justice at War,* 153–154.
89. *Korematsu v. United States,* 218.
90. Ibid., 216.
91. Yamamoto et al., *Race, Rights and Reparation,* 277–380. For the role of Aiko Herzig-Yoshinaga in the Redress movement, see Thomas Y. Fujita-Rony, "'Destructive Force': Aiko Herzig-Yoshinaga's Gendered Labor in the Japanese American Redress Movement," *Frontiers: A Journal of Women Studies* 24, no. 1 (2003): 38–60.
92. Yamamoto et al. reprinted the primary documents concerning the Justice Department's disagreements and the prepared footnote. Yamamoto et al., *Race, Rights and Reparation,* 290–316.
93. On the *coram nobis* cases, see Peter Irons, ed., *Justice Delayed: The Record of the Japanese American Internment Cases* (Middletown, Conn.: Wesleyan University Press, 1989). Legal as well as personal accounts on the *coram nobis* cases are recorded in Bannai, *Enduring Conviction,* chaps. 9 and 10.
94. Jacobus tenBroek, Edward N. Barnhart, and Floyd W. Matson, *Prejudice, War and the Constitution: Cases and Consequences of the Evacuation of the Japanese Americans in World War II* (1954; repr., Berkeley: University of California Press, 1975), 333–334. In *Trump v. Hawaii,* 138 S. Ct. 2392 (2018), Chief Justice John Roberts repudiated the Korematsu decision, saying that "it was gravely wrong the day it was decided."
95. Bannai, *Enduring Conviction,* 87.
96. *Korematsu v. United States,* 221.
97. Ibid., 223.
98. For more details about conflicts among the Supreme Court justices, see Irons, *Justice at War,* chap. 12.
99. *Korematsu v. United States,* 225–226.
100. Ibid., 233.
101. Ibid., 248.
102. The court, in principle, must decide its opinion in light of the situation at the time when the original incident occurred. Reversing the conviction, therefore, without invalidating the military order would have been difficult.
103. tenBroek, Barnhart, and Matson, *Prejudice, War and the Constitution,* 259. Jacobs tenBroek, Edward N. Barnhart, and Floyd W. Matson criticize the Supreme Court's judgment in the Japanese American cases as "one of the great failures in its history—comparable with its surrender to slavery in *Prigg v. Pennsylvania* and in *Dred Scott v. Sandford*." tenBroek, Barnhart, and Matson, *Prejudice, War and the Constitution,* 333–334.
104. *Hirabayashi v. United States,* 107.
105. Etienne Balibar, "Is There a 'Neo-racism'?" in *Nation, Race, Class: Ambiguous Identities,* ed. Etienne Balibar and Immanuel Wallerstein (London: Verso, 1991), 21. Robert Chang discusses differential racialization in his historical analysis of American immigration laws. Robert Chang, *Disoriented: Asian Americans, Law, and the Nation-State* (New York: New York University Press, 1999), 29–30.
106. Muller, "Hirabayashi," 1376.
107. Ibid., 1373–1384.
108. Ibid., 1380–1381.

109. Lotchin, *Japanese American Relocation in World War II*, 95.
110. Yamamoto et al., *Race, Rights and Reparation*, 7.
111. Jerry Kang, "Denying Prejudice: Internment, Redress, and Denial," *UCLA Law Review* 51 (2004), 994.
112. Irons, *Justice at War*, 102.
113. Wu, *The Color of Success*, 6–7.
114. Ibid., 4.
115. Ibid., 8.
116. Ibid., 80.
117. *Ex Parte Endo*, 291.
118. Ibid., 310,
119. Ibid., 300.
120. Chuman, *The Bamboo People*, 175. Also see Wu, *The Color of Success*, 78–91.
121. Chuman, *The Bamboo People*, 179.
122. Wu, *The Color of Success*, 81.
123. Ibid., 81–88.
124. Greg Robinson, *After Camp: Portraits in Midcentury Japanese American Life and Politics* (Los Angeles: University of California Press, 2012).
125. Murakawa, *Kyokaisenjo no Shiminken*, 213–215. Some of the renunciants indeed wished to be shipped to Japan, but others signed the renunciation request to avoid being forced to move to another camp or out into the mainstream society. Many of them were weary of relocation or had reasons, such as having a sick family member, that made it difficult for them to move.
126. John Howard, *Concentration Camps on the Home Front: Japanese Americans in the House of Jim Crow* (Chicago: University of Chicago Press, 2008), 235–236. I studied the WRA's agricultural reports and revealed how Japanese American Issei conducted successful farming operations within some of the camps. Masumi Izumi, "Gila River Concentration Camp and the Historical Memory of Japanese American Mass Incarceration," *Japanese Journal of American Studies* 29 (2018): 45–65.
127. The attempt to portray Japanese American internees as loyal Americans was already seen in the photographs taken in the WRA camps by some renowned photographers. See Ansel Adams, Archie Miyatake, and William H. Michael, *Born Free and Equal: The Story of Loyal Japanese Americans* (Bishop, Calif.: Spotted Dog Press, 2002); Linda Gordon and Gary Okihiro, eds., *Impounded: Dorothea Lange and the Censored Images of Japanese American Internment* (New York: W. W. Norton, 2006). On the postwar rise of racial liberalism and the emergence of the image of Asian Americans as a model minority, see Cheng, *Citizens of Asian America*.
128. Ronald Takaki, *Double Victory: A Multicultural History of America in World War II* (Boston: Little, Brown, 2001).
129. Quoted in U.S. War Relocation Authority (WRA), *People in Motion: The Postwar Adjustment of the Evacuated Japanese Americans* (Washington, D.C.: U.S. Government Printing Office, 1947; repr., New York: AMS Press, 1976), 19.
130. Ibid., 21.
131. Executive Order 9808, Establishing the President's Committee on Civil Rights, December 5, 1946.
132. President's Committee on Civil Rights, *To Secure These Rights: The Report of*

the President's Committee on Civil Rights (Washington, D.C.: U.S. Government Printing Office, 1947), 30.

133. Ibid., 31.
134. Quoted in Chuman, *The Bamboo People*, 240.
135. Ibid., 243.
136. Eugene V. Rostow, "The Japanese American Cases: A Disaster," *Yale Law Journal* 54 (1944–1945): 489–533.
137. The appropriations by the federal government to the WRA to maintain the camps between March 1942 and December 1945, including the administrative expenses to terminate the WRA program on June 30, 1946, totaled $160 million. An additional $56,482,638 was spent on the War Department to build the ten relocation centers. Still another $32,197,078 was charged by the War Department for the army personnel to guard and supervise the relocation of the Japanese Americans. Chuman, *The Bamboo People*, 237.
138. tenBroek, Barnhart, and Matson, *Prejudice, War and the Constitution*, 241.
139. Bernard Schwartz, *A Commentary on the Constitution of the United States, Part I: The Powers of Government*, vol. 2 (New York: Macmillan, 1963), 260.
140. *Ebel v. Drum*, 52 F. Supp. 189 (D. Mass. 1943); *Schueller v. Drum*, 51 F. Supp. 383 (E. D. Pa., 1943).
141. *Schueller v. Drum*.
142. Schwartz, *A Commentary*, 265.
143. *Korematsu v. United States*, 245–246.
144. Quoted in Hubert L. Dreyfus and Paul Rabinow, *Michel Foucault: Beyond Structuralism and Hermeneutics*, 2nd ed. (Chicago: University of Chicago Press, 1983), 187.

CHAPTER 2

1. Bernard Schwartz, *A Commentary on the Constitution of the United States, Part I: The Powers of Government*, vol. 2 (New York: Macmillan, 1963), 264.
2. By reviewing Supreme Court cases such as *Duncan v. Kahanamoku*, 327 U.S. 304 (1946), Bernard Schwartz concludes that the president alone may not impinge on civil liberties through preventive detention or exclusion orders, even in wartime. Schwartz, *A Commentary*, 242–244, 254–257.
3. Deirdre M. Moloney, *National Insecurities: Immigrants and U.S. Deportation Policies since 1882* (Chapel Hill: University of North Carolina Press, 2012).
4. Robin D. G. Kelley, *Hammer and Hoe: Alabama Communists during the Great Depression* (Chapel Hill: University of North Carolina Press, 1990).
5. See Jeff Woods, *Black Struggle, Red Scare: Segregation and Anti-Communism in the South, 1948–1968* (Baton Rouge: Louisiana State University Press, 2004).
6. Igor Gouzenko, the Soviet diplomat who defected to Canada in 1945, made allegations of communist atomic espionage in Canada and the United States. The Truman administration established the Atomic Energy Commission in 1947 to conduct research on atomic energy and produce nuclear weapons, but the revelations of the atomic espionage fueled opposition to civilian control of atomic energy. Gouzenko's charges, the HUAC investigation of Alger Hiss, and the trials of Julius and Ethel Rosenberg gave

conservatives in Congress grounds to believe that there were Soviet spy agents in the federal government and that the Communist Party was operating under the direction of Moscow. William K. Klingaman, *Encyclopedia of the McCarthy Era* (New York: Facts on File, 1996), 18, 160–161.

7. In fact, the connection between colonialism and racism had already been critically acknowledged by racial minorities in the United States since the early twentieth century. For example, Seema Sohi elucidates how South Asian immigrants radicalized their international colonial consciousness as they fought racial exclusion and oppression within the United States. See Seema Sohi, *Echoes of Mutiny: Race, Surveillance, and Indian Anticolonialism in North America* (Oxford: Oxford University Press, 2014). W.E.B. DuBois consistently considered capitalism "as a racialized, interconnected global system that continually produced inequality and difference." August Carbonella and Sharryn Kasmir, "W.E.B. DuBois's *Darkwater* and an Anticolonial, Internationalist Anthropology," *Dialectical Anthropology* 30, nos. 1/2 (2008): 113.

8. Richard M. Fried, *The Russians Are Coming! The Russians Are Coming! Pageantry and Patriotism in Cold-War America* (New York: Oxford University Press, 1998).

9. Benjamin Fordham points out that Truman needed support from conservatives to carry on with his foreign policy and thus was forced to compromise on domestic policies. Benjamin O. Fordham, *Building the Cold War Consensus: The Political Economy of U.S. National Security Policy, 1949–51* (Ann Arbor: University of Michigan Press, 1998).

10. Detailed analysis of the legislative process of the Internal Security Act is found in William Randolph Tanner, "The Passage of the Internal Security Act of 1950" (Ph.D. diss., University of Kansas, 1971). The process is summarized in William R. Tanner and Robert Griffith, "Legislative Politics of 'McCarthyism': The Internal Security Act of 1950," in *The Specter: Original Essays on the Cold War and the Origin of McCarthyism*, ed. Robert Griffith and Athan Theoharis (New York: New Viewpoints, 1974), 172–189.

11. Internal Security Act, 64 Stat. 987 (1950), sec. 103.

12. U.S. House of Representatives, Committee on Un-American Activities (HUAC), House of Representatives Report no. 2980, *Protection of the United States against Un-American and Subversive Activities,* 81st Congress, 2nd session, August 22, 1950.

13. *Congress and the Nation 1945–1964: A Review of Government Politics in the Postwar Years* (Washington, D.C.: Congressional Quarterly Service), 1653.

14. *Washington Post,* "The Gallup Poll: 77 Pct. of Voters Want Commie 'File,'" May 23, 1948.

15. Fordham, *Building the Cold War Consensus,* 152.

16. Robert Griffith, "American Politics and the Origins of 'McCarthyism,'" in *The Specter: Original Essays on the Cold War and the Origin of McCarthyism,* ed. Robert Griffith and Athan G. Theoharis (New York: New Viewpoints, 1974), 2–17. On McCarthyism in general, see Ellen Schrecker, *The Age of McCarthyism: A Brief History with Documents* (Boston: Bedford Books of St. Martin's Press, 1994).

17. U.S. Senate, Committee on the Judiciary, Senate Report no. 1358, *Protection of the United States against Un-American and Subversive Activities,* 81st Congress, 2nd session, March 21, 1950, 35–43.

18. Violet M. Gunther, Americans for Democratic Action, to Organizations Cooperating through the National Civil Liberties Clearing House, July 20, 1950, Senate

Subject Files, "Internal Security—Administration Bill (Pro)" C205-93, Papers of Herbert H. Lehman, Columbia University (hereafter HHL).

19. Harry S. Truman, "Special Message to the Congress on the Internal Security of the United States, August 8, 1950," in *Public Papers of the Presidents of the United States: Harry S. Truman, 1950* (Washington, D.C.: U.S. Government Printing Office, 1965), 571–576.

20. Fordham, *Building the Cold War Consensus*, 83. Truman's recollections of Senator Patrick McCarran in his memoirs are not amicable. Harry S. Truman, *Memoirs by Harry S. Truman*, vol. 2, *Years of Trial and Hope* (Garden City, N.Y.: Doubleday, 1956), 284–287.

21. U.S. Senate, Committee on the Judiciary, Senate Report no. 2369, *Protecting the Internal Security of the United States*, 81st Congress, 2nd session, August 17, 1950. McCarran had added his version of the immigration and naturalization bill to a bill that removed race and nationality barriers from naturalization rights. This bill was the product of a three-year negotiation with the JACL; it was expected to be supported by a majority in both houses because the main beneficiaries of the bill were Japanese Issei—many of whose children served in the U.S. Army—who had been barred from naturalization. The attachment of McCarran's restrictive immigration and naturalization clauses to Walter's naturalization bill stalled the process, delaying the initiation of Issei naturalization until the passage of the Walter-McCarran Act in 1952.

22. Violet M. Gunther to Organizations, HHL. Opposition to Hawaiian statehood came from senators from the South, who expressed concerns about the fact that the majority of Hawaii's population was nonwhite.

23. U.S. Senate, Committee on the Judiciary, Senate Report no. 2369, *Protecting the Internal Security of the United States*, Part 2, Minority Views, 81st Congress, 2nd session, August 28, 1950.

24. In a memorandum to the American Civil Liberties Union, dated August 5, Mary Alice Baldinger complained, "The White House is still working on the Internal Security Bills (HR4703 and S595) but, frankly they don't seem to know what they are doing. . . . They were calling around yesterday to make another check on the attitude of liberal organizations toward these bills; they were told—I believe in every case—that there was no opposition to them. . . . In other words, the situation is still confused, and so am I, and so is everybody else I know including the Democratic Policy Committee." Memorandum from M. A. Baldinger to ACLU, Re: Mundt-Ferguson-Nixon and the Internal Security Bills, August 5, 1950, Box 865, Folder 1, "Internal Security Act—Correspondence with Congressional Leaders," Papers of the American Civil Liberties Union, Seeley G. Mudd Manuscript Library, Princeton University (hereafter ACLU).

25. Oral history interview with Stephen J. Spingarn, by Jerry N. Hess, Washington, D.C., March 20, 1967, Harry S. Truman Library, Independence, Missouri (hereafter HSTL).

26. Ibid.

27. Alan D. Harper, *The Politics of Loyalty: The White House and the Communist Issue, 1946–1952* (Westport, Conn.: Greenwood, 1969), 146.

28. Ibid., 147.

29. Memorandum from Charles S. Murphy and Stephen J. Spingarn to Harry S. Truman, May 16, 1950, Papers of Harry S. Truman, Official File 2750, HSTL.

30. *Congressional Record*, August 29, 1950, 13769.

31. Warren G. Magnuson was an influential liberal senator from the state of Washington. Before becoming a senator, he served as a House representative, and during his tenure as a congressman, he proposed the Chinese Exclusion Repeal Act of 1943, also known as the Magnuson Act.

32. Stephen J. Spingarn, Memorandum for the File on Proposed Commission on Internal Security and Individual Rights, July 12, 1950, Internal Security File, National Defense and Individual Rights, vol. 1, Papers of Stephen J. Spingarn, White House Assignment, Internal Security File, Box no. 31, HSTL.

33. Letter from Herbert H. Lehman to Ralph Barton Perry, November 1, 1952, Senate Legislative Files, "Internal Security Act" C79-44, HHL.

34. *New Republic,* "Unwise, Unworkable," September 25, 1950, 7.

35. Cornelius P. Cotter and J. Malcolm Smith, "An American Paradox: The Emergency Detention Act of 1950," *Journal of Politics* 19 (February 1957): 21.

36. Paul H. Douglas, *In the Fullness of Time: The Memoirs of Paul H. Douglas* (New York: Harcourt Brace Jovanovich, 1971), 306.

37. Bruce Allen Murphy, *The Brandeis/Frankfurter Connection: The Secret Political Activities of Two Supreme Court Justices* (New York: Oxford University Press, 1982), 220–223. Also see the oral history interview with Joseph L. Rauh Jr., by Niel M. Johnson, Washington, D.C., June 21, 1989, HSTL.

38. Quoted in Peter Irons, *Justice at War: The Story of the Japanese American Internment Cases* (Berkeley: University of California Press, 1983), 54.

39. Oral history interview with Joseph L. Rauh Jr., HSTL.

40. Memorandum, Julius C. C. Edelstein to Herbert H. Lehman, September 4, 1950, Senate Subject Files, "Internal Security—Constitutionality of Bills" C205-97, HHL. Attached to the memorandum was the excerpt of the Emergency Detention Bill, with Edelstein's suggestions on the possible improvement of the bill.

41. William W. Keller, *The Liberals and J. Edgar Hoover: Rise and Fall of a Domestic Intelligence State* (Princeton, N.J.: Princeton University Press, 1989), 42.

42. Douglas, *In the Fullness of Time,* 306.

43. Ibid. Keller criticizes this comment by Douglas as "misleading," because J. Edgar Hoover's statement before the Senate Appropriations Committee about the FBI's readiness to seize twelve thousand communists followed the introduction of the Kilgore bill by one day. Keller, *The Liberals and J. Edgar Hoover,* 43–44. In any case, Hoover's statement supported the emergency detention legislation, and it was used as such during the congressional debates by supporters of the Kilgore bill.

44. Memorandum from Stephen J. Spingarn for the Internal Security File, September 6, 1950, Internal Security File, National Defense and Individual Rights, vol. 3 (folder 2 of 2), Papers of Stephen J. Spingarn, Internal Security File, Box no. 32, HSTL.

45. Ibid. Spingarn did not support the Emergency Detention Bill but rather scoffed that it was a "concentration camp bill." Stephen J. Spingarn, Memorandum for the File on Proposed Commission on Internal Security and Individual Rights, July 12, 1950, Internal Security File, National Defense and Individual Rights, vol. 1, Papers of Stephen J. Spingarn, White House Assignment, Internal Security File, Box no. 31, HSTL.

46. *Congressional Record,* September 6, 1950, 14229.

47. Douglas, *In the Fullness of Time,* 306.

48. *Congressional Record,* September 12, 1950, 14606.

49. Letter from Estes Kefauver to Ernest Angell, September 21, 1950, Box 865, Folder 1, "Internal Security Act—Correspondence with Congress," ACLU.

50. U.S. House of Representatives, Committee on Internal Security, House of Representatives Report no. 3112, *Internal Security Act of 1950, Conference Report*, 81st Congress, 2nd session, September 19, 1950, 63.

51. Memorandum from Libby Donahue to Herbert H. Lehman, September 14, 1950, Senate Subject Files, "Internal Security—Reports and Hearings" C205-100, HHL.

52. Douglas, *In the Fullness of Time*, 307.

53. Memorandum from Stephen J. Spingarn for the File on the Wood-McCarran Anti-Subversive Bill (H.R. 9490), Papers of Harry S. Truman, Files of Philleo Nash, Presidential Speeches and Messages, Box 30, Internal Security Act of 1950 (McCarran Bill) Vetoed 9–22–50, HSTL; Harper, *The Politics of Loyalty*, 156–157.

54. New Left historians interpret Truman's immediate veto as a gesture to show his liberal stance while actually supporting repressive anticommunist legislation. Athan G. Theoharis, *Seeds of Repression: Harry S. Truman and the Origins of McCarthyism* (Chicago: Quadrangle Books, 1971); Richard S. Kirkendall, ed., *The Truman Period as a Research Field: A Reappraisal, 1972* (Columbia: University of Missouri Press, 1974). Benjamin Fordham suspects that Truman compromised with conservatives so that he could get necessary support from Congress for his rearmament budget. Fordham, *Building the Cold War Consensus*, 163.

55. Letter from Harley M. Kilgore to Truman, September 14, 1950, Internal Security Legislation 2750-C, Papers of Harry S. Truman, Official File, Box 1716, HSTL; Letter from Herbert H. Lehman, James E. Murray, and Estes Kefauver to Harry S. Truman, September 20, 1950, Internal Security Legislation 2750-C, Papers of Harry S. Truman, Official File, Box 1716, HSTL.

56. Harry S. Truman, "Veto of the Internal Security Bill, September 22, 1950," *Public Papers of the Presidents of the United States: Harry S. Truman, 1950*, 645–653.

57. *Congressional Record*, September 22, 1950, 15632–15633.

58. Douglas explained his change of position in his memoir: "It was a relief when Truman vetoed the bill, with a most able message, which stressed not only the bill's weakness as an enforcement device but also its extreme stand on the toleration of dissent. On the afternoon that he did this, Truman called me on the telephone to tell me what he was doing and asked for my support in voting to uphold his veto. He said it was the greatest threat yet offered against the civil liberties of the American people. I breathed with relief at this chance to redeem myself at least partially, and pledged to uphold his veto." Douglas, *In the Fullness of Time*, 307.

59. *Congressional Record*, September 23, 1950, 15726. The organizations that opposed the bill included the American Federation of Labor; Congress of Industrial Organizations; National Lawyers Guild; Congress of American Women; Communist Party USA; Americans for Democratic Action; American Civil Liberties Union; Civil Rights Congress; American Veterans Committee; Society of Friends Committee on National Legislation; Progressive Party; Socialist Party; National Association for the Advancement of Colored People; Women's International League for Peace and Freedom; American Federation for Aid to Polish Jews; National Farmers Union; American Labor Party; National Baptist Sunday School and Baptist Training Union Congress;

National Fraternal Council of Negro Churches; Methodist Church, Boston Area; People's Lobby; and National Committee to Defeat the Mundt Bill. *Congressional Quarterly Almanac,* 81st Congress, 2nd session, 1950, 398.

60. Internal Security Act, sec. 2.6.

61. *Constitution of the United States,* "Preamble."

62. U.S. Department of War, *Final Report: Japanese Evacuation from the West Coast, 1942* (Washington, D.C.: U.S. Government Printing Office, 1943; repr., New York: Arno Press, 1978).

63. *Hirabayashi v. United States,* 93.

64. Internal Security Act, sec. 101.15.

65. To resettle Japanese Americans outside the military area, the WRA used the "Application for Leave Clearance," and those who were proven to be loyal to the United States were allowed to leave the camps and settle outside. However, the exclusion order was not lifted until December 17, 1944, so Japanese Americans could not move freely inside the country or settle in places of their choice.

66. *Congressional Record,* September 5, 1950, 14171.

67. Ibid. Former attorney general Thomas Clark testified in 1950 that among approximately five thousand militant members of the Communist Party, 91.4 percent were of foreign stock or were married to persons of foreign stock. *Hearings, Communist Activities among Aliens and National Groups,* 81st Congress, 1st session, 319, 320 (1950), quoted in Patrick A. McCarran, "The Internal Security Act of 1950," *University of Pittsburgh Law Review* 12 (Summer 1951): 482.

68. *Congressional Record,* September 5, 1950, 14186.

69. On the image of Nazis during World War II, see Francis MacDonnell, *Insidious Foes: The Axis Fifth Column and the American Home Front* (New York: Oxford University Press, 1995). John W. Dower points out that during World War II, Americans in general differentiated between ordinary German citizens and Nazi Germans but failed to make distinctions in their perception between good Japanese and bad Japanese due to their racial prejudice. See John W. Dower, *War without Mercy: Race and Power in the Pacific War* (New York: Pantheon Books, 1986), 34. During World War II, the image of Japanese as a cunning enemy "with a smile to the face and a knife in the back" repeatedly appeared in posters and cartoons. Ibid., 182.

70. *Congressional Quarterly Almanac,* 81st Congress, 2nd session (1950), 394.

71. *Congressional Record,* September 5, 1950, 14189.

72. Ibid., 14190.

73. Statement of Senator Douglas, *Congressional Record,* September 8, 1950, 14413.

74. Harry Truman was the first U.S. president who seriously took up civil rights as a major political issue. Truman's evaluation by historians as the promoter of civil rights legislation has gone through several revisions, but recent scholarship, which tends to look at the "long civil rights movement," sheds a positive light on Truman's endeavor to implement desegregation in various sectors of society. For example, Richard Gergel, *Unexampled Courage: The Blinding of Sgt. Isaac Woodard and the Awakening of President Harry S. Truman and Judge J. Waties Waring* (New York: Sarah Crichton Books, 2019) elucidates how racial violence against an African American veteran pushed Truman to establish the President's Committee on Civil Rights in 1946 and also enforce desegregation of the armed forces. His achievements, as the later sections show, were limited because of the political coalition between the anti-immigration conservatives,

such as McCarran, and the southern Democrats, who struggled to maintain the social conventions of Jim Crow.

75. Letter from William Green, President of the American Federation of Labor, to Herbert H. Lehman, September 7, 1950, reprinted in *Congressional Record,* September 8, 1950, 14395; Letter from Evelyn Dunrow, Executive Director, Americans for Democratic Action, to Herbert H. Lehman, September 5, 1950, reprinted in *Congressional Record,* September 8, 1950, 14395; Resolution on the Internal Security and Civil Liberties, Congress of Industrial Organizations, August 29, 1950, Senate Subject Files, "Internal Security—Administration Bill (Pro)" C205-93, HHL; National Civil Liberties Clearing House, Joint Statement on the National Security Legislation Now Pending before the Congress, "Internal Security—Administration Bill (Pro)" C205-93, Senate Subject Files, HHL. The Joint Statement was signed by representatives of the American Association of University Professors, the American Civil Liberties Union, Americans for Democratic Action, the American Jewish Committee, the American Jewish Congress, the American Council on Human Rights, the American Unitarian Association, the American Veterans Committee, the Anti-Defamation League of B'nai B'rith, the Association of Immigration and Nationality Lawyers, Congregational Christian Churches, the Cooperative League of the U.S.A., the Jewish Labor Committee, Jewish War Veterans of the United States of America, Friends Committee on National Legislation, the International Association of Machinists, the National Farm Labor Union, the National Community Relations Advisory Council, the Committee on Education and Social Welfare, the National Council of Jewish Women, the National Association of Jewish Center Workers, the United Council of Church Women, and the Union of American Hebrew Congregations.

76. *Congressional Record,* September 5, 1950, 14192–14193.

77. *Congressional Record,* August 29, 1950, 13725–13727.

78. Ibid., 13735.

79. Lawrence S. Wittner quotes an example of a typical anticommunist and anti–civil rights statement by Congressman Rankin: "One of the most vicious movements that has yet been instituted by the crackpots, the Communists and the parlor pinks in this country is trying to browbeat the American Red Cross into taking the labels off the blood bank . . . so that it will not show whether it is Negro blood or white blood." Lawrence S. Wittner, *Cold War America: From Hiroshima to Watergate* (New York: Praeger, 1974), 90.

80. *Congressional Record,* August 29, 1950, 13725.

81. Ibid. The Taft-Hartley Act (Labor Management Relations Act) of 1947 was a federal law that restricted laborers' collective bargaining rights and curtailed the power of labor unions. It also forced union leaders to take loyalty oaths to prove that they were not communists. The law was passed over President Truman's veto.

82. Truman, "Special Message," *Public Papers of the Presidents of the United States: Harry S. Truman, 1950,* 572–573.

83. Ibid., 573.

84. Letter from Tom C. Clark to Senator Alexander Wiley, Chairman of the Committee on the Judiciary, June 16, 1948, Internal Security File, National Defense—and Individual Rights, vol. 1 (folder 1 of 2), Papers of Stephen J. Spingarn, White House Assignment, Internal Security File, Box no. 31, HSTL.

85. Ibid.

86. *Congressional Record,* September 7, 1950, 14285.

87. Martin Arundel, "Reds Ready to Go Underground, Order Members Not to Register," *Washington Evening Star,* August 23, 1950.

88. Senator Graham was defeated in the 1950 election as a result of his opponent's campaign tactics, which used Graham's voting records to portray him as "soft on communism" and a threat to white supremacy in the South. Fordham, *Building the Cold War Consensus,* 81.

89. *Congressional Record,* August 29, 1950, 13722.

90. Ibid., 13724.

91. *Congressional Record,* September 8, 1950, 14419.

92. M. J. Heale, *McCarthy's Americans: Red Scare Politics in State and Nation, 1935–1965* (London: Macmillan, 1998), 126.

93. *Congressional Record,* September 8, 1950, 14425.

94. Ibid., 14440.

95. Yasuko I. Takezawa, *Breaking the Silence: Redress and Japanese American Ethnicity* (Ithaca, N.Y.: Cornell University Press, 1995); Don Toshiaki Nakanishi, "Beyond Redress: The Future of Japanese American Politics on the Mainland," in *The Politics of Minority Coalitions: Race, Ethnicity, and Shared Uncertainties,* ed. Wilbur C. Rich (Westpoint, Conn.: Praeger, 1996), 87–107; Alice Yang Murray, *Historical Memories of the Japanese American Internment and the Struggle for Redress* (Stanford, Calif.: Stanford University Press, 2007); Tetsuden Kashima, "Japanese American Internees Return, 1945 to 1955: Readjustment and Social Amnesia," *Phylon: The Atlanta University Review of Race and Culture* 61 (Summer 1980): 107–115.

96. *Congressional Record,* September 8, 1950, 14419.

97. Ibid., 14424.

98. Commission on Wartime Relocation and Internment of Civilians (CWRIC), *Personal Justice Denied: Report of the Commission on Wartime Relocation and Internment of Civilians* (Seattle: University of Washington Press, 1997), chap. 13; Donna K. Nagata, *Legacy of Injustice: Exploring the Cross-Generational Impact of the Japanese American Internment* (New York: Plenum Press, 1993).

99. *Congressional Record,* September 8, 1950, 14424.

100. Ibid.

101. Ibid.

102. Ibid.

103. Ibid., 14430. The original Kilgore bill had granted the president authority to proclaim the existence of an "internal security emergency" in an "invasion or imminent invasion" of the United States or its possessions. Ferguson pointed out the possibility of being enacted if the government thought that Okinawa was under the condition of "imminent invasion." As the result of this debate, the conditions for the declaration of the existence of an "internal security emergency" were limited to war, insurrection in aid of a foreign enemy, and an actual invasion of the United States.

104. *Congressional Record,* September 8, 1950, 14426.

105. Cotter and Smith, "An American Paradox," 20–33.

106. Quoted in Douglas, *In the Fullness of Time,* 306; Address of J. Edgar Hoover at the Free Mason's Dinner of the Grand Lodge of New York, May 2, 1950, Senate Subject Files, "Internal Security—Acheson and McCarthy" C205-92, HHL.

107. Douglas, *In the Fullness of Time,* 306.

108. Fordham, *Building the Cold War Consensus*, 157; Richard M. Fried, *Nightmare in Red: The McCarthy Era in Perspective* (New York: Oxford University Press, 1990), 196; Frank J. Donner, *The Age of Surveillance: The Aims and Methods of America's Political Intelligence System* (New York: Knopf, 1981), 164–165, 409–410.

109. Schwartz, *A Commentary*, 261.

CHAPTER 3

1. In February 1950, Senator Joseph R. McCarthy made a sensational speech in Wheeling, West Virginia, declaring that he had a list of known communists who were working in the State Department. Although he failed in later testimonies to actually give any names of Communist Party members among the government workers, he continued to smear people as being Russian spies and communists. In 1954, McCarthy was censured in the Senate for acting contrary to senatorial ethics.

2. Michael S. Sherry, *In the Shadow of War: The United States since the 1930s* (New Haven, Conn.: Yale University Press, 1995), 172. On the popular anti-elitist sentiments expressed during the McCarthy era, see Richard Hofstadter, *The Paranoid Style in American Politics and Other Essays* (New York: Alfred A. Knopf, 1966).

3. Red-baiting was not a purely Republican political campaign. The federal employee loyalty program, introduced by the Truman administration in 1947, systematically discharged those employees who were branded disloyal. A year before that, Henry Wallace and the Progressive Party members, along with other New Dealers, were expelled from the Truman administration.

4. Lawrence S. Wittner, *Cold War America: From Hiroshima to Watergate* (New York: Praeger, 1974), 86–87.

5. *Chicago Daily News,* "Mixed Meanings," October 3, 1950.

6. Senator Lehman's papers contain letters from his constituents between 1950 and 1954, urging repeal of the Internal Security Act. Senate Legislative Files, "Internal Security Act" C79-44, Papers of Herbert H. Lehman, Columbia University (hereafter HHL).

7. Memorandum from Stephen J. Spingarn to Harry S. Truman, "Proposal for Presidential Commission on Internal Security and Individual Rights," May 22, 1950, Papers of Harry S. Truman Official File 2750, Box no. 1716, Harry S. Truman Library, Independence, Missouri (hereafter HSTL).

8. The reason for Spingarn's removal from the White House staff was not officially explained to him. Spingarn, as well as others, suspected that he had been too aggressive in his criticism of the Internal Security Act and the Democratic senators who supported it. Oral history interview with Stephen J. Spingarn, by Jerry N. Hess, Washington, D.C., March 21, 1967, HSTL.

9. Statement by President Truman on the establishment of a Commission on Internal Security and Individual Rights, January 23, 1951, Papers of Harry S. Truman, Official File 2750-A, HSTL.

10. Alan D. Harper, *The Politics of Loyalty: The White House and the Communist Issue, 1946–1952* (Westport, Conn.: Greenwood, 1969), 179–181.

11. Truman bitterly recollected McCarran's obstruction of the Nimitz Commission. Harry S. Truman, *Memoirs by Harry S. Truman*, vol. 2, *Years of Trial and Hope* (Garden City, N.Y.: Doubleday, 1956), 287.

12. William Randolph Tanner, "The Passage of the Internal Security Act of 1950" (Ph.D. diss., University of Kansas, 1971), 482.

13. *Chicago Daily News,* "Bad Law," September 25, 1950; *Denver Post,* "Good Intentions but Bad Legislation," September 24, 1950; *St. Louis Post-Dispatch,* "An Historic Veto," September 22, 1950; *Boston Traveler,* "Congress Abdicates," September 28, 1950.

14. For example, Senator Herbert H. Lehman continued to receive letters and telegrams urging the repeal of the McCarran Act well into 1954. To name a few examples: letter from Marion Osterhout, President of Amalgamated Clothing Workers of America, to Herbert H. Lehman, June 6, 1951; letter from Julius C. C. Edelstein to Milton Lebowitz, responding to Mrs. Lebowitz urging him to repeal the Internal Security Act, December 18, 1952; letter from Eric Barnitz to Herbert H. Lehman, urging amendment to the Internal Security Act, September 21, 1953; letter from Joseph B. Kruskal Jr. to Herbert Lehman, urging repeal of the Internal Security Act, February 1, 1954. These and many more letters and telegrams are collected in the Senate Legislative Files, "Internal Security Bill (3)" C60-17c, HHL.

15. Commission on Law and Social Action, American Jewish Congress, "The Internal Security Act of 1950: Evaluation and Analysis," n.d., Box 865, Folder 3, "Internal Security Act—Outside Documents," Papers of the American Civil Liberties Union, Seeley G. Mudd Manuscript Library, Princeton University (hereafter ACLU).

16. Ibid., 3.

17. Ibid., 8.

18. Joint Memorandum from Arnold Forster and Edwin J. Lukas to CRC Offices, ADl Regional Offices, and AJC Chapters, November 27, 1950, Box 865, Folder 3, "Internal Security Act—Outside Documents," ACLU.

19. Memorandum from Sol Rabkin and Alexander Brooks to CRC Offices, ADL Regional Offices and AJC Chapters, "Summary and Analysis of the Internal Security Act of 1950, Public Law 831—81st Congress (The "McCarran Law"), November 27, 1950, 11, Box 865, Folder 3, "Internal Security Act—Outside Documents," ACLU.

20. Letter from Robert J. Silberstein, National Lawyers Guild, to Organizations Which Opposed the McCarran Bill, November 1, 1950, Box 865, Folder 3, "Internal Security Act—Outside Documents," ACLU.

21. Robert J. Silberstein, National Lawyers Guild, "Analysis of the McCarran Act," October 18, 1950, 20, Box 865, Folder 3, "Internal Security Act—Outside Documents," ACLU.

22. Ibid., 21.

23. P. L. Prattis, "The Horizon: The U.S. Is Set to Fill Its Concentration Camps Now—or Did You Know It?" *Pittsburgh Courier,* May 12, 1951, 20.

24. Letter from William L. Patterson, Civil Rights Congress, to the ACLU, October 19, 1950, Box 865, Folder 3, "Internal Security Act—Outside Documents," ACLU.

25. Board of Directors Meeting, September 25, 1950, Box 13, Folder 11, "Board of Directors—Minutes," ACLU.

26. I. H. Gordon, "Senate Omnibus Bill Will Remove Race as a Barrier to Immigration, Naturalization," *Pacific Citizen,* April 29, 1950, 8.

27. *Pacific Citizen,* "Dangers Inherent in McCarran Bill Noted by JACL Counsel," May 27, 1950. Francis Walter was a conservative Democrat who endeavored to pass a restrictive immigration law. In 1952, he sponsored, along with Senator Patrick

McCarran, the Immigration and Nationality Act of 1952, popularly known as the McCarran-Walter Act. This law retained the restrictive national-origins quota system but opened the right of naturalization to Asian Americans, who had been categorized until the passage of this law as "aliens ineligible for citizenship."

28. *Pacific Citizen,* "The Accuser and the Accused," September 23, 1950, 4.

29. Larry Tajiri, "ADC's Watch on the Potomac," *Pacific Citizen,* September 23, 1950, 4.

30. Charlotte Brooks, *Between Mao and McCarthy: Chinese American Politics in the Cold War Years* (Chicago: University of Chicago Press, 2015).

31. Larry Tajiri, "The Chinese Americans," *Pacific Citizen,* January 13, 1951, 4.

32. *Pacific Citizen,* "Civic Unity Group Will Work to Prevent Another Evacuation," January 13, 1951, 3.

33. Americans for Democratic Action, "The Internal Security Act of 1950," November 2, 1950, 8, Box 865, Folder 3, "Internal Security Act—Outside Documents," ACLU.

34. Ibid., 10.

35. Ibid., 12.

36. Ibid., 13.

37. Oral history interview with Joseph L. Rauh Jr., by Niel M. Johnson, Washington, D.C., June 21, 1989, HSTL. Joseph Rauh had other experiences in dealing with the issue of race and internal security. In June 1941, he drafted Executive Order 8802, which required government contractors in the defense industry not to discriminate. The executive order was a compromise offered by the government to dissuade Philip Randolph from organizing an antiracism march in Washington, D.C. Studs Terkel, *"The Good War": An Oral History of World War Two* (New York: Pantheon Books, 1984), 337–338.

38. Memorandum of American Civil Liberties Union on S.4061, August 23, 1950, Box 865, Folder 1, "Internal Security Act—Correspondence with Congress," ACLU.

39. Letter from Frank W. McCulloch to Herbert M. Levy, September 18, 1950, Box 865, Folder 1, "Internal Security Act—Correspondence with Congress," ACLU.

40. Telegraph from Ernest Angell and Patrick Murphy Malin, ACLU, to Senator Scott Lucas, September 11, 1950, Box 865, Folder 1, "Internal Security Act—Correspondence with Congress," ACLU.

41. The National Civil Liberties Clearing House included organizations such as the ACLU, Friends Committee on National Legislation, Americans for Democratic Action, National Education Association, Anti-Defamation League of B'nai B'rith, American Council of Education, Southern Regional Council, National Jewish Welfare Board, American Jewish Committee, Japanese American Citizens League, Congregational Christian Churches of the U.S.A., Textile Workers Union of America, Congress of Industrial Organizations, National Council of Jewish Women, and American Veterans Committee, among others. The advisory board included Zachariah Chafee Jr., Edward J. Ennis, and Francis Biddle as chairperson.

42. Memorandum from Herbert Monte Levy and George Soll to the Members of the Board of Directors, October 20, 1950, Box 864, Folder 25, "Internal Security Act," ACLU.

43. Board of Directors Meeting, November 13, 1950, Box 13, Folder 11, "Board of Directors—Minutes," ACLU.

44. Jonathan Bingham, Edward J. Ennis, Morris L. Ernst, "Majority Statement

for Committee on Emergency Detention Provisions of McCarran Act," December 18, 1950, Box 4, Folder 4, "Mailing—1951," ACLU.

45. Arthur Garfield Hays, "Minority Statement for Committee on Emergency Detention Provisions of McCarran Act," January 11, 1951, Box 4, Folder 4, "Mailing—1951," ACLU.

46. Bingham, Ennis, and Ernst, "Majority Statement," sec. 1b.

47. Ibid., sec. 1c.

48. Alfred H. Kelly, Winfred A. Harbison, and Herman Belz have pointed out that the decisions of the Supreme Court on issues of civil liberties swung between the "balancing test" approach, based on the notion that liberty and authority must be kept in equilibrium, and the "preferred freedoms" doctrine, based on the idea that individual freedom must be weighed against the interest of the larger society in maintaining public order and civility. Alfred H. Kelly, Winfred A. Harbison, and Herman Belz, *The American Constitution: Its Origins and Development,* 7th ed. (New York: W. W. Norton, 1991), 522–523.

49. On the relationship between citizenship and military service, see Linda K. Kerber, "The Meanings of Citizenship," *Journal of American History* 84 (December 1997): 833–854. On Nisei's military services and resistance to conscription, see Eric L. Muller, *Free to Die for Their Country: The Story of the Japanese American Draft Resisters in World War II* (Chicago: University of Chicago Press, 2001).

50. Bingham, Ennis, and Ernst, "Majority Statement," sec. 1f.

51. Ibid., sec. 1g.

52. After the phone conference with President Roosevelt and Henry Stimson on February 11, 1942, John McCloy told Karl Bendetsen, "We have *carte blanche* to do what we want as far as the President is concerned." The president specifically authorized the evacuation of citizens. In doing so, Roosevelt observed that the action probably would have repercussions but said that what was to be done had to be dictated by the military necessity of the situation. His only qualification was "Be as reasonable as you can." Communication from John McCloy to Karl Bendetsen, quoted in Frank F. Chuman, *The Bamboo People: The Law and Japanese Americans* (Del Mar, Calif.: Publisher's, 1976), 159.

53. Bingham, Ennis, and Ernst, "Majority Statement," sec. 1h.

54. Defence (General) Regulations, 18B-(1), "Detention Orders" (1939), emphasis added.

55. Bingham, Ennis, and Ernst, "Majority Statement," sec. 1g.

56. Ibid., sec. 2b.

57. Ibid., sec. 3a.

58. Ibid., sec. 3b.

59. Ibid., sec. 3d, emphasis in the original.

60. Ibid., sec. 3h, emphasis in the original.

61. Hays, "Minority Statement," 1.

62. Caroline Chung Simpson, *An Absent Presence: Japanese Americans in Postwar American Culture, 1945–1960* (Durham, N.C.: Duke University Press, 2001), 3.

63. Arnold Brecht, "The Concentration Camp," *Columbia Law Review* 50 (June 1950): 761–782.

64. Ibid., 762.

65. Ibid., 763.
66. Ibid., 782.
67. Arthur E. Sutherland Jr., "Freedom and Internal Security," *Harvard Law Review* 64 (January 1951): 383–416.
68. Ibid., 414.
69. Ibid., 404.
70. *Columbia Law Review*, "Note: The Internal Security Act of 1950," vol. 51 (May 1951): 606–660.
71. Ibid., 659.
72. Leslie W. Dunbar, "Beyond Korematsu: The Emergency Detention Act of 1950," *University of Pittsburgh Law Review* 13 (1952): 221–231.
73. U.S. Senate, Committee on the Judiciary, Senate Report no. 1358, *Protection of the United States against Un-American and Subversive Activities*, 81st Congress, 2nd session, March 21, 1950, 43.
74. Dunbar, "Beyond Korematsu," 223.
75. Ibid., emphasis in the original.
76. Ibid.
77. Ibid., 227.
78. Ibid., 228.
79. Charles Fairman, "Government under Law in Time of Crisis," in *Government under Law: A Conference Held at Harvard Law School on the Occasion of the Bicentennial of John Marshall*, ed. Arthur E. Sutherland (Cambridge, Mass.: Harvard University Press, 1956), 232–301.
80. Thomas C. Mack, "The Constitution and the Emergency Detention Act of 1950," *Buffalo Law Review* 13 (1964): 484.
81. Ibid., 490.
82. Ibid., 491.
83. *Times-Union*, "6 McCarran Act Camps 'Phased Out' but Usable," February 25, 1968.
84. Gila River War Relocation Center was constructed in the Gila River Indian Reservation near the town of Florence, Arizona.
85. Papers of Harry S. Truman, General File, File "McCarran Acts, Laws and Bills (only)," contains hundreds of letters and telegraphs sent to President Truman urging the repeal of the McCarran Act. Letters sent between August 1950 and November 1951 refer to the McCarran Act in general and were largely sent by liberal and labor organizations. From January 1952, most of the letters refer to the "concentration camp" provisions. They express their abhorrence at the construction of concentration camps, and many of them support the Sabath Bill calling for the repeal of the McCarran Act. Senator Lehman's files also contain a large number of letters and telegrams asking the senator to vote for the repeal of the act. Senate Legislative Files, "Internal Security Bill (3)" C60-17, HHL.
86. *Congressional Record*, January 16, 1952, 221.
87. Ibid., 222.
88. See Jeff Woods, *Black Struggle, Red Scare: Segregation and Anti-Communism in the South, 1948–1968* (Baton Rouge: Louisiana State University Press, 2004).
89. Charles R. Allen Jr., *Concentration Camps U.S.A.* (New York: Marzani and

Munsell, 1966), 59. *Concentration Camps U.S.A.* is reprinted in U.S. House of Representatives, Committee on Internal Security, *Hearings Relating to Various Bills to Repeal the Emergency Detention Act,* 91st Congress, 2nd session, March 16, 17, 19, 23, 24, and 26; April 20, 21, and 22; May 21; and September 10, 1970 (hereafter HISC, *Hearings*), 3361–3424.

90. Allen, *Concentration Camps U.S.A.*, 10.

91. Ibid., 12.

92. Ibid., 14.

93. *New York Times,* "Internment Camps Bared: Senate Group Discloses 5 Sites for Housing War Subversives," June 26, 1952.

94. Luther A. Huston, "U.S. Keeps Detention Camps Ready: Six Units Maintained for Emergency Could House Thousands," *New York Times,* December 27, 1955.

95. The Department of Justice released a report on the conditions of the former detention camps in response to the allegations of two Communist Party leaders, Benjamin Davis and Gus Hall. Davis and Hall had been indicted by a federal grand jury on a charge of failing to register as Communist Party officials under the Subversive Activities Control Act. They accused the government of maintaining "concentration camps" to detain "hundreds of thousands" of people under the 1950 Internal Security Act. *New York Times,* "6 Camps for Reds Set Up, Then Closed," May 5, 1962.

96. Ibid.

97. William W. Keller, *The Liberals and J. Edgar Hoover: Rise and Fall of a Domestic Intelligence State* (Princeton, N.J.: Princeton University Press, 1989), 56.

98. *Congressional Record,* September 11, 1950, 14463.

99. Keller, *The Liberals and J. Edgar Hoover,* 56.

100. U.S. Senate, Select Committee to Study Governmental Operations with Respect to Intelligence Activities (Church Committee), Senate Report no. 94-755, 94th Congress, 2nd session, Book 2, *Intelligence Activities and the Rights of Americans,* April 26, 1976 (hereafter Church, Book 2), 7–20.

101. William Keller argues that Title II "opened the door to ongoing investigation of a substantial and ill-defined group of individuals as the discretion of the administrator in charge." Keller, *The Liberals and J. Edgar Hoover,* 57. He further suggests that liberals contributed substantially to this development of the FBI into independent, unaccountable political police. Without disagreeing with the idea that liberals in the administration and Congress sacrificed civil liberties issues for their own political interests, I do not think it is fair to attribute the growth of the FBI during the 1950s and 1960s to liberals' veneration of the bureau. J. Edgar Hoover's policy of secrecy prevented Congress members and the administration from knowing the activities of the FBI and the information it had gathered. Hoover utilized such information for his own political ends, and he kept much better relationships with congressional conservatives than with liberals. The FBI controlled its own internal security program regardless of the intentions of Congress. However, the fact that Congress, with the passage of Title II, gave sanction to a program that necessitated domestic internal security investigations should not be taken lightly. The ultimate irony of liberals was that they helped the development of an uncontrolled political police force while trying to control and limit the possibility of governmental abuse of power as exemplified by the internment of innocent citizens.

102. Church, Book 2, 25.

103. Letter from J. Edgar Hoover to Special Agents in Charge Re: Internal Security, December 6, 1939, quoted in Keller, *The Liberals and J. Edgar Hoover*, 60. The Department of Justice also established the Special Defense Unit, which compiled a list of dangerous enemy aliens and citizens called the "ABC list." The "A" category was the people who would be subject to immediate incarceration in the event of war.

104. Biddle stated that "the notion that it is possible to make a valid determination as to how dangerous a person is in the abstract and without reference to time, environment, and other relevant circumstances, is impractical, unwise, and dangerous." Memorandum from Attorney General Biddle to Assistant Attorney General Cox and J. Edgar Hoover, Director, FBI, July 16, 1943, quoted in Church, Book 2, 35.

105. Letter from J. Edgar Hoover to FBI Field Offices, Re: Dangerousness Classification, August 14, 1943, quoted in Church, Book 2, 36.

106. Biddle and Clark show marked contrast in their attitudes toward internal security and civil liberties. While Biddle opposed the mass exclusion of Japanese Americans, Clark helped the military's takeover on this issue and did little to quell the growing public sentiment in favor of mass evacuation. See Morton Grodzins, *Americans Betrayed: Politics of the Japanese Evacuation* (Chicago: University of Chicago Press, 1949), 242–245.

107. Personal and Confidential Memorandum from J. Edgar Hoover to the Attorney General, March 8, 1946, quoted in Keller, *The Liberals and J. Edgar Hoover*, 62.

108. Keller, *The Liberals and J. Edgar Hoover*, 62. For the process by which the FBI gained authority for preventive detention, also see Athan G. Theoharis, "The Truman Administration and the Decline of Civil Liberties: The FBI's Success in Securing Authorization for a Preventive Detention Program," *Journal of American History* 64 (March 1978): 1010–1030.

109. Athan G. Theoharis, *Spying on Americans: Political Surveillance from Hoover to the Huston Plan* (Philadelphia: Temple University Press, 1978), 46.

110. U.S. Senate, Select Committee to Study Governmental Operations with Respect to Intelligence Activities (Church Committee), Final Report, Book 3, *Supplementary Detailed Staff Reports on Intelligence Activities and the Rights of Americans*, 94th Congress, 2nd session, 1976, 439–440.

111. Theoharis, *Spying on Americans*, 48.

112. Internal Security Act, 64 Stat. 987 (1950), sec. 116.

113. Ibid., sec. 104a.

114. Quoted in Theoharis, *Spying on Americans*, 49; Keller, *The Liberals and J. Edgar Hoover*, 63–64.

115. Memorandum from Peyton Ford, Deputy Attorney General, to the FBI Director, December 7, 1950, quoted in Keller, *The Liberals and J. Edgar Hoover*, 64.

116. Christopher John Gerard, "'A Program of Cooperation': The FBI, the Senate Internal Security Subcommittee, and the Communist Issue, 1950–1956" (Ph.D. diss., Marquette University, 1993).

117. James O. Eastland's worldview of white supremacy is closely decoded in Chris Myers Asch, *The Senator and the Sharecropper: The Freedom Struggles of James O. Eastland and Fannie Lou Hamer* (New York: New Press, 2008).

118. Cathleen Thom and Patrick Jung, "The Responsibilities Program of the FBI, 1951–55," *The Historian* 59, no. 2 (1997): 348.

119. Ibid., 357.

120. Ibid., 357–358.

121. Ibid., 365.

122. Ibid., 368.

123. Theoharis, *Spying on Americans,* 52, 55.

124. Ibid., 12.

125. Dwight D. Eisenhower, "Annual Message to the Congress on the State of the Union, January 7, 1954," *Public Papers of the Presidents of the United States: Dwight Eisenhower, 1954* (Washington, D.C.: U.S. Government Printing Office, 1954), 13. Eisenhower said, "I recommend that Congress enact legislation to provide that a citizen of the United States who is convicted in the courts of hereafter conspiring to advocate the overthrow of this government by force or violence be treated as having, by such act, renounced his allegiance to the United States and forfeited his United States citizenship."

126. Communist Control Act, 68 Stat. 775 (1954).

127. *Congressional Record,* August 12, 1954, 14234–14236.

128. Interview with Thomas E. Harris, November 3, 1972, Washington, D.C., quoted in Mary S. McAuliffe, "Liberals and the Communist Control Act of 1954," *Journal of American History* 63 (September 1976): 355.

129. Ibid., 358.

130. Ibid., 359.

131. *Congressional Record,* August 19, 1954, 15121, 15236–15237.

132. McAuliffe, "Liberals," 363–364. This time the liberal Democrats enjoyed their position of attacking the Eisenhower administration, which opposed the Humphrey bill, as being soft on Communism.

133. Morton J. Horwitz, *The Warren Court and the Pursuit of Justice: A Critical Issue* (New York: Hill and Wang, 1998), 59.

134. *Dennis v. United States,* 341 U.S. 494 (1951), 516–517.

135. Ibid., 579–581.

136. Ibid., 527.

137. Ibid., 589.

138. Between 1951 and 1957, the Department of Justice arrested some 128 Communist Party officers for violating the Smith Act. Nearly 100 were convicted. Kelly, Harbison, and Belz, *The American Constitution,* 572.

139. *Yates v. United States,* 355 U.S. 66 (1957), 303–304. The Communist Party of the United States was founded originally in 1919. The party went through splits and merges, and at some periods it went underground, but the Supreme Court acknowledged that the party was founded by 1945 at the latest.

140. *Yates v. United States,* 319–320.

141. Ibid., 340.

142. Ibid., 349–350.

143. *Watkins v. United States,* 354 U.S. 178 (1957).

144. *Sweezy v. New Hampshire,* 354 U.S. 234 (1957).

145. Horwitz, *The Warren Court,* 59–62.

146. Ibid., 62–65.

147. *Barenblatt v. United States,* 360 U.S. 109 (1959).

148. *Scales v. United States,* 367 U.S. 203 (1961).

149. *Communist Party v. Subversive Activities Control Board,* 352 U.S. 115 (1956).

150. *Communist Party v. Subversive Activities Control Board,* 367 U.S. 1 (1961).

151. *Albertson v. Subversive Activities Control Board,* 382 U.S. 70 (1965).
152. Ibid.
153. *Aptheker v. Secretary of State,* 378 U.S. 500 (1964).
154. *U.S. v. Robel,* 389 U.S. 258 (1967).
155. Public Law 90-237, Sec. 5, 81 Stat. 766 (1968).

CHAPTER 4

1. Quoted in William K. Klingaman, *Encyclopedia of the McCarthy Era* (New York: Facts on File, 1996), 390, 406.
2. Morton J. Horwitz, *The Warren Court and the Pursuit of Justice: A Critical Issue* (New York: Hill and Wang, 1998), 80–91.
3. Telegraph from Charles Evers and Aaron Henry to President Lyndon B. Johnson, August 20, 1967, quoted in Steven F. Lawson, "Civil Rights," in *Exploring the Johnson Years,* ed. Robert A. Divine (Austin: University of Texas Press, 1981), 122n51.
4. Studs Terkel interviewed many Americans, including veterans and civilians, and reported that most remembered the Second World War as the "Good War." Studs Terkel, *"The Good War": An Oral History of World War Two* (New York: Pantheon Books, 1984), vi.
5. The American death toll in Vietnam was somewhere over 58,000. Michael S. Sherry, *In the Shadow of War: The United States since the 1930s* (New Haven, Conn.: Yale University Press, 1995), 287.
6. *Betts v. Brady,* 316 U.S. 455 (1942).
7. *Wolf v. Colorado,* 338 U.S. 25 (1949).
8. *Mapp v. Ohio,* 367 U.S. 643 (1961).
9. The Fourth Amendment of the Constitution reads, "The right of the people to be secure in their persons, houses, papers, and effects, against unreasonable searches and seizures, shall not be violated, and no Warrants shall issue, but upon probable cause, supported by Oath or affirmation, and particularly describing the place to be searched, and the persons or things to be seized."
10. *Gideon v. Wainwright,* 372 U.S. 335 (1963).
11. *Escobedo v. Illinois,* 378 U.S. 478 (1964).
12. *Miranda v. Arizona,* 384 U.S. 436 (1966).
13. *Brown v. Board of Education of Topeka,* 347 U.S. 483 (1954).
14. Horwitz, *The Warren Court,* 65–66.
15. *Gibson v. Florida Legislative Investigation Committee,* 372 U.S. 539 (1963).
16. *NAACP v. Button,* 371 U.S. 415 (1963).
17. Many recent works have emphasized that the civil rights struggles led by African Americans were influenced by thinkers who connected domestic racial injustice with the global racial hierarchy perpetuated by colonialism. Nikhil Pal Singh, *Black Is a Country: Race and the Unfinished Struggle for Democracy* (Cambridge, Mass.: Harvard University Press, 2004). Also see Robin D. G. Kelley, *Freedom Dreams: The Black Radical Imagination* (Boston: Beacon Press, 2003).
18. Studies on radical ethnic minority movements influenced by the BPP are increasing. For example, Darrel Wanzer-Serrano elucidates how a group of Puerto Rican youths in New York City organized as the Young Lords and initiated social programs to resist urban redevelopment, improve community medical services, and assist children

of disadvantaged families. Darrel Wanzer-Serrano, *The New York Young Lords and the Struggle for Liberation* (Philadelphia: Temple University Press, 2015). Karen Ishizuka documents how radical activism was nurtured among Asian Americans who grew up in mixed-race working-class communities. Karen L. Ishizuka, *Serve the People: Making Asian America in the Long Sixties* (London: Verso, 2016).

19. The concentration camps in Siberia came to be known as the Gulag Archipelago after Aleksandr Solzhenitsyn published a novel with that title in 1973. Solzhenitsyn's earlier novel *One Day in the Life of Ivan Denisovich*, depicting a typical, grueling day of life in a Siberian labor camp, was published in 1962. This novel made Solzhenitsyn's name and also the existence of camps for political prisoners in Siberia internationally well known.

20. Letter from Raymond Okamura to the JACL Headquarters, July 20, 1967, reprinted in *Pacific Citizen,* September 8, 1967, 1.

21. Preface in Charles R. Allen Jr., *Concentration Camps U.S.A.* (New York: Marzani and Munsell, 1966). The executive secretary of the CCCL, Miriam Friedlander, was one of the forty-four individuals who had been ordered by the Subversive Activities Control Board to register as a member of the Communist Party. The order was vacated on January 28, 1966, as a consequence of the decision in *Albertson v. Subversive Activities Control Board,* 382 U.S. 70 (1965), which applied to the case the invocation of the Fifth Amendment protection against self-incrimination. U.S. House of Representatives, Committee on Internal Security, *Hearings Relating to Various Bills to Repeal the Emergency Detention Act,* 91st Congress, 2nd session (hereafter HISC, *Hearings*), 3353.

22. Allen, *Concentration Camps U.S.A.*, 59.

23. Ibid., 58.

24. Ibid., 59.

25. Scholars have researched the social significance of rumors in African American communities. Patricia A. Turner reports that there are sets of rumors and urban legends shared by most of the African American students she surveyed and not by white students. Topics of the rumors range from African American sexuality and masculinity to governmental conspiracies against African Americans. Turner explains that these stories reflect tenacious racial misunderstandings and indicate the existence of separate racialized pools of knowledge. Patricia A. Turner, *I Heard It through the Grapevine: Rumor in African-American Culture* (Berkeley: University of California Press, 1993); Gary Alan Fine and Patricia A. Turner, *Whispers on the Color Line: Rumor and Race in America* (Berkeley: University of California Press, 2001).

26. Testimony of Louis Stokes, HISC, *Hearings,* 3068.

27. Testimony of Abner J. Mikva, HISC, *Hearings,* 3154.

28. Letter from J. Walter Yeagley to Senator Thomas H. Kuchel, June 1, 1967, Box 43, File "Title II—Detention Camps," Edison Uno Papers, Special Collections, Charles E. Young Research Library, University of California, Los Angeles (hereafter Edison Uno Papers).

29. Jerome Beatty Jr., "Trade Winds," *Saturday Review,* May 7, 1966, 14.

30. Paul W. Valentine, "Negro Detention Camps: Debunking of a Myth," *Washington Post,* March 3, 1968.

31. Quoted in a letter from Okamura to Thomas H. Kuchel, May 23, 1968, File "Letters and Memoranda—From Ray Okamura and JACL National Committee," National Ad Hoc Committee for Repeal of the Emergency Detention Act, "Emer-

gency Detention Act, Campaign to Repeal," Bancroft Library, University of California, Berkeley (hereafter National Ad Hoc Committee Papers).

32. U.S. House of Representatives, Committee on Un-American Activities, House of Representatives Report no. 1351, *Guerrilla Warfare Advocates in the United States*, 90th Congress, 2nd session, May 6, 1968, 1.

33. Ibid., 59.

34. The articles from these newspapers are reprinted in a brochure published by the National Committee to Abolish HUAC (NCAHUAC) calling for Title II repeal, Box 42, File "Title II—Readings," Edison Uno Papers: *Pittsburgh Post-Gazette*, "House Un-American Activities Committee Fans the Flames," n.d.; *Evening Star*, "Un-American Proposal," May 17, 1968; *Courier-Journal*, "A Plan as Bad as Its Enemies Are Saying," May 8, 1968; *UCLA Daily Bruin*, "HUAC Report," May 7, 1968; George Lardner Jr., "Detention for Guerrillas Proposed," *Los Angeles Times*, n.d.; *Milwaukee Journal*, "Guerrilla Warfare?" n.d.; *San Francisco Chronicle*, "Ussery Hits Detention Camp Plan," n.d.

35. *Washington Afro-American*, "Concentration Camps for Ghetto? Is Rap Brown Right?" May 7, 1968.

36. William Hedgepeth, "America's Concentration Camps: The Rumor and the Realities," *Look*, May 28, 1968. According to this article, the current conditions of the six detention camps were as follows. The Allenwood camp was operated by the Bureau of Prisons as a minimum-security facility for 230 inmates, "mostly Selective Service violators." The Avon Park camp was leased in 1961 to the State of Florida, which had since "incorporated the facility into its own prison system." The Florence camp served as a minimum-security federal jail for those awaiting trial. The camp site in Wickenburg had been returned to a private lessor. In El Reno, the Bureau of Prisons had dismantled the detention barracks and maintained the property "for beef-herd pastures." The Tule Lake camp, a former Japanese American Relocation Center, had been divided among many different owners. Ibid., 89.

37. Ibid., 85.

38. Ibid., 86.

39. Martin Luther King Jr., *Why We Can't Wait* (New York: Mentor Books, 1964).

40. Quoted in Hedgepeth, "America's Concentration Camps," 86.

41. Ibid., 91.

42. L. F. Palmer Jr., "When Black Professional People Start Talking like Rap Brown (and They Are) . . . ," *Chicago Daily News*, August 10, 1968.

43. *The Nation*, "Concentration Camps?" June 3, 1968.

44. *Hokubei Mainichi*, "'Black Power' Comment on U.S. Concentration Camps Stirs 'Evacuation' Talks," February 27, 1968.

45. Edison Uno conducted a persistent campaign to demand Earl Warren to apologize for the statements he made in early 1942 regarding Japanese Americans. Warren said publicly that "if the Japs are released no one will be able to tell a saboteur from any other Jap," and "we believe that when we are dealing with the Caucasian race we have methods that will test the loyalty of them. . . . But when we deal with the Japanese we are in an entirely different field and we cannot form any opinion that we believe to be sound. Their method of living, their language, make for this difficulty." Uno's crusade appeared an impossible cause even to fellow Japanese Americans at that time. Ellen Endo, "Open End-o," *Rafu Shimpo*, April 12, 1969.

46. *Black Panther*, "Concentration Camp," July 12, 1969, reprinted in HISC, *Hearings*, 2902. "Pig" is a derogatory term for the police.

47. *New York Times*, "Back to McCarthy-McCarran," May 17, 1969. Japanese American media paid particularly close attention to the issue of Title II. *Pacific Citizen, Hokubei Mainichi*, and *Rafu Shimpo*, among others, continuously covered the story of the Title II repeal campaign until it succeeded.

48. Paul W. Valentine, "Detention Camps Rumor Sweeps Black Ghettos: Negro Leaders Cite Precedents, Claim U.S. Is Planning Mass Concentration Camps," *Los Angeles Times*, February 25, 1968; *San Francisco Chronicle*, "Official's Remark: A New Flap over Detention Camps," April 28, 1969; John Keplinger, "Candidate Asks Repeal of Detention Camp Law," *Palo Alto Times*, May 13, 1968; *Oregon Journal*, "Students Lead Drive: Repeal of U.S. Law Sought," January 13, 1970; *Honolulu Star-Bulletin*, "Erase the Blot," July 15, 1971.

49. *Time*, "The Administration Request for Repeal," December 12, 1969; Elizabeth B. Drew, "Reports: Washington," *Atlantic Monthly*, May 1969.

50. "Consensus historians" emphasize the historical uniqueness of America vis-à-vis Europe. Louis Hartz, *The Liberal Tradition in America: An Interpretation of American Political Thought since the Revolution* (New York: Harcourt, Brace, 1955). Richard Hofstadter explores the historical characteristics of American democracy. Richard Hofstadter, *The American Political Tradition and the Men Who Made It* (New York: A. A. Knopf), 1948. Arthur M. Schlesinger Jr., in his criticism of Popular Front radicalism, emphasizes the liberal tradition in America as the "vital center" that functions as an antithesis of fascism and communism, both of which amount to "totalitarianism." Arthur M. Schlesinger Jr., *The Vital Center: The Politics of Freedom* (Boston: Houghton Mifflin, 1949).

51. October 1966 Black Panther Party Platform and Program, "What We Want, What We Believe," reprinted in Kathleen Cleaver and George Katsiaficas, eds., *Liberation, Imagination, and the Black Panther Party: A New Look at the Panthers and Their Legacy* (New York: Routledge, 2001), 285.

52. "Japanese Concentration Camps," Ministry of Information, Black Panther Party, *Bulletin* no. 7, November 4, 1968, Box 43, File "Detention Camps," Edison Uno Papers.

53. National Advisory Commission on Civil Disorders, *Report of the National Advisory Commission on Civil Disorders* (Washington, D.C.: U.S. Government Printing Office, 1968).

54. In 1963 Medgar Evers, director of the NAACP in Mississippi, was shot to death on his driveway, and four African American children were killed in the Klan bombing of Sixteenth Street Baptist Church in Birmingham, Alabama. In June 1964 three civil rights activists, Michael Schwerner, Andrew Goodman, and James Chaney, disappeared near Philadelphia, Mississippi. Their bodies were discovered on August 4. On December 4, the FBI arrested twenty-one people, including the Neshoba County sheriff and his deputy.

55. William W. Keller, *The Liberals and J. Edgar Hoover: Rise and Fall of a Domestic Intelligence State* (Princeton, N.J.: Princeton University Press, 1989), 97–99.

56. William W. Keller, who studied the FBI files in detail, attributes the inaction of the FBI vis-à-vis the Klan violence to the ideological stance of J. Edgar Hoover. Even in the 1960s, the FBI's operation was based on the conventional anticommunist stance.

To justify the FBI's surveillance and disruption of Klan activities, Hoover tried to find commonality between communists and Klansmen, with little success. He thus stressed the fact that the FBI was an investigative agency and not involved with crime prevention. Keller, *The Liberals and J. Edgar Hoover*, 92–97. Others contended that Hoover's personal stance toward the issue of civil rights was not much different from the Klansmen's after all. Todd Gitlin, *The Sixties: Years of Hope, Days of Rage* (Toronto: Bantam Books, 1987), 140–141. Martin Luther King Jr. was one of the most vocal critics of the FBI's inaction in regard to the continuous violence against African Americans in the South. Hoover in turn argued that the Civil Rights Movement was influenced by the Communist Party and ordered the wiretapping of King and other civil rights leaders. Keller, *The Liberals and J. Edgar Hoover*, 103–110.

57. Keller, *The Liberals and J. Edgar Hoover*, 115.

58. Ward Churchill, "'To Disrupt, Discredit and Destroy': The FBI's Secret War against the Black Panther Party," in Cleaver and Katsiaficas, *Liberation, Imagination, and the Black Panther Party*, 95.

59. By the end of 1969, at least thirty members of the Black Panther Party were in custody facing the death penalty, another forty facing life imprisonment, fifty-five facing sentences of thirty years or more, and still another 155 forced underground or into exile to avoid prosecution. There were at least twenty-nine police-induced fatalities among the Panthers between 1968 and 1971. Churchill, "'To Disrupt, Discredit and Destroy,'" 105–109. Also see Ward Churchill and Jim Vander Wall, *Agents of Repression: The FBI's Secret Wars against the Black Panther Party and the American Indian Movement* (Boston: South End Press, 1988), 63–99.

60. A Department of Justice Memorandum from John W. Cameron, Deputy Chief, Interdivision Information Unit, to Lawrence S. Hoffheimer, Community Relations Service, November 4, 1970, Interdivisional Information Unit, 1968–1976, Department of Justice, File, National Archives, College Park, Maryland.

61. Valentine, "Negro Detention Camps."

62. Hedgepeth, "America's Concentration Camps," 87.

63. Allan R. Bosworth, *America's Concentration Camps* (New York: W. W. Norton, 1967).

64. Until this time, most books used the terms "evacuation," "relocation," or "removal" in their titles even though some of them took a critical stance toward the policy itself. See Leonard Bloom and Ruth Riemer, *Removal and Return: The Socio-economic Effects of the War on Japanese Americans* (Berkeley: University of California Press, 1949); Morton Grodzins, *Americans Betrayed: Politics of the Japanese Evacuation* (Chicago: University of Chicago Press, 1949); Jacobus tenBroek, Edward N. Barnhart, and Floyd W. Matson, *Prejudice, War and the Constitution: Cases and Consequences of the Evacuation of the Japanese Americans in World War II* (1954; repr., Berkeley: University of California Press, 1975), to name a few.

65. *Pacific Citizen*, December 22–29, 1967.

66. Earl Warren, "The Bill of Rights and the Military," *New York University Law Review* 37 (1962): 181–203.

67. Peter Novick, *The Holocaust in American Life* (New York: Houghton Mifflin, 1999), 63–84.

68. Tim Cole, *Selling the Holocaust: From Auschwitz to Schindler, How History Is Bought, Packaged, and Sold* (New York: Routledge, 1999), 47.

69. Ibid., 58.
70. Ibid., 58.
71. Hannah Arendt, *Eichmann in Jerusalem: A Report on the Banality of Evil* (1964; repr., New York: Penguin Books, 1976).
72. Novick, *The Holocaust in American Life*, 132–142.
73. Ibid., 148–155; Norman G. Finkelstein, *The Holocaust Industry: Reflections on the Exploitation of Jewish Suffering* (New York: Verso, 2000), 20–30.
74. Novick, *The Holocaust in American Life*, 6–7.
75. Ibid., 83.
76. Mike Masaoka, "Washington Newsletter: JACL Campaign against Concentration Camps," *Pacific Citizen,* March 7, 1969, 2.
77. I. F. Stone, "The Political Miracle in That Detention Camp Repealer," *I. F. Stone's Weekly*, January 12, 1970.
78. Letter from Mike Masaoka to Raymond Okamura, August 1, 1967, reprinted in *Pacific Citizen,* September 8, 1967, 1–2.
79. In the letter, Fujimoto explains the reason for his concern as follows: "In the aftermath of Martin Luther King's horrid assassination, many Americans are hearing for the first time the voices of the people who have been oppressed. Among the information that middle class America is not cognizant of—mainly because it was not listed nor even plugged into the ghetto papers, radio stations and grapevine—is the rumor circulating in the minority communities of concentration camps of 'potential subversives.' I emphasize 'rumors' though I have read enough sources to document the prevalence of this concern that I would like your help in clarifying the following questions." Letter from Isao Fumimoto to Thomas Kuchel, April 9, 1968, Box 43, File "Title II—Detention Camps," Edison Uno Papers.
80. Letter from Thomas H. Kuchel to Isao Fujimoto, April 16, 1968, Box 43, File "Title II—Detention Camps," Edison Uno Papers.
81. Letter from J. Walter Yeagley, Assistant Attorney General, to Thomas H. Kuchel, June 1, 1967, in reply to Kuchel's inquiry dated May 24, 1967, concerning the "McCarran Concentration Camp Rumors," Box 43, File "Title II—Detention Camps," Edison Uno Papers.
82. Letter from Raymond Okamura to Mike Masaoka, May 10, 1968, File "Letters and Memoranda—From Ray Okamura and JACL National Committee," National Ad Hoc Committee Papers.
83. Letter from Raymond Okamura to Congressman Jeffrey Cohelan, May 20, 1968; Letter from Raymond Okamura to Senator Thomas H. Kuchel, May 23, 1968, both in File "Letters and Memoranda—From Ray Okamura and JACL National Committee," National Ad Hoc Committee Papers.
84. Letter from Raymond Okamura to Senator Thomas H. Kuchel, May 23, 1968, File "Letters and Memoranda—From Ray Okamura and JACL National Committee," National Ad Hoc Committee Papers. Ramsay Clark appeared in ABC's *Issues and Answers* on May 11 and reiterated the comments he made in NBC's *Meet the Press* on April 7.
85. Ibid.
86. Daryl J. Maeda points out that Asian American movement emerged from concerns about American military engagements in Asia, and thus it initially had strong transnational orientation. With the movement's integration into American identity

politics and the establishment of Asian American studies programs under the rubric of ethnic studies, scholars in the movement came to focus more on domestic racial inequalities and exclusion. Daryl J. Maeda, *Chains of Babylon: The Rise of Asian America* (Minneapolis: University of Minnesota Press, 2009).

87. The Third World Liberation Front led large-scale strikes at San Francisco State College between November 1968 and March 1969 and at the University of California, Berkeley, between January and March 1969. The students demanded the establishment of ethnic studies programs for racial-minority students, controlled by the students themselves.

88. William Wei, *The Asian American Movement* (Philadelphia: Temple University Press, 1993), 19. Also see "AAPA Perspectives," *Asian American Political Alliance* 1, no. 6 (October 1969), reprinted in Amy Tachiki, Eddie Wong, Franklin Odo, and Buck Wong, eds., *Roots: An Asian American Reader* (Los Angeles: University of California Press, 1971), 251.

89. Wei, *The Asian American Movement*, 20; Maeda, *Chains of Babylon*, 52.

90. Wei, *The Asian American Movement*, 21.

91. Ibid.

92. George Woo, interview with William Wei, San Francisco, March 27, 1986, quoted in Wei, *The Asian American Movement*, 21.

93. Ibid., 21.

94. Ibid., 16.

95. William Petersen, "Success Story: Japanese American Style," *New York Times Magazine*, January 9, 1966.

96. See Ellen D. Wu, *The Color of Success: Asian Americans and the Origins of the Model Minority* (Princeton, N.J.: Princeton University Press, 2014).

97. Wu points out how Asian American politicians sought to establish political influence at local as well as federal levels through the Hawaiian statehood campaign. Wu, *The Color of Success*, chap. 7.

98. Robert G. Lee, *Orientals: Asian Americans in Popular Culture* (Philadelphia: Temple University Press, 1999), chap. 5.

99. *Pacific Citizen*, "JACL Leaders Called Upon to Support Detention Camp Repeal: Movement a Rare Show of 'Grass Roots' Effort to Get National Leaders to Press Campaign," August 23, 1968, 3.

100. *Pacific Citizen*, "JACL Urged to Push Detention Camp Repeal," August 16, 1968, 3.

101. Mike Masaoka, "Detention Camp Proviso," *Pacific Citizen*, August 2, 1968, 2.

102. Glenn Kitayama elucidates how involvement in and strategies for Title II repeal differed between the grassroots groups and the JACL. Glenn Ikuo Kitayama, "Japanese Americans and the Movement of Redress: A Case Study of Grassroots Activism in the Los Angeles Chapter of the National Coalition for Redress/Reparations" (master's thesis, University of California, Los Angeles, 1993).

103. "Delegates Shocked to Read 'Evacuation' Order," unknown newspaper, August 21, 1968, in Box 43, "Title II—Detention Camps," Edison Uno Papers.

104. As early as in the 1980s, Raymond Okamura criticized the euphemistic terms used in government documents describing the wartime incarceration of Japanese Americans and pointed out that the euphemism concealed the injustice and human rights violations of the policy. Raymond Y. Okamura, "The American Concentration

Camps: A Cover-Up through Euphemistic Terminology," *Journal of Ethnic Studies* 10 (Fall 1982): 95–109.

105. "Are You Going to Be a TYPICAL YELLOW-WHITE AMERICAN?" n.d., in Box 43, "Title II—Detention Camps," Edison Uno Papers.

106. *California Farmer Consumer Reporter*, "Civil Rights Groups Say 'No More Concentration Camps,'" vol. 29 (September 1968): 1, Box 43, "Title II—Detention Camps," Edison Uno Papers.

107. Raymond Y. Okamura, "Background and History of the Repeal Campaign," *Amerasia Journal* 2 (Fall 1974): 78–79.

108. Letter from Raymond Okamura to the JACL District Governors, September 18, 1968, File "Letters and Memoranda—From Ray Okamura and JACL National Committee," National Ad Hoc Committee Papers.

109. Memorandum from the National Ad Hoc Committee Re Detention Act of 1950 to the JACL Members, October 15, 1968, File "Letters and Memoranda—From Ray Okamura and JACL National Committee," National Ad Hoc Committee Papers.

110. Ibid.

111. Letter from Raymond Okamura to Mike Masaoka, September 18, 1968, File "Letters and Memoranda—From Ray Okamura and JACL National Committee," National Ad Hoc Committee Papers.

112. Letter from Mike Masaoka to Raymond Okamura and Paul Yamamoto, September 27, 1968, Box 43, File "Title II—Detention Camps," Edison Uno Papers.

113. Memorandum from Ray Okamura and Paul Yamamoto to Jerry Enomoto and Kaz Horita, Re: Relationship between Ad Hoc Committee and Washington Representative, November 18, 1968, File "Letters and Memoranda—From Ray Okamura and JACL National Committee," National Ad Hoc Committee Papers.

114. When Masaoka and his followers negotiated with the government at the time of mass removal, they decided that Japanese Americans should comply with the military order without resistance. They silenced the dissenting opinions within the community and therefore were disdained by some of the internees. For Masaoka's personal account of his leadership in the Japanese American community, see Mike Masaoka with Bill Hosokawa, *They Call Me Moses Masaoka: An American Saga* (New York: William Morrow, 1987).

115. *Pacific Citizen*, "JACL Leaders Called Upon," 3.

116. *Pacific Citizen*, "All-Nisei Panel Appears at S.F. Unitarian Event," November 28, 1968, 1.

117. Letter from Edison Uno to Harry Honda, Editor of *Pacific Citizen*, November 29, 1968, Box 43, File "Title II—Detention Camps," Edison Uno Papers.

118. Dorothy Kawachi, "Public Interest Still High on WRA Camps," *Pacific Citizen*, December 6, 1968, 1.

119. Ibid., 2.

120. After the meeting at the First Unitarian Church, Edison Uno asked the JACL if it could send copies of the WRA camp photographs taken by Ansel Adams so that the National Ad Hoc Committee would have some visual aids "to properly present the real conditions of camp life." Letter from Edison Uno to Mas Satow, November 29, 1968. Other letters, brochures, posters, pamphlets and booklets are contained in the Edison Uno Papers and the National Ad Hoc Committee papers.

121. *Pacific Citizen*, "Racially-Mixed Audience at Glide Methodist Church Enlightened and Disturbed by Talk of Evacuation," March 28, 1969, 6.

122. Isao Fujimoto, "The Failure of Democracy in a Time of Crisis: The War-Time Internment of the Japanese Americans and Its Relevance Today," September 29, 1968, title page, Box 43, File "Title II—Detention Camp," Edison Uno Papers.

123. Ibid., 1.

124. Quoted in Open Letter from Jerry J. Enomoto, National President of JACL, to J. Edgar Hoover, August 15, 1969, reprinted in *Gidra,* "Hoover's Yellow Peril," September 1969.

125. Ibid.

126. *Pacific Citizen,* "Title II Repeal Move Being Aired, CRCSC Help Sought," November 29, 1968, 1.

127. *Pacific Citizen* reported on January 10, 1969, that Isao Fujimoto was scheduled to talk on KPFA-FM on January 16 on his aforementioned article. *Pacific Citizen,* "UC Davis Professor to Recall WW2 Camp Experience over KPFA-FM," January 10, 1969, 3.

128. *Pacific Citizen,* "Emergency Detention Act: Half for, Half against Law," January 17, 1969, 1.

129. Memorandum from National Ad Hoc Committee to Repeal the Emergency Detention Act to National Executive Committee, March 13, 1969, File "Letters and Memoranda—From Ray Okamura and JACL National Committee," National Ad Hoc Committee Papers.

130. *Pacific Citizen,* "L.A. Human Rights Group Pushing for ISA Title II Repeal," January 31, 1969, 1.

131. Kats Kunitsugu, "Witnessing Confrontation in Silence," *Pacific Citizen,* February 14, 1969, 6.

132. The poster was contained in Box 43, File "Title II—Detention Camps," Edison Uno Papers, along with a leaflet that urges Asian American students to support the campus strike.

133. AAPA brochure urging support for the Third World strike, Box 43, File "Title II—Detention Camps," Edison Uno Papers.

134. AAPA poster, "Instructions to All Persons of ~~Japanese~~ Asian Ancestry Living in the Following Area," Box 43, File "Title II—Detention Camps," Edison Uno Papers.

135. *Barbara Bick et al. Plaintiffs v. Attorney General of the United States,* Civil Action no. 2856-2868 (1968).

136. Among the sixteen plaintiffs, those who had faced investigation by HUAC were David Dellinger, National Mobilization to End the War in Vietnam; Barbara Bick of Women's Strike for Peace; Phil Hutchins of SNCC; and Mike Kolonsky of SDS. Some organizations were cited under Title I of the McCarran Act: Jarvis Tyner of DuBois Clubs and Charlene Mitchell of the Communist Party. Those plaintiffs charged by the court were Willard Uphaus of the World Fellowship and CCCL, Carl Braden of the SCEF, Frank Wilkinson of the National Committee to Abolish HUAC, Reies Lopez Tijerina of Alianza Federal de los Pueblos, and William Epton of the Progressive Labor Party. There were also prominent members of antiwar groups: Michael Meyerson of Tri-Continental Information Center, Walter Teague of the Committee to Aid NLF, and Kay Martin of Youth against War and Fascism. *Liberty* (Newsletter of the Citizens Committee for Constitutional Liberties), "A Challenge to Concentration Camp Law!" vol. 7 (Fall 1968): 1.

137. The organization included members identified by the government as communists.

138. *Pacific Citizen,* "JACL Explains Its Role in Title 2 Court Case," March 28,

1969, 3. The case was dismissed on June 20, 1969, by Judge William B. Bryant without comment or opinion. Letter from Ray Okamura to A. Wallace Tashima, June 24, 1969; also see Memorandum from Dennis J. Roberts of the Law Center for Constitutional Rights to All Plaintiffs, Re: *Bick v. Mitchell,* June 10, 1969, both in Box 44, File "Ray Okamura," Edison Uno Papers.

139. Letter from Ray Okamura to Edward L. Peet, Chairman of the Northern Californians to Abolish HUAC, October 22, 1968; Letter from Rebecca Krieger, Executive Secretary of the Northern Californians to Abolish HUAC, to Edison Uno, October 24, 1968; Letter from Edison Uno to Frank Wilkinson, Executive Director of the NCAHUAC, November 24, 1968, all in Box 43 "Title II—Detention Camps," Edison Uno Papers.

140. For example, the brochure made by the NCAHUAC on Title II, "Would You Believe Concentration Camps for Americans?" gave ideas to the National Ad Hoc Committee members for how to make their own public relations brochures. The JACL campaign brochure, "Concentration Camps in America?" uses a cover design similar to the NCAHUAC brochure. Letter from Edison Uno to Raymond Okamura, October 13, 1968, Box 43, File "Title II—Detention Camps," Edison Uno Papers.

141. Letter from Edison Uno to Robert S. Morris, October 13, 1968, Box 43, "Title II—Detention," Edison Uno Papers.

142. For example, Uno suggested that *Pacific Citizen* provide complimentary subscriptions to the following twenty-two schools and organizations for public relations purposes: University of California (Berkeley) Library, City College of San Francisco Library, San Francisco State College Library, University of San Francisco Library, Stanford University Library, San Francisco Public Library, Chinese American Citizens Alliance, NAACP Regional Office, Urban League of the Bay Area, Council for Civil Unity, Human Rights Commission of San Francisco, ACLU of Northern California, National Conference of Christians and Jews, Japan Society of San Francisco, American Friends Service Committee, Consulate General of Japan, B'nai B'rith, Republican County Central Committee, Democratic State Central Committee, *San Francisco Examiner, San Francisco Chronicle,* and *Sun Reporter.* Letter from Edison Uno to Phil Nakamura, November 28, 1968, in Box 43 "Title II—Detention Camps," Edison Uno Papers.

143. "Ray Okamura to Appear on KBHK-TV Show to Discuss Title 2 Issue," unknown newspaper, March 29, 1969, in Box 42 "Title II—News Articles," Edison Uno Papers.

144. Letter from Grace McDonald to Raymond Okamura, September 23, 1968, Box 43, File "Title II—Detention Camps," Edison Uno Papers.

145. Bernard Schwartz, *Super Chief: Earl Warren and His Supreme Court—a Judicial Biography* (New York: New York University Press, 1983), 16.

146. Bill Hosokawa, "Is Warren's Legal Philosophy of Today a Consequence of Evacuation?" *Pacific Citizen,* December 22–27, 1967, 1.

147. "Battle of Conscience," unknown newspaper, April 14, 1969, Box 36, File "Earl Warren," Edison Uno Papers.

148. Ibid.

149. Raymond Y. Okamura, "Earl Warren Refuses to Apologize for Role in Japanese American Evacuation," a report for news release to editors of *Hokubei Mainichi (North American Daily), Nichi-bei Times,* and *Pacific Citizen* newspapers, April 11, 1969, Box 44, File "Ray Okamura," Edison Uno Papers.

150. Memorandum from Mike Masaoka to Jerry Enomoto, September 19, 1969, Box 36, File "Earl Warren," Edison Uno Papers.

151. *Pacific Citizen,* "Let's Forgive Earl Warren," April 25, 1969, 6.

152. Earl Warren Jr. had partnered with two Nisei in a business enterprise harvesting and marketing *namako* (sea cucumber). He heard about the dinner from a member of a non-Nisei farm group in San Jose "because of their mutual interest in agriculture and civil rights." "Heeds Nisei Request . . . : Judge Earl Warren, Jr. to Ask Father to Interpret Evacuation," unknown newspaper, September 28, 1969, Box 36, File "Earl Warren," Edison Uno Papers.

153. Letter from Phil Ihara to Dave (Miura?), n.d. (September 27, 1969), Box 36, File "Earl Warren," Edison Uno Papers.

154. "Wartime Evacuation Advocate Warren Offers Repeal Support," unknown newspaper, March 28, 1970, Box 36, File "Earl Warren," Edison Uno Papers.

155. Letter from Earl Warren to Jerry J. Enomoto, March 18, 1970, Box 43, File "Title II Repeal Campaign," Edison Uno Papers.

156. Warren wrote, "Recently I had an opportunity to help prevent the recurrence of such an emotional experience. Some years ago Congress gave the U.S. attorney general the authority even in peacetime to impound persons believed by him to be subversive. This was a broader and far more dangerous power than that used by President Franklin Roosevelt in removing the Japanese from the coastal areas during the War. At the request of the Japanese-American Society in California, I wrote a letter for use before the congressional committee which was studying a bill to revoke the attorney general's authority. The letter was used, and happily the nullifying bill was passed by the Congress and signed by President Richard Nixon." Earl Warren, *The Memoirs of Earl Warren* (Garden City, N.Y.: Doubleday, 1977), 149–150.

157. Guy Wright, "Finally, He Regrets," *San Francisco Examiner* (n.d.), quoted in "Finally, Mr. Warren Regrets," unknown newspaper, April 23, 1970, Box 36, File "Earl Warren," Edison Uno Papers.

158. Letter from Bob M. Suzuki to Charles Warren, June 11, 1969, Box 44, File "Ray Okamura," Edison Uno Papers.

159. The supporting organizations were

GOVERNMENTAL BODIES

1. Community Relations Conference of Southern California
2. Los Angeles County Commission on Human Relations
3. Los Angeles County Board of Supervisors
4. City of Los Angeles Human Relations Commission
5. City of San Francisco Human Rights Commission
6. City of San Francisco Board of Supervisors
7. City of Seattle Human Rights Commission
8. City of San Jose Human Relations Commission
9. City Council of San Jose

PUBLIC MEDIA

1. Editorial, *Los Angeles Times*
2. Editorial, *San Francisco Chronicle*
3. Editorial, *Chicago Daily News*

4. Editorial, *Fresno Bee*
5. Editorial, *Palo Alto Times*
6. Editorial, *East-West*
7. Editorial, *The Nation*
8. Editorial, *California Farmer-Consumer Bulletin*
9. Editorial, KGO-TV San Francisco
10. Columnist, *San Francisco Examiner*
11. Columnist, *Arizona Republic*

ORGANIZATIONS

1. Southern California Division of the American Jewish Congress
2. National Association of Social Workers
3. California Democratic Council
4. International Longshoremen and Warehousemen Union, San Francisco Local
5. International Longshoremen and Warehousemen Union, Northern California District Council
6. Chinatown Youth Council, San Francisco
7. National Association for the Advancement of Colored People, Berkeley Chapter
8. American Civil Liberties Union, Palo Alto Chapter
9. American Civil Liberties Union, San Jose Chapter
10. San Mateo City School District, Title IV Task Force
11. San Francisco Council for Civic Unity
12. San Francisco Conference on Race and Religion

A JACL Memorandum from National Ad Hoc Committee to Repeal the Emergency Detention Act to National Board, June 15, 1969, File "Letters and Memoranda—From Ray Okamura and JACL National Committee," National Ad Hoc Committee Papers.

160. Ibid.

161. A JACL Memorandum from National Ad Hoc Committee to Repeal the Emergency Detention Act and Washington Representative Mike Masaoka to Chapter Presidents, District Governors, National Officers, National Committee Chairmen, National Staff, Re: House Bill to Repeal Title II, June 15, 1969, File "Letters and Memoranda—From Ray Okamura and JACL National Committee," National Ad Hoc Committee Papers.

162. American Committee for Protection of Foreign Born, *Concentration Camps USA: It Has Happened Here, It Could Happen Again—to You!* (booklet), 1969, Box 43, File "Title II—Printed Matter," Edison Uno Papers. Kochiyama's life history can be learned in her biography, Diane C. Fujino, *Heartbeat of Struggle: The Revolutionary Life of Yuri Kochiyama* (Minneapolis: University of Minnesota Press, 2005). Kochiyama's memoir is also published. Yuri Kochiyama, *Passing It On,* edited by Marjorie Lee, 2nd printing ed. (Los Angeles: UCLA Asian American Studies Center Press, 2004).

163. Letter from Mary Kochiyama to Raymond Okamura, July 30, 1969, Box 44, File "Ray Okamura," Edison Uno Papers.

164. A JACL Memorandum from Ray Okamura to Hiroshi Kanno, Sharon Deguchi, Bill Doi, Alice Kasai, Raymond Uno, Allyn Naomi Yamanouchi, William Tashima,

Don Kazama, Don Hayashi, Bob Suzuki, Ross Harano and Jerry Enomoto, November 2, 1969, File "Letters and Memoranda—From Ray Okamura and JACL National Committee," National Ad Hoc Committee Papers.

165. *Hokubei Mainichi,* "Nisei Crusade Formed to Aid Indians on Alcatraz," December 17, 1969; Edison Uno, "Community Response to Indian Appeal 'Gratifying,'" *Hokubei Mainichi,* December 19, 1969.

166. "Nisei Collect Tons of Supplies for 150 Indians on Alcatraz," unknown newspaper, December 23, 1969, Box 47, File "Alcatraz Indians—J.A.C.L.," Edison Uno Papers.

167. "Native Americans/Alcatraz Project, Sunday, December 21, 1969," in Memorandum by the JACL National Committee to Repeal the Emergency Detention Act, Box 47, File "Alcatraz Indians—J.A.C.L.," Edison Uno Papers.

168. "Nihonmachi Church to Open Quarters to Visiting Indians," unknown newspaper, December 24, 1969, Box 47, File "Alcatraz Indians—J.A.C.L.," Edison Uno Papers.

169. "Asian Studies Staff, Students Support Alcatraz Indians," unknown newspaper, December 17, 1969, Box 47, File "Alcatraz Indians—J.A.C.L.," Edison Uno Papers.

170. Letter from Julie C. Christensen, Alcatraz Headquarters, to Edison Uno, January 25, 1970, Box 47, File "Alcatraz Indians—J.A.C.L.," Edison Uno Papers.

171. Mike Masaoka, "Washington Newsletter: JACL Campaign against Concentration Camps," *Pacific Citizen,* March 7, 1969, 2; Letter from Raymond Okamura to JACL Members, June 15, 1969, File "Letters and Memoranda—From Ray Okamura and JACL National Committee," National Ad Hoc Committee Papers.

172. This phrase was used in a *Newsweek* article along the same line of argument as William Peterson's 1966 *New York Times Magazine* article "Success Story: Japanese American Style." *Newsweek,* "Success Story: Outwhiting the Whites," June 21, 1971.

CHAPTER 5

1. Quoted in Michael S. Sherry, *In the Shadow of War: The United States since the 1930s* (New Haven, Conn.: Yale University Press, 1995), 310.

2. Ibid., 310–311.

3. Ibid., 311.

4. Daniel Inouye had achieved a high status in the Senate and the Democratic Party by the late 1960s. A World War II veteran, he was a senior member of the Senate Armed Services Committee and a ranking member of the Senate Commerce Committee. He was also the chairman of the Senate Democratic Campaign Committee, and he served as the keynote speaker for the Democratic National Convention in Chicago in the summer of 1968.

5. JACL confidential memorandum, "Urgent—Immediate Action Required," April 6, 1969, File "Letters and Memoranda—From Ray Okamura and JACL National Committee," National Ad Hoc Committee for Repeal of the Emergency Detention Act, "Emergency Detention Act, Campaign to Repeal," Bancroft Library, University of California, Berkeley (hereafter National Ad Hoc Committee Papers).

6. JACL Memorandum from Raymond Okamura and Mike Masaoka to Chapter Presidents, District Governors, National Officers, National Committee Chairmen, National Staff, National Youth Council, District Youth Council, Jr. JACL Presidents,

Re: Senate Bill to Repeal the Emergency Detention Act, April 27, 1969, File "Letters and Memoranda—From Ray Okamura and JACL National Committee," National Ad Hoc Committee Papers.

7. Ibid.

8. Mike Masaoka, "Inouye Bill to Repeal Title II," *Pacific Citizen*, May 2, 1969, 2.

9. Letter from Charles G. Gubser to *Pacific Citizen*, "Gubser Bill H.R.1157," *Pacific Citizen*, February 14, 1969, 6.

10. The JACL did not know that Gubser had introduced a repeal bill until he wrote to *Pacific Citizen* correcting *Pacific Citizen*'s report that Gubser did not respond to the Japanese Americans' call for Title II repeal.

11. Raymond Y. Okamura, "Background and History of the Repeal Campaign," *Amerasia Journal* 2 (Fall 1974): 85.

12. *Palo Alto Times*, "Candidate Denounces Detention Camp Plan," May 7, 1968; John Keplinger, "Candidate Asks Repeal of Detention Camp Law," *Palo Alto Times*, May 13, 1968.

13. JACL Confidential Memorandum from National Ad Hoc Committee to Repeal the Emergency Detention Act and JACL Washington Representative Mike Masaoka to Chapter Presidents, District Governors, National Officers, National Committee Chairmen, National Staff, Concerned Members, Re: House Bill to Repeal Title II, June 1, 1969, File "Letters and Memoranda—From Ray Okamura and JACL National Committee," National Ad Hoc Committee Papers.

14. Memorandum from National Ad Hoc Committee to Repeal the Emergency Detention Act and Washington Representative, Mike Masaoka, to Chapter Presidents, District Governors, National Officers, National Youth Council, Youth Representatives, and Concerned Members, Re: Second Round of Effort to Get Co-sponsors for Repeal Bills, n.d., File "Letters and Memoranda—From Ray Okamura and JACL National Committee," National Ad Hoc Committee Papers.

15. *Congressional Quarterly Almanac*, 92nd Congress, 1st session (1971), 480. Title 18 deals with crimes and criminal procedure.

16. Richard Ichord had been instrumental in changing the name of the committee when HUAC's notoriety peaked in the late 1960s.

17. *Pacific Citizen*, "Cranston Co-sponsors Title II Repeal Bill, Saw Nazi Concentration Camps," May 9, 1969, 1.

18. *Pacific Citizen*, "Muskie, Fong Join Title II Repeal Drive: 4 Congressmen Enter Bills," May 9, 1969, 1.

19. Elizabeth B. Drew, "Reports: Washington," *Atlantic Monthly*, May 1969, 11.

20. Inouye statement quoted in *Pacific Citizen*, "Text of Inouye Comments, JACL Letter to Kleindienst," May 16, 1969, 2.

21. *Chicago Daily News*, "Detention Law Should Go," April 26, 1969; *San Francisco Chronicle*, "Concentration Camps Should Be Outlawed," May 2, 1969; *Los Angeles Times*, "U.S. Needs No Concentration Camps," May 2, 1969; *Palo Alto Times*, "Concentration Camp Fear," May 3, 1969; *Sacramento Bee*, "Repeal Detention Camp Law," May 16, 1969.

22. *The Nation*, "Concentration Camps?" June 3, 1968; *The Nation*, "A Timely Initiative," June 9, 1969.

23. Mike Masaoka, "CBS 'Sixty Minutes' on Title II Repeal," *Pacific Citizen*, July 4, 1969, 2.

24. Ibid.
25. Ibid.
26. Ibid.
27. *Pacific Citizen*, "44 More Congressmen Join Matsunaga-Holifield Bill," June 27, 1969, 1.
28. *Pacific Citizen*, "Berkeley NAACP Votes Support of Title II Repeal: Will Seek National NAACP Involvement," June 27, 1969, 1.
29. *Pacific Citizen*, "ILWU Auxiliaries Endorse Title II Repeal Legislation," July 4, 1969, 5.
30. *Pacific Citizen*, "Arizonan Explains Title II Repeal," June 27, 1969, 5; *Pacific Citizen*, "Idaho Rep. Hansen Calls Title II of 1950 Internal Security Act 'Repugnant,'" July 4, 1969, 1; *Pacific Citizen*, "11 More Groups Support JACL's Title II Repeal," July 18, 1969, 1; *Pacific Citizen*, "Denver Group on Community Relations for Title II Repeal," August 1, 1969, 1.
31. *Pacific Citizen*, "Sentiment Growing for Title II Repeal," August 1, 1969, 1.
32. *Pacific Citizen*, "Nixon View on Title 2 Bills Sought, Hearing Requested," July 18, 1969, 1.
33. Letter from the JACL National Committee to Repeal the Emergency Detention Act to Supporters of the Title II Repeal Campaign, October 27, 1969, File "Letters and Memoranda—From Ray Okamura and JACL National Committee," National Ad Hoc Committee Papers.
34. Ibid.
35. Letter from JACL National Committee to Repeal the Emergency Detention Act to Supporters of the Title II Repeal Campaign, February 15, 1970, File "Letters and Memoranda—From Ray Okamura and JACL National Committee," National Ad Hoc Committee Papers.
36. Department of Justice Memorandum from John W. Cameron, Deputy Chief, Interdivision Information Unit, to Lawrence S. Hoffheimer, Community Relations Service, November 4, 1970, Department of Justice, File "Interdivisional Information Unit, 1968–1976," National Archives, College Park, Maryland.
37. U.S. Department of Justice, U.S. Bureau of Prisons, *Emergency Detention Manual*, January 1969.
38. Emergency Detention Act of 1950, sec. 101.7.
39. JACL Memorandum from National Committee to Repeal the Emergency Detention Act to Mike Masaoka, December 20, 1969, File "Letters and Memoranda—From Ray Okamura and JACL National Committee," National Ad Hoc Committee Papers.
40. Ibid.
41. JACL Memorandum from National Committee to Repeal the Emergency Detention Act to Mike Masaoka, January 8, 1970; JACL Memorandum from National Committee to Repeal the Emergency Detention Act to Mike Masaoka, December 20, 1969, both in File "Letters and Memoranda—From Ray Okamura and JACL National Committee," National Ad Hoc Committee Papers.
42. JACL Memorandum from Mike Masaoka to Ray Okamura, Paul Yamamoto, and Edison Uno, Re: Hearings on Title II Repeal, January 27, 1970, File "Letters and Memoranda—From Ray Okamura and JACL National Committee," National Ad Hoc Committee Papers.

43. JACL Memorandum from Raymond Okamura to Mike Masaoka, Re: California State Legislature Passes Resolution on Title II, February 27, 1970, File "Letters and Memoranda—From Ray Okamura and JACL National Committee," National Ad Hoc Committee Papers.

44. U.S. House of Representatives, Committee on Internal Security, *Hearings Relating to Various Bills to Repeal the Emergency Detention Act,* 91st Congress, 2nd session, March 16, 17, 19, 23, 24, and 26; April 20, 21, and 22; May 21; and September 10, 1970 (hereafter HISC, *Hearings*), 2951–2955.

45. Report of National Committee to Repeal the Emergency Detention Act, July 1970, File "Letters and Memoranda—From Ray Okamura and JACL National Committee," National Ad Hoc Committee Papers.

46. HISC, *Hearings*.

47. The Japanese American Evacuation and Resettlement Study (JERS) was a multidisciplinary project led by Dorothy Swaine Thomas, a sociologist from the University of California, Berkeley. She gained the cooperation of the War Relocation Authority and recruited Nisei as well as non-Japanese field workers to document and analyze the removal and incarceration of Japanese Americans during World War II. Yuji Ichioka, ed., *Views from Within: The Japanese American Evacuation and Resettlement Study* (Los Angeles: Asian American Studies Center, University of California, Los Angeles, 1989).

48. HISC, *Hearings*, 2888.

49. Ibid., 2938.

50. Ibid.

51. Ibid., 2972.

52. Ibid., 2973.

53. Letter from Earl Warren to Jerry Enomoto, n.d., reprinted in HISC, *Hearings*, 3263.

54. HISC, *Hearings*, 2994–2995.

55. For more detailed accounts of the Salt Lake City Conference, see Michael John Wallinger, "Dispersal of the Japanese Americans: Rhetorical Strategies of the War Relocation Authority, 1942–1945" (Ph.D. diss., University of Oregon, 1975), 61–76.

56. Letter from Milton Eisenhower to Richard H. Ichord, March 12, 1970, reprinted in HISC, *Hearings,* 3054.

57. Ibid., 2981.

58. Scholars, both in the United States and in Japan, are uncovering the process of resettlement. Greg Robinson, *After Camp: Portraits in Midcentury Japanese American Life and Politics* (Los Angeles: University of California Press, 2012); Sandra C. Taylor, "Leaving the Concentration Camps: Japanese American Resettlement in Utah and the Intermountain West," *Pacific Historical Review* 60 (May 1991): 169–194; Thomas M. Linehan, "Japanese American Resettlement in Cleveland during and after World War II," *Journal of Urban History* 20 (November 1993): 54–80.

59. HISC, *Hearings,* 2995.

60. Ibid., 3064–3065.

61. For details of the conflict between Congress and the WRA, see Wallinger, "Dispersal of the Japanese Americans." For personal accounts of the WRA director, see Dillon S. Myer, *Uprooted Americans: The Japanese Americans and the War Relocation Authority* (Tucson: University of Arizona Press, 1971).

62. Dorothy Swaine Thomas, "Some Social Aspects of Japanese-American De-

mography," *Proceedings of the American Philosophical Society* 94 (1950), reprinted in HISC, *Hearings*, 3239.

63. HISC, *Hearings*, 3238.
64. Ibid., 3364.
65. Ibid., 3269.
66. Ibid., 3272–3291.
67. JACL Memorandum from the National Committee to Repeal the Emergency Detention Act to Mike Masaoka, Re: HISC Hearings on Title II, March 3, 1970, File "Letters and Memoranda—From Ray Okamura and JACL National Committee," National Ad Hoc Committee Papers.
68. HISC, *Hearings*, 3291–3296.
69. Ibid., 3007.
70. In the 1960s, shortly before the repeal campaign started, several books on Japanese Americans' wartime experiences were published with the term "concentration camps" in their titles. For example, see Allan R. Bosworth, *America's Concentration Camps* (New York: W. W. Norton, 1967); and Roger Daniels, *Concentration Camps USA: Japanese Americans and World War II* (New York: Holt, Rinehart, and Winston, 1971). Before this time, many books used terms such as the "evacuation," "relocation," or "removal" in their titles even though many of them took a critical stance toward the policy.
71. HISC, *Hearings*, 3326.
72. Ibid., 3305. There are numerous accounts of the incarcerees' resentment against their wrongful incarceration among Japanese American writings. Moreover, even a lack of expressed resentment requires careful and nuanced analysis when trying to understand victims of historical atrocities. I sought to contextualize the Japanese American reaction to their removal and incarceration through the experience of Hatsuye Egami, an Issei woman in the Gila River War Relocation Center. Masumi Izumi, "Gila River Concentration Camp and the Historical Memory of Japanese American Mass Incarceration," *Japanese Journal of American Studies* 29 (2018): 67–87.
73. *Pacific Citizen*, "Washington Newsletter," April 3, 1970.
74. HISC, *Hearings*, 3266.
75. During the Twentieth JACL National Convention, the AAPA members distributed leaflets titled "Are You Going to Be a Typical Yellow-White American?" Okamura, "Background and History," 78–79. At the most radical end of the spectrum of various Japanese American groups involved in the repeal campaign, the AAPA placed the Title II repeal campaign in its wider agenda as part of the "Third World movement." On the East Coast, students at Yale University became actively involved in the repeal movement. Gail Nakahara Unno of Berkeley participated in the lawsuit arranged by CCCL and the Law Center for Constitutional Rights to have Title II declared unconstitutional on the grounds that it had a "chilling effect" on Americans' rights to freedom of speech. The National Ad Hoc Committee recommended that JACL file an *amicus curiae* brief in support of the plaintiffs, but the National Legal Council of JACL refused to get involved.
76. HISC, *Hearings*, 3029, emphasis added.
77. Ibid., 3034.
78. Ibid., 3576.
79. Ibid., 3068.

80. Ibid., 3143.

81. Statement by Daniel E. Button, a representative from New York, HISC, *Hearings,* 3514.

82. HISC, *Hearings,* 3455.

83. Ibid., 3607.

84. Ibid., 3121–3122.

85. *San Francisco Examiner,* "Support for Detention Camp Bill," August 20, 1970.

86. Confidential Memorandum from Raymond Okamura to Ken Yoshikawa, Harry Yoshikawa, Sumi Ujimori, Don Estes, Hiroshi Kanno, Sharon Deguchi, Lynn Watanabe, Allyn Yamanouchi, Bill Doi, Don Hayashi, Don Kazama, George Matsuoka, Harry Honda, David Miura, Henry Tanaka, Kaz Horita, September 14, 1970, File "Letters and Memoranda—From Ray Okamura and JACL National Committee," National Ad Hoc Committee Papers.

87. Ibid.

88. Ibid.

89. Confidential Memorandum from the National Committee to Repeal the Emergency Detention Act to All Supporters of the Title II Repeal Campaign and JACL Chapter Presidents and National Board, "Urgent—Immediate Action Required," September 23, 1970, File "Letters and Memoranda—From Ray Okamura and JACL National Committee," National Ad Hoc Committee Papers.

90. U.S. House of Representatives, Committee on Internal Security, House of Representatives Report no. 1599, *Emergency Detention Act of 1950 Amendments,* Report together with a Dissenting View to Accompany HR19163, 91st Congress, 2nd session, October 13, 1970.

91. *St. Louis Post-Dispatch,* September 17, 1970.

92. *Honolulu Star-Bulletin,* "Erase the Blot," July 15, 1971.

93. JACL Letter from National Committee to Repeal the Emergency Detention Act to Chapter Presidents, National Board, Title II Committee Members, January 28, 1971, File "Letters and Memoranda—From Ray Okamura and JACL National Committee," National Ad Hoc Committee Papers.

94. *Congressional Quarterly Almanac,* 92nd Congress, 1st session (1971), 480.

95. Memorandum from the National Committee to Repeal the Emergency Detention Act to Supporters of the Title II Repeal Campaign, JACL Chapter Presidents, National Board and Staff, Re: Progress Report on the Campaign to Repeal the Emergency Detention Act, March 26, 1971, File "Letters and Memoranda—From Ray Okamura and JACL National Committee," National Ad Hoc Committee Papers.

96. U.S. House of Representatives, Committee on the Judiciary, *Prohibiting Detention Camps,* Hearings before Subcommittee no. 3 of the Committee on the Judiciary, HR234 and Related Bills, 92nd Congress, 1st session, March 18, 1971, 44.

97. Mardian stated that Title 21 dealt with crimes involving narcotics and dangerous drugs; Title 50 involved selective service violations; Title 26 involved Internal Revenue law violations; Title 49 involved aircraft hijacking; and there were other titles involving confinement of people convicted of federal crimes. U.S. House of Representatives, Committee on the Judiciary, *Prohibiting Detention Camps,* 73.

98. JACL Memorandum from the National Committee to Repeal the Emergency Detention Act to Chapter Presidents, National Board, National Staff, National Committees, "Action for the Month of August," August 6, 1971, File "Letters and

Memoranda—From Ray Okamura and JACL National Committee," National Ad Hoc Committee Papers.

99. Richard Longaker, "Emergency Detention: The Generation Gap, 1950–1971," *Western Political Quarterly* 27 (September 1974): 405.

100. Ibid., 401–402.

101. Ibid., 407.

102. The detention of American citizens and foreign nationals in Guantanamo Bay as alleged enemy combatants drew criticism against President George W. Bush; President Barack Obama disappointed his liberal supporters by signing the National Defense Authorization Act into law. The detention of undocumented immigrants, particularly that of young children, has induced huge public outcry against President Donald Trump.

103. Richard M. Nixon, "Statement on Signing Bill Repealing the Emergency Detention Act of 1950, September 25, 1971," *Public Papers of the Presidents of the United States, Richard M. Nixon, 1971* (Washington, D.C.: U.S. Government Printing Office, 1972), 986.

104. John R. Gillis, "Memory and Identity: The History of a Relationship," in *Commemorations: The Politics of National Identity*, ed. John R. Gillis (Princeton, N.J.: Princeton University Press, 1994), 17.

105. Statement by Edward I. Koch, a representative from New York, HISC, *Hearings*, 2991.

106. Statement by Hiram L. Fong, a senator from Hawaii, HISC, *Hearings*, 3041.

107. HISC, *Hearings*, 3265.

108. Letter from Richard G. Kleindienst, Deputy Attorney General, to Richard H. Ichord, December 2, 1969, reprinted in HISC, *Hearings*, 3595.

CONCLUSION

1. Leslie T. Hatamiya, *Righting a Wrong: Japanese Americans and the Passage of the Civil Liberties Act of 1988* (Stanford, Calif.: Stanford University Press, 1993).

2. Commission on Wartime Relocation and Internment of Civilians (CWRIC), *Personal Justice Denied: Report of the Commission on Wartime Relocation and Internment of Civilians* (Seattle: University of Washington Press, 1997).

3. For the effect of Redress movement on the Japanese American community, see Yasuko I. Takezawa, *Breaking the Silence: Redress and Japanese American Ethnicity* (Ithaca, N.Y.: Cornell University Press, 1995); and Alice Yang Murray, *Historical Memories of the Japanese American Internment and the Struggle for Redress* (Stanford, Calif.: Stanford University Press, 2007).

4. Mitchell T. Maki, Harry H. L. Kitano, and S. Megan Berthold, *Achieving the Impossible Dream: How Japanese Americans Obtained Redress* (Urbana: University of Illinois Press, 1999).

5. Department of Justice Memorandum from John W. Cameron, Deputy Chief, Interdivision Information Unit, to Lawrence S. Hoffheimer, Community Relations Service, November 4, 1970, Department of Justice, File "Interdivisional Information Unit, 1968–1976," National Archives, College Park, Maryland.

6. For more on the FBI's COINTELPRO operations against African American and Native American radicals, see Ward Churchill and Jim Vander Wall, *Agents of Re-*

pression: The FBI's Secret Wars against the Black Panther Party and the American Indian Movement (Boston: South End Press, 1990); Ward Churchill, "'To Disrupt, Discredit and Destroy': The FBI's Secret War against the Black Panther Party," in *Liberation, Imagination, and the Black Panther Party: A New Look at the Panthers and Their Legacy*, ed. Kathleen Cleaver and George Katsiaficas (New York: Routledge, 2001), 78.

7. Angela Davis, a former Black Panther Party member and prominent scholar, pointed out that the U.S. penal system, which incarcerated over two million individuals, not only was biased unfavorably against people of color and the poor; it also generated great wealth for corporations that provide services for the incarcerated population and exploit prison labor. Angela Y. Davis, "Masked Racism: Reflections on the Prison Industrial Complex," *Colorlines,* October 31, 1998, 11. In the past two decades, incarceration studies, particularly in the field of African American studies, has produced many important academic works.

8. USA PATRIOT Act, Pub. L. no. 107-56, 115 Stat. 272 (codified in scattered sections of 8 U.S.C.) (2001).

9. ACLU, "America's Disappeared: Seeking International Justice for Immigrants Detained after September 11," 2004, http://www.aclu.org/FilesPDFs/un%20report.pdf, accessed September 12, 2018.

10. The U.S. government captured over seven hundred persons from more than forty countries after the 9/11 incident and held them at the U.S. Naval Base at Guantanamo Bay, Cuba. U.S. citizen Yaser Esam Hamdi and British citizen Shafiq Rasul were held in Guantanamo Bay. The U.S. government claimed the detainees were "enemy combatants." Upon their petitions for a writ of habeas corpus, the court recognized the government's power to detain enemy combatants but ruled that the detainees had the right of due process. *Hamdi v. Rumsfeld* 542 U.S. 507 (2004); *Rasul v. Bush,* 215 F. Supp. 2d 55 (D.D.C. 2002), *rev'd* 542 U.S. 466 (2004). President Barack Obama signed an executive order to close the detention facilities, but he failed to fulfill this promise during his terms of office. Forty-one prisoners were still in military custody at Guantanamo as of January 2017. CNN Library, "Guantanamo Bay Naval Station Fast Facts," CNN, March 7, 2017, http://edition.cnn.com/2013/09/09/world/guantanamo-bay-naval-station-fast-facts/, accessed September 12, 2018.

11. According to Peter Jan Honigsberg, a professor in the University of San Francisco School of Law, the Bush administration started using the term "enemy combatant" around February 2002. This term was chosen to allow the government to capture without due process individuals who were suspected to be related to al Qaeda or the Taliban and to detain and interrogate them in ways that violate the Geneva Convention, which grants prisoners of war certain human rights. Peter Jan Honigsberg, "Chasing 'Enemy Combatants' and Circumventing International Law: A License for Sanctioned Abuse," *UCLA Journal of International Law and Foreign Affairs* 12, no. 1 (2007): 46–48.

12. *Ex Parte Quirin,* 317 U.S. 1, 31 (1942).

13. For detailed comparison between *Ex Parte Quirin* and the *Hamdi* case, see James B. Anderson, "Hamdi v. Rumsfeld: Judicious Balancing at the Intersection of the Executive's Power to Detain and the Citizen-Detainee's Right to Due Process," *Journal of Criminal Law and Criminology* 95, no. 3 (2005): 689–724.

14. For example, the Bush administration maintained that citizens designated as

"enemy combatants" are protected neither under the Geneva Convention nor under the 1971 Non-detention Act.

15. Margaret Chon and Eric K. Yamamoto, "Resurrecting Korematsu: Post–September 11th National Security Curtailment of Civil Liberties," in *Race, Rights and Reparation: Law and the Japanese American Internment,* ed. Eric K. Yamamoto, Margaret Chon, Carol L. Izumi, Jerry Kang, and Frank H. Wu (New York: Aspen Law and Business, 2001), 39–48. Also see chapter 8 of this book, which is available electronically at Jerry Kang (blog), http://jerrykang.net/wp-content/uploads/2010/10/chon-yamamoto-race-rights-ch8.pdf.

16. Ibid., 48–67.

17. The American Bar Association passed a resolution to urge the president to withdraw the executive order and requested that the executive branch should "ensure that any executive orders concerning border security, immigration enforcement and terrorism respect the bounds of the U.S. Constitution and other international legal obligations and facilitate a transparent, accessible, fair and efficient system of administering U.S. immigration law and policies." American Bar Association "President Trump Drafting New Immigration Executive Order," *ABA Washington Letter,* February 2017, http://www.americanbar.org/publications/governmental_affairs_periodicals/washingtonletter/2017/february/immigrationorder.html, accessed September 12, 2018.

18. *Hawaii v. Trump,* no. 17-15589 (9th Cir. 2017).

19. Traci G. Lee, "Trump Supporter: Internment 'Precedent' for Muslim Registry to 'Protect America,'" *NBC News,* November 17, 2016, http://www.nbcnews.com/news/asian-america/trump-supporter-cites-internment-precedent-muslim-registry-n685131.

20. The Tuna Canyon Detention Station Coalition has collected information about the experiences of some two thousand men detained in the center. The organization produced an exhibit titled "Only the Oaks Remain," which is accessible in part on the Internet. Tuna Canyon Detention Station Coalition, http://www.tunacanyon.org, accessed September 12, 2018.

21. The musical premiered in September 2012 in San Diego, was performed on Broadway in 2015, and was produced again in Los Angeles and Boston between February and June 2018. In 2016 and 2017, the film recording of the Broadway production was played in several hundred theaters in the United States, and there was a showing in Japan as well.

22. Michelle Malkin, *In Defense of Internment: The Case for "Racial Profiling" in World War II and the War on Terror* (Washington, D.C.: Regnery, 2004).

23. In fact, this idea was presented by conservative scholars at the time Malkin's book was published. Charles A. Lofgren, "Hardships of War: A Review of *In Defense of Internment: The Case of 'Racial Profiling' in World War II and the War on Terror,* by Michelle Malkin," *Claremont Review of Books,* September 2005. The negative public reaction to the Trump supporters' citing of Japanese American incarceration is depicted in many newspaper articles, including Jonah Engel Bromwich, "Trump Camp's Talk of Registry and Japanese Internment Raises Muslims' Fears," *New York Times,* November 17, 2016. Roger W. Lotchin, emeritus professor of war and urban history, published a revisionist view of Japanese American wartime "relocation" in 2018, but it is unlikely that his book, which attempts to disprove that the policy was based on West Coast anti-Japanese racism, would alter the general view of internment as a race-based civil

rights violation. Roger W. Lotchin, *Japanese American Relocation in World War II: A Reconsideration* (Cambridge: Cambridge University Press, 2018.

24. *Trump v. Hawaii,* 138 S. Ct. 2392 (2018).

25. Author's telephone interview with Aiko Herzig-Yoshinaga, August 16, 2017, Los Angeles.

26. More historical records on those labeled as "disloyal" in Tule Lake have come out into the public sphere in the United States. For example, see Tatsuo Inouye, *The Tule Lake Stockade Diary,* transcribed by Nancy Kyoko Oda, translated from Japanese by Masumi Izumi, UCLA Asian American Studies Center, http://www.suyamaproject.org/?p=721, accessed September 12, 2018.

27. Franklin Odo, "The Good War and Japanese America," *American Studies Journal* 59 (2015), http://www.asjournal.org/59-2015/the-good-war-and-japanese-america/.

28. This expression was given by Alan Trachtenberg, who used it in his personal correspondence with the author, dated September 14, 2002.

Bibliography

PRIMARY SOURCES

LAWS

United States
Communist Control Act, 68 Stat. 775 (1954).
Emergency Detention Act, 64 Stat. 1019 (1950).
Internal Security Act, 64 Stat. 987 (1950).
Non-detention Act, Public Law 92-128, 85 Stat. 347 (1971).
Public Law 503, 56 Stat. 173 (1942).
Public Law 90-237, Sec. 5, 81 Stat. 766 (1968).
USA PATRIOT Act, Pub. L. no. 107-56, 115 Stat. 272 (codified in scattered sections of 8 U.S.C.) (2001).

United Kingdom
Defence (General) Regulations, 18B-(1), "Detention Orders" (1939).

COURT CASES

Abrams v. United States, 250 U.S. 616 (1919).
Albertson v. Subversive Activities Control Board, 382 U.S. 70 (1965).
Aptheker v. Secretary of State, 378 U.S. 500 (1964).
Barbara Bick et al. Plaintiffs v. Attorney General of the United States, Civil Action no. 2856-2868 (1968).
Barenblatt v. United States, 360 U.S. 109 (1959).
Betts v. Brady, 316 U.S. 455 (1942).
Brown v. Board of Education of Topeka, 347 U.S. 483 (1954).

Communist Party v. Subversive Activities Control Board, 352 U.S. 115 (1956).
Communist Party v. Subversive Activities Control Board, 367 U.S. 1 (1961).
Dennis v. United States, 341 U.S. 494 (1951).
Duncan v. Kahanamoku, 327 U.S. 304 (1946).
Ebel v. Drum, 52 F. Supp. 189 (D. Mass. 1943).
Escobedo v. Illinois, 378 U.S. 478 (1964).
Ex Parte Endo, 323 U.S. 283 (1944).
Ex Parte Milligan, 71 U.S. 2, 127 (1866).
Ex Parte Quirin, 317 U.S. 1, 31 (1942).
Gibson v. Florida Legislative Investigation Committee, 372 U.S. 539 (1963).
Gideon v. Wainwright, 372 U.S. 335 (1963).
Gitlow v. New York, 268 U.S. 652 (1925).
Hamdi v. Rumsfeld 542 U.S. 507 (2004).
Hawaii v. Trump, no. 17-15589 (9th Cir. 2017).
Hirabayashi v. United States, 320 U.S. 81 (1943).
Korematsu v. United States, 323 U.S. 214 (1944).
Mapp v. Ohio, 367 U.S. 643 (1961).
Miranda v. Arizona, 384 U.S. 436 (1966).
NAACP v. Button, 371 U.S. 415 (1963).
Rasul v. Bush, 215 F. Supp. 2d 55 (D.D.C. 2002), *rev'd* 542 U.S. 466 (2004).
Scales v. United States, 367 U.S. 203 (1961).
Schenck v. United States, 249 U.S. 470 (1919).
Schneider v. State (Town of Irvington), 308 U.S. 147 (1939).
Schueller v. Drum, 51 F. Supp. 383 (E. D. Pa., 1943).
Sterling v. Constantin, 287 U.S. 378 (1932).
Sweezy v. New Hampshire, 354 U.S. 234 (1957).
Trump v. Hawaii, 138 S. Ct. 2392 (2018).
U.S. v. Robel, 389 U.S. 258 (1967).
Watkins v. United States, 354 U.S. 178 (1957).
Wolf v. Colorado, 338 U.S. 25 (1949).
Yasui v. United States, 320 U.S. 115 (1943).
Yates v. United States, 355 U.S. 66 (1957).
Yick Wo v. Hopkins, 118 U.S. 356 (1886).

GOVERNMENT DOCUMENTS

Congress and the Nation 1945–1964: A Review of Government Politics in the Postwar Years. Washington, D.C.: Congressional Quarterly Service.
Congressional Quarterly Almanac, 81st Congress, 2nd session (1950).
Congressional Quarterly Almanac, 92nd Congress, 1st session (1971).
Congressional Record.
Constitution of the United States of America.
Executive Order 9066, Authorizing the Secretary of War to Prescribe Military Areas, February 19, 1942.
Executive Order 9808, Establishing the President's Committee on Civil Rights, December 5, 1946.
National Advisory Commission on Civil Disorders, *Report of the National Advisory*

Commission on Civil Disorders (Washington, D.C.: U.S. Government Printing Office, 1968).
Presidential Proclamation No. 2525.
Presidential Proclamation No. 2526.
Presidential Proclamation No. 2527.
President's Committee on Civil Rights. *To Secure These Rights: The Report of the President's Committee on Civil Rights*. Washington, D.C.: U.S. Government Printing Office, 1947.
Public Papers of the Presidents of the United States: Dwight D. Eisenhower, 1954. Washington, D.C.: U.S. Government Printing Office, 1954.
Public Papers of the Presidents of the United States: Harry S. Truman, 1950. Washington, D.C.: U.S. Government Printing Office, 1965.
Public Papers of the Presidents of the United States: Richard M. Nixon, 1971. Washington, D.C.: U.S. Government Printing Office, 1972.
U.S. Congress. House of Representatives, Committee on Internal Security. *Hearings Relating to Various Bills to Repeal the Emergency Detention Act*. 91st Congress, 2nd session, March 16, 17, 19, 23, 24, and 26; April 20, 21, and 22; May 21; and September 10, 1970.
———. House of Representatives, Committee on Internal Security. House of Representatives Report no. 1599. *Emergency Detention Act of 1950 Amendments*. Report Together with a Dissenting View to Accompany H.R. 19163. 91st Congress, 2nd session, October 13, 1970.
———. House of Representatives, Committee on Internal Security. House of Representatives Report no. 3112. *Internal Security Act of 1950, Conference Report*. 81st Congress, 2nd session, September 19, 1950.
———. House of Representatives, Committee on the Judiciary. *Prohibiting Detention Camps*. Hearings before Subcommittee no. 3 of the Committee on the Judiciary, HR234 and Related Bills. 92nd Congress, 1st session, March 18, 1971.
———. House of Representatives, Committee on Un-American Activities. House of Representatives Report no. 1351. *Guerrilla Warfare Advocates in the United States*. 90th Congress, 2nd session, May 6, 1968.
———. House of Representatives, Committee on Un-American Activities. House of Representatives Report no. 2980. *Protection of the United States against Un-American and Subversive Activities*. 81st Congress, 2nd session, August 22, 1950.
———. House of Representatives, Select Committee Investigating National Defense Migration. House of Representatives Report no. 1911. *Report of the Select Committee Investigating National Defense Migration*. 77th Congress, 2nd session, February 21 and 23, 1942.
———. Senate, Committee on the Judiciary. Senate Report no. 1358. *Protection of the United States against Un-American and Subversive Activities*. 81st Congress, 2nd session, March 21, 1950.
———. Senate, Committee on the Judiciary. Senate Report no. 2369. *Protecting the Internal Security of the United States*. 81st Congress, 2nd session, August 17, 1950. Senate Report no. 2369, Part 2, *Minority Views*, 81st Congress, 2nd session, August 28, 1950.
———. Senate, Select Committee to Study Governmental Operations with Respect to Intelligence Activities (Church Committee). Final Report. Book 2, *Intelligence Ac-*

tivities and the Rights of Americans. Book 3, *Supplementary Detailed Staff Reports on Intelligence Activities and the Rights of Americans.* 94th Congress, 2nd session, 1976.
U.S. Department of Justice, U.S. Bureau of Prisons. *Emergency Detention Manual.* January 1969.
U.S. Department of War. *Final Report: Japanese Evacuation from the West Coast, 1942.* Washington, D.C.: U.S. Government Printing Office, 1943; repr., New York: Arno Press, 1978.
U.S. War Relocation Authority. *People in Motion: The Postwar Adjustment of the Evacuated Japanese Americans.* Washington, D.C.: U.S. Government Printing Office, 1947; repr., New York: AMS Press, 1975.

MANUSCRIPTS

Department of Justice. File, "Interdivisional Information Unit, 1968–1976." National Archives, College Park, Maryland.
Edison Uno Papers. Special Collections, Charles E. Young Research Library, University of California, Los Angeles.
Inouye, Tatsuo. *The Tule Lake Stockade Diary.* Transcr. Nancy Kyoko Oda. Trans. Masumi Izumi. UCLA Asian American Studies Center. http://www.suyamaproject.org/?p=721. Accessed September 12, 2018.
National Ad Hoc Committee for Repeal of the Emergency Detention Act. "Campaign to Repeal the Emergency Detention Act." Bancroft Library, University of California, Berkeley.
Papers of the American Civil Liberties Union. Seeley G. Mudd Manuscript Library, Princeton University.
Papers of Harry S. Truman. Harry S. Truman Library, Independence, Missouri.
Papers of Herbert H. Lehman. Herbert H. Lehman Suite and Papers, Columbia University.
Papers of Stephen J. Spingarn. Harry S. Truman Library, Independence, Missouri.

ORAL HISTORY

Oral history interview with Stephen J. Spingarn. By Jerry N. Hess. Washington, D.C., March 20, 1967. Harry S. Truman Library, Independence, Missouri.
Oral history interview with Stephen J. Spingarn. By Jerry N. Hess. Washington, D.C., March 21, 1967. Harry S. Truman Library, Independence, Missouri.
Oral history interview with Joseph L. Rauh Jr. By Niel M. Johnson. Washington, D.C., June 21, 1989, Harry S. Truman Library, Independence, Missouri.
Telephone interview with Aiko Herzig-Yoshinaga. By Masumi Izumi. August 16, 2017, Los Angeles.

SECONDARY SOURCES

BOOKS

Adams, Ansel, Archie Miyatake, and William H. Michael. *Born Free and Equal: The Story of Loyal Japanese Americans.* Bishop, Calif.: Spotted Dog Press, 2002.
Allen, Charles R., Jr. *Concentration Camps U.S.A.* New York: Marzani and Munsell, 1966.

Arendt, Hannah. *Eichmann in Jerusalem: A Report on the Banality of Evil.* 1964; repr., New York: Penguin Books, 1976.
Asch, Chris Myers. *The Senator and the Sharecropper: The Freedom Struggles of James O. Eastland and Fannie Lou Hamer.* New York: New Press, 2008.
Azuma, Eiichiro. *Between Two Empires: Race, History and Transnationalism in Japanese America.* New York: Oxford University Press, 2005.
Bannai, Lorraine K. *Enduring Conviction: Fred Korematsu and His Quest for Justice.* Seattle: University of Washington Press, 2015.
Bencivenni, Marcella. *Italian Immigrant Radical Culture: The Idealism of the Sovversivi in the United States, 1890–1940.* New York: New York University Press, 2011.
Bloom, Leonard, and Ruth Riemer. *Removal and Return: The Socio-economic Effects of the War on Japanese Americans.* Berkeley: University of California Press, 1949.
Bosworth, Allan R. *America's Concentration Camps.* New York: W. W. Norton, 1967.
Brooks, Charlotte. *Between Mao and McCarthy: Chinese American Politics in the Cold War Years.* Chicago: University of Chicago Press, 2015.
Campbell, David. *Writing Security: United States Foreign Policy and the Politics of Identity.* Minneapolis: University of Minnesota Press, 1998.
Chang, Robert S. *Disoriented: Asian Americans, Law, and the Nation-State.* New York: New York University Press, 1999.
Cheng, Cindy I-fen. *Citizens of Asian America: Democracy and Race during the Cold War.* New York: New York University Press, 2014.
Chuman, Frank F. *The Bamboo People: The Law and Japanese Americans.* Del Mar, Calif.: Publisher's, 1976.
Churchill, Ward, and Jim Vander Wall. *Agents of Repression: The FBI's Secret Wars against the Black Panther Party and the American Indian Movement.* Boston: South End Press, 1988.
Cleaver, Kathleen, and George Katsiaficas, eds. *Liberation, Imagination, and the Black Panther Party: A New Look at the Panthers and Their Legacy.* New York: Routledge, 2001.
Cole, Tim. *Selling the Holocaust: From Auschwitz to Schindler, How History Is Bought, Packaged, and Sold.* New York: Routledge, 1999.
Commission on Wartime Relocation and Internment of Civilians (CWRIC). *Personal Justice Denied: Report of the Commission on Wartime Relocation and Internment of Civilians.* Seattle: University of Washington Press, 1997.
Daniels, Roger. *Concentration Camps USA: Japanese Americans and World War II.* New York: Holt, Rinehart, and Winston, 1971.
de Nevers, Klancy Clark. *The Colonel and the Pacifist: Karl Bendetsen, Perry Saito, and the Incarceration of Japanese Americans during World War II.* Salt Lake City: University of Utah Press, 2004.
Donner, Frank J. *The Age of Surveillance: The Aims and Methods of America's Political Intelligence System.* New York: Knopf, 1981.
Douglas, Paul H. *In the Fullness of Time: The Memoirs of Paul H. Douglas.* New York: Harcourt Brace Jovanovich, 1971.
Dower, John W. *War without Mercy: Race and Power in the Pacific War.* New York: Pantheon Books, 1986.
Dreyfus, Hubert L., and Paul Rabinow. *Michel Foucault: Beyond Structuralism and Hermeneutics.* 2nd ed. Chicago: University of Chicago Press, 1983.

Dudziak, Mary L. *Cold War Civil Rights: Race and the Image of American Democracy.* Princeton, N.J.: Princeton University Press, 2000.
Fine, Gary Alan, and Patricia A. Turner. *Whispers on the Color Line: Rumor and Race in America.* Berkeley: University of California Press, 2001.
Finkelstein, Norman G. *The Holocaust Industry: Reflections on the Exploitation of Jewish Suffering.* New York: Verso, 2000.
Fiset, Louis, and Gail M. Nomura, eds. *Nikkei in the Pacific Northwest: Japanese Americans and Japanese Canadians in the Twentieth Century.* Seattle: University of Washington Press, 2005.
Fordham, Benjamin O. B*uilding the Cold War Consensus: The Political Economy of U.S. National Security Policy, 1949–51.* Ann Arbor: University of Michigan Press, 1998.
Fried, Richard M. *Nightmare in Red: The McCarthy Era in Perspective.* New York: Oxford University Press, 1990.
———. *The Russians Are Coming! The Russians Are Coming! Pageantry and Patriotism in Cold-War America.* New York: Oxford University Press, 1998.
Fujino, Diane C. *Heartbeat of Struggle: The Revolutionary Life of Yuri Kochiyama.* Minneapolis: University of Minnesota Press, 2005.
Gergel, Richard. *Unexampled Courage: The Blinding of Sgt. Isaac Woodard and the Awakening of President Harry S. Truman and Judge J. Waties Waring.* New York: Sarah Crichton Books, 2019.
Gitlin, Todd. *The Sixties: Years of Hope, Days of Rage.* Toronto: Bantam Books, 1987.
Gordon, Linda, and Gary Okihiro, eds. *Impounded: Dorothea Lange and the Censored Images of Japanese American Internment.* New York: W. W. Norton, 2006.
Grodzins, Morton. *Americans Betrayed: Politics of the Japanese Evacuation.* Chicago: University of Chicago Press, 1949.
Harper, Alan D. *The Politics of Loyalty: The White House and the Communist Issue, 1946–1952.* Westport, Conn.: Greenwood, 1969.
Hartz, Louis. *The Liberal Tradition in America: An Interpretation of American Political Thought since the Revolution.* New York: Harcourt, Brace, 1955.
Hatamiya, Leslie T. *Righting a Wrong: Japanese Americans and the Passage of the Civil Liberties Act of 1988.* Stanford, Calif.: Stanford University Press, 1993.
Hayashi, Brian M. *Democratizing the Enemy: The Japanese American Internment.* Princeton, N.J.: Princeton University Press, 2008.
———. *For the Sake of Our Japanese Brethren: Assimilation, Nationalism and Protestantism among the Japanese of Los Angeles, 1895–1942.* Stanford, Calif.: Stanford University Press, 1995.
Heale, M. J. *American Anticommunism: Combating the Enemy Within, 1830–1970.* Baltimore: Johns Hopkins University Press, 1990.
———. *McCarthy's Americans: Red Scare Politics in State and Nation, 1935–1965.* London: Macmillan, 1998.
Hirobe, Izumi. *Japanese Pride, American Prejudice: Modifying the Exclusion Clause of the 1924 Immigration Act.* Stanford, Calif.: Stanford University Press, 2002.
Hofstadter, Richard. *The American Political Tradition and the Men Who Made It.* New York: A. A. Knopf, 1948.
———. *The Paranoid Style in American Politics and Other Essays.* New York: Alfred A. Knopf, 1966.

Horwitz, Morton J. *The Warren Court and the Pursuit of Justice: A Critical Issue.* New York: Hill and Wang, 1998.
Howard, John. *Concentration Camps on the Home Front: Japanese Americans in the House of Jim Crow.* Chicago: University of Chicago Press, 2008.
Ichioka, Yuji. *Before Internment: Essays in Prewar Japanese American History.* Edited by Gordon H. Chang and Eiichiro Azuma. Stanford, Calif.: Stanford University Press, 2006.
———, ed. *Views from Within: The Japanese American Evacuation and Resettlement Study.* Los Angeles: Asian American Studies Center, University of California, Los Angeles, 1989.
Irons, Peter. *Justice at War: The Story of the Japanese American Internment Cases.* Berkeley: University of California Press, 1983.
———, ed. *Justice Delayed: The Record of the Japanese American Internment Cases.* Middletown, Conn.: Wesleyan University Press, 1989.
Ishizuka, Karen L. *Serve the People: Making Asian America in the Long Sixties.* London: Verso, 2016.
Keller, William W. *The Liberals and J. Edgar Hoover: Rise and Fall of a Domestic Intelligence State.* Princeton, N.J.: Princeton University Press, 1989.
Kelley, Robin D. G. *Freedom Dreams: The Black Radical Imagination.* Boston: Beacon Press, 2003.
———. *Hammer and Hoe: Alabama Communists during the Great Depression.* Chapel Hill: University of North Carolina Press, 1990.
Kelly, Alfred H., Winfred A. Harbison, and Herman Belz. *The American Constitution: Its Origins and Development.* 7th ed. New York: W. W. Norton, 1991.
King, Martin Luther, Jr. *Why We Can't Wait.* New York: Mentor Books, 1964.
Kirkendall, Richard S., ed. *The Truman Period as a Research Field: A Reappraisal, 1972* (Columbia: University of Missouri Press, 1974).
Klingaman, William K. *Encyclopedia of the McCarthy Era.* New York: Facts on File, 1996.
Kochiyama, Yuri. *Passing It On.* Edited by Marjorie Lee. 2nd printing ed. Los Angeles: UCLA Asian American Studies Center Press, 2004.
Kurashige, Lon. *Two Faces of Exclusion: The Untold History of Anti-Asian Racism in the United States.* Chapel Hill: University of North Carolina Press, 2016.
Lee, Robert G. *Orientals: Asian Americans in Popular Culture.* Philadelphia: Temple University Press, 1999.
Lotchin, Roger W. *Japanese American Relocation in World War II: A Reconsideration.* Cambridge: Cambridge University Press, 2018.
MacDonnell, Francis. *Insidious Foes: The Axis Fifth Column and the American Home Front.* New York: Oxford University Press, 1995.
Maeda, Daryl J. *Chains of Babylon: The Rise of Asian America.* Minneapolis: University of Minnesota Press, 2009.
Maki, Mitchell T., Harry H. L. Kitano, and S. Megan Berthold. *Achieving the Impossible Dream: How Japanese Americans Obtained Redress.* Urbana: University of Illinois Press, 1999.
Malkin, Michelle. *In Defense of Internment: The Case for "Racial Profiling" in World War II and the War on Terror.* Washington, D.C.: Regnery, 2004.

Masaoka, Mike, with Bill Hosokawa. *They Call Me Moses Masaoka: An American Saga.* New York: William Morrow, 1987.

Michels, Tony. *Jewish Radicals: A Documentary History.* New York: New York University Press, 2012.

Moloney, Deirdre M. *National Insecurities: Immigrants and U.S. Deportation Policies since 1882.* Chapel Hill: University of North Carolina Press, 2012.

Muller, Eric L. *Free to Die for Their Country: The Story of the Japanese American Draft Resisters in World War II.* Chicago: University of Chicago Press, 2001.

Murakawa, Yoko. *Kyokaisenjo no Shiminken: Nichibei Senso to Nikkei Amerikajin* [Citizenship on the border: The Japanese Americans during the U.S.-Japanese war]. Tokyo: Ochanomizu Shobo, 2007.

Murphy, Bruce Allen. *The Brandeis/Frankfurter Connection: The Secret Political Activities of Two Supreme Court Justices.* New York: Oxford University Press, 1982.

Myer, Dillon S. *Uprooted Americans: The Japanese Americans and the War Relocation Authority.* Tucson: University of Arizona Press, 1971.

Nagata, Donna K. *Legacy of Injustice: Exploring the Cross-Generational Impact of the Japanese American Internment.* New York: Plenum Press, 1993.

Naimark, Norman M. *Fires of Hatred: Ethnic Cleansing in Twentieth-Century Europe.* Cambridge, Mass.: Harvard University Press, 2002.

National JACL (Japanese American Citizens League) Power of Words II Committee. *Power of Words Handbook: A Guide to Language about Japanese Americans in World War II.* San Francisco: Japanese American Citizens League, April 27, 2013. https://jacl.org/wordpress/wp-content/uploads/2015/08/Power-of-Words-Rev.-Term.-Handbook.pdf.

Novick, Peter. *The Holocaust in American Life.* New York: Houghton Mifflin, 1999.

Okihiro, Gary Y. *Margins and Mainstreams: Asians in American History and Culture.* Seattle: University of Washington Press, 1994.

Rich, Wilbur C., ed. *The Politics of Minority Coalitions: Race, Ethnicity, and Shared Uncertainties.* Westpoint, Conn.: Praeger, 1996.

Robinson, Greg. *After Camp: Portraits in Midcentury Japanese American Life and Politics.* Los Angeles: University of California Press, 2012.

———. *By Order of the President: FDR and the Internment of Japanese Americans.* Cambridge, Mass.: Harvard University Press, 2001.

———. *A Tragedy of Democracy: Japanese Confinement in North America.* New York: Columbia University Press, 2009.

Schlesinger, Arthur M., Jr. *The Vital Center: The Politics of Freedom.* Boston: Houghton Mifflin, 1949.

Schrecker, Ellen. *The Age of McCarthyism: A Brief History with Documents.* Boston: Bedford Books of St. Martin's Press, 1994.

Schwartz, Bernard. *A Commentary on the Constitution of the United States, Part I: The Powers of Government.* Vol. 2. New York: Macmillan, 1963.

———. *Super Chief: Earl Warren and His Supreme Court—a Judicial Biography.* New York: New York University Press, 1983.

Sherry, Michael S. *In the Shadow of War: The United States since the 1930s.* New Haven, Conn.: Yale University Press, 1995.

Simpson, Caroline Chung. *An Absent Presence: Japanese Americans in Postwar American Culture, 1945–1960.* Durham, N.C.: Duke University Press, 2001.

Singh, Nikhil Pal. *Black Is a Country: Race and the Unfinished Struggle for Democracy.* Cambridge, Mass.: Harvard University Press, 2004.
Sohi, Seema. *Echoes of Mutiny: Race, Surveillance, and Indian Anticolonialism in North America.* Oxford: Oxford University Press, 2014.
Sutherland, Arthur E., ed. *Government under Law: A Conference Held at Harvard Law School on the Occasion of the Bicentennial of John Marshall.* Cambridge, Mass.: Harvard University Press, 1956.
Tachiki, Amy, Eddie Wong, Franklin Odo, and Buck Wong, eds. *Roots: An Asian American Reader.* Los Angeles: University of California Press, 1971.
Takaki, Ronald. *Double Victory: A Multicultural History of America in World War II.* Boston: Little, Brown, 2001.
Takezawa, Yasuko I. *Breaking the Silence: Redress and Japanese American Ethnicity.* Ithaca, N.Y.: Cornell University Press, 1995.
Tchen, John Kuo Wei, and Dylan Yates. *Yellow Peril! An Archive of Anti-Asian Fear.* New York: Penguin Random House, 2014.
tenBroek, Jacobus, Edward N. Barnhart, and Floyd W. Matson. *Prejudice, War and the Constitution: Cases and Consequences of the Evacuation of the Japanese Americans in World War II.* 1954. Reprint, Berkeley: University of California Press, 1975.
Terkel, Studs. *"The Good War": An Oral History of World War Two.* New York: Pantheon Books, 1984.
Theoharis, Athan G. *Seeds of Repression: Harry S. Truman and the Origins of McCarthyism.* Chicago: Quadrangle Books, 1971.
———. *Spying on Americans: Political Surveillance from Hoover to the Huston Plan.* Philadelphia: Temple University Press, 1978.
Truman, Harry S. *Memoirs by Harry S. Truman.* Vol. 2, *Years of Trial and Hope.* Garden City, N.Y.: Doubleday, 1956.
Turner, Patricia A. *I Heard It through the Grapevine: Rumor in African-American Culture.* Berkeley: University of California Press, 1993.
Walker, Samuel. *In Defense of American Liberties: A History of the ACLU.* 2nd ed. Carbondale: Southern Illinois University Press, 1999.
Wanzer-Serrano, Darrel. *The New York Young Lords and the Struggle for Liberation.* Philadelphia: Temple University Press, 2015.
Warren, Earl. *The Memoirs of Earl Warren.* Garden City, N.Y.: Doubleday, 1977.
Weglyn, Michi Nishiura. *Years of Infamy: The Untold Story of America's Concentration Camps.* Updated ed. Seattle: University of Washington Press, 1996.
Wei, William. *The Asian American Movement.* Philadelphia: Temple University Press, 1993.
Wittner, Lawrence S. *Cold War America: From Hiroshima to Watergate.* New York: Praeger, 1974.
Woods, Jeff. *Black Struggle, Red Scare: Segregation and Anti-Communism in the South, 1948–1968.* Baton Rouge: Louisiana State University Press, 2004.
Wu, Ellen D. *The Color of Success: Asian Americans and the Origins of the Model Minority.* Princeton, N.J.: Princeton University Press, 2014.
Yamakura, Akihiro. *Shimin-teki Jiyu: Amerika Nikkeijin Senji Kyouseishuyo no Rigaru Histori (Civil Liberties: A Legal History of the Wartime Incarceration of the People of Japanese Ancestry in America).* Tokyo: Sairyu-sha, 2011.
Yamamoto, Eric K., Margaret Chon, Carol L. Izumi, Jerry Kang, and Frank H. Wu.

Race, Rights and Reparation: Law and the Japanese American Internment. New York: Aspen Law and Business, 2001; 2nd ed., 2013.

Yang Murray, Alice. *Historical Memories of the Japanese American Internment and the Struggle for Redress.* Stanford, Calif.: Stanford University Press, 2007.

ARTICLES, BOOK CHAPTERS, AND ELECTRONIC PUBLICATIONS

American Bar Association. "President Trump Drafting New Immigration Executive Order." *ABA Washington Letter,* February 2017. http://www.americanbar.org/publications/governmental_affairs_periodicals/washingtonletter/2017/february/immigrationorder.html.

American Civil Liberties Union (ACLU). "America's Disappeared: Seeking International Justice for Immigrants Detained after September 11." 2004. http://www.aclu.org/FilesPDFs/un%20report.pdf.

Anderson, James B. "Hamdi v. Rumsfeld: Judicious Balancing at the Intersection of the Executive's Power to Detain and the Citizen-Detainee's Right to Due Process." *Journal of Criminal Law and Criminology* 95, no. 3 (Spring 2005): 689–724.

Austin, Allan Wesley. "Loyalty and Concentration Camps in America: The Japanese American Precedent and the Internal Security Act of 1950." In *Last Witnesses: Reflections on the Wartime Internment of Japanese Americans,* edited by Erica Harth, 253–270. New York: Palgrave, 2001.

Balibar, Etienne. "Is There a 'Neo-racism'?" In *Nation, Race, Class: Ambiguous Identities,* edited by Etienne Balibar and Immanuel Wallerstein, 17–28. London: Verso, 1991.

Brecht, Arnold. "The Concentration Camp." *Columbia Law Review* 50 (June 1950): 761–782.

Carbonella, August, and Sharryn Kasmir. "W.E.B. DuBois's *Darkwater* and an Anticolonial, Internationalist Anthropology." *Dialectical Anthropology* 30, nos. 1/2 (2008): 113–121.

Chiasson, Lloyd. "Japanese-American Relocation during World War II: A Study of California Editorial Reactions." *Journalism Quarterly* 68 (Spring/Summer 1991): 263–268.

Chon, Margaret, and Eric K. Yamamoto. "Resurrecting Korematsu: Post–September 11th National Security Curtailment of Civil Liberties." In *Race, Rights and Reparation: Law and the Japanese American Internment,* edited by Eric K. Yamamoto, Margaret Chon, Carol L. Izumi, Jerry Kang, and Frank H. Wu, 39–48. New York: Aspen Law and Business, 2001.

CNN Library. "Guantanamo Bay Naval Station Fast Facts." CNN, March 7, 2017. http://edition.cnn.com/2013/09/09/world/guantanamo-bay-naval-station-fast-facts/.

Columbia Law Review. "Note: The Internal Security Act of 1950." Vol. 51 (May 1951): 606–660.

Cotter, Cornelius P., and J. Malcolm Smith. "An American Paradox: The Emergency Detention Act of 1950." *Journal of Politics* 19 (February 1957): 20–33.

Daniels, Roger. "Words Do Matter: A Note on Inappropriate Terminology and the Incarceration of the Japanese Americans." In *Nikkei in the Pacific Northwest: Japanese Americans and Japanese Canadians in the Twentieth Century,* edited by Louis Fiset and Gail M. Nomura, 190–214. Seattle: University of Washington Press, 2005.

Davis, Angela Y. "Masked Racism: Reflections on the Prison Industrial Complex." *Colorlines,* October 31, 1998.
Dunbar, Leslie W. "Beyond Korematsu: The Emergency Detention Act of 1950." *University of Pittsburgh Law Review* 13 (1952): 221–231.
Fairman, Charles. "Government under Law in Time of Crisis." In *Government under Law: A Conference Held at Harvard Law School on the Occasion of the Bicentennial of John Marshall,* edited by Arthur E. Sutherland, 232–301. Cambridge, Mass.: Harvard University Press, 1956.
Fujita-Rony, Thomas Y. "'Destructive Force': Aiko Herzig-Yoshinaga's Gendered Labor in the Japanese American Redress Movement." *Frontiers: A Journal of Women Studies* 24, no. 1 (2003): 38–60.
Gillis, John R. "Memory and Identity: The History of a Relationship." In *Commemorations: The Politics of National Identity,* edited by John R. Gillis, 3–24. Princeton, N.J.: Princeton University Press, 1994.
Griffith, Robert. "American Politics and the Origins of 'McCarthyism.'" In *The Specter: Original Essays on the Cold War and the Origin of McCarthyism,* edited by Robert Griffith and Athan G. Theoharis, 2–17. New York: New Viewpoints, 1974.
Honigsberg, Peter Jan. "Chasing 'Enemy Combatants' and Circumventing International Law: A License for Sanctioned Abuse." *UCLA Journal of International Law and Foreign Affairs* 12, no. 1 (2007): 1–74.
Izumi, Masumi. "Alienable Citizenship: Race, Loyalty, and the Law in the Age of 'American Concentration Camps,' 1941–1971." *Asian American Law Journal* 13 (November 2006): 1–30.
———. "Gila River Concentration Camp and the Historical Memory of Japanese American Mass Incarceration." *Japanese Journal of American Studies* 29 (2018): 45–65.
———. "Lessons from History: Japanese Canadians and Civil Liberties in Canada." *Journal of American and Canadian Studies* 17 (2000): 1–24.
———. "Prohibiting 'American Concentration Camps': Repeal of the Emergency Detention Act and the Public Historical Memory of the Japanese American Internment." *Pacific Historical Review* 74, no. 2 (2005): 165–193.
———. "Rumors of 'American Concentration Camps': The Emergency Detention Act and the Public Fear of Political Repression, 1966–1971." *Doshisha Studies in Language and Culture* 4, no. 4 (2002): 737–765.
Kang, Jerry. "Denying Prejudice: Internment, Redress, and Denial." *UCLA Law Review* 51 (2004): 933–1013.
Kashima, Tetsuden. "Japanese American Internees Return, 1945 to 1955: Readjustment and Social Amnesia." *Phylon: The Atlanta University Review of Race and Culture* 61 (Summer 1980): 107–115.
Kerber, Linda K. "The Meanings of Citizenship." *Journal of American History* 84 (December 1997): 833–854.
Lawson, Steven F. "Civil Rights." In *Exploring the Johnson Years,* edited by Robert A. Divine, 93–125. Austin: University of Texas Press, 1981.
Lee, Traci G. "Trump Supporter: Internment 'Precedent' for Muslim Registry to 'Protect America.'" *NBC News,* November 17, 2016. http://www.nbcnews.com/news/asian-america/trump-supporter-cites-internment-precedent-muslim-registry-n685131.

Linehan, Thomas M. "Japanese American Resettlement in Cleveland during and after World War II." *Journal of Urban History* 20 (November 1993): 54–80.

Lofgren, Charles A. "Hardships of War: A Review of *In Defense of Internment: The Case of 'Racial Profiling' in World War II and the War on Terror*, by Michelle Malkin." *Claremont Review of Books*, September 2005.

Longaker, Richard. "Emergency Detention: The Generation Gap, 1950–1971." *Western Political Quarterly* 27 (September 1974): 395–408.

Mack, Thomas C. "The Constitution and the Emergency Detention Act of 1950." *Buffalo Law Review* 13 (1964): 477–491.

Masaoka, Mike M. "Introduction: Some Recollections of, and Reflections on, 1942." In *Earl Warren Oral History Project, Japanese American Relocation Reviewed: Volume I, Decision and Exodus*, directed by Amelia R. Fry. Calisphere, University of California, 1976. http://texts.cdlib.org/view?docId=ft667nb2x8&doc.view=entire_text, accessed September 12, 2018.

McAuliffe, Mary S. "Liberals and the Communist Control Act of 1954." *Journal of American History* 63 (September 1976): 351–376.

McCarran, Patrick A. "The Internal Security Act of 1950." *University of Pittsburgh Law Review* 12 (Summer 1951): 481–514.

McNaughton, James C. "Japanese Americans and the U.S. Army: A Historical Reconsideration." *Army History* 99 (Summer/Fall 2003): 4–15.

Muller, Eric L. "Hirabayashi and the Invasion Evasion." *North Carolina Law Review* 88, no. 4 (2010): 1333–1388.

Nakanishi, Don Toshiaki. "Beyond Redress: The Future of Japanese American Politics on the Mainland." In *The Politics of Minority Coalitions: Race, Ethnicity, and Shared Uncertainties*, edited by Wilbur C. Rich, 87–107. Westpoint, Conn.: Praeger, 1996.

Odo, Franklin. "The Good War and Japanese America." *American Studies Journal* 59 (2015). http://www.asjournal.org/59-2015/the-good-war-and-japanese-america/.

Okamura, Raymond Y. "The American Concentration Camps: A Cover-Up through Euphemistic Terminology." *Journal of Ethnic Studies* 10 (Fall 1982): 95–109.

———. "Background and History of the Repeal Campaign." *Amerasia Journal* 2 (Fall 1974): 72–94.

Okamura, Raymond Y., Robert Takasugi, Hiroshi Kanno, and Edison Uno, "Campaign to Repeal the Emergency Detention Act," *Amerasia Journal* 2 (Fall 1974): 70–111.

Rostow, Eugene V. "The Japanese American Cases: A Disaster." *Yale Law Journal* 54 (1944–1945): 489–533.

Shaffer, Robert. "Cracks in the Consensus: Defending the Rights of Japanese Americans during World War II." *Radical History Review* 72 (Fall 1998): 84–100.

Sutherland, Arthur E., Jr. "Freedom and Internal Security." *Harvard Law Review* 64 (January 1951): 383–416.

Takei, Barbara. "Legalizing Detention: Segregated Japanese Americans and the Justice Department's Renunciation Program." *Journal of the Shaw Historical Library* 19 (2005): 75–105.

Tanner, William R., and Robert Griffith. "Legislative Politics of 'McCarthyism': The Internal Security Act of 1950." In *The Specter: Original Essays on the Cold War and the Origin of McCarthyism*, edited by Robert Griffith and Athan Theoharis, 172–189. New York: New Viewpoints, 1974.

Taylor, Sandra C. "Leaving the Concentration Camps: Japanese American Resettlement in Utah and the Intermountain West." *Pacific Historical Review* 60 (May 1991): 169–194.
Theoharis, Athan G. "The Truman Administration and the Decline of Civil Liberties: The FBI's Success in Securing Authorization for a Preventive Detention Program." *Journal of American History* 64 (March 1978): 1010–1030.
Thom, Cathleen, and Patrick Jung. "The Responsibilities Program of the FBI, 1951–55." *The Historian* 59 (Winter 1997): 347–370.
Tuna Canyon Detention Station Coalition. http://www.tunacanyon.org/.
Van Dijk, Teun A. "Discourse, Power and Access." In *Texts and Practices: Readings in Critical Discourse Analysis*, edited by C. R. Caldas-Coulthard and M. Coulthard, 84–106. London: Routledge, 1996.
Warren, Earl. "The Bill of Rights and the Military." *New York University Law Review* 37 (1962): 181–203.

Newspapers and Periodicals

Atlantic Monthly
Boston Traveler
California Farmer Consumer Reporter
Chicago Daily News
Denver Post
Gidra
Hokubei Mainichi
Honolulu Star-Bulletin
I. F. Stone's Weekly
Liberty (Newsletter of the Citizens Committee for Constitutional Liberties)
Look
Los Angeles Times
The Nation
New Republic
Newsweek
New York Times
New York Times Magazine
Oregon Journal
Pacific Citizen
Palo Alto Times
Pittsburgh Courier
Pittsburgh Post-Gazette
Rafu Shimpo
Sacramento Bee
San Francisco Chronicle
San Francisco Examiner
Saturday Review
St. Louis Post-Dispatch
Time
Times-Union (Albany, New York)

Washington Afro-American
Washington Evening Star
Washington Post

THESES AND DISSERTATIONS

Gerard, Christopher John. "'A Program of Cooperation': The FBI, the Senate Internal Security Subcommittee, and the Communist Issue, 1950–1956." Ph.D. diss., Marquette University, 1993.

Kitayama, Glenn Ikuo. "Japanese Americans and the Movement of Redress: A Case Study of Grassroots Activism in the Los Angeles Chapter of the National Coalition for Redress/Reparations." Master's thesis, University of California, Los Angeles, 1993.

Mizuno, Takeya. "The Civil Libertarian Press, Japanese American Press, and Japanese American Mass Evacuation." Ph.D. diss., University of Missouri–Columbia, 2000.

Tanner, William Randolph. "The Passage of the Internal Security Act of 1950." Ph.D. diss., University of Kansas, 1971.

Wallinger, Michael John. "Dispersal of the Japanese Americans: Rhetorical Strategies of the War Relocation Authority, 1942–1945." Ph.D. diss., University of Oregon, 1975.

Index

AAA (Asian Americans for Action), 141–142
AAPA (Asian American Political Alliance), 127–128, 130, 135–136, 139, 227n75
ABC list, 19, 209n103
absent presence, 89
ACLU. *See* American Civil Liberties Union
ADA (Americans for Democratic Action), 50–51, 82–84, 107
African Americans: in Black Power Movement, 114; in Civil Rights Movement, 114, 211n17; concentration camp rumor among, 7, 117–120, 122–123, 212n25; Lyndon B. Johnson on, 111; mass incarceration of, 172, 186n5; negative representation of, 4, 135, 143; Southern Democrats on, 24, 63; surveillance of, 215n56; tension with the police, 173; in Title II repeal movement, 8, 127, 131, 161. *See also* Black liberation movement; Black Panther Party; Civil Rights Movement; National Association for the Advancement of Colored People
Albertson v. Subversive Activities Control Board (1965), 106–107
Alcatraz Island: occupation, 142; penitentiary, 69

Alien and Sedition Acts, 15
Alien Enemy Control Unit, 20, 83, 85
Alien Registration Act (Smith Act [1940]), 18, 55, 101–105, 210n138
Allen, Charles R., 94–95, 116–117
American Bar Association, 47, 231n17
American Civil Liberties Union (ACLU): establishment of, 17; reaction to removal of Japanese Americans, 26, 192n72; reaction to Title II, 50, 82–89, 107, 120; support for Title II repeal, 135–136, 141, 154, 166
American Friends Service Committee, 154
American Indian Movement (AIM), 142. *See also* Native Americans
American Jewish Congress, 79
American Legion, 47, 73, 190n47
Americans for Democratic Action (ADA), 50–51, 82–84, 107
amnesia, 8, 69
Anti-Defamation League, 141; of B'nai B'rith, 79
antiradicalism, 5, 18
anti-Semitism, 63, 103, 124–125
antiwar activists, 7, 17, 114, 121, 128, 159, 161, 169
Arendt, Hannah, 125

248 | INDEX

Asian American Political Alliance (AAPA), 127–128, 130, 135–136, 139, 227n75
Asian Americans: Asian American activists, 8, 114, 127–129, 135–136, 139; Asian American community, 128, 212n18; in Cold War, 74; in Congress, 149; discrimination against, 205n27; as model minority, 4, 35; in Title II repeal movement, 141–143
Asian Americans for Action (AAA), 141–142
Asian American studies, 5, 217n86
assembly center, ix–x, 24, 29, 31, 175, 188n17
assimilation, 22, 33, 35, 128, 130, 132
Attorney General's Portfolio, 97–99

Balibar, Etienne, 33
Biddle, Francis, 20–21, 51, 83, 97, 109, 191n50, 205n41, 209n104, 209n106
Black, Hugo L., 30–31, 102, 104, 106
black liberation movement, 130
Black Lives Matter, 173
Black Nationalists, 118, 123
Black Panther Party (BPP), 114, 120–123, 128, 135, 160, 215n59, 230n7
Black Power, 114, 127
Bosworth, Allan, 124, 131, 133
BPP (Black Panther Party), 114, 120–123, 128, 135, 160, 215n59, 230n7
Brennan, William J., 106
Brown, H. Rap, 118–120
Brown v. Board of Education (1954), 105, 113
Bureau of Prisons, 94–96, 116, 118, 152, 213n36

Campbell, David, 23
Carmichael, Stokely, 114, 118–120
Celler, Emanuel, 49, 66, 128, 151
Chinese Americans, 81, 127, 129, 134, 153
Chinese Exclusion Repeal Act (Magnuson Act [1943]), 198n31
Chisholm, Shirley, 160
Citizens Committee for Civil Liberties (CCCL), 116, 136–137, 154, 159, 227n75
civil disobedience, 112
Civil Rights Congress, 80
Civil Rights Movement, 45, 98, 110, 113, 121, 127, 200n74, 215n56. *See also* desegregation; segregation, racial
Civil War, 15–16, 18, 32

Civil War (Spanish), 187n9
Clark, Mark, 22, 191n55
Clark, Ramsey, 118, 120, 127, 172, 216n84
Clark, Thomas C.: as attorney general, 65, 97–98, 200n67; as Supreme Court justice, 102, 104, 109, 112; during World War II, 21, 109, 209n106
clear and present danger, 17, 30, 55, 91, 100, 102–103, 106–107, 138
Commission on Wartime Relocation and Internment of Civilians (CWRIC), 30, 171, 185n1 (note on terminol.)
Communist Control Act (1954), 99–101
concentration camp law, 2, 9, 14, 73, 128, 146, 178, 184, 219n136. *See also* Emergency Detention Act (1950); Title II
Concentration Camps, U.S.A. (booklet), 116, 136, 141, 208n89
conscription, 37, 206n49. *See also* draft; Selective Service
coram nobis cases, 31, 171
critical race theory, 34
curfew, 26–29, 30, 34, 74, 92
Custodial Detention List, 97
CWRIC (Commission on Wartime Relocation and Internment of Civilians), 30, 171, 185n1 (note on terminol.)

Davis, Angela, 172, 230n7
Defence Regulation 18B, 86
Dennis v. United States (1951), 102–104
Department of Homeland Security, 172
Department of Justice: conflict with Department of War, 23, 28, 87; detention facilities, 1, 7, 95–96, 117, 150, 152, 208n95; on enemy aliens, 19–25, 83, 85, 89, 109, 174, 191n50, 209n103; and FBI, 99; and International Security Act, 59; and Japanese American exclusion, x, 14, 19–25, 30, 33, 175, 188n17; support for Title II repeal, 151–152, 154, 167, 172; surveillance on communists, 65, 97, 105, 210n138; surveillance on radicals, 123, 149, 172; during Truman administration, 49–51
Department of War, 19–25, 28
desegregation, 5, 105, 113, 122, 200n74. *See also* Civil Rights Movement; segregation, racial

Detention Review Board, 59–60, 68, 75, 79, 87, 164
DeWitt, John L., 20–32, 58, 92, 130
Dies, Martin, 24
differentialist racism, 29, 33
discourse analysis, 5, 14, 34
Douglas, Paul H., 49–54, 66, 69–71, 74, 77, 100
Douglas, William O., 26–27, 33, 36, 82, 102–104, 106, 108
draft, 16, 85, 88; of Nisei, 37, 85, 175; resistance to Vietnam War, 114, 157, 159. *See also* conscription; Selective Service

Eastland, James O., 48, 50, 94, 98, 119, 146–147, 150–151
Eichmann, Adolf, 115, 124–125, 133
Eisenhower, Dwight, 99–100, 111, 210n125
Eisenhower, Milton, 154, 156
Emergency Detention Act (1950), 1, 6, 94, 103, 178, 185n1 (intro.); bills to repeal, 166; hearings to repeal, 154, 160, 212n21; JACL National Committee to Repeal, 222n159; Japanese Americans on, 81, 116; passage of, 46; repeal of, 1, 131, 146, 153. *See also* concentration camp law; Title II
Endo, Mitsuye, 25, 35–36, 42, 44
enemy aliens, x, 6, 13–14, 25, 60, 173–174, 209n103; congressional discussion on, 70–72; detention of, 84–85; Japanese Americans as, 20–21, 23, 27–29, 37, 81, 189n40
enemy combatant, 172–173, 229n102, 230nn10–11, 231n14
Ennis, Edward J., 20, 30, 33–34, 80, 83–89, 108, 191n50, 205n41
Enomoto, Jerry, 131, 134, 136, 139–140, 158
Espionage Act (1917), 16–17, 49
ethnic cleansing, 18–19, 177
executive order, 72, 78, 82–83, 152, 230n10
Executive Order 8802 (banning discrimination in defense industry), 205n37
Executive Order 9066, 22–24, 27, 41, 43, 51, 86, 188n17, 192n72; congressional debate on, 68, 71; exhibit on, 174–176
Executive Order 10450 (federal employee loyalty program), 100

Executive Order 13767 (border security and immigration enforcement), 174
Executive Order 13769 (Muslim ban), 174, 231n17
executive power, 162, 166, 168, 172, 175, 178
Ex Parte Endo (1944), 25, 35–37, 42, 70–71, 82, 91–92
Ex Parte Milligan (1866), 16, 32

Fair Deal, 63
Federal Bureau of Investigation (FBI), 5; and civil rights activists, 7, 214n54, 215n56; expansion of, 108–109, 208n101; and Japanese Americans, 19–21, 26, 30, 188n17, 189n40; liberals on, 65–67, 74; surveillance on Chinese Americans, 129; surveillance on communists, 52, 61, 78–82, 96–99, 103; surveillance on radicals, 116–117, 122–123, 151–152, 154; Truman and, 49–50
federal employee loyalty program, 78, 98, 100, 151, 203n3
Ferguson, Homer, 53, 67–71, 83, 98, 202n103
Fifth Amendment, 2, 9, 16, 65–66, 72, 84, 101, 104–106; and Japanese American incarceration, 26
fifth column, 12, 21, 24, 53, 57, 61–62, 187n9
Fourteenth Amendment, 16, 41, 112
Fourth Amendment, 112, 211n9
Frankfurter, Felix, 51, 82, 103, 105–107, 112–113

Goldberg, Arthur J., 107, 112–113, 154–155
Guantanamo Bay Naval Base, 172, 229n102, 230n10
Gubser, Charles G., 147, 155–157, 224n10

habeas corpus, writ of, 16, 32, 82, 90, 98, 172, 230n10; in *Ex Parte Endo,* 25, 35, 70
Habeas Corpus Suspension Act (1863), 16
Harlan, John Marshall, 103–104
Hawaii, 20, 37, 48, 153–154, 158, 174, 197n22; martial law in, 14, 87, 188n17, 192n76
Herzig-Yoshinaga, Aiko, 30, 176

Hirabayashi, Gordon Kiyoshi, 25–29, 31, 34, 41, 171, 192n72
Hirabayashi v. United States (1943), x, 25–35, 42, 58, 82, 91–93, 124
HISC (House Internal Security Committee), 148, 150–151, 153–164, 166
Holifield, Chet, 147–148, 150–151, 164, 166
Holmes, Oliver Wendell, Jr., 17
Holocaust, 115, 124–125, 144
Hoover, J. Edgar, 5, 96–99, 123, 208n101; on Chinese Americans, 134, 153; on communists, 52, 61, 74, 198n43; on Ku Klux Klan, 215n56
Hosokawa, Bill, 124, 138
House Internal Security Committee (HISC), 148, 150–151, 153–164, 166
House Judiciary Committee, 49, 148, 151, 153, 165–167
House Select Committee Investigating National Defense Migration (Tolan Committee), 24, 138
House Un-American Activities Committee (HUAC): and Internal Security Act, 46–47, 54–55, 63–64, 74, 78, 104–107, 147–148, 152; investigation by, 64–68, 80, 98; National Committee to Abolish HUAC, 135–137, 159; report (1968), 118–119, 126
HR234 (Non-Detention Act [1971]), 1, 8, 165–167, 185n1 (intro.), 231n14
HUAC. *See* House Un-American Activities Committee
Humphrey, Hubert H., 39, 49, 52–54, 65, 77, 96, 100–101

Ichioka, Yuji, 128
Ichord, Richard H., 148, 151–159, 162–167, 224n16
immigration: anti-immigration, 7, 10, 18; Internal Security Act and, 46–47, 55, 57, 61, 80–82; law on, 17, 44, 81; restrictions on, 5, 15, 172, 176
Immigration and Nationality Act (McCarran-Walter Act [1952]), 81, 94. *See also* immigration; Walter-McCarran Immigration Act
Immigration and Naturalization Service (INS), 129

Inouye, Daniel K., 139, 146, 148–153, 164–167
INS (Immigration and Naturalization Service), 129
Interdivision Information Unit, 123, 151, 172
Internal Security Act (S12 [1969]), 146–147, 151–152
Internal Security Index, 96–99, 108
Issei, x, 4, 6, 20–21, 81, 188n17, 194n126, 197n21, 227n72

Jackson, Robert H., 30, 32, 42–43
Japanese American Citizens League (JACL): at HISC hearings, 154–155, 158–159; at House Judiciary Committee Hearing, 166–167; and Internal Security Act, 80; lobbying in Washington, 146–154, 163–164; and McCarran-Walter Act, 81, 197n21; on military service, 35, 37; and redress, 171; on terminology, ix–x; in Title II repeal movement, 7–8, 115, 124–126, 128–143; and Earl Warren, 124
Japanese American Evacuation and Resettlement Study (JERS), 154, 226n47
Japanese Evacuation Claims Act (1948), 40
JERS (Japanese American Evacuation and Resettlement Study), 154, 226n47
Johnson, Lyndon B., 111
judicial activism, 105, 108, 111
judicial restraint, 108, 111–112
Justice Department. *See* Department of Justice

Kennedy, John F., 100, 110, 112–114
Kilgore, Harley M., 48–49, 51–54, 60, 66, 77, 81, 198n43, 202n103
King, Martin Luther, Jr., 113, 118–119, 121, 126
KKK (Ku Klux Klan), 119, 122, 160, 214n54, 215n56
Kochiyama, Mary (Yuri), 141–142
Korean War, 2, 45, 52, 60, 81
Korematsu, Fred T., 25, 29, 31–34, 41, 44, 171, 192n72
Korematsu v. United States (1944), 25, 29–37, 42, 44; congressional debate on,

70; JACL on, 124, 142, 152; legal reviews of, 82, 91, 93; repudiation of, 176
Ku Klux Klan (KKK), 119, 122, 160, 214n54, 215n56

Labor Management Relations Act (Taft-Hartley Act [1947]), 64, 201n81
Lehman, Herbert H., 49–54, 62–63, 77, 100, 207n85
Lincoln, Abraham, 16, 32
loyalty, 5–7, 9, 40, 49, 63, 169, 179; of Chinese Americans, 81; citizenship and, 110; and detention, 70–71, 74, 92, 96; and draft, 85, 158; federal employee loyalty program, 78, 98, 100, 151, 203n3; at war, 13, 16, 32, 178; of Japanese Americans, 4, 19–20, 22–23, 25, 31–39, 43, 59, 128
loyalty question, 6, 37–38

Magnuson, Warren G., 49–50, 53, 100, 198n31
Magnuson Act (Chinese Exclusion Repeal Act [1943]), 198n31
Malkin, Michelle, 175, 231n23
Marcantonio, Vito A., 63–64
martial law, 14, 16, 26, 85, 87, 188n17
Masaoka, Mike: at HISC hearings, 158–159; lobbying in Washington, 143, 146, 150, 152–153, 163; and tension with grassroots activists, 125–127, 129, 131–132, 137, 139
Matsunaga, Spark M., 147–148, 150–151, 153, 163–164, 166
McCarran, Patrick, 46–47, 53, 60–62, 68, 77–78, 98, 101
McCarran-Walter Act (Immigration and Nationality Act [1952]), 81, 94. See also immigration; Walter-McCarran Immigration Act
McCarthy, Joseph, 46, 76, 78, 112, 203n1
McCarthyism, 2, 7, 46, 76, 89, 103–105, 115–116, 143, 178; and congressional investigations, 67, 74, 98–99, 107–108
McCloy, John, 22, 31, 37, 206n52
McGrath, J. Howard, 77, 93–94, 98
McWilliams, Cary, 78–79
Mikva, Abner J., 117, 148, 166
military tribunal, 2, 16, 173, 192n76
Mink, Patsy, 158

Miranda v. Arizona (1966), 113
model minority, 4, 35, 38, 128–130, 156–157, 159, 168
Mundt, Karl, 46–47, 52, 68, 83, 147
Murphy, Frank, 26–28, 30, 32, 36
Muslim ban, 174–176

National Association for the Advancement of Colored People (NAACP), 49, 73, 113, 141, 150, 154, 161, 214n54
National Committee to Abolish HUAC (NCAHUAC), 135–137, 159
Native Americans, 133, 142–143, 186n5
Nazi, 11, 18, 38, 62, 79, 162, 168, 200n69; historical memory of, 115, 121–122, 124–125, 148–149
NCAHUAC (National Committee to Abolish HUAC), 135–137, 159
New Left, 3, 114, 118, 121, 123, 127, 136
Newton, Huey P., 114, 128
Nisei, 6, 20, 92, 127–128, 158; as activists, 115, 129, 132, 141–143, 176; citizenship of, x, 21, 38; confinement of, 81, 84; as enemy non-aliens, 6, 23, 29, 87, 157, 162, 178; in military service, 20, 35, 37–39, 85, 175; as resisters, 25, 175
Nixon, Richard M., 1, 3, 8, 145, 151, 163, 167, 172; and communist registration bills, 46–47, 52
Non-Detention Act (HR234 [1971]), 1, 8, 165–167, 185n1 (intro.), 231n14
nuclear espionage, 2, 89, 93

Office of Strategic Services, 154, 162
Okamura, Raymond Y., 129, 131–133, 137, 139, 141–142, 150, 152; and concentration camp rumor, 115–116, 125–127; at HISC hearings, 158–159

Pacific Citizen, 81, 124, 138–140
Palmer, A. Mitchell, 17
Pearl Harbor, 11–13, 19–21, 24, 81, 122, 177
Petersen, William, 128
police brutality, 114, 168
preventive detention, 6–10, 85, 87, 90, 107–108; constitutionality of, 2–3, 93; of enemy aliens, 10; and executive power, 79, 195n2; and Fifth Amendment, 9; and

preventive detention (*continued*)
  Japanese American incarceration, 6, 44, 60, 70–72, 74, 144; as national security measure, 18, 61, 75, 91, 97, 186n5; and surveillance, 67; Title II and, 7
prison industrial complex, 172
Public Law 503, 24–25, 27–28, 41, 43, 68

racial liberalism, 35, 37–38, 74, 143
Rankin, John E., 24, 63, 76, 201n79
Rauh, Joseph L., Jr., 21, 51, 83
Reagan, Ronald, 154, 158, 171
redress, 171, 176
Responsibility Program, 98–99
Roberts, John, 176, 193n94
Roberts, Owen J., 30–31, 36
Roosevelt, Franklin Delano, 12, 19–20, 22, 97, 155, 188n17, 206n52
Rutledge, Wiley, 26–28

SACB (Subversive Activities Control Board), 56, 101, 105–106
San Francisco State College, 129, 136, 142, 217n87
Sansei, 6, 21, 129–130, 135–136, 139, 143
Schenck v. United States (1919), 17
Schueller v. Drum (1943), 41
SDS (Students for a Democratic Society), 114, 121
Sedition Act (1918), 16–17
segregation, racial, 33, 39, 45, 98, 113. *See also* Civil Rights Movement; desegregation
Segregation Center. *See* Tule Lake
Selective Service, 20, 85, 213n36, 228n97. *See also* conscription; draft
Senate Internal Security Subcommittee (SISS), 53, 60, 65, 74, 94, 98, 107, 146
Senate Judiciary Committee, 46–47, 147–148, 151
SISS (Senate Internal Security Subcommittee), 53, 60, 65, 74, 94, 98, 107, 146
Smith Act (Alien Registration Act [1940]), 18, 55, 101–105, 210n138
SNCC (Student Non-violent Coordinating Committee), 114
Solzhenitsyn, Aleksandr, 115, 212n19
Sotomayor, Sonia, 175–176
Spanish Civil War, 187n9

Spingarn, Stephen J., 49–50, 54, 78, 198n45, 203n8
Stimson, Henry, 22, 34, 37, 206n52
Stokes, Louis, 117, 161, 164
Stone, Harlan F., 26–27, 32
Student Non-violent Coordinating Committee (SNCC), 114
Students for a Democratic Society (SDS), 114, 121
S12 (Internal Security Act [1969]), 146–147, 151–152
Subversive Activities Control Board (SACB), 56, 101, 105–106
surveillance, 2, 7, 65, 115, 171–172; on Chinese American community, 81, 129; on civil rights activists, 5, 122; on communists, 78, 82, 99; on Japanese Americans, 20; on radicals, 123, 151; Title II and, 58, 82, 85, 93, 96, 108

Tachibana, Itaru, 19
Taft-Hartley Act (Labor Management Relations Act [1947]), 64, 201n81
Tajiri, Larry, 81
Takagi, Mary Ann, 129, 132, 139
Takei, George, 175
terrorism, 2, 9, 45, 122, 172–173, 227n75
Third World Liberation Front, 127, 217n87
Thomas, Dorothy Swaine, 154, 157
Title II, xi, 57–60, 107–109, 185n1 (intro.); detention camps for, 93–94; drafting of, 51; and the FBI, 7, 96–99, 208n101; and Japanese American incarceration, 3–6, 69, 71–72, 171–172, 178, 186n7, 227n75; Japanese Americans in the repeal campaign of, 125–137, 139–143, 214n47, 216n79, 217n102, 219n132, 220n140, 220n142; literature on, 3–4; passage of, 46, 53–55, 61, 67–68, 73–75; reactions to, 77, 79–84, 86–93, 213n34; repeal of, 8–10, 112, 115–117, 119–120, 125–137, 139–155, 158, 160–169, 224n10. *See also* concentration camp law; Emergency Detention Act
Tolan Committee (House Select Committee Investigating National Defense Migration), 24, 138
Truman, Harry S.: on civil rights and liberties, 45–46, 63–66; on internal

security, 48–49, 74, 77–79, 100, 107; and Japanese Americans, 39–40; tension with Patrick McCarran, 98; Title II and, 47, 52, 54, 59, 94
Trump, Donald J., 10, 174–176
Tule Lake: emergency detention camp, 7, 94–96, 116; Tule Lake Segregation Center, 6, 38, 136, 175, 177, 213n36
Tuna Canyon Detention Station, 20, 175, 190n42, 231n20
Tydings, Millard E., 52, 78
Tydings Committee, 78

Uno, Edison, 129, 132–133, 137–140, 152, 158–160, 169; and redress, 171; and Earl Warren, 120
USA PATRIOT Act (2001), 172

Vietnam War, 110–112, 114, 121–122, 127–128, 134, 145, 168

Walter, Francis, 80–81, 197n21
Walter-McCarran Immigration Act (1952), 126, 141, 197n21. *See also* Immigration and Nationality Act (McCarran-Walter Act [1952])
War Department, 19–25, 28
war on terrorism, 172–173
War Relocation Authority (WRA), x, 14, 24, 37–40, 124, 154, 156–157, 188n17; and *Ex Parte Endo,* 25, 35–36, 41
Warren, Earl: as California attorney general, 21, 23; support for Title II repeal, 154–155; as Supreme Court chief justice, 103–109, 111–113, 120, 124, 137–140, 213n45
Warren, Earl, Jr., 137, 139–140
Warren Court, 105, 107–108, 111–113, 147
Wartime Civil Control Administration (WCCA), 24
WRA. *See* War Relocation Authority

Yasui, Minoru, 25–27, 31, 41
Yasui v. United States (1943), 25, 124, 171
Yates v. United States (1957), 102–104, 111
Yeagley, J. Walter, 117–118, 154
Yellow Power, 130, 135. *See also* Asian Americans

Masumi Izumi is a Professor of North American Studies in the Department of Global and Regional Studies at Doshisha University in Kyoto, Japan. She has written numerous articles in Japanese and English on the wartime experiences and post-internment community activism of Japanese Americans and Japanese Canadians. She helped the publication of *Tule Lake Stockade Diary* by translating Tatsuo Ryusei Inouye's wartime diary, originally handwritten in Japanese. Her book *The Japanese Canadian Movement: The Little-Known Trans-Pacific History of Japanese Migration and Activism* (*Takanashi Shobo*, in Japanese) won the 2021 Pierre Savard Award by the International Council for Canadian Studies.

Also in the series *Asian American History and Culture*:

Christian Collet and Pei-te Lien, eds., *The Transnational Politics of Asian Americans*
Min Zhou, *Contemporary Chinese America: Immigration, Ethnicity, and Community Transformation*
Kathleen S. Yep, *Outside the Paint: When Basketball Ruled at the Chinese Playground*
Benito M. Vergara Jr., *Pinoy Capital: The Filipino Nation in Daly City*
Jonathan Y. Okamura, *Ethnicity and Inequality in Hawai'i*
Sucheng Chan and Madeline Y. Hsu, eds., *Chinese Americans and the Politics of Race and Culture*
K. Scott Wong, *Americans First: Chinese Americans and the Second World War*
Lisa Yun, *The Coolie Speaks: Chinese Indentured Laborers and African Slaves in Cuba*
Estella Habal, *San Francisco's International Hotel: Mobilizing the Filipino American Community in the Anti-eviction Movement*
Thomas P. Kim, *The Racial Logic of Politics: Asian Americans and Party Competition*
Sucheng Chan, ed., *The Vietnamese American 1.5 Generation: Stories of War, Revolution, Flight, and New Beginnings*
Antonio T. Tiongson Jr., Edgardo V. Gutierrez, and Ricardo V. Gutierrez, eds., *Positively No Filipinos Allowed: Building Communities and Discourse*
Sucheng Chan, ed., *Chinese American Transnationalism: The Flow of People, Resources, and Ideas between China and America during the Exclusion Era*
Rajini Srikanth, *The World Next Door: South Asian American Literature and the Idea of America*
Keith Lawrence and Floyd Cheung, eds., *Recovered Legacies: Authority and Identity in Early Asian American Literature*
Linda Trinh Võ, *Mobilizing an Asian American Community*
Franklin S. Odo, *No Sword to Bury: Japanese Americans in Hawai'i during World War II*
Josephine Lee, Imogene L. Lim, and Yuko Matsukawa, eds., *Re/collecting Early Asian America: Essays in Cultural History*
Linda Trinh Võ and Rick Bonus, eds., *Contemporary Asian American Communities: Intersections and Divergences*
Sunaina Marr Maira, *Desis in the House: Indian American Youth Culture in New York City*
Teresa Williams-León and Cynthia Nakashima, eds., *The Sum of Our Parts: Mixed-Heritage Asian Americans*
Tung Pok Chin with Winifred C. Chin, *Paper Son: One Man's Story*
Amy Ling, ed., *Yellow Light: The Flowering of Asian American Arts*
Rick Bonus, *Locating Filipino Americans: Ethnicity and the Cultural Politics of Space*
Darrell Y. Hamamoto and Sandra Liu, eds., *Countervisions: Asian American Film Criticism*
Martin F. Manalansan IV, ed., *Cultural Compass: Ethnographic Explorations of Asian America*
Ko-lin Chin, *Smuggled Chinese: Clandestine Immigration to the United States*
Evelyn Hu-DeHart, ed., *Across the Pacific: Asian Americans and Globalization*
Soo-Young Chin, *Doing What Had to Be Done: The Life Narrative of Dora Yum Kim*

Robert G. Lee, *Orientals: Asian Americans in Popular Culture*
David L. Eng and Alice Y. Hom, eds., *Q & A: Queer in Asian America*
K. Scott Wong and Sucheng Chan, eds., *Claiming America: Constructing Chinese American Identities during the Exclusion Era*
Lavina Dhingra Shankar and Rajini Srikanth, eds., *A Part, Yet Apart: South Asians in Asian America*
Jere Takahashi, *Nisei/Sansei: Shifting Japanese American Identities and Politics*
Velina Hasu Houston, ed., *But Still, Like Air, I'll Rise: New Asian American Plays*
Josephine Lee, *Performing Asian America: Race and Ethnicity on the Contemporary Stage*
Deepika Bahri and Mary Vasudeva, eds., *Between the Lines: South Asians and Postcoloniality*
E. San Juan Jr., *The Philippine Temptation: Dialectics of Philippines–U.S. Literary Relations*
Carlos Bulosan and E. San Juan Jr., eds., *The Cry and the Dedication*
Carlos Bulosan and E. San Juan Jr., eds., *On Becoming Filipino: Selected Writings of Carlos Bulosan*
Vicente L. Rafael, ed., *Discrepant Histories: Translocal Essays on Filipino Cultures*
Yen Le Espiritu, *Filipino American Lives*
Paul Ong, Edna Bonacich, and Lucie Cheng, eds., *The New Asian Immigration in Los Angeles and Global Restructuring*
Chris Friday, *Organizing Asian American Labor: The Pacific Coast Canned-Salmon Industry, 1870–1942*
Sucheng Chan, ed., *Hmong Means Free: Life in Laos and America*
Timothy P. Fong, *The First Suburban Chinatown: The Remaking of Monterey Park, California*
William Wei, *The Asian American Movement*
Yen Le Espiritu, *Asian American Panethnicity*
Velina Hasu Houston, ed., *The Politics of Life*
Renqiu Yu, *To Save China, To Save Ourselves: The Chinese Hand Laundry Alliance of New York*
Shirley Geok-lin Lim and Amy Ling, eds., *Reading the Literatures of Asian America*
Karen Isaksen Leonard, *Making Ethnic Choices: California's Punjabi Mexican Americans*
Gary Y. Okihiro, *Cane Fires: The Anti-Japanese Movement in Hawaii, 1865–1945*
Sucheng Chan, *Entry Denied: Exclusion and the Chinese Community in America, 1882–1943*

www.ingramcontent.com/pod-product-compliance
Lightning Source LLC
Chambersburg PA
CBHW032020230426
43671CB00005B/152